CROSSCURRENTS

INTERNATIONAL

DEVELOPMENT

EDITED BY

MARK CHARLTON
TRINITY WESTERN UNIVERSITY

AND

PAUL ROWE
TRINITY WESTERN UNIVERSITY

TH
N

D1445527

Australia   Canada   Mexico   Singapore   Spain   United Kingdom   United States

THOMSON

NELSON

Crosscurrents: International Development

Edited by Mark Charlton and Paul Rowe

Associate Vice President, Editorial Director:
Evelyn Veitch

Editor-in-Chief, Higher Education:
Anne Williams

Executive Editor:
Cara Yarzab

Acquisitions Editor:
Bram Sepers

Executive Marketing Manager:
Lenore Taylor

Developmental Editor:
My Editor Inc.

Permissions Coordinator:
Melody Tolson

Content Production Manager:
Imoinda Romain

Production Service:
ICC Macmillan Inc.

Copy Editor/Proofreader:
Wendy Yano

Production Coordinator:
Ferial Suleman

Design Director:
Ken Phipps

Cover Design:
Katherine Strain

Cover Image:
© Adams Picture Library t/a apl/Alamy

Compositor:
ICC Macmillan Inc.

Printer:
Thomson/West

Library and Archives Canada Cataloguing in Publication

Crosscurrents : international development / edited by Mark Charlton and Paul Rowe.

Includes bibliographical references.

ISBN-13: 978-0-17-610477-1

ISBN-10: 0-17-610477-1

1. Economic development—Textbooks. I. Charlton, Mark, 1948– II. Rowe, Paul, 1972– III. Title: International development

HD82.C755 2007   338.91
C2007-900264-1

Contents

Contributors

Brian Ames is an economist with the International Monetary Fund.

George Ayittey is the Distinguished Economist in Residence at the Department of Economics, American University, Washington, D.C.

Ward Brown is an economist with the International Monetary Fund.

Michael Clemens is a Research Fellow at the Center for Global Development, Washington, D.C.

Gregory Conko is the Director of Food Safety Policy at the Competitive Enterprise Institute, Washington, D.C.

Adam Davidson-Harden is an Assistant Professor in the peace and conflict stream of Wilfrid Laurier University's interdisciplinary Global Studies program.

Hernando de Soto is an economist and the President of the Institute for Liberty and Democracy, Peru.

Shanta Devarajan is an economist with the World Bank.

Gavin Fridell is an Assistant Professor in Political Studies at Trent University.

Sakiko Fukuda-Parr is a Research Fellow at the Belfer Center for Science and International Affairs, John F. Kennedy School of Government, Harvard University, and was director and lead author of the *Human Development Report 2003: A Compact Among Nations to End Human Poverty.*

Alan Gilbert is a Professor of Geography at University College, London.

Ted Robert Gurr is the Director of the Minorities at Risk Project, Center for International Development and Conflict Management, University of Maryland.

Barbara Harff is a Professor of Political Science at the U.S. Naval Academy.

Robert Isaak is the Henry George Professor of International Management at Pace University.

Alejandro Izquierdo is a Senior Economist at the Inter-American Development Bank.

Paul Krugman is a Professor of Economics and International Affairs at the Woodrow Wilson School, Princeton University.

Adrian Leftwich is a Senior Lecturer in the Department of Politics, University of York, UK.

John Miller is a Professor of Economics at Wheaton College.

Todd Moss is a Senior Fellow at the Center for Global Development.

John Mueller holds the Woody Hayes Chair of National Security Studies, Mershon Center, and is a Professor of Political Science at Ohio State University.

Moses Ochonu is an Assistant Professor, History College of Arts & Sciences, Vanderbilt University.

C.S. Prakash is a Professor in Plant Molecular Genetics and the Director of the Center for Plant Biotechnology Research at Tuskegee University.

Aruna Rao has served as President of the Association for Women's Rights in Development (AWID) and is currently a Commissioner of the Commission on Globalization convened by State of the World Forum.

Dexter Samida is formerly a research economist at the Fraser Institute.

Richard Sandbrook is a Professor of Political Science at the University of Toronto.

Liane Schalatek is the Associate Director of the Heinrich Böll Foundation's Washington office.

Amartya Sen is the Lamont University Professor at Harvard University and winner of the Nobel Prize in economics.

Hugo Slim is the Chief Scholar at the Centre for Humanitarian Dialogue, Geneva, Switzerland. .

Rebecca Tiessen is an Assistant Professor of International Development Studies at Dalhousie University.

Barbara Unmüssig is a board member of the Heinrich Böll Foundation, which is connected to Germany's Green party.

Peter Uvin is the Henry J. Leir Professor of International Humanitarian Studies and Director, the Institute for Human Security, Tufts University.

Henry Veltmeyer is a Professor of Sociology at St. Mary's University, Halifax.

Laure Waridel is the co-founder of Équiterre, a non-profit organization based in Montreal.

Martin Wolf is an Associate Editor and Chief Economics Commentator, *The Financial Times,* and a Special Professor, School of Economics, University of Nottingham.

Introduction

The study of international development has gone through several phases. In its earliest phase, beginning with the mid-nineteenth century and continuing into the 1960s, studies of development were characterized by a set of assumptions known as the modernization thesis. In a broad sense, modernization argued that developing societies moved from backward, rural, traditional, and non-institutionalized economies with a simple division of labour toward modern, urbanized, progressive, and industrialized economies with a complex division of labour. Modernization implied the movement from feudal to capitalist societies. In the Marxist variant, capitalism was a stage in the concentration of the forms of production to the point where revolutionary change would be necessary, causing a redistribution of resources. But beyond the imperatives of economic systems, Marxism was equally a form of modernization.

Since the 1960s, a wide variety of critiques have been levelled against modernization theory. The most influential of these from the 1960s was dependency theory, a set of contentions flowing out of the colonial experience and championed in particular by Latin American scholars. Dependency faulted modernization for ignoring the context of the colonial age, in which colonial societies were forced into a dependent relationship on industrialized states in the core of the modern capitalist system and suffered due to declining terms of trade for their exports.

The relationships illuminated by dependency theory have come to be an important part of how we conceptualize development. Dependency theorists of the 1960s and 1970s prescribed income-substitution industrialization (ISI) strategies to developing states so as to promote industrialization and the replication of the modern division of labour in the developing world. But in the late 1970s and early 1980s, major macroeconomic challenges and a crippling debt crisis largely forced these states to abandon ISI. Other postcolonial economies had adapted to the rapidly globalizing economy through opening their markets to export-oriented industrialization (EOI), and by the 1980s, countries such as Japan, South Korea, Taiwan, and Hong Kong were demonstrating the apparent success of this project. The growth of neoliberalism through the collapse of the communist alternative and the ascendance of international trade and financial institutions encouraged the expansion of the EOI model. To many, however, the triumph of neoliberalism only served to confirm the adoption of the flawed mantras of modernization theory and still did not open development thinking to the creative impulses of scholars and practitioners of development in the rapidly expanding "two-thirds" world.

The late 1980s and 1990s saw an explosion of new approaches to development, a group of theories that Bjorn Hettne tentatively labelled "another development".[1]

---

1. Bjorn Hettne, *Development Theory and the Three Worlds*, second edition (Essex: Longman Scientific and Technical, 1995), pp. 160–206.

Here the indigenization of development strategies was lauded, as were counter-points to the statist assumptions of prior development policy. The role of women and of feminist (re)interpretation began to have an important role to play, adding a gendered dimension to our study. Development was further refined through the lens of environmental sustainability, critiquing the forms of development based on the extent to which it did not compromise the abilities of future generations to meet their own needs.

Nevertheless, throughout the 1990s, the neoliberal "Washington Consensus" remained the bedrock foundation upon which attempts at international development were constructed. The growing association of the neoliberal order with American leadership only came to be underscored by developments in the political sphere. The events of September 11, 2001 and the ensuing extension of American power into central and southwest Asia have undoubtedly had an important impact on relations between North and South for some time to come. New organized resistance to neoliberal globalization has also arisen in areas of the developing world, inspired in part by growing resource wealth and the limitations of US power. As we proceed past the first decade of the twenty-first century there is no doubt that these polarizing changes will continue to be felt.

This first edition of *Crosscurrents: International Development* reflects some of the historic debates of the past century as well as those emerging questions that vex development today. It considers prominent alternative strategies of development such as fair trading networks, debt cancellation, and provision of property titles to the poor. It explores the ideas being debated about reform of the international financial and trading system and the intellectual traditions that we use to interpret development. It considers some of the key questions of political development in developing societies, such as ethnic diversity, gender, and democratization. Finally, it explores some of the technical and environmental concerns that have arisen over the way we engage in development.

The political economy of international development is a study that benefits from a great deal of interdisciplinarity. There are likely as many facets to international development as there are disciplines, and indeed development theory has been shaped over the years by sociologists, political scientists, economists, historians, geographers—and the list goes on. This text equally takes into account the cross-disciplinary nature of the field by bringing into dialogue individuals from a broad array of disciplinary areas. For these reasons, we believe that *Crosscurrents: International Development* will be a useful contribution to education in a variety of courses in development, from studies in sociology, political economy, geography, and various of the social sciences.

NOTE FOR STUDENTS USING THE TEXT

We hope that this text will prove useful to you in your study and research on international development issues. To enhance your ability to find additional resources for both participating in class debates and discussions and for writing papers, we provide two useful features at the end of each issue, in addition to a list of suggested readings:

Website resources: At the end of the each postscript, we provide an annotated list of suggested website resources. Especially in the area of international development, a large number of international institutions, research institutes, and non-governmental agencies provide useful websites. To facilitate your online research you may also want to consult Grant Heckman, the *Thomson Nelson Guide to Web Research 2007–2008* (Scarborough: Thomson Nelson, 2008). This manual not only provides useful tips on conducting web research, but also includes information on citing web resources in both MLA and APA formats. For further information on finding and documenting resources you may wish to consult Lucille Charlton and Mark Charlton, *Thomson Nelson Guide to Research and Writing in Political Science* (Scarborough: Thomson Nelson, 2006).

InfoTrac®: Students purchasing a new copy of *Crosscurrents: International Development* will receive a free four-month subscription to InfoTrac® College Edition. This is an online library containing full-text articles from a large number of scholarly journals and popular news magazines. In each postscript, we have provided a few sample article references and then suggested useful keywords that students may wish to use when doing research. A separate User Guide for Instructors is available from Nelson.

NOTE FOR FACULTY ADOPTING *CROSSCURRENTS: INTERNATIONAL DEVELOPMENT*

Crosscurrents: International Development continues the structure of the *Crosscurrents* series of framing discussion of issues for students in the debate format. Issues are raised by formulating them as a question and then presenting students with two readings reflecting contrasting approaches to the issue. *Crosscurrents: International Development* can be incorporated into courses in a variety of ways:

i) You may wish to use *Crosscurrents: International Development* as a means of organizing weekly discussion sessions or tutorial groups using a structured debate format. On each topic, two students, or groups of students, may be asked to argued the case for the opposing sides, followed by a group discussion. This format requires students to adopt a particular point of view and defend that position. Because the necessary background material is provided in the readings, this format is very easily adapted to large courses in which teaching assistants are responsible for weekly tutorial sessions.

ii) Some may wish simply to assign the chapters as supplementary readings, either to reinforce material covered in the lectures, or to use them to illustrate particular points that have been made in the course. In this way, the text can be used as a more traditional supplementary course reader, with the instructor have the option of assigning only one of the readings under a given topic.

iii) Others may wish to use the readings as a point of departure for essay assignments in the course. The readings and the list of suggested readings, and websites at the end of each issue may serve as a starting point for researching the topic under discussion. In other cases, the instructor might want to encourage students to develop their critical skills by having them write an assessment of the arguments and evidence presented by the writers on a particular issue. Alternatively, students could be asked to select one side of the debate and write a persuasive essay developing their own arguments in favour of that point of view.

We hope that you find *Crosscurrents: International Development* to be a flexible and useful tool. As you use this text in your courses, the editors would welcome suggestions or recommendations that you have from experience.

ACKNOWLEDGMENTS

We would like to express our thanks to the reviewers who provided many valuable suggestions and comments:

Mario E. Blaser, York University
Rex Brynen, McGill University
Derek Hall, Trent University
Richard Sandbrook, University of Toronto
Jeffrey Steeves, University of Saskatchewan
Rebecca Tiessen, Dalhousie University

Appreciation is also expressed to the authors and publishers who have given permission to include their work in this volume. At Thomson Nelson, we would like to acknowledge the excellent and patient support of Bram Sepers, Katherine Goodes, and other members of the staff. Thanks also to Chris Charlton for his work as research assistant on parts of the book.

Mark Charlton
Paul Rowe
Trinity Western University
Langley, B.C.

About the Editors

Mark Charlton is a Professor of Political Studies and Dean of Research and Faculty Development at Trinity Western University. He has written *The Making of Canadian Food Aid Policy* (1992) and has co-edited with Paul Barker, *Crosscurrents: Contemporary Political Issues,* fifth edition (2005) and edited *Crosscurrents: International Relations,* fourth edition (2005). He also co-authored the *Thomson Nelson Guide to Research and Writing in Political Science.* In addition, he has published a number of articles in *International Journal, Etudes Internationales,* and *The Canadian Journal of Development Studies.*

Paul Rowe is an Assistant Professor of Political Studies and Coordinator of International Studies at Trinity Western University. His research interests surround the politics of religion in developing countries and at the global level. He has published articles on the relationship between religion and politics in Middle Eastern states and among diaspora groups, included in *Nationalism and Minority Identities in Islamic Societies* (Montreal and Kingston: McGill-Queen's, 2005) and in *Journal of Church and State.*

PART ONE

CONTENDING PERSPECTIVES ON DEVELOPMENT

Are development and globalization a form of imperialism?

Are Development and Globalization a Form of Imperialism?

✔ **YES**
HENRY VELTMEYER, "Development and Globalization as Imperialism,"
Canadian Journal of Development Studies, 26, no. 2 (2005): 89–106

✗ **NO**
ECONOMIC COMMISSION FOR LATIN AMERICA AND THE CARIBBEAN,
Globalization and Development (New York: ECLAC, 2002), pp. 17–27

The modern study and pursuit of developmentalist thinking has evolved over the course of the past few decades and was strongly shaped by the dominant world order of which it was a part. At the end of the Second World War, the victorious allies sought to create international institutions that would help to guide the new international system out of the economic and strategic ruts that had led to war. Inevitably, this led to the division of the international system between the capitalist and liberal-democratic West and the communist East. Each of these power blocs sought to prescribe their own approaches to improving and developing those areas of the world that were in the process of "modernizing." The Western pattern of development prescribed liberal economics, the expansion of freer trade, and management of international economic relations through the Bretton Woods institutions, including the International Monetary Fund and the World Bank. The Eastern bloc sought to expand the influence of revolutionary movements and to overturn the erstwhile orders in traditional societies through central planning and, in some places, enforced modernization and industrialization.

By the early 1950s, the pursuit of developmental strategies was seen by both sides in the Cold War to be a key means of extending ideological and political sway in areas of the developing world. The Marshall Plan of 1947 proffered aid for European nations if they would accept liberal domestic and international reforms. As the reforms were unacceptable to the Soviet Union, Eastern bloc satellites were unable to accept. After the successful spread of Communist revolution in a set of developing countries sponsored in whole or in part by Soviet influence, Western nations deliberately set out to provide aid as a means of leveraging developing countries toward liberalizing their economies and following the capitalist model. For example, the Colombo Plan of 1950 was a deliberate attempt by the developed nations of the Commonwealth to provide overseas development assistance (ODA) to fellow Commonwealth partners as a means of forestalling Communist revolution and supporting the American Cold War policy of containment.

The theoretical bases upon which the development project proceeded were equally dependent upon contending theoretical bases. The doctrinaire development perspective emerging out of the Second World War was the modernization perspective that had taken hold over the preceding century. This held that backward traditional, rural, and pre-industrial societies moved inexorably toward modern, urban, industrial societies with a complex new division of labour. Development implied concerted effort to move underdeveloped societies toward modern societies. Among the Western capitalist countries, it was assumed that this would take place through the provision of developmental aid to enhance a country's industrialization through specialization and integration into the world economy. The Soviet bloc sought to promote modernization instead through collectivization and central planning. While challenges were applied to the predominant modernization theory by critics of dependency, the modernization paradigm remained largely unchallenged when industrialization strategies promoted by dependency theory failed to provide sustainable solutions for developing countries in the midst of the macroeconomic shocks of the 1970s and 1980s.

For these reasons, the international institutions and development agencies that are most significant today were birthed in a political environment in which they were designed to be extensions of Cold War foreign policy and to spread modernization via the prevailing developmental paradigm. In the late 1980s came the decline of Soviet power and the disappearance of the contending force of Communism. By the early 1990s, developing countries were increasingly forced to adapt their economies to the neoliberal economic system in order to receive financial assistance and aid to further develop their economies. International financial institutions (IFIs) such as the International Monetary Fund and the World Bank came to be extremely influential in this process. Since most developing nations were suffering significant balance of payments difficulties and needed to support continued development through agencies that would provide to countries with a proven poor track record in repayment, they were forced to accept the neoliberal reforms demanded by the IFIs. Developing countries increasingly came to be influenced by these reforms (known as Structural Adjustment Policies or SAPs) and to be integrated into the globalized world economy.

As a result, the practice and theory of development today takes place within a system that has largely embraced the neoliberal economic system fostered and spread during the Cold War, a system designed to promote the political and economic values that underpinned American primacy. In the 1990s, the United States emerged from the Cold War as the most powerful and dominant force in world politics, with the largest economy and the highest degree of influence on the international financial institutions. What is more, American primacy has come to be reinforced in world politics through the doctrine of pre-emption (the "Bush doctrine") and the unchallenged use of coercive force to promote American interests abroad.

It has become common for some scholars of international political economy to see US power in the model of a new global empire, in which American foreign policy is to use US influence to extend its dominance. In this view, the institutions that support the global economy and the development assistance that seeks to enhance development in the global South are still vehicles for the promotion of American power, as they were during the Cold War. Today this no longer takes place in the midst of bipolar competition for world power but in the context of American primacy—hence it is said to be imperialistic. Others argue that no matter the challenges implicit in the process of structural adjustment and the fact that these reforms take place in the context of American dominance, development that takes place by embracing globalization and the adoption of neoliberal norms can come to serve the needs of developing countries and help to improve their performance.

In the following piece, Henry Veltmeyer argues that development and globalization cannot be understood outside the growth of American power and imperialism. On the other hand, the Economic Commission for Latin America and the Caribbean (ECLAC) emphasizes the progressive nature of development and globalization and the extent to which it promotes improvement in societies of the South in spite of the inherent political challenges that have arisen over the years.

✔ **YES**
Development and Globalization as Imperialism
HENRY VELTMEYER

INTRODUCTION

The epoch-defining changes of recent years are constructed three different ways in academic discourse.[1] One is in recent terms of development, a project initiated after the Second World War but which, after the onset of a system-wide production crisis and a series of systemic involutions and strategic responses, was reconstituted as globalization. A second makes reference to globalization as a progress designed to release the "forces of freedom, democracy and private enterprise," to quote from George W. Bush's 2002 *National Security Report.* In this conception of the transformative social change that has characterized world development in recent years, "globalization" is viewed as the irresistible and desirable outcome of economic and political adjustments to the requirements of a new world order, a process in which—to return to George W. Bush—"good" (the forces of economic and political freedom, prosperity, and peace) will vanquish "evil" (constraints on these forces, opponents of freedom, rogue regimes). A third way of understanding these changes and associated developments is as imperialism in its diverse forms. That is how these changes and developments are understood and presented in this paper. In fact, it is argued that both development and globalization can be understood in this way, as different faces of the same dynamics arising out of a project of world domination and longstanding efforts of the United States to establish its hegemony over the whole system.

[...]

[...] Given the unabashed transparency of the new imperialism and its call for, and reliance on, overt coercive force and unilateral action (justified in terms of advancing the forces of economic and political freedom) there is in fact no further need for the dissimulation, ideological covering, or covert operations that have characterized imperialism over the years. However, the guardians of the new world order, if not the White House neoconservatives, have discovered that the iron fist of military force still needs to be gloved in politically acceptable terms. The point is that the economics of adjustment to the requirements of the new world order (international economic integration) require corresponding politics to ensure a successful outcome of the process involved—or, in the neoliberal conception, "good governance." The neoliberal model of capitalist development and globalization is profoundly exclusionary and destabilizing, generating powerful forces of resistance that make the entire process ungovernable. This is where "development" comes in—or back, rather—not as a model and strategy for reviving the capital accumulation (and economic growth) process (globalization is called upon in this regard) but to provide conditions of political stability for the neoliberal world order and a local benign or human face to imperialism. The paper ends on this point, concluding that nongovernmental development organizations and other elements of civil society have been pressed into imperial service, providing strategic assistance to the empire in its concern and effort to quell the fire of revolutionary ferment on the southern periphery of the system, particularly in the countryside of rural development and social movements.

I. DEVELOPMENT AS IMPERIALISM

Although it can be traced to the 18th century Enlightenment and the idea of progress, development as we know it (as a macroproject involving, or based on, international cooperation) had its birth in US foreign policy and the Cold War—in its diverse efforts, orchestrated by the US State Department, to ensure that the post-colonial state in the economically "backward" areas of the developing world would not fall prey to the lure of communism or the example for rapid growth and national development set by the USSR.

A. Aid in the 1940s and 1950s: The War against Communism

According to Wolfgang Sachs (1992) and his associates in postdevelopment theory (inter alia, Esteva and Prakash 1998), development was "invented" in the late 1940s as a form of imperialism—a means of imposing relations of domination on peoples and states struggling to liberate themselves from the yoke of colonialism. The idea of development itself is here traced back to the program of overseas development assistance (ODA) announced by US President Truman on 10 January 1949. But in its multilateral form it originates in various projects funded by the International Bank of Reconstruction and Development (subsequently known as the World Bank) in Chile in 1948 and in Brazil and Mexico the year after. The World Bank is a pillar of the Bretton Woods system designed to resurrect the global form of capitalist development and international trade (and international economic integration) characteristic of earlier epochs.[2]

In regard to ODA, the US government was by far the major donor, and the foreign policy geopolitical and strategic considerations of the US government the most relevant in shaping the form that uses foreign aid. The central issue had to do with how the broader geopolitical strategic interests of the United States could be served by it. Some voices were raised to the effect that it would not be in the economic interest of the United States to promote economic development in the backward areas of the world and that efforts to contain the underdeveloped countries within the Western bloc would be unrealistic and not fruitful for American interests. But the view that prevailed was that ODA was indeed a useful means of advancing the geopolitical interests of the United States (to prevent the spread of communism) without damaging its economic interest (Cohen et al. 1968).

B. Aid in the 1960s and 1970s: Reform or Revolution?

In the developing world, the emphasis of aid was on building the administrative capacity of the state and providing the infrastructure for both public and private enterprise—"nation-building" in the parlance of imperial policy. In Latin America, however, as well as in parts of Asia, the main concern was to stave off pressure for revolutionary change—to prevent another Cuba (and China). To this end, the US Agency for International Development (USAID) promoted state-led reforms and the public provision of credit and technical assistance to the rural poor.

Much of ODA took a bilateral form but USAID also turned to nongovernmental organizations (NGOs) as their executing arm, bypassing governments to channel funds more directly to the local communities. These NGOs (private voluntary organizations as they were termed) not only provided a useful channel for ODA but also for various collateral services to benefit to donors, such as the strengthening of local organizations that were prepared to opt for social reform and local development rather than social revolution, and the weakening of class-base anti-systemic/anti-capitalist state organizations. In this context, NGOs were also used—somewhat innocently from the perspective of their middle-class workers—not only to elude revolution and promote economic and social development but to promote the virtues of democracy and capitalism: the use of electoral mechanism in politics, the market mechanism (free trade, mobile capital) in economics, and reform as the modality of change.

In effect, as noted by Bombarolo, Coscio Perez, and Stein (1990) and argued more recently by Petras (in Petras and Veltmeyer 2001), many if not most NGOs have tended to serve as executing agents of US imperialism, promoting values and behaviour functional for the economic and political interests of the growing US Empire.[3] In this they resembled the missionaries of the old imperialism in the promotion of change in the next rather than in this world and the vocation to spread the gospel— in this case the good word about reform and democracy—and information about the evil forces (communism, revolutionary change) that were lurking the land.

The difference between the new missionaries of old—then again perhaps there is no fundamental difference in that more often than not they were unaware of the broader implications of their interventions—is that NGOs were not apparatuses commissioned to spread the gospel. Generally they were, as they are today, composed of well-intentioned individuals concerned to make a difference, albeit small, in the lives of people they touched with their assistance. Nevertheless, in their micro-projects and mediations between the donors and recipient organizations, they could not help but promote an alternative to the politics of revolutionary change, and it was to this end that they were contracted and funded. USAID and the broader donor community used NGOs as partners in the shared development enterprise. They helped turn local communities away from revolution and promote reform, and, in the process, create conditions that would allow the empire to advance its economic and geopolitical interests.[4]

C. Foreign Aid and System in Transition: 1973–83

The years 1948–1973 have been described as the "golden age of capitalism" (Marglin and Schor 1990). But in the late 1960s cracks began to appear in the foundations of the system. The result was an extended period of crisis and diverse strategic efforts to restructure the system as a way out. One strategic response involved a direct assault by capital on labour—attacking its share of national income to that point linked to productivity gains, its organizational capacity, and political power (Davis 1984; Crouch and Pizzorno 1978).[5] The aim of this counteroffensive was in increase the pool of capital available for productive investment. The result was a compression of wages to the point that in many cases their value or purchasing power in 2003 was still below levels achieved in 1973 (Weisbrot 2002). In the United States, for example, wages fell 10% in as many years (1974–83) and continued to fall subsequently, particularly in the years of Reaganomics in which the individuals in the upper reaches (the top 1%) of the wealth and income hierarchy appropriated all of the proceeds of economic growth. In Latin America, the power of organized labour regarding the capacity to negotiate collective agreements for higher wages and improved conditions was so reduced that the share of labour (wages and salaries) in national income (and value added to production) in many cases fell by over 50 percentage points—from over 40% in the 1970s to below 20 after a decade and more of "structural" (neoliberal) reform. This process of income concentration, and associated conditions of wealth and poverty on the extremes of the income distribution, unfolded on a global scale but in some countries and regions the results were particularly dramatic. In Argentina, for example, even today, after more than a decade of economic restructuring and neoliberal reform the level of per capita income is still well below that achieved in 1970. And Argentina is by no means an isolated or the most exemplary case.

Other less direct strategic responses to the worldwide capitalist crisis included a process of technological conversion and productive transformation; the evolution of a new more flexible form of regulation (postfordism); a global restructuring of finance, provided primarily in the form of "official" ODA, which at the time dominated global North–South capital flows ("international transfer of resources" in official discourse); and a restructuring of national macroeconomic policy on the basis of what the World Bank economists dubbed "structural adjustment."

Regarding financial capital flows, the dominant stream took the form of ODA, offered as a supplemental form of finance needed to stimulate economic growth. Until 1983 such official transfers of financial resources were channelled into projects designed to establish the infrastructure for economic activity and nation-building. However, after the onset of a region-wide debt crisis, official transfers began to assume a different form: loans conditioned by policy reforms oriented toward the free market and democracy (Burnside and Dollar 1997; Carothers 1999; Rodrik 1995).

Until this point the World Bank and other international financial institutions (IFIs) took the position that ODA would service development strategies that were "owned" by countries pursuing their own development path. But with the leverage provided by the debt crisis, bank lending was conditional on structural reforms designed by economists at the World Bank—reforms that were market friendly and conducive to good governance (Kaufmann, Kraay, and Zoido-Lobatón 1999; World Bank 1994).

In the wake of the global production crisis in the early 1970s, US and European commercial banks initiated a lending policy that led to an explosion of private capital and debt financing. The flows involved in this form of capital would come to exceed the official resource transfers (ODA) and, for some years (particularly in the first half of the 1990s), the flow of capital associated with the multinational corporations (MNCs). The following table provides a historic picture of these capital flows as well as some of the returns on the investments involved.

These data reflect global trends in "international resource transfers," including the eclipse of ODA by private capital flows, a dramatic decline of commercial lending in the 1980s and then again after the Asian financial crisis in 1997, and

TABLE 1.1

LONG-TERM NORTH–SOUTH FINANCIAL FLOWS, 1985–2001 (IN US$ BILLIONS)

	'85–89	'90–94	'95	'96	'97	'98	'99	'00	'01
ODA	200.0	274.6	55.3	31.2	43.0	54.5	46.1	37.9	36.2
Private	157.0	547.5	206.1	276.6	300.8	283.2	224.4	225.8	160.0
FDI	76.0	268.5	106.8	130.8	172.5	178.3	184.4	166.7	168.2
Portfolio Inv	6.0	111.5	36.1	49.2	30.2	15.6	34.5	50.9	18.5
Other	75.0	172.5	63.2	126.2	98.1	−10.7	25.5	8.2	−26.7
Net Resource Inflow	357.0	822.5	261.4	307.8	343.8	337.7	270.5	263.7	196.2
FDI Profits	66.0	96.5	26.5	30.0	31.8	35.2	40.3	45.4	55.3
Debt Payments	354.0	356.5	100.8	106.6	112.9	118.7	121.9	126.7	122.2
Net Resource Outflow	420.0	453.0	227.3	136.6	144.7	153.9	162.2	172.1	177.5

Source: IMF (2000); World Bank (2002).

the growth of foreign direct investment (FDI) as the dominant flow of capital (the "backbone of private sector external financial flows," as the International Monetary Fund puts it) and used primarily to acquire the assets of privatized enterprises or merge with other firms. The data also reflect the imperial agency of the world's largest transnational corporations, the basic operating units of the Euromerican Empire, whose operations in Latin America alone—facilitated by a process of financial liberalization—netted over US\$ 100 billion profits in the 1990s (Saxe-Fernández and Núñez 2001). And these net resource transfers do not take into account the surplus value extracted from the direct producers and workers through wage exploitation, relations of international trade, and other means (Petras, Veltmeyer, and Vasapollo 2005).

D. The Imperialism of Foreign Aid and Debt

With the onset of the debt crisis, creditors lined up behind the World Bank and the International Monetary Fund (IMF) and capital in the form of loans dried up. Table 1.1 suggests that in the 1980s, more than US\$ 350 billion was diverted from the developing countries (primarily Latin America) to the head offices of the commercial banks—a capital drain that led directly to a "decade lost to development" in Latin America. As of 1995, virtually no new loans have been extended to developing countries by the commercial banks, while another US\$ 800 billion were lost to development due to policy reforms set by the World Bank as a conditionality of further "aid" (Burnside and Dollar 1997; Mosley 1999; World Bank 1998). Saxe-Fernández and Núñez (2001) documented a huge net outflow from Latin America to the American and European centres of the empire by diverse means, primarily financial mechanisms of surplus transfer. The United Nations Conference on Trade and Development (UNCTAD 2004) has extended this study to all developing societies on the periphery of the world capitalist system. According to UNCTAD, in 2004 alone the developing countries made a net financial contribution of close to US\$ 240 billion to the rich countries of the North.

These policy reforms and their dynamics have been subjected to considerable study, particularly as regards their socioeconomic impacts (see, for example, Collier 1997; Gwin and Nelson 1997; Veltmeyer and Petras 1997, 2000). They are based on what has become known as the "new economic model" or, more revealingly, "neolilberalism," a doctrine that argues the need for countries to integrate their economies into a single global economy. These policies include the privatization of public enterprises; liberalization or trade and financial flows; deregulation of product, capital, and labour markets; and downsizing of the state, particularly as regards economic and social programming. The point of these structural reforms, aimed at substituting the institutions or private enterprise for the state, is to unleash the forces of economic freedom from their tethers, allowing them to operate with as few constraints as possible (Bulmer-Thomas 1996).

The 1990s saw the global spread of a virus that first affected Mexico and then Southeast Asia in mid-1997. By most accounts caused by the volatile and deregulated movement of hundreds of billions of dollars in capital in search of short-term profit, the Asian financial crisis devastated economy after economy in the region, stilling talk (and much writing) about the "economic miracle" of rapid growth in parts of Asia.

The financial crisis resurrected the spectre of a more generalized economic crisis, even a collapse of the system. Under these conditions the multinational commercial banks again pulled out, leaving a vacuum only partially filled by FDI (the privatization bonanza was largely over), leading to another half decade lost to development (ECLAC 2002). Official aid flows in this context were minimal and largely unproductive, as were FDI flows, destined as they largely were to the purchase and acquisition of privatized assets. The results of these developments are not hard to find. They are exemplified in the experience of Argentina, hitherto the strongest economy in Latin America but now in the throes of a far-reaching crisis and in default on its debt payment obligations to its external creditors, incurring the wrath of the IMF.

E. Alternative Development and Imperialism in an Era of Globalization: 1983–2003

ODA, as noted, originated as a policy for meeting the strategic foreign policy requirements of the US state. In retrospect it can quite properly be described as an imperial policy in the service of a long-established project of world domination and hegemony.[6] Subsequently, with the agency of the NGOs, the development project was constructed as a means of defusing pressures for revolutionary change within its client states. The history of the US state intervention in Central America—one of the more successful arenas for the projection of US state power—testifies that more often than not development did not work. True, no other Cuba emerged in the region but this was the result not so much of the operations of USAID as the projection of military force and the extensive "aid" provided to counterinsurgency forces in the region.

In the 1980s an entirely new context was created for ODA by a new neoliberal project of globalization based on a program of free market policy reforms. In this context the development project was not abandoned but it was reconstructed—designed as an alternative, more participatory form of development based on the partnership of intergovernmental ODA organizations and nongovernmental organizations that would mediate between the donors and the grassroots in the execution of a new generation of development projects targeted at the problem of poverty. The actual flow of funds channelled through NGOs, many of which were unwittingly converted into agents of the new imperialism—bearers of the gospel about free market capitalism and democracy—was actually very modest (less than 10% of the total) but enough to induce many organizations in the popular sector to turn away from direct collective action against the system and to opt for a participatory form of local development.

This form of development is predicated on the accumulation not of natural, physical, and financial assets but of "social capital," which, unlike the accumulation of other forms of capital, requires neither political confrontation with the power structure nor substantive change (Knack 1999; Woolcock and Narayan 2000). Development in this form is predicated on changing not the structures of economic and political power but rather how people feel about themselves and their capacity for action, and is oriented toward empowerment, providing the poor with a sense of participation and involvement in decision-making (albeit limited to decisions as to how to spend the meagre poverty alleviation funds that come their way or financing their micro-enterprises). It is in this context that Heloise Weber (2002, 146) could write of micro-finance and microcredit as a "coherent set of tools that may facilitate as well as govern the globalization agenda." From "the perspective of the architects of global development," she writes, "the micro-credit agenda (and thus, the 'poverty alleviation' strategy of the World Bank—'Sustainable Banking with the Poor') ... is conducive to facilitating policy changes at the local level according to the logic of globalization ... while at the same time advancing its potential to discipline locally in the global governance agenda" (Weber 2002, 146).

[...]

II. GLOBALIZATION AS IMPERIALISM

A. Crisis and Restructuring under a New Economic Model

One aspect of the class was unleashed by capital in the 1970s was a direct assault on labour. Another was a turn toward a new economic policy agenda based on a neoclassical economic theory that held up the world market as the fundamental engine of economic growth and the private sector multinational enterprises as its driver. In the orthodoxy of development theory in the 1950s and 1960s the absence or weakness of the capitalist class in economically backward countries required the state to step in and assume the function of capital (investment, entrepreneurship, management) and a leading role in the economy. With reference to this idea the pioneers of development economists designed a model that was highly functional for governments in the developing world. It emphasized the need for, and resulted in a policy emphasis on (1) nationalization—state takeover of firms in strategic industries—as well as the need for state enterprises not just in the area of infrastructure, utilities, and social programming but in the leading or strategic sectors of the economy; (2) the regulation of economic activity and commodity, capital, and labour markets; (3) import substitution based on the protection of domestic industry from outside competition; (4) an inward orientation of national production; and (5) increased programming in the areas of economic development and social welfare.

Under conditions of a by-then decade-long and system-wide production crisis, a growing fiscal crisis, and an impending debt crisis, this model succumbed to the attacks on it from the Right, which had achieved state power in the Southern cone of South America in the 1970s and managed to capture the state power in the United States, the United Kingdom, and elsewhere in the developing and developed world. On the basis of several Latin American experiments with the "most sweeping economic reforms in history," economists at the World Bank designed a new economic model intended to halt and reverse a decade-long trend toward the slow but steady incorporation of the working class and non-capitalist producers into the economic and political development process. This model, dubbed and subsequently known as "neoliberalism," prescribed a package of policies (presented as structural reforms) that make up what Williamson (1990) has termed the "Washington Consensus."

B. The Economics of Adjustment: Globalization in Theory, Neoliberalism in Practice

The new economic model, and the policy reform program derived from it, was presented by the World Bank as a development program, i.e., as the only way of moving forward, placing countries on the path of economic growth and prosperity, and, in the process, providing necessary and possible conditions for attacking the problem of widespread poverty. However, it was clear enough that the agenda behind these policies was not economic development but rather globalization, the creation of a new world economy based on economic freedom within the policy and institutional framework of the new world order. The first clear reference to this agenda was in 1996 at a conference convened by the US Council for Foreign Relations, a major part of what Salbuchi (2000) dubs the "'braintrust' of the system" (Ostry 1990). At this point globalization was presented not as it would be some years later—as a process (i.e., as the inevitable outcome of the workings of a system that did not allow for any alternatives)—but as a project with desirable outcomes (economic growth, etc.).

The object of this consensus was to create a system in which, to paraphrase George W. Bush's 2002 *National Security Report,* the forces of economic and political freedom could flourish, vanquishing the enemies of freedom and obstacles such as government regulation, capital controls, and restrictions on the movement of goods and capital. The necessary condition for this "development" was the structural adjustment of national economies to the requirements of this new world economic order (adoption of the specified structural reforms in their national policy) and thus their integration into the world economy. By the end of the decade in Latin America all the four countries were more or less—to various degrees and unevenly in regard to different policies in the program—integrated under conditions of privatization and financial liberalization, so much so that private capital (the IFIs and MNCs) had managed to achieve dominion over the global economy, generating an enormous influx and reflux of capital. The bulk of this capital—more than 95%, it has been estimated—is either speculative or unproductive in nature, used to acquire privatized and other firms or speculate on exchange rates or future contracts rather than productive investment in new technology.

Studies by Saxe-Fernández, cited above, have established some of the outcomes of the process, which, in the 1990s, was extended to Argentina, Brazil, and Peru, three of the holdout countries relatively slow to get on the globalization train but once they did moved with alacrity and speed (Veltmeyer and Petras 1997, 2000). The negligible economic growth and increase social inequalities in the distribution of global (and national) incomes, and conditions of poverty and wealth at the extremes of this distribution, are, of course, well known.[7] They have been subject of considerable study and the facts are well established albeit with diverse interpretation.[8] However, what Saxe-Fernández established is a pronounced trend toward asset denationalization and a system that allowed the MNCs to generate an enormous pool of capital and siphon off financial resources in the form of profit on direct investments, interest on bank loans and portfolio investments, royalty payments, not to mention labour exploitation and unfair trade. According to UNCTAD (2004), taking a global view, this process in 2004 generated a net outflow of capital from the developing countries on the periphery of the system to the tune of US\$ 239 billion.[9]

[...]

CONCLUSION

Globalization has been presented as a form of development, the best if not only way of bringing about economic growth and placing countries on the road toward a future of prosperity. But both the project of international cooperation for development and globalization are shown to be masks for an entirely different project: US imperialism. As a point of fact, over the post-war years since the late 1940s, imperialism has taken the most diverse forms, the explanation of the most diverse dynamics of worldwide developments. It first emerged in the form of a system designed to ensure the economic dominance of the United States and advance the economic interests of its economic enterprises. In this system the economically backward countries were cast in the role of exporters of raw materials needed for the industrial centre of the empire.

In the same context imperialism also took the form of international cooperation for international development, a policy designed to ensure that the economically backward countries of the post-colonial world would pursue a capitalist path for their national development, sticking to a system set up to advance the economic and geopolitical interests of the United States, the hegemony of the post-war era. Soon thereafter, in the 1960s and 1970s, imperialism took the form of integrated rural development, a policy designed as a means of defusing pressure for revolutionary change as well as creating local conditions for penetration of US capital.

In the 1970s, under conditions of a system-wide crisis the entire liberal world order was under threat of falling apart, necessitating an overhaul of the economic model used to guide national economy policy, a model that assigned the predominant (political) role of allocating the productive resources of the system, and determining who gets what, to the nation-state.

In the 1980s a major strategic response to the crisis took the form of a new economic model used to launch a program of structural reforms in national policy that would usher in a new era, and create a new world in which national economies are integrated into a uniquely global economic system that would liberate the forces of economic and political freedom. The new world order was designed to create optimum conditions for liberating the constraints of the nation-state on the mobility of capital—on its capacity to find emerging markets and penetrate and dominate them (capital control and regulation of trade and markets)—and thereby accumulate more capital. The new world order also created conditions for several new forms of imperialism—from the imperialism of aid to the domination of trade and investment—based on a new world order, a new international division of labour, a process of economic globalization, and a Washington Consensus on correct policy. Under these conditions, the nation-state was restructured to better meet the new requirements of global capital and the nongovernmental organizations of civil society were enlisted in the service of empire, to participate in the construction of a good governance regime and thereby help advance the imperial project, to ensure the political and economic order needed for another round of economic imperialism.

In the 1990s we saw a decided shift in the dominant form of imperialism. The US economy, on the basis and by means of a multifaceted restructuring of the system,[10] was well on the road toward economic recovery and a renewal of the imperial project. But the US project of world domination was in jeopardy, beset by all sorts of countervailing forces and difficulties. Despite advances in its Central American backyard and increased influence in the less important Balkan states of Kosovo, Macedonia, and Serbia, US political and economic power throughout the 1990s was in decline in key areas of the world with a series of reverses and setbacks in other parts of the empire, particularly in the Middle East/Persian Gulf region, Latin America, Asia, and Europe (Petras 2001).

Under these conditions, as well as the advance of a neoconservative counter-attack, the project of the new imperialism was designed and put into motion. By most accounts it is a form of imperialism that is not afraid to be named and hide itself behind development or globalization; disposed to use whatever means at its disposal: the coercive apparatus and power of military force. The UN was designed as a bulwark against a unilateral quest for world domination, to force any world power to act multilaterally within a system of checks and balances, and to create an institutional mechanism for settling inter-imperialist conflicts. However, with the emergence of the United States as a sole superpower, the self-appointed defender of the forces of freedom, the constraints of this system by and large have been superseded or ignored.

In the 1990s, imperialism in its various forms, from the covert and overt projection of state power, from local development to war, from the war against poverty to the war against Iraq and international terrorism, can be viewed as a multifaceted effort to escape its constraints. The multiple and heavy costs of this effort and ultimate consequences warrant a closer look and further study, as do the forces of resistance generated in the process, forces that have been mobilized by diverse anti-systemic social movements. The weight and meaning of these forces, and their political dynamics, are of particular importance to an assessment of the outcome of the imperialist project. Scholars and activists should focus their attention and analysis on the resulting process.

NOTES

1. These three forms of understanding can be compared in their theoretical scope with the three meta-narratives that have dominated our understanding of the great historic transformation of society since the 18th century: modernization (from tradition to modernity or pre-modern to modern in terms of culture—the values that underpin institutional functioning); industrialization (from pre-industrial to industrial forms of economic activity and organization); and capitalist development (from pre-capitalist to a capitalist mode of production). From a poststructuralist (postmodern/postdevel-opment/postimperialist) perspective—it is hotly debated—this great transformation was essentially completed (at least in some places) in the 1970s and/or 1980s, leading to notions of a theoretical impasse or a crisis of understanding and the exhaustion (and thus irrelevance) of associated ideologies such as liberalism and socialism used to promote social changes (Booth 1985). Be this as it may, and notwithstanding a gen-eralized attack against all forms of structuralism, the concepts of "development," "globalization," and "imperialism," and their associated understandings, have been elaborated within different forms of structuralist discourse.

2. In this connection, many analysts have identified the current era as a third period of economic globalization characterized by the internationalization of capital, free trade, and the integration of nation economies into the world capitalist system. See Wolf (2004) and Pteras and Veltmeyer (2001) for radically opposed interpretations of the dynamics of this process.

3. Wallace (2004), perhaps more accurately, portrays NGOs not as executing agents but as unwitting "Trojan horses for global neoliberalism."

4. As for these economic interests, a number of studies have documented the resulting penetration of US capital in the Central (and South) American countryside, in the form of its multinational corporations, extracting huge volumes of surplus capital used to create or expand markets and pay dividends to shareholders.

5. The principal theatres of this class war were in Europe (Davis 1984; Crouch and Pizzorno 1978) and in Latin America, in the context of Operation Condor and other "dirty wars" waged against subversion and subversives (peasants in arms, human rights, union, and political activists), by Latin America's military regimes at the time.

6. In academic and political circles there is much talk and writing today about the "new imperialism," with reference to a project of empire building constructed by a group of neocons that have surrounded and entered the administration of George W. Bush. The literature on this is becoming voluminous. However, there is considerable evi-dence that this project, even in its projection of naked military power and resort to

unilateral action and pre-emptive strikes, is not at all new, that it can be traced out in virtually every administration in the 20th century, both republican and democratic, liberal and conservative, and not least in Clinton's administration (Leffler 2004).

7. The statistics related to these trends, if not their connection to globalization, have been acknowledged by one of the foremost defenders of the new economic model (neoliberalism, globalization): Martin Wolf (2004), chief economics commentator of the *Financial Times*.

8. Wolf (2004), like other hyper-globalists and apologists for free market capitalism, argues that non-globalization (the failure or refusal of a government to enter the process of international economic integration) is as much, if not more, at fault than globalization-inducing/supportive policies. However, there is a broad consensus in the academic community and key operating agencies of the UN that the increased social inequalities and the polarization of wealth and income, and new forms of poverty, can be directly attributed to the new economic model of neoliberal reforms. After all, they have been in place for over two decades in many countries and a decade or more in most.

9. Table 1.1 also points toward an enormous outflow of productive and financial resources from the developing countries to those at the centre—a veritable hemorrhage of the system's lifeblood. In this regard it is estimated that over the last decade, just in Latin America, outflows of capital in the form of various types of return on investments (profit repatriation, interest payments on debt and equity investments) were in excess of $750 billion (ECLAC, 2002). These transfers represent a huge drain of potential capital that could have been used to expand production in the developing countries. Even ODA in this connection has served as a mechanism of capital drain: in 2002 repayments by the developing countries to the World Bank exceeded total outlays of new financial resources. According to ECLAC (2002) over $69 billion in interest payments and profits were remitted from the region to the US home offices of the multinational corporations and banks in just one year. Saxe-Fernández notes that if we were to take account of the billions in royalty payments, shipping, insurance, and other service fees and the billions more illegally transferred by Latin American elites via US and European banks to overseas accounts, the total pillage for 2002 was closer to $100 billion. And this is in just one year in one part of the US Empire.

10. This restructuring process took a number of forms, each contributing conditions of a US recovery from what Brenner (2000) has termed the "long crisis," a capitalist production crisis that ended the "Golden Age of Capitalism" or what French historians have termed "the thirty glorious years" (Marglin and Schor 1990).

✗ **NO**

Globalization and Development
ECONOMIC COMMISSION FOR LATIN AMERICA
AND THE CARIBBEAN

In the past decade the concept of globalization has been employed widely in academic and political debate, but the meanings attributed to the term are far from consistent. In this document it is used to refer to the growing influence exerted at the local, national and regional levels by financial, economic, environmental, political, social and cultural processes that are global in scope. This definition of the term highlights the multidimensional nature of globalization. Indeed, although the economic facet of globalization is the most commonly referred to, it acts concomitantly with non-economic processes, which have their own momentum and therefore are not determined by economic factors. In addition, the tension that is generated between the different dimensions is a pivotal element of the process. In the economic sphere but also—and especially—in the broadest sense of the term, the current process of globalization is incomplete and asymmetric, and is marked by major shortcomings in the area of governance.

The dynamics of the globalization process are shaped, to a large extent, by the fact that the actors involved are on an unequal footing. Developed-country governments, together with transnational corporations, exert the strongest influence, while developing-country governments and civil society organizations hold much less sway. Moreover, these actors, particularly developed-country governments, reserve and exercise the right to take unilateral and bilateral action and to participate in regional processes, concurrently with their participation in debates and negotiations of global scope.

The meaning of the term "globalization" as used in this document is positively couched and is intended to serve the purposes of analysis. It does not embrace the normative use of the concept as referring to the only possible road to the full liberalization and integration of world markets, which is seen as the inevitable and desirable fate of all humankind.[1] The history of the twentieth century refutes such a view, as the period between the world wars was marked by a long and conflictive reversal of the internationalization process. The development of multilateral institutions which has accompanied this process over the last two centuries and the current debate on global governance show that there is not just one possible international order, nor is there a single way of dividing responsibilities among global, regional and national institutions and agencies. Moreover, the course of events in developed and developing countries has revealed that there are many ways to carve out a position in the global economy (ECLAC, 2000; Albert, 1991; Rodrik, 2001a). The differences are a reflection of each country's history and its perception of the opportunities and risks involved in becoming integrated into the world economy.

[...]

I. THE GLOBALIZATION PROCESS

The contemporary process of internationalization dates back to the emergence of capitalism in Europe in the late Middle Ages, the new scientific and cultural thinking embodied by the Renaissance and the establishment of the great European nations and their empires. The expansion of capitalism is the only historical phenomenon to have been truly global, albeit incomplete, in scope. To a greater extent than other parts of the developing world, the history of Latin America and the Caribbean has been strongly influenced by this phenomenon ever since the late fifteenth century.

Modern historians distinguish a number of stages[2] in the last 130 years of globalization which, with a few adaptations, will be employed here. The first phase, from 1870 to 1913, was marked by great capital and labour mobility, together with a trade boom which was the result of dramatically reduced transport costs rather than of free trade. This phase of globalization was cut short by the First World War. As a result, in the 1920s it was impossible to resume the trend of previous years, and in the 1930s the globalization process was openly reversed.

After the Second World War, a new stage of global integration began. This period consisted of two entirely different phases. The watershed events of the early 1970s that marked the changeover from the first to the second included the disintegration of the macroeconomic regulation regime established in 1944 in Bretton Woods, the first oil crisis, the increasing mobility of private capital—intensified by the first two phenomena—and the end of the "golden age" of growth in the industrialized countries (Marglin and Schor, 1990). If the early 1970s are taken as the turning point, then an earlier phase of globalization can be identified, which lasted from 1945 to 1973. This period was characterized by a major effort to develop international institutions for financial and trade cooperation and by a significant expansion of trade in manufactures between developed countries. It was also marked by widely varying models of economic organization and limitations on the mobility of capital and labour. The final quarter of the twentieth century ushered in a third phase of globalization, with the gradual spread of free trade, the growing presence on the international scene of transnational corporations operating as integrated production systems, the expansion and notable mobility of capital and a shift towards the standardization of development models. At the same time, restrictions on the movement of labour persisted.

This long process has been fuelled by successive technological revolutions and—most of all—by advances that have cut the costs of transportation, information and communications.[3] The shortening of distances, in the economic sense of the term, is a cumulative effect of cost reductions and of the development of new means of transport, in combination with the capacity for the "real time" transmission of information, starting with the invention of the telegraph and expanding with the telephone and the television. Access to information on a mass scale, however, became possible only with the development of information and communications technologies in recent years. These technologies have drastically reduced the cost of access to information, though not, obviously, the cost of processing it or, therefore, of making effective use of it.

Advances in transportation, information and communications are part of a wider range of technological innovations which have resulted in unprecedented leaps in productivity, economic expansion and increased international trade. In the European countries, the large capital cities have been engaged in international trade since inception of modern capitalism (Braudel, 1994). The internationalization of corporate production dates back to the late nineteenth century, when it emerged as a by-product of economic concentration in the industrialized countries. In fact, this is the phenomenon that marked the birth of transnational corporations. From the 1970s on, it became increasingly common for labour-intensive tasks, such as assembly or *maquila* activities, to be outsourced in other countries, in a trend facilitated by the reduction in transport costs and the trade regulations established by the industrialized countries. This was the first step towards the development of integrated production systems, in which production can be divided into various stages ("dismemberment of the value chain"). In such systems, the outsourcing plants or firms in different countries can then specialize in the production of certain components, in particular phases of production, or in the assembly of specific models.

These changes in the structure of production and trade have made major players of large corporations and business conglomerates. In fact, the development of integrated production systems and increased flows of trade and foreign direct investment go hand in hand with the growing influence of transnational corporations. The key factor has undoubtedly been the liberalization of trade, financial flows and investment in developing countries, whose pace has increased in the last two decades. These phenomena are partly to account for the huge wave of foreign investment and the marked concentration of production at the world level which were a hallmark of the final decade of the twentieth century.

As in the case of trade, international financial transactions originated in Europe at about the same time as modern capitalism (Kindleberger, 1984; Braudel, 1994). In the nineteenth century, London was the main international financial centre and presided over the consolidation of the gold standard as a system of international payments and macroeconomic regulation. Paris and—by the early twentieth century—New York were its closest competitors. The subscription of capital for large-scale projects, especially in infrastructure and natural resources, and the creation of an international market in public debt bonds were the predominant modalities of long-term international capital movements during the first phase of globalization. These developments were then joined by systems for financing international trade, with the emergence of an incipient international banking network.

Long-term financing arrangements were then hit by a series of crises, however, and nearly disappeared as a result of the worldwide depression of the 1930s, the collapse of the gold standard and the massive moratoriums that ensued. As a response to this situation, the Bretton Woods agreements were adopted in 1944 with a view to creating a multilateral system of macroeconomic regulation based on fixed but adjustable exchange rates and on financial support for countries threatened with balance-of-payments crises. Another response was the establishment of an official international banking system at both the national level (export and import banks) and the multilateral level (World Bank and, later, Inter-American Development Bank and other regional banks).

In the 1960s, long-term international private flows reappeared, thanks in part to a new phase of global economic stability, but also to other factors: the surplus of dollars that built up in the 1960s and of petrodollars in the 1970s; the abandonment of the Bretton Woods system of fixed rates and the flotation of the main currencies in the early 1970s; the rapid development of institutional saving in the 1980s, led by the United States and the United Kingdom; and the emergence of an increasingly large financial derivatives market in the last decade of the twentieth century, which made it possible to hedge the risks associated with different financial assets and liabilities.

Globalization has proceeded at a faster pace in the financial sphere than in trade and production, and it can reasonably be argued that we live in an era in which the financial sphere holds sway over the real sector of the economy (ECLAC, 2001a). Both processes are taking place within a framework of profound institutional restructuring at the global level. And the essence of that process has been the liberalization of international current and capital transactions. The design of new global economic rules continues to be inadequate, however, and clearly suffers from institutional gaps.

[...]

II. NON-ECONOMIC DIMENSIONS

1. Ethical and Cultural Dimensions

Economic globalization is taking place alongside other processes that have a dynamic of their own. One of the most positive of these processes is what ECLAC has termed the "globalization of values". This concept refers to the gradual spread of shared ethical principles (ECLAC, 2000a) and is manifested most clearly in declarations on human rights. The two main dimensions of concern here are: (i) civil and political rights, by virtue of which individuals have autonomy from the power of the State and are entitled to participate in public decision-making; and (ii) economic, social and cultural rights, which reflect the values of economic and social equality, solidarity and non-discrimination. This process has also found expression in the accession to

United Nations human rights conventions by a growing number of governments (see figure 1.1). This phenomenon is reflected in the declarations issued by the participants in world summits held under United Nations auspices on the environment, social development, population, women and the rights of the child, among others. The Millennium Declaration (United Nations, 2000) is one of the most comprehensive expressions of the principles agreed upon at those summits.

[...]

At the same time, it is important to note that this "globalization of values" sometimes comes into conflict with a diametrically opposed type of globalization that reflects the penetration of market-economy values into social relations (in the areas of production, culture and even the family). The tension generated between these shared ethical principles and the extension of market relations into the sphere of values, which is implicit in the concept of a "market

FIGURE 1.1

RATIFICATION OF HUMAN RIGHTS CONVENTIONS (TOTAL COUNTRIES)

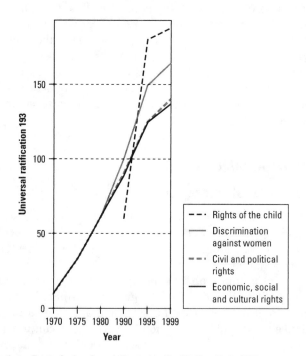

Source: United Nations, *Treaty Series. Cumulative Index,* No. 25, New York, 1999.

society," is another distinctive feature of the globalization process. This tension sometimes reaches the level of conflict because the international market lacks the mediation mechanisms which the political sphere has traditionally provided at the national level.

In recent years, the long history of social movements has taken on a new dimension: the effort to preserve the identity of peoples and social groups that feel threatened by the tendency towards cultural homogeneity imposed by globalization. This "right to be different" is interrelated in various ways with human rights in the traditional sense, which highlight the equality of citizens, both among themselves and with the State. Thus at the global level, equality and identity are interrelated in quite complex ways.

Globalization simultaneously undermines and fosters cultural diversity. Indeed, whole segments of the world population feel that their unique histories and the values that govern their communities are under threat. At the same time, however, globalization builds closer relationships among different cultural traditions and ways of life, and promotes a plurality of interpretations of the global order.

The speed of this process poses unprecedented challenges. On the one hand, it threatens to turn the enriching dialogue of cultures into a monologue. On the other, interaction opens up cultural opportunities, including those related to the mixture of different cultures, to new and varied groups and individuals. This process of incorporation through participatory and exclusionary mechanisms has given rise to new forms of organization. New networks, including virtual ones, are replacing the traditional forms of organization of protest movements.

[...]

The unprecedented development of the communications media has strongly influenced these processes and has also given rise to new problems. First, it has widened the gap between the cultural norms most broadly disseminated through global channels and the cultural and artistic roots of countries and regions. Second, control of the media, at the national and international levels, is concentrated in the hands of a few. This situation threatens the ideal of cultural diversity, since the control of symbolic exchanges affects identity-building and the formation of opinions and beliefs.[4] Third, the development of audiovisual media has led to greatly heightened personal expectations. Access to information is not always in balance with opportunities for steady employment and incomes, and, accordingly, for well-being and consumption. Today, more than ever before, the demonstration effect cuts across national boundaries. Lastly, participation in or exclusion from the electronic exchange of information has become a crucial factor for the exercise of citizenship, thereby posing the basic problem of how to prevent the emergence of a gap between those with access to information technology and those who suffer from "electronic invisibility".

2. The Political Dimension

International political relations have also undergone far-reaching changes in recent decades. The end of the cold war produced a dramatic change in the climate prevailing among sovereign States, while the exacerbation and increased visibility of a number of local conflicts generated international tensions of a very different nature than those seen before. While these trends had been in evidence since the 1970s, they became consolidated in the closing decade of the twentieth century, particularly as a result of the profound changes that took place after the fall of the Berlin Wall. The heightened predominance of the United States, European efforts to form a bloc capable of playing a leading role in global economic and political life, the setbacks suffered by Japan, the increased prominence of China and India, and the sudden transition experienced in the former socialist countries were the most salient features of this period.

These sweeping political changes have placed representative democracy in a position of unparalleled predominance. Political discourse is being shaped by an acceptance of the principles of pluralism, alternation of power, division of the powers of the State, election of authorities as a basis for legitimacy and recognition of the majority and respect for minorities, and these principles have begun to be applied much more widely.

Nevertheless, the transformations now under way have raised questions with respect to the functioning of all democratic institutions in societies where information, "image" and the power of money play a fundamental role. These criticisms extend to political parties, legislatures, the relationship between voters and representatives, and even the very meaning of politics, especially, though not exclusively, in the parts of the developing world that suffer from exclusion and poverty. Although democracy is the choice of the majority, there is certainly no scarcity of negative views regarding its workings and its effectiveness in meeting the population's needs. Since the peace dividend resulting from the end of the cold war has not yielded significant benefits, it has not yet been possible to cash in on the "democracy bonus".

Despite these difficulties, it is recognized that democracy is the best means of setting a development agenda (Sen, 1999) and that good governance is characterized by a focus on improving the design, management and evaluation of public policy, understood as the analytical and operational unit of government (Lahera, 1999). Nonetheless, government authorities and political leaders are under pressure to win broad local support and, at the same time, to respect the rigid rules deriving from specific forms of globalization. In this connection, it may be categorically stated that the promotion of democracy as a universal value is meaningless if national processes to provide for representation and participation are not allowed to influence the definition of economic and social development strategies or to mediate the tensions inherent in the globalization process.

The reduced capacity of the State has a bearing on the role which the public sector can play in reducing the cost of the "creative destruction" associated with rapid structural change and may exacerbate the difficulties involved in the modernization of the State. However, it is less than realistic to sing the praises of both globalization and the disintegration of the State at one and the same time. The role of the social State as a generator of technological and institutional externalities is and will remain very important. In a world of global risks, the claim that economic forces can and should take the place of public policy and the State is less and less convincing. It is helpful, in this connection, to recall the categorical warning issued by Polanyi (1957) in his analysis of the collapse of the first phase of globalization: if the market seeks to take precedence over society, it will end up destroying its own foundations.

III. OPPORTUNITIES AND RISKS

In the area of access to new technologies, as in the area of trade, the globalization of markets offers developing countries ample opportunity to integrate themselves more fully into the world economy. The sustained growth of international trade and the strengthening of multilateral rules and dispute settlement mechanisms within the framework of the World Trade Organization (WTO) are promising signs in this regard, as is regionalism when understood in the positive sense of open regionalism proposed by ECLAC (1994). However, the inroads being made in these directions run up against the incomplete liberalization of developed-country economies. The partial nature of this process is itself a reflection of the protectionist practices that still predominate in the world today, as well as the oversupply of certain goods in international trade, particularly raw materials. In addition, the developing countries face the challenge of adapting their policies to the institutional mechanisms required by WTO. This task has not been easy, and it may even have consequences that are more restrictive than desired. In fact, as will be shown later on in this study, global standards only generate greater disparities in the absence of genuine equality of opportunity at the international level.

The explosive pace of global financial development has created opportunities for financing and for hedging financial risk, but it has also revealed the enormous problems caused by the asymmetry existing between the strength of market forces and the weakness of the institutional frameworks that regulate them.[5] The coexistence of financial globalization and national macroeconomic policies, which are still formulated on the basis of domestic interests and contexts, creates considerable tension for developing countries. Their governments are subject to the uncertainty generated by the macroeconomic policies of developed countries, which do not adequately internalize their effects on the rest of the world and lack coordination mechanisms to ensure global coherence. These difficulties are compounded by the problems inherent in the financial market, particularly those of volatility and contagion, which have strongly affected the Latin American and Caribbean countries in recent decades. These phenomena are related to the market's inability to distinguish properly between different groups of borrowers, which elicits herd behaviour in the financial market during both booms and busts. The developing countries are also threatened by the globalization of financial volatility, which can have adverse effects on economic growth and social equity (French-Davis and Ocampo, 2001; Rodrik, 2001b).

Financial instability is the clearest, but not the only, manifestation of the progressive asymmetry between the power of the market and the lack of adequate economic governance. Other manifestations include the considerable economic concentration in evidence throughout the world and the multiple distributive tensions caused by the globalization process both between and within countries.[6] These phenomena reflect, among other factors, the stringent educational and knowledge requirements imposed by global technologies and markets, which threaten to marginalize those who are not fully prepared and to further confine the availability of these technologies and of new knowledge to just a few countries, social groups and enterprises. This process is part of a whole series of old and new threats to the economic and social security of the population, whose position is being made all the more precarious by a progressive weakening of the entire range of social safety nets, starting with those provided by the family and ending with those furnished by the State.

Globalization can also promote the emergence and appraisal of environmental comparative advantages, including the sustainable use of natural capital having economic value (forests, fisheries, tourist attractions), ecological value (natural sinks for the absorption of carbon and other pollutants) or aesthetic, historical or scientific value. This can give rise to countless policies on the development of ecotourism, research on new medicines, the use of empirical knowledge concerning natural resources management and the economic properties of local biological diversity, the use of the regional ecological supply (such as biomass and natural resources), the productive utilization of unique ecological niches and international negotiations on regional ecological services of global interest. At the national level, globalization can promote the improvement of public policies by raising the cost of implementing unsustainable strategies that adversely affect long-term development. One of the risks that arises in this connection, however, is the possibility that traditional comparative advantages may be lost without necessarily being replaced by new ones.

By definition, global environmental processes affect all countries, but small tropical countries, particularly island States, are especially vulnerable to global environmental changes, as is demonstrated by the increasing frequency and intensity of natural disasters. Indeed, unless specific national and international policies are adopted, the trend towards the overexploitation of certain natural resources, the underutilization of others and the transfer of ecological costs from major polluting countries to the region can be expected to intensify.

Globalization also provides unprecedented opportunities in non-economic areas. As noted earlier, the spread of global values, the struggle for the right to be different and the establishment of international mechanisms to defend the exercise of citizenship are notable advances that are reflected in the consolidation, insufficient though it may be, of respect for human rights, democracy, gender equality and ethnic diversity. The breakdown of archaic structures of domination and the control of abuses of power at the country level are some of the advances of this new global era. Nonetheless, this has not done away with the tensions created by the lack of channels, in some cases, for the legitimization of international actions and the reduction of the enormous imbalances of power existing at the global level. The globalization of the communications media and their concentration in the hands of a few also pose new problems. One of these problems is the strong tensions this generates between homogeneity and cultural diversity. Another is the enormous distance between symbolic integration into the globalized world and the insufficient capacity for actual integration owing to the sharp inequalities that exist in today's world.

Many of these problems stem from the incomplete and asymmetrical nature of the policy agenda associated with the current phase of the globalization process. This is largely because of the disparities, in terms of power and organization, found among the international players influencing the formulation and implementation of that agenda. In the terms used in the financial debates of recent years, all of this underscores the need for a new "international architecture" for the era of globalization based on a wide-ranging agenda and a representative and pluralistic negotiation process.

Such a global agenda should encompass both the provision of global public goods and the correction of major international inequalities and asymmetries. The international structure reveals, first, a contrast between the rapid development of markets and the slow development of global governance, which has resulted in a suboptimal supply of global public goods (Kaul, Grunberg and Stern, 1999). A second category of problems has to do with the lack of effective international instruments for guaranteeing the achievement of the development goals that have been reiterated so often, most recently in the United Nations Millennium Declaration. A third category is related to the correction of the asymmetries faced by developing countries in the global order in the areas of production, technology, finance and macroeconomics as a result of the contrast between the high international mobility of capital and the tight restrictions imposed on the mobility of labour (Ocampo, 2001a).

In the first decades following the Second World War, the need to correct the asymmetries of the international economic system was expressly acknowledged. The commitments entered into in relation to official development assistance and preferential treatment for developing countries in international trade were some of the partial, albeit relatively unsatisfactory, results of this effort to build a "new international economic order". This vision has been radically eroded in recent decades and has been replaced with an alternative paradigm whereby the basic objective of changes in the international economic order should be to provide a "level playing field" for the efficient operation of free market forces. The evidence of a further exacerbation of inequalities over the past half century, which represents a continuation of more long-standing trends, shows that both approaches have fallen short.

The lack of global governance, which encompasses all these issues, reflects another deep-rooted conflict: the contrast between global problems and local political processes. This discrepancy basically means that there are no decision-making mechanisms at the global level to ensure that the interests of the least powerful countries and social sectors are adequately represented. Obviously, this situation gives rise to tensions because the exercise of citizenship and democracy remains confined to the national and local spheres.[7] In fact, in today's world, this is still the most important meaning attached to the concept of a nation, although globalization has also heightened the tensions between the demands of citizenship, which have been increased by democracy, and the limitations which globalization has imposed on the ability of governments to take action.

NOTES

1. Helleiner (2000) presents a comparison of these two visions.

2. See Maddison (1991, 1995 and 2001); O'Rourke and Williamson (1999); Dowrich and DeLong (2001); Lindert and Williamson (2001) and O'Rourke (2001). The starting point, set at around 1870, is somewhat arbitrary, but it reflects the incipient and still limited integration at the international level (and even at the domestic level, in large countries) of goods, capital and labour markets up to that time, as well as the restricted scope of the industrialization process in most of the countries that formed the nucleus of the world economy.

3. In fact, globalization could not have come about without the railway, the steamship and the telegraph in the nineteenth century; the construction of canals connecting oceans (Suez in 1869 and Panama in 1903); automobiles, aeroplanes, telephones and television in the twentieth century; and, of course, the revolution in information and communication technologies in the final decades of the twentieth century.

4. None of the world's 20 largest multimedia groups is Ibero-American, and four of the five largest conglomerates are from the Anglo-Saxon world. In 1999, just four agencies controlled the international flow of news in print. If there is a correlation between these figures and the degree of symbolic influence, it may well be wondered how audible and visible the Latin American and Caribbean region is in the world of today.

5. See United Nations (1999a), UNCTAD (1998, 2001a) and ECLAC (2001).

6. See UNCTAD (1997), UNDP (1999), Cornia (1999a), Rodrik (1997), Bourguignon and Morrison (2002) and chapter 3 of this report.

7. Certainly, there are areas in which a form of "global citizenship" is emerging, as manifested in civil-society participation in United Nations world summits and in global debates on the environment and trade. This was demonstrated very clearly by the civil society event that took place in parallel with the Ministerial Meeting on Trade of the Summit of the Americas (Toronto, 1999) and by the clashes surrounding the WTO Ministerial Conference in Seattle (1999), the annual meeting of the International Monetary Fund and the World Bank in Prague (2000), the meeting of the Group of Eight in Genoa (2001) and the World Social Forum in Porto Alegre (2001 and 2002), among others.

POSTSCRIPT_____

The unprecedented dominance of the United States at the heart of the global economic system inevitably tailors the context in which attempts at development are undertaken. In the 1990s, the process of adaptation to globalization among developing countries was generally viewed in multilateral terms, even if the multilateral financial and development agencies at the heart of the system were largely reflective of the neoliberal Western and capitalist world. With the greater assertiveness of the United States in the strategic realm, the neoliberal world system has come to be associated more strongly with the hegemonic role of the world's largest economic and military power.

For these reasons, coverage of imperialism in the international economic order is usually associated with the military-strategic interests of the United States. For example, David Harvey has contributed a full theory of American primacy as a broad worldwide project designed to maintain the place of American material interests.

On the other hand, many such as Jagdish Bhagwati contend that globalization and development are essentially benign processes that help to make developing nations contenders for world power. The increasing size and importance of the Indian and Chinese economies in particular suggest that globalization might actually be sowing the seeds for an alternative world order in which economic power is far more diffuse than that implied by imperialism. For the time being, however, the United States remains by far the greatest world economic power.

Suggested Additional Readings

Bhagwati, Jagdish. *In Defense of Globalization* (New York: Oxford University Press, 2004).

Chomsky, Noam. *Hegemony or Survival: America's Quest for Global Dominance* (New York: Metropolitan Books, 2003).

Cox, Robert. "Beyond Empire and Terror: Critical Reflections on the Political Economy of World Order," *New Political Economy*, 9, no. 3 (September 2004): 307–323.

Harvey, David. *The New Imperialism* (Oxford: Oxford University Press, 2005).

Hettne, Bjorn. *Development Theory and the Three Worlds* (New York: Wiley, 1990).

Ikenberry, John G. *Liberal Order and Imperial Ambition: Essays on American Power and World Politics* (Cambridge: Polity Press, 2006).

Mooers, Colin, ed. *The New Imperialists: Ideologies of Empire* (Oxford: Oneworld, 2006).

Poole, Lisette. "The Americanization of Globalization: Reflections of a Third World Intellectual," *Global Policy Forum* (September–October 2005). www.globalpolicy.org/empire/analysis/2005/09specialreport.htm

Stokes, Doug. "The Heart of Empire? Theorising US Empire in an Era of Transnational Capitalism," *Third World Quarterly*, 26, no. 2 (2005): 217–236.

Wallerstein, Immanuel. "U.S. Weakness and the Struggle for Hegemony," *Monthly Review*, 55, no. 3 (July–August 2003): 23–29.

Williams, Gavin. "Studying Development and Explaining Policies," *Oxford Development Studies* 31, no. 1 (2003): 37–58.

InfoTrac® College Edition

Search for the following articles in the InfoTrac® database:

Finnegan, William. "The Economics of Empire: Notes on the Washington Consensus," *Harper's Magazine* (May 2003): 41–54.

LaFeber, Walter. "The Post September 11 Debate over Empire, Globalization, and Fragmentation," *Political Science Quarterly*, 117, no. 1 (Spring 2002): 1–17.

Mielants, Eric. "The 'New' World Order?" *International Journal of Comparative Sociology*, 45, no. 5 (October 2004): 385–389.

For more articles, enter:
"imperialism," "economics and empire," or "globalization and empire" in the keyword search.

Web Resources

UNITED NATIONS HUMAN DEVELOPMENT REPORTS

hdr.undp.org/

The United Nations Development Programme publishes an annual review highlighting the top concerns of world development.

WORLD BANK WORLD DEVELOPMENT REPORTS

web.worldbank.org/WBSITE/EXTERNAL/EXTDEC/EXTRESEARCH/EXTWDRS/0,,contentMDK: 20227703~pagePK:478093~piPK:477627~theSitePK:477624,00.html

The World Bank's annual development reports provide background on key issues in the pursuit of development worldwide. Consider other publications that are also provided on the site.

THE AMERICAN EMPIRE PROJECT

www.americanempireproject.com

Several high-profile American critics have contributed polemics against American foreign policy under the rubric of imperialism. These are gathered under the American Empire Project.

GLOBAL POLICY FORUM RESOURCES ON EMPIRE

www.globalpolicy.org/empire/

The Global Policy Forum has created a set of links to discussions of US Empire from economic, strategic, and cultural points of view.

PART TWO

POLITICAL ECONOMY AND DEVELOPMENT

Is the present trading regime beneficial to the world's poor?

Do fair trade networks create a fairer trading system?

Can sweatshops and cheap labour benefit the poor?

Does outright debt cancellation ignore the real problems of Africa?

Are property titling systems the key to increased economic growth?

Is the Present Trading Regime Beneficial to the World's Poor?

✔ **YES**

MARTIN WOLF, *Why Globalization Works* (New Haven, CT: Yale Nota Bene, 2005), pp. 138–172

✗ **NO**

ROBERT ISAAK, "How the Rules Rule the Poor," *The Globalization Gap* (Upper Saddle River, NJ: Prentice-Hall, 2005), pp. 183–202

The theoretical basis that formed the core of modern neoliberalism held that the world economy would grow as a whole through specialization. On the premise that "a rising tide lifts all ships," the argument went that a growing aggregate economy would benefit everyone, including the poorest nations in the world. As an increasing number of states dropped tariff barriers to trade over the years since the end of the Second World War, a rapidly expanding global economy bore out the promise. Nations that pursued import-substitution saw initial gains but rapidly fell behind economies that embraced the neoliberal impulse through export-led growth. Poor nations that accepted the neoliberal consensus in favour of freer trade managed to move ahead while others stagnated.

Indeed, the rapid industrialization of the "Asian Tigers," beginning with Japan in the 1960s and 1970s and followed by newly industrializing countries from Taiwan to Singapore, provided a model for the future of developmental strategies worldwide. In spite of the challenge to the East Asian economies that arose with the "Asian Flu" currency crisis of 1997, more and more developing economies sought market liberalization in deeper and deeper ways. By the time of the accession of China to the World Trade Organization in 2001 a massive proportion of the population of the developing world had come into the world trading system. For many countries, this has been associated with rapid integration into the world market, accelerating the insertion of developing countries into a global division of labour.

In Western developed states, this process has been perceived by some as a threat, causing Americans in particular to be concerned with the extent to which productive jobs have been transferred to the global South through "outsourcing". The process of globalization of production through expansion of trading relationships thus sometimes pits the developed nations of the world against the global South, given that they frequently have divergent interests. Trade rules that have evolved over the past 60 years through negotiations among the capitalist nations of the

Western world matched the interests of industrial or industrializing societies. They did not seek to integrate underdeveloped agrarian societies in the same fashion. In fact, most developed economies saw the agricultural sector to be a key strategic and political interest that needed to remain outside the international trading system. Western trading nations also did not see a need to deepen the trading system to streamline technical regulations, safety and labour standards, and the like. As a result, developing nations joining the pre-existing arrangements approved under the World Trade Organization are frequently at a disadvantage.

These disadvantages and the perception that trading rules set unfair and irresponsible standards for world trade fuelled large-scale demonstrations against the World Trade Organization and other international institutions associated with globalization in the late 1990s. The most famous of these demonstrations was the "Battle of Seattle" of December 1999, when anti-globalization activists disrupted the ministerial summit of the World Trade Organization. They claimed that the present trading regime set rules that were ultimately unfair to large numbers of the world's poor and privileged corporate globalization of production over labour standards, environmental protection, and an egalitarian distribution of the world's resources. The complaints of anti-globalization activists have had an important impact, motivating reform of the world trading system as well as the practices of international financial institutions.

The chief complaint against the international trading regime today is also one of the most major sticking points in negotiating changes to the venerable General Agreement on Tariffs and Trade that forms the legal authority behind the operation of the World Trade Organization. The latest in a series of "rounds" of trade discussions involving the members of the WTO, known as the Doha Round, has bogged down over the dicey and very political issue of agricultural subsidies. The Doha Round began in 2001 with the goal of liberating remaining sectors of world trade that have been left out of previous agreements. Agricultural products in Europe and North America in particular remain protected through the use of various mechanisms, including farm subsidies, quotas, and supply management regimes. At the same time, this sector and others (such as the highly protected textile industry) are those in which many developing countries have a comparative advantage. This suggests that if the poorest countries are to benefit from world trade, trade rules need to change to include many of the products and services that will benefit underdeveloped nations.

These are the basic issues that underpin the debate over the world trading system and its ability to benefit the world's poor through globalization of production. Martin Wolf, a British commentator for the *Financial Times* and former economist with the World Bank, defends the current world trading regime from charges that it promotes inequality by promoting growth over social justice. He argues that although inequality has increased in the age of neoliberalism, the aggregate effect of globalization of production has been to improve the standard of living of everyone, even as some benefit far more than others. While income inequality persists, it is not indicative of a decline in the living standards of the poorest of the poor.

On the other hand, Robert Isaak argues that the contemporary world trading regime contributes to widening the "globalization gap": the massive inequality between the rich and poor in the world economy. This gap remains unjust not only because it represents the worldwide acceptance of the division of wealth between rich and poor but because the wealthy have the ability to set rules that minimize the upward mobility of the poorest in the world economy.

✔ **YES**
Why Globalization Works
MARTIN WOLF

Globalization has dramatically increased inequality between and within nations, even as it connects people as never before. A world in which the assets of the 200 richest people are greater than the combined income of the more than 2bn people at the other end of the economic ladder should give everyone pause.

> —Jay Mazur, president of the Union of Needletrades,
> Industrial and Textile Employees.[1]

Jay Mazur is not alone. Ignacio Ramonet has written on similar lines, in *Le Monde Diplomatique*, that:

> the dramatic advance of globalization and neoliberalism ... has been accompanied by an *explosive growth in inequality* and a return of mass poverty and unemployment. The very opposite of everything which the modern state and modern citizenship is supposed to stand for.
>
> The net result is a *massive growth in inequality*. The United States, which is the richest country in the world, has more than 60 million poor. The world's foremost trading power, the European Union, has over 50 million. In the United States, 1 per cent of the population owns 39 per cent of the country's wealth. Taking the planet as a whole, the combined wealth of the 358 richest people (all of them dollar billionaires) is greater than the total annual income of 45 per cent of the world's poorest inhabitants, that is, 2.6bn people.[2]

Let us, for a moment, ignore the assumption that the number of poor (how defined?) in two of the richest regions in the world tells one anything about global inequality, or about poverty for that matter, or even about inequality within the US and the European Union. Let us also ignore the comparison between the *assets* of one group of people, the richest, and the *incomes* of another, the poor, which is a comparison of apples and oranges. (In order to obtain the permanent incomes of the rich, one would need to divide the value of their assets by at least twenty.) These absurdities merely make Romonet's diatribe representative of the empty rhetoric of many critics of globalization. But the questions that underlie his remarks need to be tackled. Here are seven propositions that can be advanced about what has happened in the age of so-called 'neo-liberal globalization' over the past two decades.

First, the ratio of average incomes in the richest countries to those in the poorest has continued to rise.

Second, the absolute gap in living standards between today's high-income countries and the most developing countries has also continued to rise.

Third, global inequality among individuals has risen.

Fourth, the number of people in extreme poverty has risen.

Fifth, the proportion of people in extreme poverty in the world's population has also risen.

Sixth, the poor of the world are worse off not just in terms of incomes, but in terms of a wide range of other indicators of human welfare.

Seventh, income inequality has risen in every country and particularly in countries most exposed to international economic integration.

[...]

ECONOMIC GROWTH AND GLOBALIZATION

In the mid-1970s I was the World Bank's senior divisional economist on India during the country's worst post-independence decade. After a spurt of growth in the early phase of its inward-looking development, growth in incomes per head had the ground virtually to a halt. Hundreds of millions of people seemed, as a result, to be mired in hopeless and unending poverty. I a book published in 1968, a well-known environmentalist doomsayer, Paul Ehrlich, had written the country off all together.[3] For a young man from the UK, work in India as an economist was both fascinating and appalling: so much poverty; so much frustration; so much complacency. Yet I was convinced then, as I am now, that, with perfectly feasible policy changes, this vast country could generate rapid rates of economic growth and reductions in poverty. No iron law imposed levels of real output (and so real incomes) per head at only 10 per cent of those in high-income countries.

Since those unhappy days, India has enjoyed the fruit of two revolutions: the green revolution, which transformed agricultural productivity; and a liberalizing revolution, which began, haltingly, under Rajiv Gandhi's leadership, in the 1980s and then took a 'great leap forward' in 1991, in response to a severe foreign exchange crisis, under the direction of one of the country's most remarkable public servants, Manmohan Singh, the then finance minister. Slowly, India abandoned the absurdities of its pseudo-Stalinist 'control raj' in favour of individual enterprise and the market. As a result, between 1980 and 2000, India's real GDP per head more than doubled. Stagnation has become a thing of the past.

India was not alone. On the contrary, it was far behind a still more dynamic and even bigger liberalizing country—China, which achieved a rise in real incomes per head of well over 400 per cent between 1980 and 2000. China and India, it should be remembered, contain almost two-fifths of the world's population. China alone contains more people than Latin American and sub-Saharan Africa together. Many other countries in east and south Asia have also experienced rapid growth. According to the 2003 *Human Development Report* from the United Nations Development Programme, between 1975 and 2001, GDP per head rose at 5.9 per cent a year in east Asian developing countries (with 31 per cent of the world's population in 2000). The corresponding figure for growth GDP per head for south

Asia (with another 22 per cent of the world's population) was 2.4 per cent a year. Between 1990 and 2001, GDP per head rose at 5.5 per cent a year in east Asia, while growth rose to 3.2 per cent a year in south Asia.

Never before have so many people—or so large a proportion of the world's population—enjoyed such large rises in their standards of living. Meanwhile, GDP per head in high-income countries (with 15 per cent of the world's population) rose by 2.1 per cent a year between 1975 and 2001 and by only 1.7 per cent a year between 1990 and 2001. This then was a period of partial convergence: the incomes of poor developing countries, with more than half the world's population, grew substantially faster than those of the world's richest countries.

This, in a nutshell, is why Mazur and the many people who think like him are wrong. Globalization has not increased to inequality. It has reduced it, just as it had reduced the incidence of poverty. How can this be, critics will demand? Are absolute and proportional gaps in living standards between the world's richest and poorest countries not rising all the time? Yes is the answer. And is inequality not rising in most of the world's big countries? Yes, is again the answer. So how can global inequality be falling? To adapt to Bill Clinton's campaign slogan, it is the growth, stupid. Rapid economic growth in poor countries with half the world's population has powerful effects on the only sort of inequality which matters, that among individuals. It has similarly dramatic effects on world poverty. The rise of Asia is transforming the world, very much for the better. It is the 'Asian drama' of our times, to plagiarize the title of a celebrated work by a Nobel-laureate economist, the late Gunnar Myrdal.

What, the reader may ask, has this progress to do with international economic integration? In its analysis of globalization, published in 2002, the World Bank divided seventy-three developing countries, with aggregate population, in 1997, of 4 billion (80 per cent of all people in developing countries), into two groups: the third that had increased ratios of trade to GDP, since 1980, by the largest amount and the rest.[4] The former group, with an aggregate population of 2.9 billion, managed a remarkable combined increase of 104 per cent in the ratio of trade to GDP. Over the same period, the increase in the trade ratio of the high-income countries was 71 per cent, while the 'less globalized' two-thirds of countries in the sample of developing countries experienced a decline in their trade ratios.

The average incomes per head of these twenty-four globalizing countries rose by 67 per cent (a compound rate of 3.1 per cent a year) between 1980 and 1997. In contrast, the other forty-nine countries managed to rise of only 10 per cent (a compound rate of 0.5 per cent a year) in incomes per head over this period. As Table 2.1 shows, these more globalized countries did not have particularly high levels of education in 1980. At that time, they were also a little poorer, as a group, than the rest. Subsequently, the new globalizers, as the World Bank calls them, cut their import tariffs by 34 percentage points, on average, against 11 percentage points for the other group. They also achieved a better reading on the rule of law

TABLE 2.1

CHARACTERISTICS OF MORE GLOBALIZED AND LESS GLOBALIZED DEVELOPING ECONOMIES (POPULATION-WEIGHTED AVERAGE)

Socioeconomic characteristics	More globalized (24)	Less globalized (49)
Population, 1997 (billions)	2.9	1.1
Per-capita GDP, 1980	$1,488	$1,947
Per-capita GDP, 1997	$2,485	$2,133
Compound annual growth rate of GDP per head 1980–1997	3.1%	0.5%
Rule of law index, 1997 (world average = 0)	–0.04	–0.48
Average years primary schooling, 1980	2.4	2.5
Average years primary schooling, 1997	3.8	3.1
Average years secondary schooling, 1980	0.8	0.7
Average years secondary schooling, 1997	1.3	1.3
Average years tertiary schooling, 1980	0.08	0.09
Average years tertiary schooling, 1997	0.18	0.22

Source: World Bank, *Globalization, Growth & Poverty: Building an Inclusive World Economy* (Washington DC: World Bank, 2002), Table 1.1.

than the other. The World Bank's conclusion is that, 'as they reformed and integrated with the world market, the "more globalized" developing countries started to grow rapidly, accelerating steadily from 2.9 per cent in the 1970s to 5 per cent in the 1990s'.[5]

While what the Bank says is both true and important, it should be observed that its notion of a group of twenty-four countries is something of a fiction. China and India contain, between them, 75 per cent of the group's combined population. With Brazil, Bangladesh, Mexico, the Philippines and Thailand, one has 92 per cent of the group's population. Moreover, Asian countries dominate: they make up 85 per cent of the population of this group of globalizing countries.

What then do we learn from the success of the countries picked out as globalizers by the World Bank? We can say, with confidence, that the notion that international economic integration necessarily makes the rich richer and the poor poorer is nonsense. Here is a wide range of countries that increased their integration with the world economy and prospered, in some cases dramatically so. A subtler question, to which we shall return in subsequent chapters, is precisely what policies relatively successful developing countries have followed. Critics are right to argue that success has not required adoption of the full range of so-called 'neo-liberal' policies— privatization, free trade and capital-account liberalization. But, in insisting upon this point, critics are wilfully mistaking individual policy trees for the market-oriented forest. What the successful countries all share is a move towards the market economy, one in which private property rights, free enterprise and competition increasingly took the place of state ownership, planning and protection. They chose, however haltingly, the path of economic liberalization and international integration. This is the heart of the matter. All else is commentary.

If one compares the China of today with the China of Mao Zedong or the India of today with the India of Indira Gandhi, the contrasts are overwhelming. Market forces have been allowed to operate in ways that would have been not just unthinkable but criminal a quarter of a century ago. Under Mao, economic freedom had been virtually eliminated. Under the Indian control system, no significant company was allowed to produce, invest or import without government permission. From this starting-point, much of the most important liberalization was, necessarily and rightly, internal. Given where it was in the 1970s, liberalizing agriculture alone started China on the path towards rapid development. Similarly, eliminating the more absurd controls on industry permitted an acceleration in Indian economic growth. In both cases then these initial reforms and the abundance of cheap and hard-working labour guaranteed accelerated growth.

Yet in neither case can the contribution of economic integration be ignored. This is spectacularly true of China. The volume of China's exports grew at 13 per cent a year between 1980 and 1990 and then at 11 per cent between 1990 and 1999. Between 1990 and 2000 the ratio of trade in goods to Chinese GDP, at market prices, jumped from 33 to 44 per cent, an extraordinarily high ratio for such a large economy. The ratio of merchandise trade to output of goods in the economy rose from 47 per cent to 66 per cent over the same period.[6] In 2001, China's gross merchandize exports of $266 billion amounted to 4.3 per cent of the world total, up from a mere 0.7 per cent in 1977.[7] By that year, China was the world's sixth largest merchandise exporter (including intra-European Union trade in the total), just behind the UK, but already ahead of Canada and Italy. Meanwhile, private capital flow into China jumped from 3 per cent of GDP in 1990 to 13 per cent in 2000. By 2001, the stock of inward foreign direct investment in China was $395 billion, 6 per cent of the world's total, up from $25 billion in 1990. In 2000, inward direct investment financed 11 per cent of the giant's gross fixed capital formation, while foreign affiliates generated 31 per cent of China's manufacturing sales and, more astonishingly so, 50 per cent of its exports.[8] It is possible to argue that China's dramatic economic growth somehow had nothing to do with its headlong rush into the global market economy. But it would be absurd to do so.

India's integration was much less spectacular. So, not coincidentally, was its growth. Yet here, too, the change was palpable. India's volume of merchandise exports fells in the 1980s, which contributed mightily to the foreign exchange crisis that brought to an end its overwhelmingly inward-looking liberalization of the 1980s. But export volume rose at 5.3 per cent a year between 1990 and 1999, after external liberalization had begun. India's share in world merchandise exports had fallen from 2.1 per cent in 1951 to a low of 0.4 per cent in 1980. But by 2001 this share was modestly back up, to 0.7 per cent, putting it in thirtieth place globally. Between 1990 and 2000, the share of trade in goods also rose from 13 to 20 per cent of GDP. India did achieve a significant success in exports of commercial services (particularly software). By 2001, its exports of such services were $20 billion, almost half as much as its $44 billion in merchandise exports. Its share in world exports of commercial services was 1.4 per cent, double its share in exports and goods, while its rank in the world was nineteenth, though even here it was behind China's exports of $33 billion (2.3 per cent of the world total). India also lagged in openness to inward direct investment, which only reached $3.4 billion in 2001. But even this was close to revolutionary in a country that had, for decades, discouraged all inward FDI. In 1990, the total stock of inward FDI was a mere $1.7 billion. By 2001, it had reached $22 billion. The 1990s were, in all, India's most economically successful post-independence decade. They were also the decade in which the country liberalized both internal and external transactions and increased its integration into the global economy. An accident? Hardly.

Now consider an even more fascinating example in the Bank's list of globalizing economies—Bangladesh, certainly the poorest sizeable country in the world in the 1970s and, as I remember well, almost universally deemed a hopeless case. Even this country has benefited from international economic integration. The GDP per head of Bangladesh rose at 2.3 per cent a year between 1975 and 2001, generating a 60 per cent rise in real income per head over more than a quarter of a century. Between 1990 and 2001, GDP per head grew considerably faster, at 3.1 per cent a year, as the economy opened. In 1975, Bangladesh's real GDP per head (measured at purchasing power parity) was roughly half that of sub-Saharan Africa. By 2000, its real GDP per head was close to the average level of sub-Saharan Africa. In the 1980s, Bangladesh's volume of merchandise exports barely rose. In the 1990s, it rose at a remarkable 15 per cent a year. Between 1990 and 2000, the ratio of exports to GDP jumped from 18 to 32 per cent. The volume of trade also grew 6 percentage points a year faster than GDP in the decade. Bangladesh did not suddenly become a magnet for foreign direct investment. That is hardly surprising, since it has been ranked bottom of seventy-five countries in the cost of corruption.[9] But the stock of inward direct investment did reach $1.1 billion by 2001, up from $150 million in 1990. Even for Bangladesh, international economic integration has paid off. It is only a start. But it is, at least, that.

[...]

GROWTH AND INEQUALITY

Now what does the performance of those who have succeeded in growing through economic integration mean for inequality? Inequality is a measure of relative incomes. If the average real incomes of poor countries containing at least half of the world's population have been rising faster than those of the relatively rich, inequality among countries, weighted by population, will have fallen. This will be true even if the ratio of the incomes of the world's richest to the world's poorest countries and the absolute gaps in average incomes per head between rich countries and almost all developing countries have risen (as they have).

These two points may need a little explanation. First, compare, say, the US with China. Between 1980 and 2000, according to the World Bank, Chinese average real incomes rose by about 440 per cent. Over the same period, US average real incomes per hand rose by about 60 per cent. The ratio of Chinese real incomes per head, at purchasing power parity, to those of the US rose, accordingly, from just over 3 per cent in 1980 to just under 12 per cent in 2000. This is a big reaction in relative inequality. But the absolute gap in real incomes between China and the US rose from $20,600 to $30,200 per head (at PPP). The reason is simple: since China's standard of living was, initially, about a thirtieth of that of the US, the absolute gap could have remained constant only if China's growth had been thirty times faster than that of the US. That would have been impossible. If China continues to grow faster than the US, however, absolute gaps will ultimately fall, as happened with Japan in the 1960s and 1970s.

Second, while the *ratio* of the average incomes per head in the richest country to those in the world's least successful countries is rising all the time, the *proportion* of the world's population living in the world's poorest countries has, happily, been falling. Thirty years ago, China and India were among the world's poorest countries. Today, the poorest seems to be Sierra Leone, a country with a population of only 5 million. China's average real income per head is now some ten times higher than Sierra Leone's. The largest very poor country today is Nigeria, with a population of 127 million in 2000 and a real income, at PPP, just a fortieth of that of the US (and a fifth of China's). Again, this means that rising ratios between the average incomes of the world's richest and poorest countries are consistent with declining inequality among countries, weighted by their populations. Moreover, it is also perfectly possible for inequality to have risen in every single country in the world (as Mazur alleges, wrongly) while global inequality has fallen. Unless the increase in inequality among individuals within countries offsets the reduction in population-weighted inequality among countries, not only inequality among (population-weighted) countries, but also inequality among individuals will have declined.

Andrea Boltho of Oxford University and Gianni Toniolo of Rome University have computed population-weighted among forty-nine countries that contain 80 per cent of the world's population, back to 1900.[10] To compute their measure of inequality, the gini coefficient, the authors weight the average income, at purchasing power parity (in order to compare standards of living), of each country by its population.[11] They conclude that inequality among countries, weighted in this way, reached its maximum in 1980, at a value of 0.54, but has fallen by 9 per cent since then, to 0.50, a level not seen since some six decades ago. This decline in inequality among countries, weighted by their population size, is exactly what one would expect.

The reason for weighting distribution among countries by population is that it is people who matter, not countries. Then the right thing to do must be to take account of changes in distribution of income within countries as well.

[...]

GROWTH AND POVERTY

On all measures, global inequality rose until about the early 1980s. Since then, it appears, inequality among individuals has declined as a result of the rapid growth of much of Asia and, above all, China. But it is also important to understand what drove the long-term trend towards global inequality over almost two centuries. It is the consequence of the dynamic growth that spread, unevenly, from the UK in the course of the nineteenth and twentieth centuries. In the process a growing number of people became vastly better off than any one had ever been before, but few can have become worse off. Such dynamic growth is bound to be uneven. Some regions of the world proved better able to take advantage of the new opportunities for growth, because of superior climates, resources and policies. In just the same way, some parts of countries, particularly huge countries such as China or India, are today better able to take advantage of new opportunities than others. To bemoan the resulting increase in inequality is to bemoan the growth itself. It is to argue that it would be better off for everybody to be equally poor than for some to become significantly better off, even if, in the long run, this will almost certainly lead to advances for everybody.

For this reason, it makes more sense to focus on what has happened to poverty than to inequality. Again, the statistical debate is a vexed one. But some plausible conclusions can be reached.

The World Bank has, for some time, defined extreme poverty as an income of a dollar a day at 1985 international prices (PPP). Bourguignon and Morrison also used that figure in an analysis of extreme poverty since 1820, on the same lines as their analysis of inequality (see Figure 2.1).[12] It comes to three intriguing conclusions. First, the number of desperately poor people rose from about 900 million in 1820 to a peak of from 1.3 to 1.4 billion between 1960 and 1980, before falling, modestly, to just under 1.3 billion in 1992. Second, the proportion of the world's population living on less than a dollar a day fell dramatically, over time, from over 80 per cent in 1820, a time when living on the margins of subsistence was the norm, to about two-thirds at the beginning of the twentieth century, to

FIGURE 2.1

EXTREME POVERTY IN THE LONG RUN (LESS THAN A DOLLAR A DAY AT PPP, IN 1985 PRICES, MILLIONS AND WORLD POPULATION SHARE)

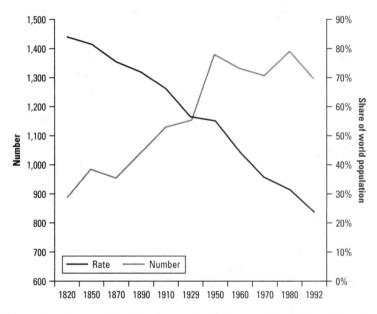

Source: François Bourguignon and Christian Morrison, 'Inequality among World Citizens,' *American Economic Review,* Vol. 92, No. 4 (September 2002), pp. 727–44.

close to 50 per cent by 1950, then 32 per cent in 1980 and, finally, 24 per cent by 1992. The contrast between the rising numbers and falling proportions of the world's population in extreme poverty reflects the race between higher output and rising population, particularly in poor countries. In 1820, the world's population was a little over a billion. By 1910 it was 1.7 billion and by 1992 it had risen to 5.5 billion.

Again, the results from Bourguignon and Morrison are cause for qualified optimism. From being universal, extreme poverty has become, if not rare, the affliction of less than a quarter of a vastly increased human population. But, again, it is necessary to look more closely at what has happened in the supposed period of globalization, the years since 1980. Here, the authoritative voice is that of the World Bank, the institution whose 'dream is a world without poverty.'[13] The numbers in Tables 2.2 and 2.3 come from two recent World Bank publications.[14] They reach the following conclusions.

TABLE 2.2

INCOME POVERTY, BY REGION (MILLIONS OF PEOPLE LIVING ON LESS THAN $1.08 A DAY AT 1993 PPP)

Regions	1987	1990	1999
East Asia and Pacific	418	486	279
(Excluding China)	114	110	57
China	304	376	222
Europe and Central Asia	1	6	24
Latin America and Caribbean	64	48	57
Middle East and North Africa	9	5	6
South Asia	474	506	488
Sub-Saharan Africa	217	241	315
Total	1,183	1,292	1,169
Total, excluding China	880	917	945

Sources: World Bank, *World Development Report 2000/2001: Attacking Poverty* (Washington DC: World Bank, 2000), Table 1.1, and World Bank, *Global Economic Prospects and the Developing Countries 2003: Investing to Unlock Global Opportunities* (Washington DC: World Bank, 2003), Table 1.9.

First, the number of people in extreme poverty fell from 1.18 billion in 1987 to 1.17 billion in 1999, but not before jumping upwards to 1.29 billion in 1990, underlining the extent to which the 1988–93 period chosen by Milanovic was exceptional.

Second, enormous declines in the number of people in extreme poverty have occurred in dynamic east Asia, from 486 million in 1990 to 279 million in 1999, including China, and from 114 million to 57 million, excluding China. In China itself, the decline, between 1990 and 1999, was from 376 million to 222 million. Rapid growth reduces poverty dramatically. This remains today, as it has been for two centuries, an abiding truth.

Third, the number of people in extreme poverty fell very modestly in south Asia between 1990 and 1999, while it rose sharply in eastern Europe and central Asia (the former Soviet empire) and, above all, sub-Saharan Africa, from 217 million in 1987 to 241 million in 1990, and then 315 million in 1999.

Fourth, the regional incidence of poverty fell dramatically in east Asia, from 30.5 per cent of the population in 1990 to just 15.6 per cent in 1999. Excluding

TABLE 2.3

REGIONAL INCIDENCE OF INCOME POVERTY (SHARE OF PEOPLE LIVING ON LESS THAN $1.08 A DAY AT 1993 PPP, IN REGIONAL POPULATIONS, PER CENT)

Regions	1987	1990	1999
East Asia and Pacific	26.6	30.5	15.6
(Excluding China)	23.9	24.2	10.6
China	27.8	33.0	17.7
Europe and Central Asia	0.2	1.4	5.1
Latin America and Caribbean	15.3	11.0	11.1
Middle East and North Africa	4.3	2.1	2.2
South Asia	44.9	45.0	36.6
Sub-Saharan Africa	46.6	47.4	49.0
Total	28.3	29.6	23.2
Total, excluding China	28.5	28.5	25.0
World total	23.7	24.6	19.5

Sources: World Bank, *World Development Report 2000/2001: Attacking Poverty,* Table 1.1, and World Bank, *Global Economic Prospects 2003,* Table 1.9.

China, it fell from 24.2 to 10.6 per cent. In China it fell from 33 per cent of the population to just under 18 per cent over nine years. This was, without doubt, the most rapid reduction in the incidence of extreme poverty anywhere, ever.

Fifth, the incidence of poverty also fell sharply in south Asia (dominated by India) in the 1990s, from 45.0 per cent of the population in 1990 to 36.6 per cent in 1999. But it rose sharply in eastern Europe and central Asia and also increased in sub-Saharan Africa, from 47.4 per cent of the population to 49.0 per cent.

[...]

POVERTY AND HUMAN WELFARE

[...] As an independent analyst, Indur Goklany, persuasively argues, it is possible, in addition, for people to enjoy better health and longer lives, at lower incomes, than before.[15] This is the result of technological and organizational improvements that have come from the world's rich countries. In 1913, life expectancy at birth in the US was fifty-two years. US GDP per head, at PPP, was then about 50 per cent higher than China's would be in 2000, and 150 per cent higher than India's.[16] Yet, in 2000, life expectancy in China was seventy and in India sixty-three. In 1900, Sweden seems to have had the world's highest life expectancy, at fifty-six. In 2000, only very poor countries, mostly in Africa, had life expectancy as low as (or lower) this. As Goklany shows, the curve relating life expectancy to average GDP per head has shifted upwards over time. Similarly, the curve relating infant mortality to incomes has shifted downwards over time. Much the same desirable pattern can be observed for the relationship between other indicators of human welfare and income.

In the developing world as a whole, life expectancy rose by four months each year after 1970, from fifty-five years in 1970 to sixty-four years in 2000. It rose from forty-nine in 1970 to sixty-two in south Asia and from fifty-nine to sixty-nine in east Asia. Tragically, life expectancy fell in thirty-two countries in the 1990s, mostly because of the AIDS epidemic, or the gross incompetence (or worse) of governments, as in North Korea and Zimbabwe.[17] It also fell because of western hysteria about DDT, which removed the only effective way of controlling that dreadful curse, malaria. Improvements in life expectancy have meant a decline in global inequality as well. In 1950, average life expectancy in developing countries was two-thirds of the levels in high-income countries (forty-four and sixty-six years of age, respectively). By 2000, it was 82 per cent (sixty-four and seventy-eight).

Meanwhile, in the developing world as a whole, infant mortality rates have fallen from 107 per thousand in 1970 to eighty-seven in 1980 and fifty-eight in 2000. In east Asia, the region with the fastest-growing economy, they have fallen from fifty-six in 1980 to thirty-five in 2000. In south Asia, infant mortality fell from 119 in 1980 to seventy-three in 2000. In sub-Saharan Africa progress was, once again, slower. But infant mortality fell even there, from 116 in 1980 to ninety-one in 2000.

Losing a child must inflict the sharpest grief human beings can suffer. The decline in infant mortality is thus a tremendous blessing in itself. So, too, is the rise in life expectancy. But these improvements also mean that it makes sense to invest in education. The world increasingly produces smaller families with much better-educated children. On average, adult literacy in developing countries rose from 53 per cent in 1970 to 74 per cent in 1998. By 2000, adult male illiteracy was down 8 per cent in east Asia, though it was still 30 per cent in sub-Saharan Africa and (a real scandal this) 34 per cent in south Asia. Adult female illiteracy was more widespread than that for men, but was also improving. Between 1990 and 2000, female illiteracy fell from 29 per cent to 21 per cent in east Asia. In south Asia, it fell from 66 per cent to 57 per cent (an even worse scandal than the low rate for men), while in sub-Saharan Africa it fell from 60 to 47 per cent. Illiteracy is much lower among the young. This guarantees that rates will continue to fall as time passes.

The reduction in fertility rates has also been remarkable. In the developing world as a whole, births per woman (the fertility rate) have fallen from 4.1 in 1980 to 2.8

in 2000. In east Asia, the fertility rate, down from 3.0 to 2.1, is already at close to the replacement rate. In Latin America, the fertility rate has fallen from 4.1 to 2.6. Even in south Asia it has fallen from 5.3 in 1980 to 3.3 in 2000. Again, progress has been slowest in sub-Saharan Africa, where the birth rate has only fallen from 6.6 in 1980 to 5.2 in 2000. But, in all, these reductions tell us of improved control by women of their fertility, of fewer children with more parental investment in each and of far stronger confidence that children will survive to maturity. The demographic transition that is now under way in the developing world is immensely encouraging. It is also an indication—as well as a source—of rising welfare.

Now, let us look at hunger. Growth in food production has substantially outpaced that of population. Between 1961 and 1999, the average daily food supply per person increased 24 per cent globally. In developing countries, it rose by 39 per cent, to 2,684 calories. By 1999, China's average daily food supply had gone up 82 per cent, to 3,044 calories, from a barely subsistence level of 1,636 in 1961. India's went up by 48 per cent to 2,417 calories, from 1,635 calories in 1950-1. According to estimates by the United Nations Food and Agricultural Organization, the average active adult needs between 2,000 and 2,310 calories per person. Thus the developing-country food supply has gone, on average, from inadequate to adequate. Hunger persists. But the FAO estimates that the number of people suffering from chronic undernourishment fell from 920 million in 1969-71 to 790 million in 1997-9, or from 35 to 17 per cent of the population of developing countries. Trends in sub-Saharan Africa, the continent that did not grow, were far worse. Between 1979-81 and 1997-9, the share of the population that was undernourished declined from 38 to 34 per cent, but absolute number, in a rapidly growing population, rose from 168 million to 194 million.[18]

Now, turn to what has become one of the most controversial indicators: child labour. One would expect that more prosperous parents, with fewer children, who are also expected to live longer, would wish to see their children being educated rather than at work. So, happily, it has proved. The proportion of children aged ten to fourteen in the labour force has, according to the World Bank, fallen from 23 per cent in all developing countries in 1980 to 12 per cent in 2000. The fall in east Asia has, once again, been astonishing, from 26 to 8. In south Asia, it has fallen from 23 to 15 per cent. In sub-Saharan Africa, the decline has been less impressive, from 35 to 29 per cent. China's transformation has been breathtaking, with a fall from 30 per cent in 1980 to just 8 per cent in 2000. In lagging India, the fall was from 21 to 12 per cent. Thus just as one would expect, countries whose economies have done well in the era of globalization have been ones in which parents have chosen to withdraw their children from the labour force. Parents have never put their children to work out of indifference or malevolence, but only out of necessity.

Finally, let us remember some of the other feature of the last two decades: the world-wide shift to democracy, however imperfect; the disappearance of some of the worst despotisms in history; the increase in personal economic opportunity in vast swathes of the world, notably China and India; and the improving relative position of women almost, although not quite, everywhere.

All these are very encouraging trends. People in developing countries and, particularly, in the fast-growing ones are enjoying longer and healthier lives than before. They are better fed and better educated. They treat their fewer children better. All these good things have not happened only because of rising incomes. Learning from the high-income countries has helped. Developing countries are reaching higher levels of social progress at lower levels of income than the high-income countries of today. But, as one would expect, social progress has been greatest where incomes have risen fastest. It remains 'the growth, stupid'.

[...]

NOTES

1. 'Labour's New Internationalism', *Foreign Affairs*, Vol. 79, January–February 2000.

2. Ignacio Ramonet, *Le Monde Diplomatique*, May 1998. Cited in Xavier Sala-I-Martin, 'The Myth of Exploding Income Inequality in Europe and the World', in Henryk Kierzkowski (ed.), *Europe and Globalization* (Basingstoke: Palgrave MacMillan, 2002), p. 11.

3. Paul Ehrlich, *The Population Bomb* (New York: Ballantine Books, 1968).

4. World Bank, *Globalization, Growth & Poverty: Building an Inclusive World Economy* (Washington DC: 2002), Table 1.1, p. 34.

5. *Ibid.*, p. 36.

6. These data are from World Bank, *World Development Indicators 2002* (Washington DC: World Bank, 2002).

7. World Trade Organization, *International Trade Statistics 2002* (Geneva: WTO, 2002), and T. N. Srinivasan, *Eight Lectures on India's Economic Reforms* (New York: Oxford University Press, 2000), p. 73, for the data on China in the 1970s and a comparison between China and India.

8. United Nations Conference on Trade and Development, *World Investment Report 2002: Transnational Corporations and Export Competitiveness* (New York: United Nations, 2002).

9. World Economic Forum, *The Global Competitiveness Report 2001–02* (New York: Oxford University Press, 2002).

10. The measure used is the 'gini coefficient', a measure that falls between zero for absolute equality and unity for extreme in equality. The coefficient is calculated as follows. Draw a curve showing cumulative shares in incomes against cumulative shares in the population, with the two axes of the same length. Draw also the line showing perfect equality, which would be a 45 degree line. Then the ratio of the area between the 45 degree line and the curve showing the cumulative shares in incomes, to the total area under the 45 degree line is the gini coefficient. If all income belonged to one person, the curve drawn would follow the axes, in which case the coefficient would be unity. If all incomes were evenly shared, the curve would be the 45 degree line, in which case the coefficient must be zero. Gini coefficients for the countries of

the world vary between close to 0.25 for egalitarian high-income countries such as Denmark and Japan, and close to 0.6 for Brazil, the world's most inegalitarian country. In 1997, the US index was 0.41 and the UK's 0.37. See World Bank, *World Development Indicators 2002,* Table 2.8.

11. Data come from Angus Maddison, *Monitoring the World Economy,* 1820–1992 (Paris: Development Centre of the Organization for Economic Co-operation and Development, 1995 and 1998) and the International Monetary Fund's *World Economic Outlook.* See Andrea Boltho and Gianni Toniolo, 'The Assessment: The Twentieth Century–Achievements, Failures, Lessons', *Oxford Review of Economic Policy,* Vol. 15, No. 4 (Winter 1999), pp. 1–17, Table 4.

12. François Bourguignon and Christian Morrison, 'Inequality among World Citizens,' *American Economic Review,* Vol. 92, No. 4 (September 2002), Table 1.

13. Cynics might suppose this is the Bank's nightmare. Fortunately for the Bank, though not for the world, poverty seems most unlikely to be eliminated in the near future, particularly since richer societies tend to define their poverty lines upwards, more or less *pari passu.*

14. Poverty lines are defined as $1.08 a day at 1993 PPP.

15. Indur M. Goklany, "The Globalization of Human Well-Being", Policy Analysis No. 447, Cato Institute, Washington DC, 22 August 2002.

16. Maddison, *The World Economy.*

17. It is worth noting that if drugs are to prove a remedy for the AIDS catastrophe in Africa, it will only be because the wealth and technology of the high-income countries allowed them to invent the treatments activists argue should be provided to Africans at very low cost. As Goklany remarks,' a certain level of global inequality may even benefit the poor as rich countries develop and invest in more expensive medicines and technologies that then become affordable to the poor'. See Goklany, 'The Globalization of Human Well-Being,' p. 1.

18. The data from the FAO are cited in *ibid.,* p. 7.

✗ NO
How the Rules Rule the Poor
ROBERT ISAAK

The mere mention of a "cartel" usually strikes fear in the hearts and wallets of consumers and regulators around the globe. Its members are the world's leading foreign aid organizations, which constitute a near monopoly, relative to the powerless poor.

—William Easterly, *The Cartel of Good Intentions* (2002)

The poor are set up by the rules to remain dependent while the rich are aided in maintaining their way of life.

Poor people in poor countries suffer the consequences of the rules of the world economy set by the rich countries every day. Consider, for example, two telling international events of September of 2003[1]:

Trade ministers from 146 nations met in Cancun, Mexico. They held talks to assess the Doha Round of trade tariff reduction discussions launched in Doha, Qatar two years before. The guiding idea of the Doha Round of the World Trade Organization (WTO) talks was presumably to raise the prospects of the economies of the poor nations. But remember who set up the rules. The developing countries had appealed to the wealthy countries, such as the United States and the European Union (EU), to lower tariffs against the agriculture and mineral commodities on which many of the poor countries' livelihood depend. The response by the United States and the EU was to ask the developing countries to lower *their* tariffs in order to liberalize their markets and increase global trade. This alliance between the developed countries was not concerned that the playing field is not exactly "level" for rich and poor countries in terms of comparative advantage. Their initial starting positions give a huge competitive edge to those most prepared to benefit from the new globalized economy.

A protest movement gathered in front of the place in Cancun where the world trade talks were taking place. One of the protesters was a 56-year-old rice farmer, a former president of the Korean Advance Farmers Federation, who wore a sign: "The WTO kills farmers." He stabbed himself in the chest and died in the hospital, leaving a handout behind in which he stated that he had tried but failed to organize opposition to economic forces that had become "waves that destroyed our lovely rural communities."[2] The WTO talks later collapsed, leaving the status quo in place. Meanwhile, another event was unfolding that also illustrates how developing countries suffer the consequences of the rules established by the wealthy.

Argentina defaulted on its $2.9 billion debt payment due to the International Monetary Fund (IMF) after both sides could not agree on the terms of a new three-year aid program. For most of the past decade, Argentineans acceded to stringent

IMF demands, only to see their economy sink into deeper malaise. The Argentinean government staked out a tough bargaining position against the governments of France and Italy, who sought to protect their companies and investors in Argentina. The government of Argentina lost in these negotiations. Thus, Argentina joined Iraq, Somalia, Liberia, Zimbabwe, and Sudan—the group of countries in arrears with the IMF. Never mind that the bargaining position is not exactly level between an economically depressed Argentina and two of the richest countries in the world, which help to set the rules in the IMF.

What both of these examples have in common is the starting position of the poor in negotiations: A take-it-or-leave-it bargaining stance by developed countries typically pushes the poor even further into dependence.

As Thucydides observed in ancient Greece, **the powerful exact what they can, and the weak grant what they must.**

HOW TO INCREASE POVERTY WITH TRADE

In Mali, where the per capita income is $270 annually, cotton is a critical raw commodity to export for economic sustainability of the people. The native people grow corn and millet to eat and produce unprocessed cotton to export. With a level playing field in trade, Mail could develop a stable economy to match its democratic system.

However, the trade rules are tilted to create more *poverty*, not more wealth in Mali. The U.S. government subsidizes its own farmers to grow cotton. Without having to compete with these American subsidies, the income for cotton producers in Mali would go up 30%. The government in Mali can't afford to subsidize its own cotton production.

In terms of global agricultural production, the picture becomes even darker for countries such as Mali because the EU and Canada subsidize agriculture more than the United States does. In fact, the developed countries subsidize agriculture to the tune of a billion dollars a day, making it extremely difficult for developing nations to compete with them.

In Mali, there is a saying: "The hand that gives is always higher than the one that receives." But this is not the principle of the global trade regime. A focal point of developing nations at the WTO talks in Cancun was to push the WTO to lower the cotton subsidies granted to largely rich American cotton farmers that prevent cotton producers in poor countries such as Mali from maintaining themselves.

The difficulty is that farmers in wealthy nations correctly argue that without subsidies, many of them will go broke. There are tremendous domestic political pressures on the side of developed countries coming up against the threat of survival perceived by many developing nations.

Mali is not alone. Consider Senegal. The World Bank demanded that this developing country cut its tariffs by 90% as a condition for receiving further financing.

The WTO required Senegal not to limit its imports. The people in Senegal could be closer to self-sufficiency if they could afford to eat the chicken that they themselves produce. But subsidized frozen chicken imported from the EU in Senegal is half the price of home-grown chicken: The people of Senegal cannot afford to buy their own. They are becoming more dependent, less self-sufficient, and hence, poorer.

Or consider Ethiopia. The United States provides generous "food aid" in the form of surplus *American* wheat, corn, or beans on a regular basis, to the point of undermining the economic ability of the Ethiopians to grow and sell their own wheat, corn, and beans. The rules (in this case, American laws) say that the United States must send its own home-grown food for aid, rather than spend cash on foreign produce in all but very exceptional cases.

American agribusinesses use high technology and efficiency to overproduce, given their ability to count on selling at least some 20% of their food as food aid at government subsidized prices. Almost 70% of the farm subsidy payments by the U.S. government go to the largest 10% of producers: It is a corporate welfare program. However, it also keeps American farmers employed, increases their income, and maintains the value of their land.

Meanwhile, Ethiopian farmers cannot earn enough selling their crops to pay for this year's harvest of the space to store it, not to speak of the loans needed to plant next year's crop. The cycle of famine and poverty in Ethiopia is preprogrammed by the existing rules. (Recall that international organizations support Egypt's restriction on the use of most of the Nile's water by Ethiopia, where the Nile originates.) And the welfare mentality of dependence is continually subsidized by the American food coming in, leading Ethiopians to expect and accept it, rather than motivating them to try to stand on their own feet. Thus, American farmers continue to produce much more wheat than they need. The U.S. government buys much of their wheat to ship to Ethiopia and other developing countries as food aid to get rid of the surpluses. The Ethiopians are socialized into consuming American brand products. And the cycle of poverty is deepened and made inevitable for the future.[3]

One might think that Mali, Senegal, and Ethiopia are possible exceptions to the rule. But how does one explain the statistics? During 1960–1969, Africa's average share of total world exports was 5.3% and of imports, 5.0%. Compare this with 1990–1998, when the African share of world exports dropped to 2.3% and of imports, 2.2%.[4] Of course, many factors could explain this decline, apart from the existing global trade rules: the restrictive nature of African's own trade regimes, high costs of transport, the distance of the region from major markets, and the slow growth of per capita income. But substantial efforts made by African countries to liberalize their economies in the 1990s do not change the fact that Africa is poorer today than several decades ago, as measured by world market share of exports and imports. Naturally, poverty, as always, is relative because world imports and exports as a whole have risen significantly during the past few decades. But the existing trade rules seem designed more to increase the gap between the poorest countries and the rich ones than to bridge it.

Moreover, without the barriers of protectionism, the United States, Germany, France, Japan, and the East Asian "tigers" could not have become wealthy and powerful. These barriers included such means as government-targeted subsidies for forms and for R&D (research and development), export subsidies, import substitutions, and government regulations to bolster the domestic savings rate and keep down the cost of capital for local companies.[5] As journalist Tina Rosenberg noted, free trade is a religion, and religions come with hypocrisy.[6]

Powerful economic states became so by protecting their markets until they were ready to compete globally. But the existing "free trade" rules block developing countries from following this strategy. Meanwhile, rich countries take protectionist exceptions to the rules in order to lock in their global position.

Not able even to protect their commodities, the poorest developing countries hardly stand a chance of modernizing their economies beyond dependence on agriculture and natural resources. Not surprisingly, between 1960 and 2002, there has been a long-term downward trend in nonfuel commodity prices. Indeed, the commodity price recession of the 1980s was more severe and more prolonged than that of the Great Depression of the 1930s. A clear link between dependence on the export of these primary commodities and the incidence of extreme poverty is well known but often ignored by richer nations. Over the last three decades of the twentieth century, UNCTAD studies confirm that the long-term decline in the price of primary commodities, relative to the world's poorest commodity-exporting countries (including Burkina Faso, Burundi, Chad, the Democratic Republic of the Congo, Ethiopia, Guinea-Bissau, Madagascar, Malawi, Mali, Niger, Rwanda, Sierra Leone, Sudan, Tanzania, and Zambia).[7]

Check out the Congo, for instance. Here, miners dig up coltan by chopping down huge chunks of rain forest, which serves as the habitat for the Mbuti people (pygmies), who live by hunting, gathering, and trading. The wireless world of the rich depends on coltan. It is refined in the United States and Europe to become tantalum powder, a conductor of electricity vital for the capacitors used inside miniature circuit boards installed on almost all laptops, pagers, personal digital assistants, and cell phones.

To illustrate the social consequences of this resource dependence, miners in the Congo buy temporary "wives" (teenage girls) for the price of a kilogram of coltan, which can fetch up to $80 (compared with the 20 cents the average worker in the Congo takes home daily). Almost anyone with a shovel can dig up coltan, which is often near the surface. The profit from its sale is so high that it stimulates perpetual civil war and bands of armed predators. According to the WHO, the monthly toll of "avoidable deaths" in the Congo averages about 72,800. And not just human beings suffer from the coltan trade. In the Kahuzi-Biega National Park alone, a population of 8,000 eastern lowland gorillas has been reduced to about

1,000 as some 10,000 miners and traders use the gorillas for food or as bait to trap other animals.[8] For the Congo, the rules of globalization have straightforward consequences: **The greater the number of laptops and cell phones sold worldwide, the greater the violence, the more sparse the rain forests, and the fewer gorillas and pygmies will survive.**

Thus, the rules of the free market often become perverse. Without effective rule of law and a government that can keep a balance between environmental sustainability and growing economic markets, free market ideology alone can spell disaster. Rich countries are in a position to continue to protect their own vital resources and sectors, imposing agricultural tariffs averaging over 40% (and on some products, above 300%) on the least developed countries. And this does not include nontariff barriers applied by developed nations. Consider the case of EU regulations banning the import of foods with aflatoxins—toxic fungi in maize and groundnuts that possibly retard the growth in West African children who consume these products. The World Bank has calculated that this health regulation costs Africa $750 million annually in exports of dried fruit and nuts. Perhaps because of the EU regulations, the life of one European citizen is saved from aflatoxin poisoning every two years. This must be weighed against many African lives that are dependent on the export of these commodities: Without their livelihood from this trade, the Africans have little sustenance or medical treatment and are apt to die young from malnutrition or endemic disease.[9]

The international community has taken the special needs of poor countries into account in some exceptional arrangements in the past. But with rising global competition, existing multinational agreements to buffer the harsh effects of free markets for trade in the poorest countries are coming to an end. For example, the Multifiber Arrangement, which regulates the $350 billion of world trade in garments, is scheduled to expire in 2005. Millions of families in Bangladesh and other developing countries that depend on the garment industry will be devastated economically. In a Muslim nation of 140 million such as Bangladesh, with rising crime and a strong conservative Islamic movement, the timing of the expiration of the trade quotas could not be worse for regional stability.[10]

Left to the free market rules alone, large corporate lobbies dominate the globalization agenda to the point that thousands can die from the results. The most notorious case is the pharmaceutical lobby. Until August 2003, the conservative Bush administration supported the U.S. pharmaceutical lobby's demand that the patents on expensive medicines should be strictly enforced and that no cheap generic versions should water down these profits, no matter what the consequences (i.e. epidemics of devastating diseases in African countries).

Fortunately, this time the Anglo-Saxons free market model did not prevail. The pharmaceutical companies of the EU and Switzerland accepted an accord with African leaders that enables poor countries to import generic versions of expensive drugs to fight AIDS, malaria, and tuberculosis from countries such as India and Brazil without violating the trade laws protecting patent rights. The United States officially backed down. But governments in developing countries courting the good will of the United States, such as in Guatemala, choose to let their people die rather than to distribute inexpensive drugs to treat AIDS, even when these drugs become available. The Free Trade Area of the Americans (FTAA) initiative of the U.S government was targeted to maximize profits for pharmaceutical companies at the potential cost of thousands of human lives.[11] The pressure of thousands of protestors at the FTAA governmental negotiations in Miami, Florida in 2003 helped to slow down, if not to derail, this proposal—at least temporarily.

The question is, **How many lives in poor countries must be at stake before exceptions to the globalization rules of the rich are enforced for the sake of human needs?** Poor people do not have effective lobbies.

Recall the strategy of the rich countries at the WTO meeting in Cancun—to demand tariff reductions from the developing nations before a discussion of agricultural subsidy reductions could take place. Otherwise, the American Trade Representative, Robert Zoellick, threatened to go ahead with his declared strategy of bilateral agreements between the United States and other countries, circumventing the WTO. To counter this strategy, Brazil and India, among others, created a "Group of 22" alliance of developing countries. This initiative inspired other groupings of developing countries to hold firm in opposing the approval of trade-enhancing measures on investment, antitrust, and transparency on government procurement that the Europeans and Japanese demanded before they would talk about agricultural tariffs. The talks at Cancun broke down. Everyone left before any agricultural subsidy reductions could take place. The so-called victory for the Group of 22 was a hollow one because the United States went ahead with its plan to make bilateral deals with 14 countries, with additional countries lining up for their own deals with the United States because the WTO failed to get them any relief. It was more in the interest of American governmental elites than those of the low-income countries to have the talks break down, given the rising protectionism in the United States before the presidential election of 2004. The EU, on the other hand, had put all of its chips on a WTO compromise. Pascal Lamy, the head negotiator of the EU, called the U.S. strategy of cutting separate deals outside the WTO (which would not have any benefits spilling over to poorer nations in the world) "a form of bilateral imperialism."[12] Meanwhile, the EU farmers were no doubt relieved that their agricultural subsidies were not going to be cut—a politically convenient outcome for developed countries all around.

[...]

THE COMPETITIVENESS MANTRA: CONSOLIDATE, RAISE PRODUCTIVITY, DOWNSIZE, OUTSOURCE

Globalization, guided by the Anglo-Saxon principles, not only defies private property; it puts a premium on the value of competition. This blueprint (favoring those with lots of property contracts) constitutes what can be called the ideology of corporate social Darwinism: The rules of society should be set up to maximize the profits of the best organized and funded "national" teams, which prove themselves on the global fields of competition. Innovation leads to power and wealth. To succeed in a global economy, there must be tolerance for big and fast organizations. These nationally based cartels, conglomerates, or multinational companies will bring the nation great market share within their sectors and, in the process, raise the GDP and employment at home.

The consequences of this grand vision, however, do not live up to its promises. Using the strategy of what Bennett Harrison, in *Lean and Mean*,[13] called "concentration without centralization," the big multinational firms consolidate power through global networking. These organizations reduce in-house operations to "core competencies" by downsizing their personnel, outsourcing peripheral activities to low-cost labour sites at home or abroad (usually without benefits), computerizing and automating to increase productivity, and creating mergers, acquisitions, and strategic alliances in order to counter potential global competition.

This model generates unemployment and underemployment in the process of "creative destruction" in both rich and poor nations as the obsolete and unneeded are let go. It makes it impossible for poor countries to create multinational firms sophisticated enough to compete.

For starters, the unrestrained competitiveness model assumes that the social ideal is export-oriented growth in order to capture the maximum global market share, thus increasing employment at home. But because the world is one system, when one country builds up export surpluses, another must necessarily run trade deficits. Just as the global economy was subsidized throughout much of the post–World War II era by the printing and distribution of U.S. dollars, so too has the recent global economy been subsidized by huge U.S. trade deficits allowing other countries (e.g., China) to run large trade surpluses. But just as the dollar's value fixed to gold was eventually undermined by this extravagant liquidity, bringing down the money system, so does the extreme American trade deficit threaten to undermine the world's trade system. Protectionism has come home to roost in the United States: Unemployment near 6% is pushing toward European levels without European-style safety nets to catch those cast aside. With a huge external debt and a rising current account deficit (trade deficit plus interest payments on old government debt), the U.S. currency is pre-programmed to go down, putting pressure on Americans to save and on foreigners to buy lots of American goods and services. Income mobility stagnated beginning in the 1970s, and the real pay (adjusted for inflation) of workers in the United States in 2003 was lower than in 1973. The real value of the legal *minimum wage* in 2003 was lower than in 1968.[14]

Meanwhile, in the early twenty-first century, the conservative elite in Washington D.C. set a tone of permissiveness for the big, the powerful, and the wealthy to consolidate their positions. For example, pushed by the lobby for the media conglomerates, Republican Michael Powell, appointed head of the Federal Trade Commission, proposed in 2003 that single media giant could expand its "penetration" in the United States from reaching one third of all American television viewers to almost one half of viewers. The U.S. Congress diluted the proposal after the Senate rejected it while facing a Presidential veto. Yet the over-riding rationale of market efficiency through size—up to the point of irrefutable monopoly—is still perceived to be legitimate.

[...]

Not only have the basic services of developing economies been cartelized by large, private concerns, but the foreign aid bureaucracies aimed to help devel-oping countries have become costly, cartelized organizations, as well. Former advisor to the World Bank William Easterly notes that the global aid bureaucracies constitute a "cartel of good intentions." This cartel is made up of the United Nations Conference on Financing for Development, the World Bank, the U.S. Agency for International Development, the IMF, the United Nations, and the Inter-American Development Bank. Like all cartels, the aid cartel thrives when customers cannot find alternative suppliers and have little chance to complain, just as OPEC dictated severe terms to its oil customers during its peak in the 1970s.[15]

A case in point is Niger, which wanted debt forgiveness and new loans. The World Bank and IMF requirements forced the understaffed government offices there to spend 15 months preparing a participatory Poverty Reduction Strategy paper. This included not only a 14-point World Bank check list (the Comprehensive Development Framework) stretching from lumber to labor practices, but also a Financial Information Management System report, a report on Observance of Standards and Codes, a Medium Term Expenditure Framework, and a Debt Sustain-ability Analysis for the Enhanced Heavily Indebted Poor Countries Initiative. Niger's report was 187 pages long. It had to itemize spending for 2002–2005, including the annual cost of detailed items down to the level of sensitizing population to traffic circulation.

Good business practice would require the aid bureaucracies to "keep it simple, stupid!" But each well-intentioned, well-paid aid organization adds its own regulations (reaffirming its own need to exist), making for a regulatory morass that would challenge even the best educated and best staffed government seeking funding. Meanwhile, the many at the bottom of the society become poorer while the exhaustive paperwork is being filled out.

Indeed, the developing countries have adopted a much simpler approach to support themselves—money sent home annually by immigrant workers in devel-oped countries. From such family members working abroad, poor countries receive about $80 billion—*twice* as much as they do from foreign aid and *ten times* as much as they do from private investment.[16] But restrictions on immigration by developed countries due to the fears of terrorism and of domestic unemploy-ment may complicate even this last source of finance for low-income nations, despite the growing need for immigrant workers in most aging rich nations whose native populations are shrinking.

The rules of globalization set by the wealthy are extremely complex and make it difficult for individuals in any country to cope—particularly for the poor, who lack education, opportunity, and resources. The acceleration of change due to the process of globalization has only made things worse. To become competitive, organizations must become quick while still having a large enough size to benefit from economies of scale and to "socialize" some of their costs—that is, to pass them on to others. A social reality has been created that is characterized by increasing uncertainty in the name of freedom on the one hand and by the search for security on the other. Plutocracy reigns. Meanwhile, even in developed nations, social security nets are being trimmed back for the disadvantaged who can't make it or who fall behind because of lack of opportunity, bad luck, illness, or old age. Let's examine some of the trends that make up this social reality and will structure our life chances.

NOTES

1. Scott Miller and Neil King, "Poor Nations Bristle over New Push," and Michael Casey, "Argentina Ends Standoff with IMF by Defaulting on $2.9 Billion Debt," *The Wall Street Journal,* September 10, 2003, p. A22.

2. Elizabeth Becker and Finger Thompson, "Poorer Nations Plead Farmers' Case at Trade Talks," *The New York Times,* September 11, 2003.

3. Roger Thurow and Scott Kilman, "Bitter Harvest: As U.S. Food Aid Enriches Farmers, Poor Nations Cry Foul," *The Wall Street Journal,* September 11, 2003.

4. S. Ibi Ajayi, "What Africa Needs to Do to Benefit from Globalization," *Finance and Development,* Vol. 38, No. 4 (Washington, D.C.: 2001), pp. 6–8.

5. R. Isaak, *Managing World Economic Change,* 3rd edition (Upper Saddle River, NJ: Prentice Hall, 2000), p. 252.

6. Tina Rosenberg, "The Free-Trade Fix," *The New York Times Magazine,* August 18, 2002.

7. "Commodity Export Dependence, the International Poverty Trap and New Vulnerabilities," *The Least Developed Countries Report 2002* (UNCTAD, 2002), p. 138, 142–143.

8. Blain Harden, "The Dirt in the New Machine," *The New York Times Magazine,* August 12, 2001.

9. Kofi Annan, "Best Hope for Least-Developed Countries," *Presidents & Prime Ministers,* Vol. 10, No. 3 (Glen Ellyn: May/June 2001), pp. 18–19.

10. Peter Frisch, "As End of a Quota System Nears, Bangladesh Fears for Its Jobs," *The Wall Street Journal,* November 20, 2003.

11. Nicholas D. Kristof, "Death by Dividend," *The New York Times,* November 22, 2003.

12. Neil King and Scott Miller, "Cancun: Victory for Whom?" *The Wall Street Journal,* September 16, 2003.

13. Bennett Harrison, *Lean and Mean: The Changing Landscape of Corporate Power in the Age of Flexibility* (New York: Basic Books. 1993), pp. 9–12. Also see David C. Korten, *When Corporations Rule the World* (West Hartford, CT: Kumarian Press, 1996).

14. *NOW with Bill Moyers,* Public Broadcasting System, November 21, 2003.

15. William Easterly, "The Cartel of Good Intentions," *Foreign Policy,* July/August 2002, pp. 40–41.

16. "A Lifeline for Poor Nations," *Business Week,* November 24, 2003, p. 28.

POSTSCRIPT

Trade negotiations that have characterized the apparently ill-fated Doha Round illustrate that although wealthy nations are aware of the unfairness of limited free trade in agricultural sectors and others, there is little political impetus to compromise for the sake of the poor in developing nations. At the same time, poor nations have been compelled to embrace neoliberalism to deepen structural adjustment reforms that will improve their ability to service long-term debt. States such as the "Asian Tiger" economies ranging from China to Singapore to India, which enjoy a comparative advantage in the production of industrial goods and the provision of services to the global economy, have benefitted well through export-oriented growth. Predominantly agrarian societies remain peripheral, at least in some ways marginalized by the very same trade rules that allow others to prosper.

Assuming that modern globalization is beneficial to the world's poor, what are the best ways to enhance and improve the "trickle-down" effects of trade liberalization? Can the lot of the world's poor be improved without resorting to the major changes to the trade regime envisioned by the most optimistic analysts of world trade? Or are the rules that presently govern the process of globalization unredeemable? Doubtless these questions will be important themes in world development for the next decade.

Suggested Additional Readings

Berg, Andrew, and Anne Krueger. "Lifting All Boats: Why Openness Helps Curb Poverty," *Finance and Development,* 39, no. 3 (2002). www.imf.org/external/pubs/ft/fandd/2002/09/berg.htm

Birdsall, Nancy, Dani Rodrik, and Arvind Subramanian. "How to Help Poor Countries," *Foreign Affairs,* 84, no. 4 (July–August 2005): 136–152.

Moss, Todd, and Alicia Bannon. "Africa and the Battle over Agricultural Protectionism," *World Policy Journal,* 21, no. 2 (Summer 2004): 53–62.

Pauwelyn, Joost. "The Transformation of World Trade," *Michigan Law Review,* 104, no. 1 (October 2005): 1–66.

Rodrik, Dani. "Globalization for Whom?" *Harvard Magazine* (July–August 2002). www.harvardmagazine.com/on-line/070280.html

Stiglitz, Joseph E., and Andrew Charlton. *Fair Trade for All: How Trade Can Promote Development* (New York: Oxford University Press, 2005).

Sutherland, Peter D. "Why We Should Embrace Globalization," *Finance and Development,* 39, no. 3 (2002). www.imf.org/external/pubs/ft/fandd/2002/09/sutherla.htm

Wade, Robert Hunter. "Is Globalization Reducing Poverty and Inequality?" *World Development,* 32, no. 4 (2004): 567–589.

Wise, Timothy A. "The WTO's Development Crumbs," *Foreign Policy in Focus* (23 January 2006). www.fpif.org/fpiftxt/3083

InfoTrac® College Edition

Search for the following articles in the InfoTrac® database:

Bachelet, Michelle. "For Global Progress, Focus on Fair Trade," *Christian Science Monitor,* 9 (January 2006): 9.

Miles, Mark A. "Trade and Justice," *Harvard International Review,* 28, no. 2 (Summer 2006): 78–79.

For more articles, enter:
"trade justice," "world trade organization," "trade regime," or "trade negotiations" in the keyword search.

Web Resources

THE WORLD TRADE ORGANIZATION

www.wto.org

The World Trade Organization oversees the application of trade rules based on the General Agreement on Tariffs and Trade and related trade agreements.

INTERNATIONAL CENTRE FOR TRADE AND SUSTAINABLE DEVELOPMENT

www.ictsd.org

ICTSD is an international non-governmental organization that seeks to promote education and dialogue in regard to environmental concerns in the system of international trade.

UNITED NATIONS CONFERENCE ON TRADE AND DEVELOPMENT

www.unctad.org

UNCTAD is a subsidiary organ of the United Nations General Assembly founded in 1964. It serves as an intergovernmental forum and research institute for issues affecting development and the world trading system.

TRADE JUSTICE MOVEMENT

www.tjm.org.uk

The UK-based Trade Justice Movement is a coalition of dozens of non-governmental organizations and charitable foundations dedicated to challenging the prevailing trading regime through multilateral action.

Do Fair Trade Networks Create a Fairer Trading System?

✔ **YES**

LAURE WARIDEL, *Coffee with Pleasure: Just Java and World Trade* (Montreal: Black Rose Books, 2002), pp. 93–115

✗ **NO**

GAVIN FRIDELL, "The Fair Trade Network in Historical Perspective," *Canadian Journal of Development Studies,* 25, no. 3 (2004): 411–428

The 1990s saw the triumph of the neoliberal world economic order with the assumption of the Washington Consensus, the creation of the World Trade Organization, and the expansion of capitalism throughout portions of the post-communist and developing world. At the same time there arose a group of widely varied movements that criticized neoliberalism for a set of discriminatory trading practices and the imposition of structural adjustment. Among other things, it was argued that the modern trading system gave an unfair advantage to large corporations that were able to sell finished goods in developed nations far above the price paid for the raw materials that were purchased in the South. What was more, it was found that the gap in terms of trade was only widening as multi-nationals gained from the expansion of economies of scale. While big multinational suppliers and retailers benefitted handsomely through cornering the market in retail products, the farmers, miners, loggers, and other suppliers at the heart of the production process continued to work in substandard conditions, earning substandard pay and enjoying little upward mobility.

While developing nations as a whole tend to suffer from declining terms of trade, trade in export commodities tends to draw the clearest picture. Among these, coffee stands out as a telling example. Like most agricultural commodities, the market in coffee beans is subject to rapid and dramatic fluctuations in price, based in part on the size of local harvests and levels of demand in a global economy. Over the course of the 1990s, changes in the structure of the coffee market came with the liberalization of agricultural industries in several key coffee-exporting nations, the collapse of the International Coffee Agreement, and the spread of new technologies and developmental strategies to increase production. This served to increase the supply of coffee beans to the world economy. At the same time, the distribution and retailing of coffee came to be controlled by a small coterie of large-scale multinational corporations that concentrated the coffee industry. Put together, these developments caused a significant shift in market power to the distribution and retail side of the industry and caused a corresponding reduction in the share of market price going to coffee producers. Over the course of the 1990s, producers came to make far less by selling their beans on the open market and suffered similar reductions in working and living standards.

The publicity generated by the plight of peasants and wage labourers in many developing nations led by critics of neoliberal globalization contributed to calls for alternative modes of production. Small networks set up by international nongovernmental organizations (INGOs) over the years had sought to create parochial infant industries that would help to bypass the larger market distributors who might either exploit or ignore small producers in the developing world. Organizations such as Oxfam and the Mennonite Central Committee (MCC) had long been working with small producers of consumer commodities like coffee and handicraft artists to seek fair market value for their work. Known as alternative or fair trade, these businesses developed partnerships with local communities where they could also monitor working standards and engage in a form of collective bargaining. Fair trade retailers now distribute and sell a wide variety of commodities, including sugar, rice, coffee, and tea, as well as a growing variety of handicrafts made in small workshops.

By the 1990s, these small efforts had grown and inspired private-sector corporations that saw value in marketing goods that were procured through fair trade. Interest in fair trade as an ethical business venture as well as a successful marketing strategy led to the further "mainstreaming" of fair trade. In order to service and regulate the fair trade industry, a spate of labelling organizations has arisen to monitor and certify that products are produced according to widely accepted fair trade practices. More recently, an international organization, Fairtrade Labelling Organizations International (FLO) was created to coordinate these efforts. Fair trade has grown most significantly in Europe up until the 1990s, but it has taken great strides in the North American market as well in the past decade. In 2000, massive coffee retailer Starbucks responded to popular pressure to sell fair trade coffee in its stores. Likewise, many other retailers have decided to publicize their commitment to ethical business practices either through in-house agreements with third world suppliers or by selling fair trade certified products.

In spite of the great gains made by fair trade retailers and networks over the past few years, fair trade initiatives are marginal to the worldwide trade that takes place between North and South. So long as alternative trade organizations remain marginal to the world economy, they are unlikely to effect widespread change in the structure of international system that is said to benefit large multinationals based in the developed world. Increased success risks mainstreaming and watering down the distinctiveness of the fair trade industry. In the following essays, Laure Waridel explores the motivations and benefits of fair trade, while Gavin Fridell admits the limitations of the fair trade movement in seeking to change the patterns of world trade.

✔ YES
Coffee with Pleasure: Just Java and World Trade
LAURE WARIDEL

ORIGINS OF THE FAIR-TRADE MOVEMENT

Awareness of the rights and responsibilities of consumers began to gather momentum during the 1960s, when a young lawyer named Ralph Nader won a battle with General Motors over their manufacturing of unsafe cars. More recently, consumers' concern over the social and environmental effects of various products has manifested itself in campaigns to persuade such companies as The Gap, Shell, Nike, the Disney Corporation and Starbucks to change their business practices.

Fair trade is part of this wave of interest in ethical consumption. It is difficult to pinpoint exactly when the fair-trade movement started: a number of initiatives seem to have begun at about the same time on several continents. In North America, the Mennonite International Development Agency (now known as the Mennonite Central Committee) instigated the first direct-purchasing project with impoverished Latin American craftspeople, as early as 1946. Their first stores, Self-Help Crafts (today known as Ten Thousand Villages), were opened by volunteers who wanted to educate their communities about the inequities of international commerce and the need to pay a fair price to producers. In Europe, in 1950 Oxfam began planning sales of crafts made by Chinese refugees in its British stores, and soon afterwards a group of young Dutch activists started directly importing Haitian wood sculptures in order to help the craftspeople become economically independent.

Initially named alternative trade, the burgeoning movement originally was aimed not at reforming conventional trading practices, but rather at creating a parallel system that would open markets to disadvantaged Southern producers and craftspeople. The organizations involved in this movement wanted to build relationships based on justice, not charity, in order to put an end to exploitation. As one project followed another, the concept of alternative trade started to strengthen into what is now usually known as fair trade, with the organizations involved establishing a set of core principles that they strive to respect in their dealings with all their partners.

Specific criteria have been established by fair-trade certification organizations for different products such as coffee, tea, bananas, cocoa, etc. [...] In general, however, a fair-trade product must be bought from democratically organized small-scale producers at a price that will provide them with a decent standard of living. The purchasing must be as direct as possible in order to prevent speculation and to cut out unnecessary intermediaries. Southern partners must have access to credit from their Northern counterparts and both parties must be encouraged to develop long-term relationships. Production techniques must be environmentally friendly and the producer organizations must be democratically managed.

A Growing Success Story

Thanks to consumer support, fair-trade projects have sprung up on all continents. But although fair trade originated in North America, its greatest impact on consumers has been in Europe. In the case of coffee, between 75 and 80 percent of the world's certified fair-trade production is distributed in European shops, offices, and restaurants.[1] Consumers in Switzerland, the Netherlands, Belgium and Germany can find fair-trade coffee in the stores of any nationwide grocery chain.[2] There are currently over 70,000 points of sale for fair-trade products in Europe. Besides coffee, they sell sugar, tea, bananas, spices and nuts, as well as a wide range of crafts: woven baskets, jewellery, clothing, ceramics, cards, and toys.[3] At the production end, fair trade benefits more than 800,000 producer families in the South—over 5 million people in 45 countries.[4]

Fair-Trade Organizations

Over the years, the fair-trade movement has achieved a considerable degree of organization and collaboration. Two important umbrella organizations are the International Federation for Alternative Trade (IFAT) and the European Fair Trade Association (EFTA), which bring together about a hundred fair-trade organizations (FTOs) from all over the world. Their main role is to facilitate the exchange of information on markets and sources for fair-trade products. They also lobby public institutions and attempt to raise public awareness of fair-trade issues.

An important role is played by independent certification organizations. As large numbers of new fair-trade products arrived on the market in the 1980s, it became vital to develop a method of guaranteeing that such products were in fact equitably traded, and that the production process compiled with certain well-defined criteria. It all started with coffee.

The first fair-trade certification program began in 1988, in the Netherlands. The Max Havelaar Foundation was named after the hero of a Dutch novel who denounced the treatment of Indonesian coffee planters during the Dutch colonial period. By establishing a certification process, it was hoped that fair-trade coffee could be marketed more easily through conventional channels and thus reach a larger number of consumers. Several conventional coffee roasters warmed to the idea and soon began marketing Max Havelaar's certified fair-trade coffee. For the first time, certified fair-trade products could be found on the shelves of major supermarkets and in restaurants rather than only in the stores of nonprofit organizations and church groups.

After the Netherlands, certification was adopted in other European countries, then in North America and Asia. These initiatives have greatly increased fair-trade coffee sales. Many European countries now also certify fair-trade bananas, sugar, tea, chocolate, honey and orange juice. Although there is no independent certification process for crafts, the members of the International Federation of Alternative Trade share principles similar to those of certified fair trade.

FAIR-TRADE LABELS

TransFair, Max Havelaar and the Fair Trade Foundation are all international certification organizations which put their logo on fair-trade food products such as coffee, tea, cocoa, bananas, honey and sugar. Beyond simply respecting the certification criteria, companies must pay the certification organization a license fee which, in the case of coffee, costs between about $0.18 and $0.29 per kg ($0.08 and $0.13 per lb.) depending on the country. This money finances the monitoring process and the promotion of the seal.[5] All these certification initiatives are united under the umbrella of Fairtrade Labelling Organizations International (FLO-International) which has been working to standardize the certification process since 1997.

TransFair

In Canada and the USA, TransFair puts its label on certified fair-trade coffee. The same seal is used in Germany, Japan, Austria, Luxembourg and Italy. Although a recent addition to packages of North American coffees, this logo is sought after by a growing number of consumers.

	TransFair Canada	TransFair USA
Founded	1994	1995
Number of licensees (August 2001)	70	103
Amount of fair-trade coffee sold in 2000	191,000 kg (420,000 lb.)	1.95 million kg (4.3 million lb.)

Max Havelaar

Since 1988, the Max Havelaar certification label has met with great success in Europe. In Holland, for example, 90 percent of consumers are familiar with this label. Over 130 brands of certified fair-trade coffee are sold at 35,000 outlets in Europe.[6] In Switzerland one can find Max Havelaar in the vast majority of grocery stores. Many European supermarkets have entire sections devoted to fair-trade coffee, tea, sugar, chocolate, bananas and other produce certified by Max Havelaar.

Fair Trade Foundation

The Fair Trade Foundation is the fair-trade certification mark in Britain and Ireland. Fair-trade coffee is served in the British parliament and many government buildings, and is available in most supermarkets. The British government has strongly supported the fair-trade movement.

Players	Tasks performed by certification organization
Cooperatives	• Selects which cooperatives are eligible for FLO-International's Registry of Coffee Growers. Regular inspection to ensure that criteria are being met (democratic procedures and sustainable development).
Northern importers and roasters	• Accredits importers and roasters.
	• Gives introduction to cooperatives in the Registry.
	• Ensures contractual agreements are respected (e.g. minimum price and prefinancing).
	• Grants seal of certification.
Distributors	• Support in the marketing of their products.
Individual consumers/collective consumer	• Public-information campaigns on fair trade.

Source: Information sheet, Max Havelaar France, 1998

THE CERTIFICATION PROCESS FOR FAIR-TRADE COFFEE

Every player in the fair-trade chain has a role to play in abiding by the agreed rules of the game. The criteria decided upon by the certification organizations are applied in as fair a manner as possible, while accounting for cultural and economic differences that exist both in the North and in the South.

Inspectors visit Southern cooperatives every one to two years, depending on their volume of production and the needs of the producers. In May 2001, 363 producers' organizations from 22 countries were listed in the FLO's fair-trade registry. Of these, 110 have been only provisionally accepted and may be granted permanent status after two coffee seasons, once they have demonstrated an ability to honour their commercial agreements. The coops registered on the FLO list can be found in Bolivia, Brazil, Cameroon, Colombia, Costa Rica, the Democratic Republic of Congo, the Dominican Republic, El Salvador, Guatemala, Haiti, Honduras, Mexico, Nicaragua, Papua-New Guinea, Peru, Tanzania, Uganda, Ecuador, Venezuela, Ethiopia, Indonesia and Thailand.

As for the roasters, inspection procedures vary somewhat for each certification organization, usually depending on their financial resources. In Switzerland, visits are made every six to 12 months, whereas in Canada and in the USA such visits are less frequent. After these inspections, certifiers have the authority to revoke the licenses of cooperatives and roasters that do not meet their criteria and have done so.

In contrast to organic certification, certification fees are paid by the roasters, rather than the producers. For a coffee to be certified fairly traded, it is not enough that its cooperative of origin be listed in FLO-International's Registry of Coffee Growers. The coffee's movements must also be strictly controlled, which is beyond the cooperatives' sphere of operation. Roasters must show their books and warehouses in order to assure certifiers that they too have complied with the rules of fair trade and are entitled to affix a fair-trade logo to their products when appropriate.

[...]

FAIR-TRADE COFFEE IN NORTH AMERICA

Thanks to a growing awareness of the injustice of our economic system, fair trade has begun to catch on quickly in North America during the last few years. Between 1998 and 2000, sales of fair-trade coffee quadrupled in Canada and multiplied 37-fold in the USA.[7] Today more than 60 roasters are offering over 200 different blends of fair-trade coffee across Canada. In the USA, the number of roasters has reached 100. The demand is growing every day to the point that the certification organizations are facing challenges posed by rapid growth.

The price of fair-trade coffee, like that of any other product, varies from one brand to another depending on the business practices and expenditures of the supplier. Product quality, salaries, rent, spending on marketing, profit margins, packaging, transportation and investors' returns are all covered in the price charged to consumers. Fair-trade products are not necessarily more expensive than regular market products of the same quality. In some cases they can be cheaper. Some fair-trade roasters claim that they are able to offer a cheaper product than conventional competitors at equivalent quality because buying directly from coops saves money by reducing the number of intermediaries. Others argue that trading directly is more complicated and time-consuming than dealing with brokers and thus entails higher costs, making their fair-trade coffee more expensive. A survey by the Specialty Coffee Association of America found that quality rather than price, customer demand, or convenience of supply was the overwhelming criterion for industry purchasing decisions regarding fair-trade, organic and shade-grown coffees.[8] Price is thus one factor among a number of others that influence the development of sustainable coffee.

Almost all the fair-trade coffee available in North America is gourmet coffee. Approximately 79 percent of it is certified organic.[9] In contrast with the situation of a few years ago, the majority of customers can now find a variety of fair-trade blends to choose from in their area. The list of companies offering at least one fair-trade coffee is growing almost daily.

[...]

WHEN THE BIG BOYS MOVE IN: MULTINATIONAL CORPORATIONS IN THE FAIR-TRADE MOVEMENT

In recent years, North American sales of fair-trade coffee have boomed and some big players have contributed to this. What was originally the province of a few small roasters has been adopted by multinationals such as Starbucks, Sara Lee and Van Houtte. Like smaller companies, they have signed licensee agreements with TransFair and have committed themselves to abiding by the criteria of fair trade for a certain amount of their coffee. Their wide distribution network has made fair-trade coffee much more widely available across North America—Starbucks alone has over 2,300 stores across the USA.

The involvement of such big names is unquestionably very good news for thousands of small coffee farmers. But the fact that big corporations are eligible to use the fair-trade seal has raised questions in the minds of some activists and long-established fair-trade coffee roasters. They wonder why small-scale production and democratic principles of organization should be criteria for coffee growers but not for roasters. What does "fair" mean—and fair for whom? On this point, opinions are numerous.

What should be recognized is that, generally speaking, the rich countries where fair-trade coffee is being bought have stronger labour regulations and better social safety nets than most of the countries where coffee is grown. Exploitative working conditions and poverty are much more visible in coffee-growing areas than in richer countries. The coffee industry can no longer ignore the plight of small coffee growers, especially now that farmers are facing severe economic hardships as a result of the catastrophic slump in prices on the New York and London coffee markets. The consequences of "unfair trade" are borne by those who pick the coffee more than anyone else. This is undeniable. The coffee industry is starting to wake up to its own unsustainability.[10]

In practice, the extent of the commitment by some companies is questionable. Some roasters appear to be using fair trade to shield themselves against criticism from consumers and are making little effort to promote their fair-trade brands. Some appear to have adopted fair-trade coffee in order not to lose customers rather than as a means of assuming their responsibility towards coffee farmers. They talk about it as a new trend, like flavoured coffees. Some retailers show a serious lack of information in answering questions about fair trade, which does not help its development.

However, despite the fact that some businesses seem to be using fair trade to protect or enhance their public image rather than out of a real commitment, it must be acknowledged that this is a first step in a positive direction. It is then up to us consumers to keep on the pressure every time we have the chance. We need to make sure that the coffee we choose wears the fair-trade certification logo. We can decide whether to buy it from a small local company or a bigger one. The more people buy fair-trade coffee, the sooner it will become a must for all businesses, large and small.

CAMPAIGNING FOR FAIR TRADE

All over the developed world, men and women of all ages and all walks of life are coming together to raise awareness of fair trade and pushing to make fairly traded products more accessible to consumers—as individuals simply asking for fair-trade coffee in restaurants and stores, or as groups of volunteers armed with various tools. Organizations such as Équiterre, Global Exchange, the Canadian Council for International Cooperation, Ten Days for Global Justice and Oxfam have organized very effective campaigns to make people realize the political power of their consumer choices.

Internationally, Oxfam has been leading the way in promoting fair trade for over 40 years. Oxfam-UK alone currently works with over 160 producer organizations in some 30 countries around the world. In Belgium, the popular "world shops" selling fair-trade products arose out of the Oxfam movement. Over the last 10 years, Oxfam International has increased its campaigning and lobbying activities denouncing the negative social and environmental effects of the dominant trading system. It publishes and distributes well-researched policy papers and raises consumer awareness of the issues of ethical trade and child labour.[11]

In Canada, Équiterre has developed many education-for-action tools aimed at creating a snowball effect for fair trade. The organization has mobilized groups across Québec and Canada which have used Équiterre's material to build their own local campaigns. A variety of public-information activities have been organized and an information kit put together to encourage businesses to make fair-trade coffee more accessible. Équiterre has aroused the interest of the media, organized slide-show lecture tours, staged a photo exhibition, and has organized debates, street theatre, and letter-writing campaigns, with a view to moving both consumers and retailers into fair trade.

Rather than initiating a boycott to put pressure on coffee companies, Équiterre (like TransFair Canada and other groups) has chosen another strategy: so-called "buycotting" campaigns. These encourage consumers to ask for fair-trade coffee and buy it where available, to prove to corporations that the public is interested in fair-trade products, thereby creating a demand.

This was the strategy behind the postcard campaign directed at Paul-André Guillotte, head of Van Houtte, one of the largest players in the Canadian coffee industry. [...] Van Houtte owns many brands and is especially strong in the office coffee-service market. After meetings with Équiterre representatives and after receiving thousands of postcards mailed by consumers over three years, the company finally signed on. The company is now offering one kind of fair-trade coffee through its organic line, "Les Amoureux du café." Many consumers are hoping for more choices, especially in view of the company's recent record profits—profits fuelled by the current low prices paid to producers on the conventional market.

In the USA, the nonprofit organization Global Exchange has put forward a more assertive strategy. Across the country, a network of activists, church groups, students, labour unions and environmentalists has been mobilized against sweatshop labour practices in coffee production. Global Exchange has targeted companies and organized protests in front of cafes. Starbucks was one of the first companies they approached. Deborah James, Fair Trade Director at Global Exchange, explains:

> We chose Starbucks because it is the largest specialty coffee retailer, with one fifth of all cafes in the country. In the fall of 1999, Global Exchange approached then CEO Howard Schultz and requested that Starbucks offer fairtrade certified coffee in all its stores. The company was initially very hesitant, alleging the beans were of low quality. Shortly thereafter, we organized several peaceful demonstrations in front of Starbucks stores in Seattle.
>
> In February 2000, an investigative report by San Francisco's ABC TV affiliate exposed child labour and scandalously low wages on Guatemalan coffee plantations, some of which sell coffee to Starbucks. Immediately after the program aired, we organized a local protest. We then petitioned Starbucks stockholders at their annual meeting in Seattle to offer fair-trade certified coffee. That same week, the company announced a one-time shipment of 34,000 kg (75,000 lb.) of fair-trade coffee. We responded that for a firm as big as Starbucks, this represented a "Drop in the Cup"—an average of only about 14 kg (30 lb.) per store, and the coffee was not certified! We then circulated an open letter, signed by 84 student, environmental, church, and social-justice organizations, again asking Starbucks to pay farmers a living wage and offer their customers fair-trade certified coffee. We helped plan 30 demonstrations that were scheduled for April 13 across the country at Starbucks shops. Meanwhile, hundreds of people faxed letters to Starbucks from our website or sent postcards asking the giant retailer to pay farmers fair prices.
>
> Three days before our scheduled demonstrations, Starbucks announced an agreement with TransFair USA to offer fair-trade certified coffee at all its stores nationwide, beginning October 2000. They will also be developing educational material and training for coffee-bar workers, so that millions of consumers can learn about fair trade. This is a huge victory for farmers, whose incomes will triple when they can sell their coffee at fair-trade prices. It is also an important win for the corporate-accountability movement. Starbucks' quick capitulation in the face of nationwide protest illustrates that grassroots organizing and education can indeed bring major results.[12]

The success of this campaign is a clear illustration of the fact that, once organized, consumers have much more power over companies than they think. They are the *raison d'être* of all companies.[13] Without consumers, there is no business.

[...]

TRANSFERRING RESPONSIBILITY TO THE CONSUMER

Although more and more citizens may wish to make a political statement with their consumer choices, they need access to information in order to make judicious decisions. (They don't have time to read a book about everything they buy!)

In an ideal world, people would be able to learn about the environmental and social impacts of what they buy simply by reading product labels. These impacts would need to be adequately measured before we could properly judge and compare the product's "real value." Such a label might resemble the "nutritional content" labels found on many food items sold in North America, and ideally it would become mandatory to provide this information everywhere in the world. This is unlikely to happen in the near future, considering that most governments are refusing to insist on labelling genetically modified food and that the World Trade Organization is restricting eco-labelling schemes. The right to know what we buy is a new concept, and has a long way to go before being officially recognized.

Not only is the WTO failing to address the issue of sustainable trade, it could also threaten existing initiatives. Under the Technical Barriers to Trade (TBT) agreement, many environmental and social regulatory standards are obstacles to free trade.[14] Voluntary, nongovernmental eco-labelling schemes may be judged to discriminate against "like" products on the basis of how they are produced rather than what they are. This means that "fair-trade", "shade-grown" and even "organic" certification labels could be challenged in front of the secretive WTO ruling panel.

To avoid the threat of WTO action, the leading international standard-setting, accreditation and labelling organizations in social and environmental certification have united under the International Social and Environmental Accreditation and Labelling (ISEAL) Alliance. One of ISEAL's objectives is to gain international recognition and credibility for their programs in the eyes of intergovernmental trade bodies and in the international arena. Consequently, they are working to secure acceptance of their criteria as international standards in order to avoid their initiatives' being considered technical barriers to trade.[15] The organizations currently participating in ISEAL are: Fairtrade Labelling Organizations International (FLO), the Conservation Agriculture Network (CAN), the Forest Stewardship Council (FSC), the International Federation of Organic Agriculture Movements (IFOAM), the International Organic Accreditation Service (IOAS), the Marine Stewardship Council (MSC), and Social Accountability International (SAI).

At first sight, sustainable-trade initiatives might appear like David fighting Goliath. Free-trade policies are buttressed by WTO rules and other trade agreements. Citizens often find themselves disempowered in the face of such structures and left without much governmental support to respond to the environmental and social problems exacerbated by increased international trade. Slowly however, people all around the world are becoming organized to make their voices heard and to take action. Nongovernmental organizations (NGOs) are springing up around the globe to defend various issues. These groups encompass a wide range of viewpoints and plans for action, and each in its worn way is seeking to influence the beliefs and behaviour of people throughout the world. Some promote human rights, others international cooperation, environmental action, and justice. Every initiative is important and many are complementary. The ethical consumer's choice movement is only one strategy among many, but one which we can practice in our day-to-day lives, by buying according to our values. Goliath is facing many Davids.

NOTES

1. Interview with Mr. Hans Bolscher, Max Havelaar Netherlands. Utrech, May 26, 1998.

2. Waridel, Laure and Teitelbaum, Sara. Research Report *Fair Trade in Europe: Contributing to equitable commerce in Holland, Belgium, Switzerland, and France.* Montreal: Équiterre, 1999.

3. European Fair Trade Association (EFTA). *Fair trade in Europe: Facts and figures on the fair-trade sector in 16 European countries.* Maastricht: European Fair Trade Association, 1998.

4. Ibid.

5. Fair TradeMark Canada. Campaign Kit, 1996, 3.

6. Équiterre, "What is fair-trade coffee?" *Fair Trade: a growing trend in the coffee industry.* May, 2000.

7. Data obtained directly from TransFair Canada and TransFair USA. June 2001.

8. Giovannucci, Daniele. *Sustainable Coffee Survey of the North American Specialty Coffee Industry.* Conducted for the Summit Foundation, the Nature Conservancy, the North American Commission for Environmental Cooperation, the Specialty Coffee Association of America and the World Bank. May, 2001.

9. Ibid., 24.

10. Participation in the SCAA Coffee Conference. San Francisco, April 14–18, 2001.

11. Oxfam-UK: www.oxfam.org.uk.

12. James, Deborah. "Justice and Java: Coffee in a Fair Trade Market." *North American Congress on Latin America.* Vol. 34, No. 2 (October 2000).

13. Seybold, Patricia B. *The Customer Revolution: How to thrive when customers are in control.* New York: Crown Business, 2001.

14. Shrybman, op. cit. 11.

15. Mallet, Patrick. *ISEAL Alliance Strategic Role: Background Paper.* Knowlesville: Falls Brook Centre, May 2001.

✗ NO
The Fair Trade Network in Historical Perspective
GAVIN FRIDELL

Over the past few decades the fair trade network has emerged as a significant development project that seeks to address underdevelopment in the South by challenging the unequal terms of exchange for Southern handicrafts and commodities. Generally speaking, goods are certified as fair trade by fair trade umbrella organizations if they are exchanged under the terms of a minimum guaranteed price and are produced in a manner deemed to be in line with the principles of democratic organization, no utilization of child labour, recognized trade unions for workers, and environmental sustainability. While little systematic empirical work on fair trade has been carried out, the evidence that does exist reveals that the network has the potential to provide much-needed higher income, technical advice, and social and physical infrastructure for hundreds of thousands of Southern partners worldwide. In recent years, a small but growing body of literature on fair trade has emerged that has begun to assess the network's potential for poverty alleviation, local capacity building, and North-South solidarity (LeClair 2002; Raynold 2002; Renard 1999; Simpson and Rapone 2000; VanderHoff Boersma 2001; Waridel 2002). Most authors, to varying degrees, depict the fair trade network as an innovative challenge to neoliberal globalization and view the growth of fair trade sales as a small but important victory in the struggle against market deregulation, social spending cuts, and the assault on labour rights imposed by neoliberal reformers. However, this paper contends that the depiction of the fair trade network as a victory against neoliberal globalization fails to situate the network historically within the broader context of post-war development. A historical perspective reveals that the growth of the fair trade network has in fact been indicative of the current triumph of neoliberal globalization, which has imposed on the network a voluntarist, nonstatist development strategy while at the same time defeating the broader fair trade movement and its vision of a regulated international market with strong state intervention.

[...]

II. THE FAIR TRADE NETWORK: PHASE ONE, 1940s–1988

The fair trade network was significantly influenced by the broader fair trade movement, which set the context within which it evolved. From the movement, the fair trade network drew an emphasis on combating unfair commodity prices and on attaining "trade not aid." Moreover, during the first phase of its history the network was influenced by dependency theory, its critique of the world capitalist system, and its emphasis on the need to develop alternatives to the existing system.

Convinced by dependency theorists that the world capitalist system was incapable of providing developmental benefits to the poor majority in the South because of the mechanism of unequal exchange, fair traders aspired to create a parallel trading system that would open alternative markets for Southern products. In these alternative markets, prices would not be determined by the vagaries of supply and demand, but would be formed through a process of negotiation between producers and consumers based on the premise of fairness to all parties.

The multiple origins of the fair trade network can be traced back to the 1940s and 1950s when Christian mission-driven NGOs in Europe and North America began selling handicrafts produced by disadvantaged Southern artisans in direct-purchase projects. In Europe, these efforts were led by Oxfam UK and the Dutch Catholic group Fair Trade Organisatie (originally known as S.O.S. Wereldhandel). In North America, these efforts were led by the Mennonite Central Committee (MCC) (then called the Mennonite International Development Agency), and the Sales Exchange for Refugee Rehabilitation (SERRV) program of the Church of the Brethren. In the 1950s and 1960s, these NGOs developed Alternative Trade Organizations (ATOs) and initiated the import and sale of fair trade handicrafts through mail-order and church solidarity groups. In 1969, the first fair trade "world shop" was established in the Netherlands, which was soon followed by the opening of the MCC's first SELFHELP (later changed to Ten Thousand Villages) retail store in the United States in 1972 (EFTA 2001a, 2001b, 1995; Littrell and Dickson 1999, 61–112).

Throughout the 1970s and 1980s the fair trade network grew steadily. In 1973, Fair Trade Organisatie first introduced coffee into fair trade markets in Europe. The turnover of fair trade coffee soon exceeded those of handicrafts and sparked further growth for the network. By the early 1990s, there were more than 60 fair trade importing organizations and thousands of world shops throughout Europe. Oxfam Trading had developed into an organization with 625 shops in the United Kingdom and a retail turnover of $15.4 million in 1994. Fair Trade Organisatie had grown even larger with a retail turnover of $24 million in 1994 (EFTA 1995). In North America, the fair trade network grew at a significantly slower pace and remained in the hands of a small number of fair trade ATOs. At the end of the 1970s there were more than 60 SELFHELP stores across the United States and Canada, which doubled to over 120 by the late 1980s. By 1989, SERRV had grown into an ATO with annual sales of more than $3 million (Littrell and Dickson 1999, 61–112).

The ATOs that developed the fair trade network were motivated by the desire to assist Southern partners in their immediate needs and to lay the groundwork for a new international trading system.[1] Perhaps one of the clearest examples of the ideas that were prominent in the fair trade network during its formative decades is provided by the work of Michael Barratt Brown, the Founding Chair and Trustee of Third World Information Network (TWIN) and Twin Trading Ltd., a fair trade organization in the United Kingdom that has played an important role in promoting fair trade. In his work, Barratt Brown draws explicitly on the concepts of dependency theory and argues for the need to expand the fair trade network to combat underdevelopment in the South, which he asserts stems primarily from unequal exchange (Barratt Brown 1993, 23–43). He argues that fair trade can provide important solutions to the causes of unequal exchange by giving Southern producers greater access to technology, education, credit, and value-added processing and storage facilities, while at the same time protecting them from the whims of the global market through guaranteed prices, strict labour standards, and bonds of solidarity between producers and consumers.

Yet, while asserting that the fair trade network is key to confronting underdevelopment in the South, Barratt Brown argues that its benefits can only be broadened and sustained if it is combined with strong international market regulation. In an unregulated global market, he argues, giant TNCs will always be able to profit through speculation and market manipulation, while small producers will always suffer the most as a result of the unpredictable market swings caused by these actions. Consequently, Barratt Brown proposed a model for a new economic order composed of democratically controlled state marketing boards, with grassroots control at all levels, and direct links between Northern consumers and Southern producers. Central to his vision is an alternative trade clearing union, designed to address Southern countries' lack of access to hard currency and credit needed to diversify and develop trade. The clearing house would make multiple deals between Southern countries in cases where direct exchanges would not satisfy any one country. Fair trade standards, green consumerism, and consumer-producer unions would be essential to promote the rights of workers and consumers. The final outcome would be a decentralized economy based on "a parallel trading system and an alternative trade network within that system growing up side by side with the present organisation of world trade by giant companies" (Barratt Brown 1993, 134).

Since the late 1980s, the fair trade network has undergone a significant reorientation to meet the demands of the capitalist market and neoliberal reformers and most fair traders and fair trade analysts have, to varying degrees, departed significantly from Barratt Brown's vision of a new economic order. Two key aspects of Barratt Brown's work have been left behind. First, most fair traders have abandoned his focus on the nation-state as a primary agent in development, which derives from dependency theory's focus on the goal of national self-sufficiency. To Barratt Brown, a democratically run, interventionist state is required to regulate the economy both internationally and domestically; to provide much needed infrastructure, credit, and technology to domestic prodders; and to coordinate various sectors within a national economy to ensure diversification and a degree of self-reliance. In contrast to this, most fair traders now focus on NGOs as the primary agents of development. The state is viewed as having the potential to provide benefits to fair traders through the provision of such things as basic social welfare, protection for weak sectors of the domestic economy, and labour and environmental legislation, but its role is generally viewed as subsidiary, not central, to the fair trade network (Bolscher 2002; VanderHoff Boersma 2002, 2001). An important exception to this is Oxfam International, which continues to lobby for such things as international commodity agreements and state-enforced social and environmental standards while at the same time promoting the fair trade network's non-statist project (Oxfam International 2002a, 2002b).

The second key aspect of Barratt Brown's analysis that has been sidelined by most fair traders is his focus on creating a parallel trading network that presents itself as a distinct alternative to the existing global market. In his work, Barratt Brown argues against the concept of de-linking promoted by some dependency theorists because of his assertion that Southern nations require access to Northern technology. However, he is convinced of the need to break to some degree from the global capitalist system and develop an alternative model for a new international trade system that, in the long run, aspires to be free from the pressures imposed by profit-driven TNCs and the imperatives of the capitalist market. In contrast to his vision, over the past two decades, fair traders have moved increasingly toward attempting to reform the existing trade system rather than forging an alternative to it.

[...]

III. THE FAIR TRADE NETWORK: PHASE TWO, 1988–PRESENT

The Max Havelaar Foundation[2] was founded in the Netherlands in 1988 in response to arguments made by Southern fair trade producers about the need to gain access to "real markets" (Bolscher 2002). The objective was to promote the fair trade label and its mission, and offer it to conventional importers who met Max Havelaar's standards in exchange for a certification fee. Conventional importers would be encouraged to participate in free trade because of the "added value" the fair trade label—injected with symbolic social meaning—would give them on the market (Renard 1999, 484). After its original formation, the fair trade labelling movement spread quickly so that by the late 1990s there were 17 national initiatives (NIs) throughout Europe, North America, and Japan, variously under the names of Max Havelaar, TransFair, or the Fair Trade Foundation (FTF). Since 1997, these NIs have been coordinated under the umbrella group Fairtrade Labelling Organizations International (FLO), headquartered in Bonn, Germany (FLO 2001).

[...]

FLO's eagerness to do business with conventional importers and distributors and gain access to conventional markets has caused some commentators to view fair trade as a subset of ethical business practices, which include such things as "corporate citizenship" and "codes of conduct." However, FLO licensers argue that the goals of fair trade transcend those of ethical business practices, which are generally little more than window dressing and are limited by the minimal desire of corporations to protect themselves from public criticism (Bolscher 2002; FLO 2001).

Whereas ethical business practices are profit-driven and top-down, fair trade is focused on long-term developmental aims and the organization and empowerment of marginalized workers and peasants from below.[3]

Since its establishment in 1988, FLO's strategy has been a relative success and the fair trade label has gained growing popularity among consumers, small-scale importers, and mainstream supermarkets in Europe and, to a lesser extent, North America. Sales of FLO-certified goods grew by 35% from 1997 to 2000. The total retail turnover of FLO-certified goods in 2000 was worth more than $196 million, of which more than $49 million went directly to producers. This is about 40% more than would have been justified by conventional prices. Consumers in Switzerland have purchased the greatest quantity of FLO-labelled goods (34.8% of the total from 1997–2000), followed by the Netherlands (24.7%), Germany (17.6%), the United Kingdom (9.8%), and the remaining fair trade countries (13.1%). Canada and the United States each accounted for only 0.2% of the total during this period (FLO 2001).

Due to its growing popularity, FLO-certified goods have made some notable inroads to mainstream markets in Europe.[4] In 2000, sales of fair trade coffee, traditionally the largest fair trade sector, accounted for 3% of the coffee market in Switzerland, 2.7% in the Netherlands, 1.8% in Denmark, and around 1% or less in the remaining fair trade countries (EFTA 2001b, 1995). To meet this demand, FLO had 163 coffee co-operatives on its register, representing 516,544 coffee-producer families out of a total of nearly 25 million coffee-producer families worldwide. Other fair trade sectors have shown similar trends, with fair trade bananas accounting for 15% of the banana market in Switzerland and 4.2% in the Netherlands, and fair trade tea accounting for 4% of the tea market in Switzerland and 2.5% in Germany (FLO 2001).

[...]

FLO's rapid growth since the 1980s has been accompanied by the emergence of other fair trade organizations that have also played a key role in promoting its new mainstream orientation. The International Federation for International Trade (IFAT) was formed in 1989 and currently consists of 148 ATOs from 48 countries in Africa, Asia, Australia, Europe, North America, and South America (IFAT 2004). This was followed by the establishment of the European Fair Trade Association (EFTA) in 1990, consisting of 11 of the largest fair trade organizations in Europe, and European World Shops (NEWS!) in 1994, composed of more than 2,700 world shops throughout Europe (EFTA 2001b). These organizations facilitate the co-operation and exchange of information between members on product development, marketing and management strategies, and professional training, and jointly promote fair trade and lobby government for support.

IFAT, EFTA, and NEWS! have focused on a different role than FLO in the reorientation of the fair trade network. Whereas FLO's main objective has been to gain the participation of conventional corporations in the network, IFAT, EFTA, and NEWS! have focused on enhancing the marketing skills and efficiency of existing fair trade ATOs so that they are better able to compete against conventional corporations. They have been at the head of the "professionalization" of fair trade, which has involved ATOs adopting marketing and managerial strategies common to mainstream corporations. Beginning in the 1990s, ATOs have placed greater emphasis on staff training, computerization, better promotional strategies, and new, stylish packaging and storefronts (EFTA 2001b). For some handicraft ATOs, professionalization has involved abandoning their tradition of honouring artisans' indigenous knowledge and artistic skills through limited product intervention in favour of purchasing products based on saleability and suggesting changes to meet market trends (Littrell and Dickson 1999).

Despite the fact that IFAT, EFTA, and NEWS! have a different focus than FLO, they share the same essential principles and goals. Often their efforts are intertwined. For example, many fair trade ATOs, such as Oxfam UK and GEPA in Germany (both members of IFAT and EFTA), import and distribute commodities certified by FLO. Thus, it is best to view all of these actors as part of the same international fair trade network. In 1998, FLO, IFAT, NEWS! and EFTA created the informal umbrella network FINE, which in 2001 established a single definition of fair trade. It states:

> Fair Trade is a trading partnership, based on dialogue, transparency and respect, that seeks greater equity in international trade. It contributes to sustainable development by offering better trading conditions to, and securing the rights of, marginalised producers and workers—especially in the South. Fair Trade organisations (backed by consumers) are engaged actively in supporting producers, awareness raising and in campaigning for changes in the rules and practice of conventional international trade. (EFTA 2001a)

IV. LIMITS OF THE FAIR TRADE MARKET

The combined efforts of all the actors in the fair trade network resulted in substantial sales growth throughout the 1990s. EFTA estimates that the net retail value of all fair trade products in Europe in 1998 was more than 200 million Euros, representing an increase of over 400% since the early 1990s. In 2001, EFTA put this figure at more than 260 million Euros, an increase of 30% over a three-year period. Of this figure, the net retail value of fair trade commodities certified by FLO represented around 80% of the total net retail value. While these numbers are dwarfed when compared with conventional international trade—in 2001 fair trade represented around 0.01% of all global trade—they represent significant growth within the network itself (Barratt Brown 1993, 10; EFTA 2001a, 2001b).

Despite the rapid growth of the fair trade network it has still not been able to meet the needs of many of its Southern partners. In many cases, Southern organizations are only able to sell a small proportion of their total production on fair trade markets. For example, by one estimate fair trade coffee co-operatives are currently selling on average only 20% of their coffee on fair trade markets, with the remainder being sold on conventional markets at less than half the price (Raynold 2002). Moreover, recently there have been signs that the impressive growth rate for fair trade markets could soon level off.

According to EFTA, while the average annual growth rate in total retail value for its members from 2995 to 1999 was 3.3%, this varied greatly from country to country. In European countries where the concept of fair trade was relatively recently introduced, annual growth rates of EFTA members were substantial: as high as 31% in Spain and 17% in Italy. In these countries, fair trade sales started from a very small base and expanded rapidly. However, in countries where fair trade was well developed, such as the Netherlands, Switzerland, Germany, and the United Kingdom, EFTA members registered sluggish growth, and sometimes even decline and crises. According to EFTA, "This reflects the attainment of a certain threshold level of sales or market shares which then seems very difficult to surpass" (EFTA 2001a, 33–36).

Similar evidence was also reported by FLO in its annual report for 2000–2001. While recording an increase in total sales from 1999 to 2000 for fair trade cocoa and fair trade bananas, other commodities showed signs of slowing sales growth or even stagnation. Sales of fair trade tea grew only by 1.8%, sales of fair trade honey declined by 3.5%, and sales of fair trade orange juice declined significantly in Germany. Perhaps most alarming has been the declining growth of the fair trade coffee market. Although sales of fair trade coffee grew substantially throughout the 1990s, they did not grow fast enough to match the increase of new coffee co-operatives. In 2000 this matter came to a head as FLO recorded stagnant growth for fair trade coffee and stated that it was reluctant to register any new coffee co-operatives (FLO 2001; Renard 1999, 498).

According to FLO, fierce competition from outside the fair trade network is the primary cause of these trends. The fair trade network has been hit hard by unprecedented declines in the prices of tropical goods and by price wars among giant supermarket chains, which have further increased the gap between the prices of fair trade and mainstream goods, thus damaging fair trade's competitiveness (FLO 2001). This has particularly been the case with the conventional coffee sector, which has experienced a staggering dive in world export prices for specialty coffee since 2000 from around $1 to as low as $0.41 per pound, tying a record low set back in 1882. The primary cause of this has been global oversupply in the wake of the collapse of the International Coffee Agreement (ICA) in 1989, a commodity control scheme that had provided some price stability. The oversupply has been driven by the rise of Vietnam—encouraged by advice and loans from the World Bank—from an insignificant coffee exporting nation a decade ago to the world's second largest today. Throughout the crisis, the fair trade minimum price has remained at $1.26 per pound, which has damaged fair trade's competitiveness but also saved many fair traders from the bankruptcy, mass migration, and hunger experienced by tens of thousands of small-scale coffee farmers worldwide (Oxfam International 2002a).

In response to these global market pressures, fair traders have sought to escalate their efforts to promote fair trade and expand the fair trade market, especially in the United States and Canada. The primary strategy employed by activists has been "buycotting" campaigns. Rather than boycott corporations to force them to adopt fair trade standards, activists have sought to create a demand for fair trade products among consumers and then demonstrate to corporations that this demand exists and can be capitalized on. Perhaps the most notable buycotting campaign has been the one headed by Global Exchange, a San Francisco-based human rights NGO, which compelled Starbucks Coffee, the world's largest specialty coffee roaster, to agree to sell fair trade coffee in its 2,300 stores across the United States in April 2000. After a series of protests and letter-writing campaigns, Starbucks agreed to sell fair trade coffee just three days before Global Exchange had planned to initiate a nationwide protest. The decision of the giant coffee TNC nearly doubled the number of fair trade sales outlets in the United States. It also had spillover effects in other nations and in 2002 Starbucks began offering fair trade coffee in its stores in the United Kingdom and Canada (Waridel 2002, 107–109). Similar pressures have recently compelled other corporations, including Proctor & Gamble and Sara Lee, two of the world's largest coffee roasters, and Van Houtte, one of the largest roasters in Canada, to begin offering limited quantities of fair trade coffee.

The growing involvement of giant TNCs in the fair trade network, generally celebrated by fair trade activists (Waridel 2002, 105–106), raises serious concerns about the limits imposed on the network by the imperatives of the market. These TNCs are concerned only with the need to protect their public image for the sake of profitability. For making relatively minor commitments to fair trade (Starbucks only sells around 1% to 2% of its beans certified as fair trade), TNCs attain positive publicity, which masks their devotion to a broader neoliberal project. Procter & Gamble and Sara Lee, for example, successfully lobbied the US government to abandon the ICA in 1989 and are currently making huge profits as a result of the global coffee crisis while at the same time showing growing support for fair trade coffee. In addition, the relatively minor commitment of these TNCs is a major one for the fair trade network—Starbucks is now among the largest fair trade roasters in North America—which promises to give TNCs immense influence on the future direction of the network. At the same time, TNCs may pose a significant threat to the viability of small-scale fair trade ATOs (which generally sell 100% of their beans as fair trade), which lack the formers' financial and marketing resources (Fridell 2004a). These realities have given way to growing controversy within the network. A handful of smaller fair trade coffee roasters in the United States have recently broken with TransFair and aspire to form a new association composed entirely of 100% fair trade coffee roasters (Rogers, 2004).

In addition to buycotting campaigns, fair traders have also sought to expand the fair trade market by gaining the support of public institutions, whose procurement policies can be a significant avenue for increasing sales. This has proven to be the case in Europe. Over the past decade, the EU has passed a series of resolutions in support of fair trade and, presently, all of the European Union Institutions use fair trade coffee, although not exclusively, and some also use fair trade tea. In addition, fair trade coffee is used at an array of national, regional, and municipal institutions throughout Europe, including the office of the President of the Republic and the national Parliament in Germany, and the Scottish Parliament and the House of Commons in the United Kingdom (EFTA 2001a, 2001b).

In North America, the support of public institutions for fair trade has been relatively insignificant, and procurement policies have only recently become a focus for fair trade activists. Much of their energy has been directed at university campuses, where student groups have organized information tables, teach-ins, fair trade coffee tastings, petitions, and letter-writing campaigns to gain the support of campus food services. In the United States, these campaigns have yet to result in a university or college adopting an official fair trade purchasing policy. Yet, there are hopes that the recent success of campus "no-sweat" campaigns, which have compelled more than 100 colleges and universities to adopt anti-sweatshop codes of conduct for trademark licensees, can be extended to include fair trade purchasing policies in the near future. In Canada, in 2002 McMaster University in Hamilton, Ontario became the first university in North America to adopt a no-sweat code of conduct *and* a fair trade purchasing policy that forces all retailers on campus to offer the choice of fair trade coffee (Fridell 2004b). This was followed by the adoption of a similar fair trade code at Trent University in Peterborough, Ontario in early 2004 and activists now hope to compel other universities to follow suit.

Due to the growing emphasis on expanding the public procurement of fair trade, concern has been raised among fair traders over the potential barriers posed to the network's further expansion by the WTO and its Technical Barriers to Trade (TBT) agreement. Under the TBT agreement, many social and environmental regulations are considered obstacles to free trade, and it is possible that fair trade goods may be judged to discriminate against like products on the basis of how they are produced. In response to this threat, FLO has joined with some of the world's leading accreditation and labelling organizations in social and environmental standards in forming the International Social and Environmental Accreditation and Labelling Alliance (ISEAL) (Waridel 2002, 113–114). The primary goal of ISEAL is to gain credibility in the eyes of international trade bodies and demonstrate that its members' initiatives do not pose a barrier to free trade and neoliberal restructuring.

As is the case with the growing involvement of TNCs, the expansion of the public procurement of fair trade also raises serious concerns about the limits of the network. While public institutions in Europe and North America have shown increasing support for the fair trade network, they have also continued to reject the greater demands of the fair trade movement and have pushed forward with neoliberal reforms. This suggests that to these institutions, the fair trade network is increasingly being employed as an "ethical fig leaf" to mask their devotion to a broader neoliberal agenda. Thus, while the EU institutions and many national and local governments in Europe have thrown their support behind the fair trade network, they have at the same time continued with neoliberal restructuring and have refused to lower high tariff barriers to Southern commodities, a long-standing demand of the fair trade movement. A similar case can be made for universities in North America, which have shown growing support for ethical procurement policies like fair trade and no-sweat codes while at the same time pushing forward with their own neoliberal restructuring. This has entailed the corporatization of the university as administrators have turned increasingly toward relying on TNCs to provide donations, directly fund courses, finance endowed chairs, and sponsor research centres, all of which pose a serious threat to academic freedom. To these institutions, the fair trade network is not being adopted as a challenge to neoliberal globalization but as an ethical fig leaf designed to mask its negative impact (Fridell 2004b).

CONCLUSION

The rapid growth of the fair trade network since the late 1980s can be attributed to its nongovernmental development strategy, which has focused on voluntarism and mainstreaming. It is owing to this strategy that the network has survived and thrived while the fair trade movement has staggered and declined. This has been part of a broader transformation in the international trade and development regime, which has involved the decline of state intervention and market regulation and the rise of neoliberal political–economic agreements and NGO-led development projects. Throughout the 1980s and 1990s, thousands of new NGOs have emerged to fulfill the social welfare and developmental role once played by the state. Many of these NGOs receive funding from official institutions, such as the World Bank, which view NGOs as a non-statist solution to the negative social and environmental consequences of neoliberal reforms (Petras 1997). Thus, in the era of neoliberal globalization, just as NGO-provided health care is moving to the fore of official development discourse in place of state-provided health care, so the fair trade network, with its voluntary, non statist program, is moving to the fore over commodity control schemes and state-enforced ILO labour standards.

While the growth of the fair trade network has marked the decline of the fair trade movement, the latter has not disappeared and there have even been signs of a potential revival in recent years as Southern governments and NGOs have grown increasingly resistant to the demands of Northern governments and international financial institutions. One of the most important examples of this has been the emergence of a coalition of developing countries, the G20, headed by India, Brazil, China, and South Africa, which derailed the 5th ministerial meetings of the WTO in Cancun, Mexico in September 2003. The G20 has demanded the elimination of Northern protectionist barriers to Southern commodities and an end to Northern agricultural export subsidies (Bullard 2004). Such demands are compatible with both the aims of the fair trade movement and the needs of the fair trade network. Due to such compatibility, Oxfam International continues to actively support both the movement and the network, and sees the network as a stepping stone toward achieving the broader aims of the fair trade movement (Oxfam International 2002a).

However, Oxfam International's vision is not one shared by the TNCs, public institutions, and international organizations that have thrown their support behind the fair trade network over the past few years. To these organizations, the fair trade network represents not a step toward a regulated international market but an alternative to it. Recently, the World Bank, a primary architect of neoliberalism, has begun to take notice of fair trade due to its growing interest in "private (market driven) standards that encourage employers to adopt desirable labour practices," which stems from the bank's desire to combat a growing crisis of legitimacy in the wake of global justice protests (World Bank 2001, 74). The World Bank has met several times with fair trade representatives, has begun promoting the fair trade network, and has even started serving fair trade coffee at its head office in Washington, DC (World Bank 2002; Zonneveld, 2003). Many fair traders have responded favourably to these moves, and some have felt compelled to disavow the radical aims of the Global Justice Movement, whose participants they have pejoratively referred to as "globaphobes," in an attempt to present themselves as responsible stakeholders worthy of further consideration at future meetings of the World Bank and the WTO (Bello 2002; Oxfam 2002b; VanerHoff Boersma 2002). To neoliberal organizations such as the World Bank, as well as TNCs and public institutions in Europe and North America, the fair trade network is a digestible pill to swallow precisely because it is not seen as a radical challenge to the central tenets of neoliberal globalization (Bolscher 2002).

One need not romanticize past attempts at international market regulation to see how the development of the fair trade network's voluntarist approach has been part of an overall setback for the fair trade movement. CFSs such as STABEX frequently lacked appropriate funding and encouraged producers to continue to grow primary commodities for swamped Northern markets. International commodity agreements tended to encourage increased production or led to the development of substitutes and were based on tenuous alliances between competitive states, which made them subject to eventual collapse. Various proposals for an end to Northern protectionist barriers, enforced ILO labour standards, reforms to the international monetary system, and codes of conduct for TNCs have failed in the wake of strong resistance from rich countries in the North. Nonetheless, despite their weaknesses, these projects did represent a movement toward a model for a new international economic order in which price stability, labour rights, and a more equitable distribution of wealth would be state-enforced and universally applied.

In contrast to the broader vision of the fair trade movement, the fair trade network represents a model that is voluntarist, market-dependent, and member-specific. The prices for fair trade goods and the size of the fair trade market niche (and by extension the number of producers that can get access to fair trade standards) are entirely dependent on the whims of Northern consumers. The need to continually expand market access has compelled fair traders to deal increasingly with TNCs whose interest in fair trade is contingent entirely on corporate profitability and the need to protect their corporate image. To gain the support of these TNCs, along with public institutions, fair traders have had to abandon their vision of an alternative trading system and confine their struggles to the niches of an international market directed by the neoliberal aims of the World Bank, the WTO, and the IMF. Within these confines, fair trade activism has become limited to scrambling for market access in an oversaturated international market; for example, in response to the global coffee crisis initiated by World Bank policies, fair traders have had little recourse other than to encourage TNCs to buy more fair trade coffee. This situation represents a victory for neoliberal reformers, and reveals that the growth of the fair trade network can only be properly understood historically as the flip side of the decline of the fair trade movement and its broader objectives. As such, the future of the fair trade movement, if it is to be a challenge to neoliberalism, lies not in the voluntarist direction of the fair trade network but in struggling to recover the gains of the past.

NOTES

1. For examples of fair trade ATOs that have had to significantly modify their earlier version of an alternative trading system, see the accounts of Ten Thousand Villages and SERRV in Littrell and Dickson 1999, 61–112.

2. Max Havelaar is named after the hero of a Dutch novel who denounced the treatment of Indonesian coffee planters under colonial rule. See Multatuli (1987).

3. Naomi Klein (2000, 428–436) provides an excellent critique of corporate codes of conduct, which she asserts are driven by corporations' needs to protect their brand image. However, she fails to properly distinguish these top-down codes from fair trade, which focuses on empowering workers and peasants from below (Bolscher, 2002).

4. According to EFTA (2001b, 1995), the total points of sale for fair trade labelled products for Europe grew from 45,000 retail channels in 1994 to more than 63,800 in 2000. One of FLO's greatest successes in this regard has been in the Netherlands, where Max Havelaar labelled products in 2000 were available for sale in nearly 90% of all Dutch supermarkets.

POSTSCRIPT

In the final analysis, assessing the relative success or failure of fair trade networks is likely based on the level of change one seeks to achieve through the process. To the extent that fair trading networks inspire incremental change in the way we do business which gradually changes terms of trade to benefit producers in the South, its success is a long-term objective that may never be entirely within reach. There will always be ways in which the system will need to be reformed through behavioural strategies such as alternative or fair trade, but the system will slowly improve for Southern producers over time. Some might argue, however, that in an ultimate sense there is little that can be gained by fair trading networks that might not simply be gained through the inexorable movement in prices of commodities, demands for organized labour and political change in developing countries, and the market-based fluctuations of supply and demand.

On the other hand, if the goal of fair trade is to set up a fully parallel trading system that can come to rival the neoliberal framework and effect change in a more revolutionary fashion, success is perhaps even more remote. If this is the aim of fair trading networks, their continued marginality compared to large multinational retailers and the tendency for large corporations to "mainstream" the practice within the dominant neoliberal order are challenges to the relevance of the fair trade strategy. Systemic change is a long way off, and fair trade will not effectively see off the concentration of big distributors in the global market that causes structural marginalization of producers in the South.

In large part, fair trading networks have been pleased with the gains achieved through mainstreaming fair trade and in mobilizing an educated public to demand more incremental changes in the neoliberal framework. While behavioural initiative to change the way individuals do business may see success, wholesale change at the level of world trade is less likely, given the challenges that have arisen in negotiating any revisions of the General Agreement on Tariffs and Trade to make it more friendly to fair trading practices.

Suggested Additional Readings

Bacon, Christopher. "Confronting the Coffee Crisis: Can Fair Trade, Organic, and Specialty Coffees Reduce Small-Scale Farmer Vulnerability in Northern Nicaragua?" *World Development,* 33, no. 3 (2004): 497–511.

Leclair, Mark S. "Fighting the Tide: Alternative Trade Organizations in the Era of Global Free Trade," *World Development,* 30, no. 6 (2002): 949–958.

Levi, Margaret, and April Linton. "Fair Trade: A Cup at a Time?" *Politics & Society,* 31, no. 3 (2003): 407–432.

Maseland, Robert, and Albert De Vaal. "How Fair Is Fair Trade?" *De Economist,* 150, no. 3 (2002): 251–272.

Moore, Geoff. "The Fair Trade Movement: Parameters, Issues, and Future Research," *Journal of Business Ethics,* 53 (2004): 73–86.

Nicholls, Alex, and Charlotte Opal. *Fair Trade: Market-Driven Ethical Consumption* (London: Sage, 2005).

Ponte, S. "The 'Latte Revolution'? Regulation, Markets and Consumption in the Global Coffee Chain," *World Development,* 30, no. 7 (2002): 1099–1122.

Rice, Robert A. "Noble Goals and Challenging Terrain: Organic and Fair Trade Coffee Movements in the Global Marketplace," *Journal of Agricultural and Environmental Ethics,* 14 (2001): 39–66.

Talbot, J.M. "Where Does Your Coffee Dollar Go? The Division of Income and Surplus along the Coffee Commodity Chain," *Studies in Comparative International Development,* 32, no. 1 (1997): 56–91.

Taylor, Peter Leigh. "In the Market but Not of it: Fair Trade Coffee and Forest Stewardship Council Certification as Market-Based Social Change," *World Development,* 33, no. 1 (2005): 129–147.

InfoTrac® College Edition

Search for the following articles in the InfoTrac® database:

De Pelsmacker, Patrick, Liesbeth Driesen, and Glenn Rayp. "Do Consumers Care about Ethics? Willingness to Pay for Fair Trade Coffee," *Journal of Consumer Affairs* 39, no. 2 (Winter 2005): 363–385.

MacLachlan, Amy. "Mad about the Bean: Fair Trade Is Good to the Last Drop," *Presbyterian Record,* 129, no. 5 (May 2005): 20–24.

Tester, Frank, Glenn Drover, and Howard Espin. "Offsetting Corporate Trade: Free Trade, Community Development, and Alternative Trade in the South Pacific," *Alternatives Journal,* 22, no. 1 (January–February 1996): 16–22.

For more articles, enter:
"fair trade," "alternative trade," or "fair trade coffee" in the keyword search.

Web Resources

Fairtrade Labelling Organizations International (FLO)

www.fairtrade.net

FLO is the coordinating authority for the largest fair trade labelling organizations worldwide.

FairTrade Federation (FTF)

www.fairtradefederation.org

An association of businesses involved in the fair trade sector, the Fair Trade Federation serves to provide information, resources, and networking opportunities in fair trade.

TEN THOUSAND VILLAGES

www.tenthousandvillages.ca

The most venerable fair trade network, Ten Thousand Villages began in 1946 out of the efforts of the Mennonite Central Committee (MCC).

MAX HAVELAAR FOUNDATION

www.maxhavelaar.ch/en/

Max Havelaar is one of the pre-eminent fair trade certification and labelling authorities, based in Switzerland.

TRANSFAIR CANADA

www.transfair.ca

TransFair is actively involved in certifying and labelling fair trade products in Canada.

Can Sweatshops and Cheap Labour Benefit the Poor?

✔ **YES**

PAUL KRUGMAN, "In Praise of Cheap Labor," *Slate*, 1997.
web.mit.edu/krugman/www/smokey.html

✘ **NO**

JOHN MILLER, "Why Economists Are Wrong about Sweatshops and the Antisweatshop Movement," *Challenge*, 46, no. 1 (January/February 2003): 93–122

In 1995, Craig Kielburger, a 12-year-old Canadian boy, read about the tragic story of Iqbal Masih, a child of the same age who had been murdered in Pakistan. Iqbal had been sold into child labour by his parents at the age of four. This practice was common among many poor Pakistani families who, having accumulated debts to landlords and local merchants, were desperate to find a means of paying them off. For the next six years, Iqbal worked in deplorable and dangerous conditions, putting in up to 16 hours a day, 6 days a week.

In 1992, Iqbal came into contact with activists working for the Bonded Labor Liberation Front (BLLF), a human rights organization campaigning against bonded child labour. Iqbal soon became a spokesperson for the organization, travelling overseas to tell his story to consumers in Western countries. He became a symbol for the movement and was awarded the Reebok Human Rights Youth in Action Award and a future scholarship to an American university. However, in 1995, at the age of 12, while visiting relatives in a Pakistani village, Iqbal was murdered, reportedly by those associated with interests in the Pakistani carpet industry who see the BLLF campaign as a threat. The news of Iqbal's story catalyzed Craig Keilburger into action, leading him to form his own award-winning *Free the Children* campaign, aimed at abolishing exploitative child labour practices throughout the world.

Stories like those of Iqbal have focused attention not only on the problem of child labour but also on the role of sweatshops and cheap labour practices in the development of economies throughout the world. Much of this debate has focused on the practice of retailing multinationals in industrialized countries that turn to low-wage workers in developing countries as a way of procuring cheap goods. This allows them to maximize profits while undercutting the prices of competitors. The term "sweatshop" is often associated with the garment industry, where companies seek to boost profits by prohibiting collective bargaining and paying low wages with no benefits. Workers are often forced to work in unsafe conditions and are vulnerable to physical and sexual abuse. Workers in a developing country labour at 16 cents an hour, 12 hours a day, 7 days a week to make a running shoe that sells for $150 in North America, while basketball stars receive multimillion dollar contracts to endorse them.

Critics of such practices see sweatshops as an example of the "race to the bottom" phenomenon that has come to characterize globalization. Big corporations head-quartered in industrialized countries seek to escape rigorous labour wage and safety guidelines by looking to factories in countries with more relaxed labour and safety standards. Many developing countries in turn compete for the opportunity to attract these corporations by offering lower labour, safety, and environmental standards than their neighbours. In his book *The Race to the Bottom* (Westview Press, 2000), Alan Tonelson argues that it is often workers in developing countries who are called upon to shoulder the burdens of globalization, while Western multinationals continue to amass profits. Rather that contributing to the development of these countries, corporations supporting these sweatshops simply exploit the poverty and desperation of the poor and vulnerable. As a result, a number of campaigns, including *Free the Children,* have emerged in industrialized countries to publicize the dangers and costs of such cheap labour policies. A growing number of anti-sweatshop organizations have demanded that corporations increase wages, improve safety, observe human rights and environmental standards, and adopt codes of conduct for operating in developing countries. A number of boycott campaigns have been organized against high profile corporations such as Nike, Reebok, and Fruit of the Loom.

While some of these boycotts and public campaigns have been successful, others have not always produced results that are in the best interests of sweatshop workers themselves. In some cases, corporations such as Nike and The Gap simply pulled out of developing countries, leaving the workers out of work and costing the local economies millions of dollars.

Another argument is that this is simply a necessary phase that all countries go through on the road to prosperity. Great Britain and the United States both saw the widespread use of cheap labour and sweatshop conditions in the early phase of their industrialization. As their economies developed and matured, these policies were gradually phased out. For many developing nations, cheap labour is the only commodity that they can offer the industrialized world on a competitive basis. If corporations are not allowed to invest and take advantage of these conditions, labourers in these countries will simply be forced back into agricultural subsistence. It is preferable that these countries go through a transitional period of low wages and poor working conditions in the short run. Once they have been able to build stronger economies, better labour conditions will emerge. The current policies simply mark an important first step toward greater future prosperity.

In the following two essays, we find two quite different takes on the role that cheap labour policies and sweatshops play in the process of development. In the first essay, Paul Krugman, a noted American economist who now teaches at Princeton University, presents his widely read essay, "In Praise of Cheap Labor," which has become somewhat of a classic statement of the pro-sweatshop argument. As his provocative title suggests, Krugman argues that "cheap labour" is really a relative economic concept. What appears as abysmal wages to us may for someone be a vast improvement over even greater poverty in the rural areas. In the second essay, John Miller, an economics professor at Wheaton College and an anti-sweatshop activist himself, provides a critique of the economic assumptions underlying Krugman's argument.

✔ **YES**
In Praise of Cheap Labor
PAUL KRUGMAN

For many years a huge Manila garbage dump known as Smokey Mountain was a favorite media symbol of Third World poverty. Several thousand men, women, and children lived on that dump—enduring the stench, the flies, and the toxic waste in order to make a living combing the garbage for scrap metal and other recyclables. And they lived there voluntarily, because the $10 or so a squatter family could clear in a day was better than the alternatives.

The squatters are gone now, forcibly removed by Philippine police last year as a cosmetic move in advance of a Pacific Rim summit. But I found myself thinking about Smokey Mountain recently, after reading my latest batch of hate mail.

The occasion was an op-ed piece I had written for the *New York Times,* in which I had pointed out that while wages and working conditions in the new export industries of the Third World are appalling, they are a big improvement over the "previous, less visible rural poverty." I guess I should have expected that this comment would generate letters along the lines of, "Well, if you lose your comfortable position as an American professor you can always find another job— as long as you are 12 years old and willing to work for 40 cents an hour."

Such moral outrage is common among the opponents of globalization—of the transfer of technology and capital from high-wage to low-wage countries and the resulting growth of labor-intensive Third World exports. These critics take it as a given that anyone with a good word for this process is naive or corrupt and, in either case, a de facto agent of global capital in its oppression of workers here and abroad.

But matters are not that simple, and the moral lines are not that clear. In fact, let me make a counter-accusation: The lofty moral tone of the opponents of globalization is possible only because they have chosen not to think their position through. While fat-cat capitalists might benefit from globalization, the biggest beneficiaries are, yes, Third World workers.

After all, global poverty is not something recently invented for the benefit of multinational corporations. Let's turn the clock back to the Third World as it was only two decades ago (and still is, in many countries). In those days, although the rapid economic growth of a handful of small Asian nations had started to attract attention, developing countries like Indonesia or Bangladesh were still mainly what they had always been: exporters of raw materials, importers of manufactures. Inefficient manufacturing sectors served their domestic markets, sheltered behind import quotas, but generated few jobs. Meanwhile, population pressure pushed desperate peasants into cultivating ever more marginal land or seeking a livelihood in any way possible—such as homesteading on a mountain of garbage.

Given this lack of other opportunities, you could hire workers in Jakarta or Manila for a pittance. But in the mid-'70s, cheap labor was not enough to allow a developing country to compete in world markets for manufactured goods. The entrenched advantages of advanced nations—their infrastructure and technical know-how, the vastly larger size of their markets and their proximity to suppliers of key components, their political stability and the subtle-but-crucial social adaptations that are necessary to operate an efficient economy—seemed to outweigh even a tenfold or twentyfold disparity in wage rates.

And then something changed. Some combination of factors that we still don't fully understand—lower tariff barriers, improved telecommunications, cheaper air transport—reduced the disadvantages of producing in developing countries. (Other things being the same, it is still better to produce in the First World—stories of companies that moved production to Mexico or East Asia, then moved back after experiencing the disadvantages of the Third World environment, are common.) In a substantial number of industries, low wages allowed developing countries to break into world markets. And so countries that had previously made a living selling jute or coffee started producing shirts and sneakers instead.

Workers in those shirt and sneaker factories are, inevitably, paid very little and expected to endure terrible working conditions. I say "inevitably" because their employers are not in business for their (or their workers') health; they pay as little as possible, and that minimum is determined by the other opportunities available to workers. And these are still extremely poor countries, where living on a garbage heap is attractive compared with the alternatives.

And yet, wherever the new export industries have grown, there has been measurable improvement in the lives of ordinary people. Partly this is because a growing industry must offer a somewhat higher wage than workers could get elsewhere in order to get them to move. More importantly, however, the growth of manufacturing—and of the penumbra of other jobs that the new export sector creates—has a ripple effect throughout the economy. The pressure on the land becomes less intense, so rural wages rise; the pool of unemployed urban dwellers always anxious for work shrinks, so factories start to compete with each other for workers, and urban wages also begin to rise. Where the process has gone on long enough—say, in South Korea or Taiwan—average wages start to approach what an American teenager can earn at McDonald's. And eventually people are no longer eager to live on garbage dumps. (Smokey Mountain persisted because the Philippines, until recently, did not share in the export-led growth of its neighbors. Jobs that pay better than scavenging are still few and far between.)

The benefits of export-led economic growth to the mass of people in the newly industrializing economies are not a matter of conjecture. A country like Indonesia is still so poor that progress can be measured in terms of how much the average person gets to eat; since 1970, per capita intake has risen from less than 2,100 to more than 2,800 calories a day. A shocking one-third of young children are still malnourished—but in 1975, the fraction was more than half. Similar improvements can be seen throughout the Pacific Rim, and even in places like Bangladesh. These improvements have not taken place because well-meaning people in the West have done anything to help—foreign aid, never large, has lately shrunk to virtually nothing. Nor is it the result of the benign policies of national governments, which are as callous and corrupt as ever. It is the indirect and unintended result of the actions of soulless multinationals and rapacious local entrepreneurs, whose only concern was to take advantage of the profit opportunities offered by cheap labor. It is not an edifying spectacle; but no matter how base the motives of those involved, the result has been to move hundreds of millions of people from abject poverty to something still awful but nonetheless significantly better.

Why, then, the outrage of my correspondents? Why does the image of an Indonesian sewing sneakers for 60 cents an hour evoke so much more feeling than the image of another Indonesian earning the equivalent of 30 cents an hour trying to feed his family on a tiny plot of land—or of a Filipino scavenging on a garbage heap?

The main answer, I think, is a sort of fastidiousness. Unlike the starving subsistence farmer, the women and children in the sneaker factory are working at slave wages *for our benefit*—and this makes us feel unclean. And so there are self-righteous demands for international labor standards: We should not, the opponents of globalization insist, be willing to buy those sneakers and shirts unless the people who make them receive decent wages and work under decent conditions.

This sounds only fair—but is it? Let's think through the consequences.

First of all, even if we could assure the workers in Third World export industries of higher wages and better working conditions, this would do nothing for the peasants, day laborers, scavengers, and so on who make up the bulk of these developing countries' populations. At best, forcing developing countries to adhere to our labor standards would create a privileged labor aristocracy, leaving the poor majority no better off.

And it might not even do that. The advantages of established First World industries are still formidable. The only reason developing countries have been able to compete with those industries is their ability to offer employers cheap labor. Deny them that ability, and you might well deny them the prospect of continuing industrial growth, even reverse the growth that has been achieved. And since export-oriented growth, for all its injustice, has been a huge boon for the workers in those nations, anything that curtails that growth is very much against their interests. A policy of good jobs in principle, but no jobs in practice, might assuage our consciences, but it is no favor to its alleged beneficiaries.

You may say that the wretched of the earth should not be forced to serve as hewers of wood, drawers of water, and sewers of sneakers for the affluent. But is the alternative? Should they be helped with foreign aid? Maybe—although the historical record of regions like southern Italy suggests that such aid has a tendency to promote perpetual dependence. Anyway, there isn't the slightest prospect of significant aid materializing. Should their own governments provide more social justice? Of course—but they won't, or at least not because we tell them to. And as long as you have no realistic alternative to industrialization based on low wages, to oppose it means that you are willing to deny desperately poor people the best chance they have of progress for the sake of what amounts to an aesthetic standard—that is, the fact that you don't like the idea of workers being paid a pittance to supply rich Westerners with fashion items.

In short, my correspondents are not entitled to their self-righteousness. They have no thought the matter through. And when the hopes of hundreds of millions are at stake, thinking things through is not just good intellectual practice. It is a moral duty.

✗ NO
Why Economists Are Wrong about Sweatshops and the Antisweatshop Movement
JOHN MILLER

The student-led antisweatshop movement that took hold on many college campuses during the late 1990s should have pleased economists. Studying the working conditions faced by factory workers across the globe offered powerful lessons about the workings of the world economy, the dimensions of world poverty, and most students' privileged position in that economy.

On top of that, these students were dedicated not just to explaining sweatshop conditions, but also to changing them. They wanted desperately to do something to put a stop to the brutalization and assaults on human dignity suffered by the women and men who made their jeans, t-shirts, or sneakers. On many campuses, student activism succeeded in pressuring college administrators by demanding that clothing bearing their college logo not be made under sweatshop conditions, and, at best, that it be made by workers earning a living wage (Featherstone and United Students Against Sweatshops 2002).

But most mainstream economists were not at all pleased. No, they did not dispute these tales from the factory floor, many of which had been confirmed in the business press (Roberts and Bernstein 2000) and by international agencies (ILO 2000). Rather, mainstream economists rushed to defend the positive role of low-wage factory jobs, the very kind we usually call sweatshops, in economic development and in alleviating poverty.

What is more, these economists were generally dismissive of the student-led antisweatshop movement. [...]

The response of mainstream economists to the antisweatshop movement was hardly surprising. Economists have a penchant for playing the contrarian, and, for the most part, they oppose interventions into market outcomes, even interventions into the labor markets of the developing world.

No matter how predictable, their response was profoundly disappointing. Although it contains elements of truth, what economists have to say about sweatshops misses the mark. That was my conclusion after spending summer and fall of 2000 reading much of what economists and economic journalists had written about sweatshops as I prepared to teach my undergraduate seminar, "Sweatshops and the Global Economy." First, the propositions that mainstream economists rely on to defend sweatshops are misleading, rooted in an exchange perspective that obscures sweatshop oppression. Sweatshop oppression is not defined by labor market exchanges but by the characteristics of a job. Second, policy positions based on these propositions are equally flawed. Economists' claim that market-led economic development, independent of labor and social movements and government regulation, will put an end to sweatshop conditions distorts the historical record. Finally, their assertion that demands for better working conditions in the world-export factories will harm third-world workers and frustrate poverty alleviation is also suspect.

With that said, the challenge issued by mainstream economists to the anti-sweatshop movement remains a formidable one. What economists have to say about the sweatshops has considerable power in the way of persuasion and influence. [...] Often it is their writings that are being distilled in what journalists, government officials, and the general public have to say about sweatshops.

[...]

JUST ENFORCE THE LAW

What to do about sweatshops? That is not a difficult question for most mainstream economists to answer. Just enforce the law, they say (Weidenbaum 1999, 26–28). And avoid other "institutional interventions" that might impair a market-led development that will enhance productivity and thereby raise wages and improve working conditions (Irwin 2002, 214; Sengenberger 1994, 10). By law, they mean local labor law, not some labor standard that ill-informed protesters (or even the International Labor Organization, for that matter) would impose on multinational corporations and their subcontractors in developing economies.

No one in the antisweatshop movement would quarrel with the insistence that the law be obeyed. In fact, several U.S. antisweatshop groups define a sweatshop in legal terms. According to Feminists Against Sweatshops (2002), for instance, sweatshop operators are employers who violate two or more labor laws, from the prohibition of child labor, to health, safety, fire, and building codes, to forced overtime and the minimum wage.

Effective enforcement of local labor law in the developing world, where labor legislation in many countries—on paper, at least—is quite extensive, would surely help to combat sweatshop abuse as well (Portes 1994, 163). For instance, *Made in China,* a report of the National Labor Committee, the leading U.S.-based antisweatshop group, found that subcontractors producing goods for U.S. corporations, including Wal-Mart and Nike, "routinely violate" Chinese labor law. In some of these factories, young women work as long as seventy hours a week and are paid just pennies an hour after pay deductions for board and room, clear violations of China's labor law (Kernaghan 2000). A three-month Business Week investigation of the Chun Si Enterprise Handbag Factory in southern China, which makes Kathie Lee Gifford handbags sold by Wal-Mart stores, confirmed that workers there confronted labor practices that included illegally collected fines, confiscated identity papers, and beatings (Roberts and Bernstein 2000).

But the limitations of this legal prescription for curing sweatshop abuse become obvious when we go to apply it to countries where local labor law, even on paper, does not measure up to the most minimal, internationally agreed-upon labor standards. Take the case of the high-performance economies of Southeast Asia, Indonesia, Malaysia, and Thailand. In those countries, several core labor conventions of the International Labor Organization (ILO) have gone unratified—including the right to organize. Minimum wages are well below the level necessary to lift a family of three above the poverty line, the usual definition of a living wage. And in those countries (as well as China), independent trade union activity is systematically and sometimes brutally suppressed.

[...]

A DEFENSE OF SWEATSHOPS?

The defense of sweatshops offered up by mainstream economists turns on two elegantly simple and ideologically powerful propositions. The first is that workers freely choose to enter these jobs, and the second is that these sweatshop jobs are better than the alternative employments available to them in developing economies. Both propositions have a certain truth to them.

An Exchange Perspective

From the perspective of mainstream economics, every exchange, including the exchange between worker and boss, is freely entered into and only takes place because both parties are made better off. Hiring workers to fill the jobs in the world-export factories is no exception.

Of course, in some cases, workers do not freely enter into sweatshop employment even by the usual standards of wage labor. Sometimes workers are held captive. For example, a 1995 police raid of a fenced-in compound of seven apartments in El Monte, California, found a clandestine garment sweatshop where some seventy-two illegal Thai immigrants were held in virtual captivity as they sewed clothes for brand-name labels (Su 1997, 143). Other times, workers find themselves locked into walled factory compounds surrounded by barbed wire, sometimes required to work fifteen hours a day, seven days a week, subject to physical abuse, and, after fines and charges are deducted from their paycheck, left without the money necessary to repay exorbitant hiring fees. That was the case for the more than 50,000 young female immigrants from China, the Philippines, Bangladesh, and Thailand who were recently discovered in Saipan (part of the Commonwealth of the Northern Mariana Islands, a territory of the United States) working under these near-slavelike conditions as they produced clothing for major American distributors bearing the label "Made in the United States" (ILO 2000).

But in most cases, workers do choose these jobs, if hardly freely or without the coercion of economic necessity. Seen from the exchange perspective of mainstream economics, that choice alone demonstrates that these factory job are neither sweatshops nor exploitative.

Listen to how mainstream economists and their followers make this argument. In response to the National Labor Committee's exposé of conditions in the Honduran factories manufacturing Kathie Lee clothing for Wal-Mart, El Salvadoran economist Lucy Martinez-Mont assured us that "People choose to work in maquila shops of their own free will, because those are the best jobs available to them" (Martinez-Mont 1996, sec. A, p. 14). For economic journalist Nicholas Kristof (1998), the story of Mrs. Tratiwoon, an Indonesian woman, makes the same point. She sustains herself and her son by picking through a garbage dump outside of Jakarta in search of metal scraps to sell. She tells Kristof of her dreams for her three-year-old son as she works. "She wants him to grow up to work in a sweatshop."

Stories such as this one are powerful. The fact that many in the developing world are worse off than workers in the world-export factories is a point that economists supportive of the antisweatshop movement do not deny. For instance, a few years back, economist Arthur MacEwan, my colleague at *Dollars & Sense,* a popular economics magazine, made much the same point. He observed that in a poor country like Indonesia, where women working in agriculture are paid wages one-fifth those of women working in manufacturing, sweatshops do not seem to have a hard time finding workers (MacEwan 1998). And the Scholars Against Sweatshop Labor statement (2001) admits that "Even after allowing for the frequent low wages and poor working conditions in these jobs, they are still generally superior to 'informal' employment in, for example, much of agriculture or urban street vending."

This is not meant to suggest that these exchanges between employers and poor workers with few alternatives are in reality voluntary or that world-export factory jobs are not sweatshops or places of exploitation. Rather, as political philosopher Michael Waltzer argues, these exchanges should be seen as "trades of last resort" or "desperate" exchanges that need to be protected by labor legislation regulating such things as limits on hours, a wage floor, and guaranteed health and safety requirements (Rodrik 1997, 35).

Prevailing Wages and Working Conditions

What mainstream economists say in defense of sweatshops is limited in other ways as well. For instance, an ACIT letter (2000) misstates the argument. The ACIT writes that multinational corporations "commonly pay their workers more on average in comparison to the prevailing market wage for similar workers employed elsewhere in the economy." But, as the SASL authors correctly point out, "While this is true, it does not speak to the situation in which most garments are produced throughout the world—which is by firms subcontracted by multinational corporations, not the MNCs themselves." The ACIT authors implicitly acknowledge as much, for in the next sentence they write that, "in cases where subcontracting is involved, workers are generally paid no less than the prevailing market wage."

The SASL statement also warns that the ACIT claim that subcontractors pay the prevailing market wage does not by itself make a persuasive case that the world export factories we commonly call sweatshops are anything but that. The SASL authors (2001) emphasize that

> the prevailing market wage is frequently extremely low for garment workers in less developed countries. In addition, the recent university-sponsored studies as well as an October 2000 report by the International Labor Organization consistently find that serious workplace abuses and violations of workers' rights are occurring in the garment industry throughout the world.

The same can be said about other world-export factories. Consider for a minute the working conditions at the Indonesian factories that produce footwear for Reebok, the Stoughton, Massachusetts–based international corporation that "goes to great lengths to portray itself as a conscientious promoter of human rights in the Third World" (Zuckoff 1994). Despite its status as a model employer, working conditions at factories that make Reebok footwear became the focus of the *Boston Globe* 1994 series entitled "Foul Trade" (Zuckoff 1994). The *Globe* tells the story of Yati, a young Indonesian woman in Tangerang, Indonesia. She works sewing bits of leather and lace for tennis shoes sold as Reeboks.

Yati sits at a sewing machine, which is one of sixty in her row. There are forty-six rows on the factory floor. For working sixty-three hours a week, Yati earns not quite $80 a month—just about the price of a pair of Reeboks in the United States. Her hourly pay is less than 32 cents per hour, which exceeds the minimum wage for her region of Indonesia. Yati lives in a nearby ten-by-twelve-foot shack with no furniture. She and her two roommates sleep on the mud and tile floor.

A factory like the one Yati works in is typically owned by an East Asian company. For instance, PT Tong Yang Indonesia, a South Korean–owned factory, pumped out 400,000 pairs of Reeboks a month in 1993. In return, Reebok paid its owner, Tan Chuan Cheng, $10.20 for each pair of shoes and then sold them for $60 or more in the United States. Most of Tan's payment went to purchase materials. Tan told the *Globe* that wages accounted for as little as $1.40 of the cost of a pair of shoes (Zuckoff 1994).

A More Effective Response

As I taught my seminar on sweatshops, I settled on a more effective response to the mainstream economic argument. It is simply this: Their argument is irrelevant for determining if a factory is a sweatshop or if workers are exploited. Sweatshop conditions are defined by the characteristics of a job. If workers are denied the right to organize, suffer unsafe and abusive working conditions, are forced to work over-time, or are paid less than a living wage, then they work in a sweatshop, regardless of how they came to take their jobs or if the alternatives they face are worse yet.

A careful reading of what the mainstream exchange perspective suggests about sweatshop jobs is not they are "good news" for the world's poor but "less bad news" than the usual conditions of work in the agricultural and informal sectors. The oppressive conditions of the work in the world-export factories are not denied by their argument. For instance, ACIT leader Jagdish Bhagwati says sweatshop jobs are a "ticket to slightly less impoverishment" (Goldberg 2001, 30).

[...]

CONFRONTING CRITICS OF THE ANTISWEATSHOP MOVEMENT

Still, none of the above speaks directly to the contention of mainstream economists that imposing "enlightened standards" advocated by the antisweatshop activists onto conditions for employment in the export factories of the developing world will immiserate the very workers the movement intends to help (ACIT 2000).

Core Labor Standards

To begin with, as labor economist Richard Freeman (1994, 80) writes, "Everyone, almost everyone is for some standards" (emphasis in the original). Surely that includes economists who would combat sweatshops by insisting that local labor law be respected. Even their position recognizes that the "voluntary" exchange of labor for wages must be delimited by rules, collectively determined and obeyed by all.

The relevant question is: What are those rules, and are any so basic that they should be applied universally, transcending the normal bounds of sovereignty? For the most part, economists, trained after all as economists and not political philosophers, have little to say on this matter other than to caution that outside of the condemnation of slavery, there is no universal agreement about the appropriateness of labor standards even when it comes to bonded labor and child labor (Bhagwati 1995, 754; Brown 2001, 94; Irwin 2002, 216).

Nonetheless other economists, even some critical of the antisweatshop movement, are favorably disposed toward international labor standards about safety and health, forced labor, and the right to organize. For instance, Alice Amsden, an economist who opposes establishing wage standards on developing economies, favors the imposition of other labor standards. "The issue," she says, "is not health and safety conditions, the right of workers to be treated like human beings—not to be murdered for organizing unions, for example. These rights are inviolate" (Amsden 1995). At times, even Jagdish Bhagwati has taken a similar position (Bhagwati 2002, 60).

The International Labor Organization, in its 1998 Declaration on Fundamental Principles at Work, took a similar position. The ILO held that each of its 175 members (even if they have not ratified the conventions in question) was obligated "to respect, to promote and to realize" the fundamental rights of "freedom of association and the effective recognition of the right to collective bargaining, the elimination of all forms of forced or compulsory labour, the effective abolition of child labour and the elimination of discrimination in respect of employment and occupation" (2002a).

The empirical evidence of the effect of these core labor standards on economic development is ambiguous. For instance, the Organization for Economic Cooperation and Development (OECD) found that countries that strengthen these core labor standards "can increase economic growth and efficiency" (OECD 2000, 14). International trade economist Jai Mah, on the other hand, found that ratification of the ILO Conventions on freedom of association and on the right to nondiscrimination negatively affected the export performance of developing countries (Mah 1997, 781). And a study conducted by Dani Rodrik, another international trade economist, suggested that low core labor standards enhanced a country's comparative advantage in the production of labor-intensive goods but deterred rather than attracted direct foreign investment (Rodrik 1996, 59).

The Living Wage

Nevertheless, almost all mainstream economists draw the line at labor codes designed to boost wages as opposed to leaving the determination of wages to labor market outcomes. That surely goes for labor codes that call for the payment of a living wage, usually defined as a wage adequate to lift a worker and two dependents out of poverty. The ACIT worries that if multinational corporations are persuaded to increase their wages (and those of their subcontractors) "in response to what the on-going studies by the anti-sweatshop movement may conclude are appropriate wage levels, the net result would be shifts in employments that will worsen the collective welfare of the very workers who are supposed to be helped." (2001). And ACIT leader Bhagwati dismisses the call for multinationals and their subcontractors to pay a living wage as so much first-world protectionism cloaked in the language of "social responsibility" (Bhagwati 2000, 11). As he sees it, students' demand that a "living wage" be paid in developing countries would dull the one competitive advantage enjoyed by these countries, cheap labor.

But, in practice, would a labor standard demanding that multinational corporations and their subcontractors boost their wages beyond the local minimum wage and toward a living wage be a jobs killer? On that point the ACIT letter is silent, as journalists Featherstone and Henwood point out (2001a).

These economists may be short on evidence about the effects of higher wages on the demand for labor by multinational corporations and their subcontractors, but they are long on authority. Their proposition is as simple as this: "Either you believe labor demand curves are downward sloping, or you don't," as a neoclassical colleague said to me. Of course, not to believe that demand curves are negatively sloped would be tantamount to declaring yourself an economic illiterate.

Still, we can ask just how responsive are the hiring decisions of multinational corporations and their subcontractors to higher wages. There is real reason to believe that the right answer is, not very responsive.

Economists Robert Pollin, James Heintz, and Justine Burns recently looked more closely at this question (Pollin et al. 2001). They examined the impact that a

100 percent increase in the pay for apparel workers in Mexico and in the United States would have on costs relative to the retail price those garments sell for in the United States. Their preliminary findings are that doubling the pay of nonsupervisory workers would add just 50 cents to the production costs of a men's casual shirt sold for $32 in the United States, or just 1.6 percent of the retail price. And even if the wage increase were passed on to consumers, which seems likely because retailers in the U.S. garment industry enjoy substantial market power, Pollin et al. argue that the increase in price is well within the amount that recent surveys suggest U.S. consumers are willing to pay to purchase goods produced under "good" working conditions as opposed to sweatshop conditions. (See Elliot and Freeman [2000] for a detailed discussion of survey results.) More generally, using a sample of forty-five countries over the period 1992–97, Pollin et al. found no statistically significant relationship between real wages and employment growth in the apparel industry. Their results suggest that the mainstream economists' claim that improving the quality of jobs in the world export factories (by boosting wages) will reduce the number of jobs is not evident in the data (Pollin et al. 2001).

Even if this counterexample is not convincing, it is important to recall that the demand curve that defines the responsiveness of multinational corporations and their subcontractors to wage increases for factory workers is a theoretical device drawn while holding other economic circumstances constant, including public policy. In reality, those circumstances are neither fixed nor unalterable. In fact, to counteract any negative effect that higher wages might have on employment, the SASL statement calls for the adoption of new polices, which include

> measures to expand the overall number of relatively high quality jobs; relief from excessive foreign debt payments; raising worker job satisfaction and productivity and the quality of goods they produce; and improving the capacity to bring final products to retail markets. (SASL 2001)

"Shifting the demand curve for labor outward," says economic sociologist Peter Evans (2002), "is almost the definition of economic development-making people more valuable relative to the commodities they need to live." This "high road" approach to development, adds Evans, has the additional benefit of augmenting the demand for the commodities that workers produce.

Historical Change and Social Improvement

A labor code that requires multinational corporations and their subcontractors to pay a living wage, provide safe and healthy working conditions, and allow workers to organize would be likely to have yet more profound effects on these developing economies. On this point, the antisweatshop activists and their critics agree. What they disagree about is whether these broader effects will be a help or hindrance to economic development and an improved standard of living in the developing world (Freeman 1992).

Mainstream critics argue that labor codes are likely to have widespread debilitating effects. The institutionalization of these labor standards proposed by activists, they argue, would derail a market-led development process (Irwin 2002, 214; Sengenberger 1994, 10–11).

As they see it, labor-intensive sweatshops are good starter jobs—the very jobs that successful developing economies and developed countries used as "stepping-stones" to an improved standard of living for their citizens. And in each case, these countries outgrew their "sweatshop phase" through market-led development that enhanced productivity, not through the interventions of an antisweatshop movement (Krugman 1994, 116).

These economists often use the Asian economies as examples of national economies that abandoned "sweatshop practices" as they grew. Their list includes Japan, which moved from poverty to wealth early in the twentieth century, and the tiger economies—South Korea, Hong Kong, Singapore, and Taiwan—which grew rapidly in the second half of the century to become middle income countries (Irwin 2002; Krugman 1994; Krugman 1997; Lim 1990; Weidenbaum 1999). Paul Krugman (1997) allows that some tigers relied on foreign plant owners (e.g., Singapore) while others shunned them (e.g., South Korea). Nonetheless, he maintains that their first stage of development had one constant: "It's always sweat-shops" (Meyerson 1997).

For anyone who doubts that market-led development that begins with a sweatshop phase produces intergenerational progress, Murray Weidenbaum (1999) invokes the personal story of Milton Friedman, the Nobel Prize–winning economist. "If his parents were not willing to work so long and hard under sweatshop conditions, they could not have earned the money to invest in his education," writes Weidenbaum. "We should all be grateful for that investment by a previous generation of Friedmans and for the circumstances that enabled them to make that enlightened choice."

But these arguments distort the historical record and misrepresent how social improvement is brought about with economic development. First, the claim that developed economies passed through a sweatshop stage does not establish that sweatshops caused or contributed to the enhanced productivity that they say improved working conditions. Second, in the developed world, the sweatshop phase was not extinguished by market-led forces alone but when economic growth combined with the very kind of social action, or enlightened collective choice, that defenders of sweatshops find objectionable.

Even Nobel Prize–winning economist Simon Kuznets, whose work did much to inspire economists' faith in the moderating effects of capitalist development on inequality, would find the mainstream economists' story of market-led social progress questionable. Kuznets based his famous hypothesis—that after initially increasing, inequality will diminish with capitalist economic development—not on the operation of market forces alone, but on the combined effect of economic growth and social legislation. For instance, in his famous 1955 *American Economic Review* article, Kuznets writes,

In democratic societies the growing political power of the urban lower-income groups led to a variety of protective and supporting legislation, much of it aimed to counteract the worst effects of rapid industrialization and urbanization and to support the claims of the broad masses for more adequate shares of the growing income of the country. (1955, 17)

The labor codes called for by the antisweatshop movement would seem to be an example of the "protective and supporting legislation" that Kuznets says is key to spreading the benefits of economic growth more widely.

To be sure, labor standards in the absence of economic growth will be hard put to make workers better off. Economist Ajit Singh and Ann Zammit of the South Centre, an intergovernmental organization dedicated to promoting cooperation among developing countries, make exactly this point in their article opposing compulsory labor standards (Singh and Zammit 2000, 37). As they note, over the last few decades, wages in rapidly growing South Korea increased much more quickly than those in slowly growing India, even though India had much better labor standards in the 1950s than South Korea did.

[...]

Finally, no matter how mistaken these mainstream economists might be about how societies have rid themselves of sweatshops, they are perhaps right that past economic developments have gone through a sweatshop stage. On that score, I would reply exactly as one well-known economist did to a 1997 *New York Times* article that made the same point. His letter read this way:

Your June 22 Week in Review article on sweatshops quotes some prominent economists to the effect that sweatshops, which they confuse with "low-wage factories," are "an essential first step toward modern prosperity in developing countries." Sweatshops indeed existed in 19th-century Britain during early industrialization, leading to a burst of social legislation to rid the country of these ills. But nothing requires us to go that route again. Nations should join nongovernmental groups like the International Labor Organization to rid the world of sweatshops. In addition, we can require multinationals to apply our own labor, safety and environmental standards when they manufacture abroad. In Rome, they must do not as Romans do but as we do. Their example would spread.

Surprisingly, the author is none other than Jagdish Bhagwati (1997). I would only add to Bhagwati's powerful pre-ACIT letter that the student-led antisweatshop movement has increased the likelihood that future economic developments might avoid the sweatshop stage. Unlike earlier periods, when labor standards were imposed in response to the demands of labor organizations and an urban population of the developing world alone, first-world consumers today are also pushing multinational corporations to improve the working conditions in the factories of their subcontractors (Brunett and Mahon 2001, 70).

Fastidiousness or Commodity Fetishism?

Mainstream economists have one last probing question for antisweatshop activists: Why factory workers?

Krugman (1997) asks the question in a most pointed way: "Why does the image of an Indonesian sewing sneakers for 60 cents an hour evoke so much more feeling than the image of another Indonesian earning the equivalent of 30 cents an hour trying to feed his family on a tiny plot of land, or of a Filipino scavenging on a garbage heap?"

It is a good question. There are plenty of poor people in the world. Some 1.2 billion people, about one-fifth of the world population, had to make do on less than U.S. $1 a day in 1998 (World Bank 2001). The world's poor are disproportionately located in rural areas. Most scratch out their livelihood from subsistence agriculture or by plying petty trades, while others on the edge of urban centers work in the informal sector as street-hawkers or the like (Todaro 2000, 151). In addition, if sweat is the issue, journalist Kristof (1998) assures us that "this kind of work, hoeing the field or working in paddies, often involves more perspiration than factory work."

So why has the plight of these rural workers, who are often poorer and sweat more than workers in the world-export factories, not inspired a first-world movement dedicated to their betterment?

"Fastidiousness" is Krugman's answer. "Unlike the starving subsistence farmer," says Krugman, "the women and children in the sneaker factory are working at slave wages *for our benefit*—and this makes us feel unclean. And so there are self-righteous demands for international labor standards" (1997; emphasis in the original).

Ironically, Krugman's answer is not so different from the one Marx would have given to the question. Marx's answer would be commodity fetishism or that commodities become the bearers of social relations in a capitalist economy (Marx 1967). Purchasing commodities brings us in contact with the lives of the factory workers who manufacture them. Buying jeans, t-shirts, or sneakers made in Los Angeles, Bangkok, or Jakarta, or the export zones of southern China and Latin America, connected students in my seminar to the women and men who work long hours in unhealthy and dangerous conditions for little pay in the apparel and athletic footwear industries. And it was the lives of those workers that my most political students sought to improve through their antisweatshop activism. Beyond that, as consumers and citizens they are empowered to change the employment practices of U.S. corporations and their subcontractors.

Krugman's complaint is no reason to dismiss the concerns of the antisweatshop movement. Historically, the organization of factory workers has been one of the most powerful forces for changing politics in the democratic direction that Kuznets outlines. Krugman's complaint does, however, suggest that the plight of sweatshop workers needs to be seen in the context of pervasive world poverty and the gaping inequalities of the global economy.

The global economy, to the extent that we live in a truly unified marketplace, connects us not just with sweatshop workers, but with oppressed workers outside the factory gates as well. By pointing out these connections to my students, I hoped to demonstrate the need to build a movement that would demand more for working people across the multiple dimensions of the world economy. Campaigns to improve conditions in the world-export factories should, of course, be part of that movement. But that movement must also tackle the often worse conditions of low-wage agricultural workers, poor farmers, street vendors, domestic servants, small-shop textile workers, and prostitutes. Only when conditions for both groups of workers improve might economists be able to say honestly, as something other than a Faustian bargain, that more world factory jobs are good news for the world's poor.

POSTSCRIPT

As John Miller mentions in his article, a number of fairly active transnational advocacy networks have organized around the issues of child labour and sweatshops. These campaigns are essentially a subset of a larger network of advocacy groups focusing on issues of corporate accountability. The strategies of these groups vary, ranging from efforts to tighten international labour standards and pressuring multinational corporations to voluntarily adopt codes of conduct for their operations in developing countries, to more aggressive public awareness campaigns aimed at organizing boycotts of products believed to be produced under sweatshop conditions.

While such campaigns have certainly raised awareness of these issues, some analysts have asked whether the results have always been beneficial. As the previous debate illustrates, the issues surrounding sweatshops are complex and cause-and-effect relationships are not always clear cut. Stories that may work great for grabbing public attention and sympathy may not necessarily accurately reflect the economic and social dynamics of what is taking place. Some researchers have even suggested that boycott campaigns frequently lead to detrimental results such as situations where child labourers thrown out of work due to a boycott campaign are forced to turn to more dangerous forms of work or prostitution in order to earn income for their families. This has led some to suggest the need for NGOs to take the issue of research on such issues much more seriously and to invest in building up their research capacity. For a discussion of these issues as they relate specifically to child labour and sweatshops, see Caroline Harper, "Do the Facts Matter? NGOs, Research, and International Advocacy," in Michael Edwards and John Gaventa, eds., *Global Citizen Action* (Boulder: Lynne Rienner, 2001).

Suggested Additional Readings

Amsden, Alice. "International Labor Standards: Hype or Help?" *Boston Review,* 20, no. 6 (1995). bostonreview.mit.edu/BR20.6/amsden.html

Bhagwati, Jagdish. "Trade Liberalization and 'Fair Trade' Demands: Addressing the Environmental and Labour Standards Issues," *World Economy,* 18, no. 6 (1995): 745–759.

Brown, Drusilla K. "Labor Standards: Where Do They Belong on the International Trade Agenda?" *Journal of Economic Perspectives,* 15, no. 3 (summer 2001): 89–112.

Elliot, K.A., and R.B. Freeman. "White Hats or Don Quixotes? Human Rights Vigilantes in the Global Economy," National Bureau of Economic Research Conference on Emerging Labor Market Institutions (2000). www.nber.org/~confer/2000/si2000/elliot.pdf

Elson, Diane, and Ruth Pearson. "The Subordination of Women and the Internationalization of Factory Production," in Naline Visvanathan et al., eds., *The Women, Gender, and Development Reader,* pp. 191–202 (London: Zed Books, 1997).

Freeman, Richard B. "Labour Market Institutions and Policies: Help or Hindrance to Economic Development?" in Proceedings of the World Bank, *Annual Conference on Development Economics,* pp. 117–156 (Washington, DC: 1992).

Howard, Alan. "Labor, History, and Sweatshops in the New Global Economy," in Andrew Ross, ed., *No Sweat: Fashion, Free Trade, and the Rights of Garment Workers,* pp. 151–172 (New York: Verso, 1997).

Krugman, Paul. "Does Third World Growth Hurt First World Prosperity?" *Harvard Business Review* (July–August 1994): 113–121.

Lim, Linda. "Women's Work in Export Factories," in Irene Tinker, ed., *Persistent Inequalities,* pp. 101–119 (New York: Oxford University Press, 1990).

Martinez-Mont, Lucy. "Sweatshops Are Better Than No Shops," *Wall Street Journal* (June 25, 1996): sec. A, p. 14.

Meyerson, Allen R. "In Principle, a Case for More 'Sweatshops,'" *New York Times* (June 22, 1997): sec. 4, p. 5.

Piore, Michael. "The Economics of the Sweatshop," in Andrew Ross, ed., *No Sweat: Fashion, Free Trade, and the Rights of Garment Workers,* pp. 125–142 (New York: Verso, 1997).

Singh, A., and A. Zammit. "The Global Labour Standards Controversy: Critical Issues for Developing Countries" (Geneva: South Centre, 2000). www.southcentre.org/publications/labour/toc.htm

InfoTrac® College Edition

Search for the following articles in the InfoTrac® database:

Bigelow, Bill. "The Human Lives Behind the Labels: The Global Sweatshop, Nike, and the Race to the Bottom," *Phi Delta Kappan,* 78, no. 2 (October 1997): 112–119.

Cawthorne, Pamela, and Gavin Kitching. "Moral Dilemmas and Factual Claims: Some Comments on Paul Krugman's Defense of Cheap Labor," *Review of Social Economy,* 59, no. 4 (December 2001): 455–466.

De Winter, Rebecca. "The Anti-sweatshop Movement: Constructing Corporate Moral Agency in the Global Apparel Industry," *Ethics & International Affairs,* 15, no. 2 (October 2001): 99–115.

Spar, Debora L. "The Spotlight on the Bottom Line: How Multinationals Export Human Rights," *Foreign Affairs,* 77, no. 2 (March–April 1998): 7–12.

For more articles, enter:
"cheap labor" and "sweatshops" in the keyword search.

Web Resources

BEHIND THE LABEL

www.behindthelabel.org

This site contains news items regarding various international anti-sweatshop campaigns.

SCHOLARS AGAINST SWEATSHOPS

www.peri.umass.edu/Scholars-Against.252.0.html

This site, which is housed at the Political Economy Research Institute, has links to a number of articles relating to sweatshops, the idea of a living wage, and international labour standards.

INTERNATIONAL LABOUR ORGANIZATION

www.ilo.org

This official website of the United Nation's International Labour Association has an extensive amount of materials on issues such as child labour and international labour standards.

GLOBAL EXCHANGE

www.globalexchange.org/campaigns/sweatshops/backgroundandresources.html

This website contains resources on a number of global issues including sweatshops. Look under the resource section for an extensive list of links to various anti-sweatshop campaigns and organizations.

THE UNOFFICIAL PAUL KRUGMAN ARCHIVE

www.pkarchive.org

You will find here an archive of many of the academic writings, newspaper articles, and interviews by Paul Krugman on international trade and other economic issues.

CLEAN CLOTHES CAMPAIGN

www.cleanclothes.org

A leading Dutch anti-sweatshop campaign, the Clean Clothes site contains information regarding a variety of campaigns around the world. Reflecting European sports interests, it contains extensive information about cheap labour and the production of soccer balls.

Does Outright Debt Cancellation Ignore the Real Problems of Africa?

✔ **YES**
GEORGE AYITTEY, "Smart Aid for Africa," *African Dialogue Series,* no. 773 (2005). www.utexas.edu/conferences/africa/ads/773.html

✘ **NO**
MOSES OCHONU, "The Case for Debt Cancellation and Increased Aid to Africa," *The Nigerian Village Square* (2005).
www.nigeriavillagesquare.com/content/view/1137/55/

In the run-up to the G8 Summit scheduled for Gleneagles, Scotland in 2005, a group of high-profile celebrities gathered to present the case for debt relief as a solution to the problem of poverty in African states. A campaign for broad-based debt relief for all developing nations had been gaining steam at the grassroots for several years. The Jubilee 2000 Campaign, based in the United Kingdom and spreading to dozens of other countries, had been working hard to publicize its case for massive debt elimination as a means of giving developing nations a leg up. In 1998, it had mobilized a massive group of demonstrators for the G8 Summit in Birmingham. In the years following, a series of networked groups began to press "drop the debt" campaigns in order to redress the massive dislocations that had come of debt accumulation and structural adjustment throughout the global South.

There had been policy responses to these debt campaigns. Back in 1996, the IMF had launched the Heavily Indebted Poor Country (HIPC) Initiative. The initiative offered debt restructuring and eventual reduction of debt to heavily indebted countries that displayed an ongoing commitment to reducing their dependence on sustained debt. Amid complaints that the criteria for the HIPC Initiative were overly stringent, the program was modified in 1999 and supplemented by the Multilateral Debt Relief Initiative (MDRI) in 2005. Outside debt relief programs, the United Nations' set of Millennium Development Goals (MDGs) laid out in 2000 committed the world to addressing some of the chronic problems of poverty and underdevelopment.

Likewise, previous G8 Summits had occasioned hope for consideration of African economic problems. In 2001 in Genoa, African leaders had presented the New Africa Initiative (NAI), a pledge to own up to African leadership on economic issues while seeking a financial partnership with developed nations. The following G8 Summit held in Kananaskis, Alberta in 2002 had been billed as the summit for African development, featuring an updated version of the NAI known as the New

Partnership for African Development (NEPAD), whereby government aid and debt forgiveness would come with demonstrated improvements in governance and curtailment of corruption. However, African development had been consigned to secondary status in the 2003 and 2004 summits and it was not clear that poverty would remain a significant point in the agenda of the organization.

So in the months previous to the Gleneagles Summit, debt relief activists and concerned celebrities combined to organize a live around-the-world series of concerts in combination with a campaign that came to be known as "Make Poverty History". The key spokesmen for the cause were Bob Geldof and U2 frontman Bono, both of whom came to become the public faces of the global drop-the-debt campaign. Well-known actors, musicians, and entertainers lent their time and their images to publicize the event and a multinational petition was launched to be proffered to host Prime Minister Tony Blair at Gleneagles. The "Live 8" concerts held on July 2, 2005 were pitched not as a worldwide benefit as in the case of 1985's Live Aid so much as a means to bring public pressure to bear on the leaders of the G8 to make debt relief a priority.

Despite the remarkable public attention brought to the debt relief campaign, economists and policy makers are by no means united on the utility of debt relief as a means of improving the lot of developing nations in Africa and other areas of the global South. In particular, the G8 and IMF initiatives reflect the general feeling that it is inappropriate to reward developing nations with debt relief if the underlying governance and economic dysfunctions are not addressed. For this reason, debt relief has largely been tied to improvements in the record of transparency, respect of human rights, and financial management on the part of third world governments. Many argue, however, that conditions of such relief have largely remained inconsequential and ineffective. By contrast, others suggest that debt relief programs still reflect the colonial assumptions that developing nations need to be improved through Western intervention and tutelage, and that Western states have not yet come to grips with their own role in promoting the underdevelopment and dependency of the global South.

In this exchange, George Ayittey argues that the improvement of governance through a policy of "smart aid" is a better strategy than outright debt relief. On the other hand, Moses Ochonu points out that the problem of governance is more deep-seated and requires a solution that combines debt relief with reformation of Western aid and development agencies.

✔ **YES**
Smart Aid for Africa
GEORGE AYITTEY

Mired in grinding poverty and social destitution, Africa cries for help. A cacopho-nous galaxy of rock stars, anti-poverty activists, and heads of state are calling on the G-8 countries to cancel Africa's $350 billion crippling foreign debt and double aid to the continent. British Prime Minister Tony Blair will make aid to Africa the center-piece in Britain's presidency of the G-8 meeting in Gleneagles, Scotland in July. Live 8 is planned for July 2. After meeting with President Bush on June 10, modalities are being worked out to cancel at least $34 billion in debt of 27 of the world's poorest nations, mostly African. Will this African Marshall Aid Plan work?

Africa's plight follows a ten-year attention deficit cycle. Every decade or so, mega-plans are drawn up and rock concerts held to whip up international rescue missions for Africa. Acrimonious wrangling over financing modalities ensues. Years slip by, then a decade later, another grand Africa initiative is unveiled. Back in 1985, there was Live Aid and a "Special Session on Africa" held by the United Nations to boost aid to Africa. Then in March 1996, the U.N. launched a $25 billion Special Initiative for Africa. In September 2005, the plight of Africa will again take center-stage at a U.N. conference with clockwork precision. Expect another major initiative for Africa in 2015.

Helping Africa of course is noble but has now become a theater of the absurd—the blind leading the clueless. A recent IMF study estimated that Africans in the diaspora remit $32 billion annually back to Africa, with the main destinations being Ghana, Nigeria, and Kenya. About $7 billion is sent to southern Africa (Ghana News Agency, Accra, May 31, 2005). The amount Africans abroad remit back exceeds the $25 billion Tony Blair seeks to raise.

Nigerian President Olusegun Obasanjo says corrupt African leaders have stolen at least $140 billion (£95 billion) from their people since independence. The World Bank estimates that 40 per cent of wealth created in Africa is invested outside the continent. Even the African Union, in a stunning report last August, claimed that Africa loses an estimated $148 billion annually to corruption—or 25 percent of the continent's Gross Domestic Product (GDP). Rather than plug the huge hemor-rhage, African leaders prefer to badger the West for more money. And the West, blinded by its own racial over-sensitivity and guilt over the iniquities of the slave trade and colonialism, obliges. This is the real tragedy of Africa.

Between 1960 and 1997, the West pumped more than $450 billion in foreign aid—the equivalent of four Marshall Aid Plans—into Africa with nothing to show for it. Contrary to popular misconception, foreign aid is not free but a soft loan. Outright debt relief and massive inflow of aid without any conditionalities, safe-guards or monitoring mechanisms is absurd. It is akin to writing off the credit card debt of a drunken sailor and allowing him to keep the same credit cards.

No African government has been called upon to give a full public accounting of who took what loan and for what purpose since many of Africa's foreign loans taken in the past were misused and squandered. No government official has been held accountable; instead, irresponsible past borrowing behavior is being rewarded.

More distressing, much of the new aid money will flow directly into an African government budget—a huge black maze of vanishing tax receipts, extra-budgetary expenditure items, perks and off-budget "presidential privy accounts," redolent with graft, patronage and waste. Over the past few decades, African budgets have careened out of control. State bureaucracies have swollen, packed with political supporters. Back in 1996, 20 percent of Ghana's public sector workforce was declared redundant by the Secretary of Finance and Guinea's 50,000 civil servants were consuming 51 percent of the nation's wealth. In Kenya, civil service salaries take up half the budget; in Uganda, it is 40 percent. Zimbabwe has 54 ministers; Uganda with a population of 35 million has 70, while Ghana, with a population of 22 million, has 88 ministers and deputy ministers. With bloated bureaucracies, soaring expenditures and narrow tax bases, budget deficits have soared.

They are covered with World Bank loans and foreign aid (Ghana's budget is 50 percent aid-financed and Uganda's is 60 percent). If the aid is insufficient, the rest of the budget shortfall is financed by printing money. Even when aid is available for "budgetary support," there is no guarantee that it will be used productively to generate a return to repay the soft loan. It could well be "consumed" when it pays for the salaries of civil servants. Writing off Uganda's debt does not eliminate the aid dependency. In fact, when the World Bank canceled $650 million of Uganda's debt in 1999, the first item President Yoweri Museveni purchased was a new presidential jet!

The British Prime Minister thinks he can cajole or browbeat African leaders into curbing corruption and ensuring that resources released by debt relief are put to some good use—such as increased spending on education and health care. But the push for good governance and reform must come from within—from African civil society groups, organizations and the people. However, in country after country, chastened by diabolical restrictions, these groups have no freedom or political space to operate.

Carlos Cardoso, an investigative journalist, was murdered in November 2000 for uncovering a bank scandal in which about $14 million was looted from Mozambique's largest bank, BCM, on the eve of its privatization. The official in charge of banking supervision, Antonio Siba Siba, was also murdered while investigating the banking scandals. Such was also the fate of Norbert Zongo, a popular journalist in Burkina Faso, who was gunned down on Dec 13, 1998, while investigating official corruption. In September 2001, [Eritrean] President Isaias Afwerki closed down all the independent media and arrested its staff, quashing calls for democratic reforms. In all, the government shut down eight private newspapers and arrested its journalists, picking them up in their newsrooms and homes and from the streets. They were held in a central jail until April 2002, when they threatened to begin a hunger strike to protest their detention. They were then transferred to an undisclosed location.

In neighboring Ethiopia, President Meles Zenawi, a member of Tony Blair's Africa Commission, just held fraudulent elections. Anticipating public outrage, he banned street demonstrations for one month and assumed full control of the country's security forces. When the opposition rallied to protest the results dribbling in, the police opened fire, killing 26; opposition leaders have been placed under house arrest. Witness the election machinations in Egypt.

The paucity of good leadership has left a garish stain on the continent. Worse, the caliber of leadership has distressingly deteriorated over the decades to execrable depths. The likes of Charles Taylor of Liberia and Sani Abacha of Nigeria even make Mobutu Sese Seko of formerly Zaire look like a saint. In an unusual editorial, *The Independent* newspaper in Ghana wrote: "Most of the leaders in Africa are power-loving politicians, who in uniform or out of uniform, represent no good for the welfare of our people. These are harsh words to use on men and women who may mean well but lack the necessary vision and direction to uplift the status of their people" (*The Independent*, Ghana, July 20, 2000; p. 2).

The crisis in leadership remains a major obstacle to poverty reduction and has many manifestations. It is characterized, among others, by the following dispositions and failings: the "Big Man" syndrome, subordination of national interests to personal aggrandizement, super-inflated egos, misplaced priorities, poor judgment, reluctance to take responsibility for personal failures, and total lack of vision and understanding of even such basic and elementary concepts as "democracy," "fairness," "rule of law," "accountability," and "freedom"—among other deficiencies. In some instances, the leadership is given to vituperative utterances, outright buffoonery, stubborn refusal to learn from past mistakes, and complete absence of cognitive pragmatism.

Believing that their countries belong to them and them only, they cling to power at all costs. Their promises are worth less than Al Capone's. They stipulate constitutional term limits and then break them: Angola, Chad, Gabon, Guinea, and Uganda. African leaders themselves drew up a New Economic Partnership for Africa's Development (NEPAD) in 2001, in which they inserted a Peer Review Mechanism (PRM), by which they were to evaluate the performance of fellow African leaders in terms of democratic governance. What happened? To be fair, they acted in reversing the "military coup" in Togo in February but went on vacation when elections were stolen in Zimbabwe and Togo.

Ask them to cut bloated state bureaucracies or government spending and they will set up a "Ministry of Less Government Spending." Then there is the "Ministry of Good Governance" (Tanzania). They set up "Anti-Corruption Commissions" with no teeth and then sack the Commissioner if he gets too close to the fat cats (Kenya) or issue a Government White Paper to exonerate corrupt ministers (Ghana in 1996). To be sure, multi-party elections have been held in recent years in many African countries but the electoral process was contumaciously manipulated to return incumbents to power. Four such "coconut elections" have so far been held this year: Zimbabwe, Togo, Congo (Brazzaville), and Ethiopia.

Ask them to place more reliance on the private sector and they will create a Ministry of Private Enterprise (Ghana). Ask them to privatize inefficient state-owned enterprises and they will sell them off at fire-sale prices to their cronies (Uganda). Or ask them to move a foot and they will demand foreign aid in order to do so. In 2003, some 30,000 ghost names were discovered on the payroll of the Ministry of Education, costing the government $1.2 million a month in salaries heisted by living workers. When Ghana demanded foreign aid to purge the payroll of these ghost names, Japan coughed up $5 million.

The reform process has stalled through vexatious chicanery, willful deception, and vaunted acrobatics. Only 16 out of the 54 African countries are democratic, fewer than 8 are "economic success stories," only 8 have a free and independent media.

No amount of debt relief and increased aid will help Africa until Africa cleans up its own house. But the leadership is not interested in reform. Thus, without new leadership and genuine reform, debt relief and increased aid would compound Africa's problems and more African countries will implode. The continent is stuck in a veritable conundrum. What can Western donors do?

Smart aid would do one of two things. One, bypass the vampire state and target the people, who produce Africa's real wealth. An African economy consists of three sectors: the traditional, informal, and the modern sector. The people who produce Africa's real wealth—cash crops, diamonds, gold and other minerals—live in the traditional and informal sectors. Meaningful development and poverty reduction cannot occur by ignoring these two sectors. But in the 1960s and 1970s, much Western development aid was channeled into the modern sector or the urban area, the abode of the parasitic elite minority. Industrialization was the rage and the two other sectors—especially agriculture—were neglected. Huge foreign loans were contracted to set up a dizzying array of state enterprises, which became towering edifices of gross inefficiency, waste and graft. Economic crises emerged in the 1980s and billions in foreign aid money were spent in an attempt to reform the dysfunctional modern sector. Between 1981 and 1994, for example, the World Bank spent more than $25 billion in Structural Adjustment loans to reform Africa's dilapidated statist economic system. Only 6 out of the 29 "adjusting" African countries were adjudged to be "economic success stories" in 1994. Even then, the success list was phantasmagoric. Ghana, declared a "success story" in 1994, is now on HIPC life-support system.

At some point, even the most recklessly optimistic donor must come to terms with the law of diminishing returns: that pouring in more money to reform the modern sector is futile. Greater returns can be achieved elsewhere—by focusing on the traditional and informal sectors.

Second, smart aid would empower the African people (African civil society groups) to monitor how the aid money is being spent and to instigate reform from within. Empowerment requires arming the African people with information, the freedom and the institutional means to unchain themselves from the vicious grip of poverty and oppression.

Africa already has its own Charter of Human and Peoples' Rights (the 1981 Banjul Charter), which recognizes the right to liberty and to the security of his person (Article 6); to receive information, to express and disseminate his opinions (Article 9); to free association (Article 10); to assemble freely with others (Article 11); and to participate freely in the government of his country, either directly or through freely chosen representatives in accordance with the provisions of the law (Article 13). Though the Charter enjoins African states to recognize these rights, few do so. When President Thabo Mbeki called on June 3, President Bush should have handed him a signed copy of this Charter to be delivered to President Robert Mugabe of Zimbabwe.

The institutional tools Africans need are an independent central bank (to assure monetary stability and stanch capital flight), an independent judiciary (for the rule of law), a free and independent media (to ensure free flow of information), an independent Electoral Commission, an efficient and professional civil service, and a neutral and professional armed and security forces.

Recent events in Ukraine (November), Ghana (December), Zimbabwe (March), Lebanon (April), and Togo (April) unerringly underscore the critical importance of these institutions. Without them, President Bush's plan to spread democracy may stall. Democracies are not built in a vacuum but in a "political space" in which the people can air their opinion, petition their government without being fired on by security forces and can choose who should rule them in elections that are not rigged by electoral commissions packed with government goons.

On May 13, thousands of Egyptian judges, frustrated by government control over the judiciary, agitated for full independence from the executive in their oversight of the electoral process. "The institutions are presenting Mr. Mubarak with an unexpected challenge from within, one that will be difficult to dismiss. The fact is, major changes in this country are going to come out of those institutions, not from the streets," said Abdel Monem Said, director of the Ahram Center for Strategic Studies in Cairo.

In the past 24 years, Egypt has received more than $55 billion in U.S. aid in direct government-to-government transfers. Smart aid would assist civil society in instigating institutional reform. Since this approach carries some risks, the same objective can be achieved by funneling aid through diaspora Africans and their organizations, as was the case with Soviet dissidents during the Cold War.

Africa's long term growth prospects do not lie in rock concerts and increased dependency on Western aid but on the ability of the African people or civil society groups to instigate reform from within. Assistance to such groups—both at home and abroad—constitutes much smarter aid to Africa than all the LIVE AID concerts Bob Geldof can organize.

✗ NO
The Case for Debt Cancellation and Increased Aid to Africa
MOSES OCHONU

Recently, George Ayittey of American University went before the standing committee of the Canadian Parliament on Foreign Relations to present his thoughts and recommendations on the subject of aid to Africa. Ayittey expanded the talking points for that presentation to respond to the new British-led initiative for debt cancellation, increased aid, and Africa-friendly trade practices.

Ayittey's write up on Africa's debt crises (published as dialogue 773) raises a lot of contentious issues. Because aid and debt are two extremely important issues on which Africa's economic and social future partly hinge, it is important to respond strongly to some of the issues in the piece. I will preface this write-up with a declaration of my disagreement with the ideological and philosophical premise of Ayittey's presentation on the subject of aid in and debt "relief" in Africa. Ayittey's presentation is steeped in the widespread but erroneous notion that aid and foreign loans are charitable acts on the part of the West toward Africa and that their forgiveness, being undeserved, should be considered as acts of remarkable benevolence. This is one of the biggest myths being naively reproduced in current discussions on Africa's economic predicament. I do not subscribe to this naïve and simplistic rendering of two institutions which have been used by the West as mechanisms for controlling and self-interestedly tele-guiding African economies. As very perceptive and informed commentators have opined, the reluctance of Western countries to sign on to a program of total debt cancellation is informed partly by their anxieties regarding the potential loss of these key tools of Western economic hegemony in Africa. Back to Ayittey's talking points.

First of all, Ayittey's write-up does a disservice to the Blair plan by reducing it to yet another attempt to raise and throw money at Africa's myriad problems. This is an unfair caricature of a three-pronged, nuanced proposal, of which aid is only one aspect. Debt relief is another aspect. For me, though, the most important aspect of this proposal—and this is what makes it radical in an unprecedented way—is its courage in calling for the elimination of many anti-Africa Western trade practices, not the least of which are the agricultural subsidies which not only close Western markets to African producers but also belies the West's rhetoric of free trade and globalization. If this proposal is embraced at next month's WTO talks, it will do infinitely more for Africa than aid or debt forgiveness can do over the long term.

Secondly, the write-up's comparison of African aid to the Marshall plan is outrageous, misleading, and disingenuous. By Ayittey's own assertion, the $450 billion purportedly "pumped" into Africa between 1960 and 1997 was not free money but a plethora of soft loans, with conditions that are anything but soft. The Marshall plan, on the other hand, was direct, free America aid, the only condition being that the nations of Europe should form a collective and devise a comprehensive plan on how to spend the money. One could say that the world has changed and that the political threats and goals which made the case for the Marshall Plan no longer exist today. That may be so, but who is to say that hunger, disease, destitution, and anger in Africa pose a lesser threat to the United States than did the advancing wave of Soviet Socialism?

Yes, aid without conditionalities is counterproductive. However, does Ayittey not know that all previous aid to Africa carried stringent conditionalities but that African leaders and states, with the active support and encouragement of Western actors and financial institutions circumvented these conditions, thus getting us into this debt conundrum? If these conditionalities have been applied to African regimes and haven't worked, isn't it time we looked at applying the same set of ethical conditionalities to the Western institutions and actors who facilitate the merry-go-round of aid, embezzlement, Swiss accounts, and more recycled aid-loans?

Ayittey argues that no African government has been called to "give full public accounting of who took what loan for what purpose." This is sadly true, and I have no doubt in my mind that the day of reckoning is coming for all the African leaders who mortgaged our collective patrimony and destiny by taking and squandering foreign loans and aid on behalf of expectant and needy Africans. I have no illusions, however, that the West will be the champion of such a project of accountability. The West will not demand such an accounting, NOT because of its historical hangovers over past injustices, as Ayittey erroneously alleges—as anyone can see, the West has since shrugged off the guilt of the slave trade and colonialism, and mainstream revisionist histories which exonerate and assuage the West's conscience now abound. The West will not initiate a full process of soul searching and accountability because such a full accounting will inevitably lead the indictment of the West itself and its complicit financial institutions. Such a probe may also implicate some respectable Western figures who have done and still do business with corrupt African leaders and who are either in power in Western countries or have politicians in these countries who are beholden to them. In short, such a process of accounting will open Pandora's Box and reveal the underbelly of the fraudulent, two-sided aid-loan-corruption poverty producing machine. This is why the West will not demand full public accounting. It will not investigate its own institutions and practices.

Ayittey's analysis is thus a one-sided one at best. If African kleptocrats have yet to be held accountable for collecting and misusing dubious aid, no Western contractors, financial institutions, bankers, and economic hitmen (apologies to John Perkins), who wickedly pushed (read imposed) dubious waste-pipe projects on greedy African bureaucrats and politicians, have been called to account for their destructive adventures on the continent. They, too, must not go scot-free.

A big chunk of the write-up is really a simplistic and uncritical regurgitation of boring, outmoded IMF and World Bank-inspired free market postulations bemoaning the size of African civil services and recommending the drastic down-sizing of the public sector. If this overly theoretical and textbookish prescription hadn't already been discredited in many reputable intellectual and academic circles as a one-size-fits-all, I would spend some time on it. Perhaps Ayittey and other small government advocates can tell us how the innocent civil servants to be massively retrenched will be absorbed into other niches without further burdening the informal and traditional sectors, since the private sector is either non-existent or stagnant in most African countries. It seems that in the journey toward the neoclassical economic Holy Grail of small government, real humans and their economic fates are expendable.

Ayittey's most contentious postulation is his argument that "no amount of debt relief and increased aid will help Africa until Africa cleans up its own house." This would be a noble assertion were it not for the fallacy which inheres in it. How can Africa not be better off, even with all the corruption and waste, if it no longer has to pay the billions of dollars that it pays annually to service debts which were dubiously collected and which ended up for the most part in the West with the active collaboration of Western institutions and persons? In any case, the example of Nigeria, where the country has spent more than four times the amount of the original debt amount in servicing and interest payment and is still left with a rapidly appreciating principal, makes repayments of the foreign debts and the withholding of so-called debt relief immoral. Both Nigeria and her creditors know that this debt can never be repaid under the existing arrangements, which are actually designed to keep the principal unpaid while the creditors reap billions of dollars in annual servicing and interest payments. Nigeria's example is a microcosm of the African debt situation. Isn't it morally unacceptable for a country to continue to pay interests and service charges on dubious debts for which servicing payments alone have eclipsed the original debt amount? If only the Ayitteys of this world would temper their economics with some morality, they'd be able to grasp the moral dimension of this discourse of debt cancellation.

Let me therefore restate that I do not believe that debt relief is a charitable gesture on the part of the West; Western countries are merely trying, rather belatedly and half-heartedly, to make right what they messed up (by design) in Africa. The recent debt cancellation gesture is an incomplete atonement and a small restitution for the Western crime of willfully participating in questionable loan schemes and dubious monetary imports from Africa, which have left the continent comatose.

Nor do I subscribe to the notion of aid as aid or aid as charity. These aids—and they need to become completely free—are also token restitutive and compensatory payments deserved by Africa and Africans as a negligible material compensation, not for the slave trade and colonialism, as Ayittey insinuates, but for ONGOING devastation of the continent through the wanton extraction of the continent's resources by environmentally nonchalant Western companies, and the resultant destruction of the environment, livelihoods, lifestyles, not to mention the instigation and exacerbation of armed conflict and the massive repatriation of tax-free profits to Western capitals. No amount of aid will adequately compensate Africans for these Western schemes or atone for their amoral and immoral aftermaths.

It sounds good to call for a reform of African states and institutions as a prelude to increased aid and debt relief. Ayittey wants Africa to cleanse its own house before the West goes further with these new projects. But is this complete cleansing feasible or possible in Africa (or anywhere else) in the foreseeable future? Is this insistence on cleansing as a condition for aid in the interest of the suffering (and innocent) mass of Africans, some of who depend solely on foreign aid handouts for survival? Is this not tantamount to withholding food and medicine from a child until its parents "clean up their acts" and start being financially responsible?

Finally, Ayittey calls for smart aid, which he argues would bypass the "vampire state" and deliver help directly the Africans in the traditional and informal sectors through civil society organs. First, let me welcome Ayittey to the club of the realists—those who believe that needy Africans should not be starved of aid because their governments are corrupt, and that aid, especially of the non-soft loan variety, cannot be tied to slow or non-existent political and institutional reforms. I recall that when the moderator of USA/Africa dialogue posted a *New York Times* editorial some months ago calling for the same kind of aid—aid which sidesteps corrupt state institutions and delivers help directly to those who need it—Ayittey was very vehement in his opposition to it. Since Ayittey himself is cynical and pessimistic about the prospects for the expansion of liberal reform on the continent, I wonder how he expects Africa "to clean its own house" and thus attract increased aid and debt relief.

In his response to the *New York Times* piece, Ayittey had argued that bypassing the vampire state with aid was a practical impossibility since the greedy state operatives would frustrate such a project. I would like to repeat this same criticism to him as an answer to his idea of channeling aid through civil society organizations. Since the African state is quite ubiquitous in terms of the exercise of power, the so-called smart aid will not work as state officials will resist and/or undermine this usurpation of what they consider their jurisdictional prerogative. It is illusory to expect that state bureaucrats will not pounce on or interfere with the implementation of such a smart aid package.

More importantly, the idea that civil society organizations and the informal sector are corruption-free and could thus serve as an accountable, efficient, and effective channel for aid distribution and implementation reveals a mindset that is hopelessly out of touch with African realities on the ground. It is founded on an overly theoretical insistence on separating African leaders from their people, the modern sector from the informal and traditional sectors. Such insistence on separateness ignores the symbiotic relationships between the public and private sectors of African political and economic life. These sectors, contrary to Ayittey's argument, are separated by the thinnest and blurriest of lines. In fact, they are connected in a complex web of patron-client, familial, lineage, clan, ethnic, political, and socio-economic ties of mutual dependence and benefits.

My own knowledge, which is experientially rooted in Nigeria, reveals a more nuanced and variegated picture of corruption in which there are both private and public actors, in which there are actors from the so-called traditional and informal sectors and civil society. Corruption is not only rampant in the private and informal sectors of the Nigerian economy; the civil society organizations that Ayittey venerates are also very corrupt. In fact, the corruption in the Nigerian NGO and human rights communities, which no one talks about, is just as alarming as governmental graft. It is now so bad that human rights advocacy and NGO affairs have become autonomous domains of profit-oriented business and money-making. In this domain, the relationship between donors and recipient and partner organizations has an unsettling resemblance to that between so-called Western lenders and financial institutions on the one hand and African governments and leaders on the other.

So, what do we do?

Tony Blair's set of proposals, which actually falls short of the 100% debt cancellation (not forgiveness or relief) which many people of good conscience advocate, is a good place to start. It does not commit the error of simply throwing money at a bad situation. It marries the concerns of reform and the urgent need to save and improve lives on the continent. More importantly, it attempts to redress the anti-Africa trade practices of Western nations, who in effect have stifled African agricultural and proto-industrial production through their hypocritical subsidies and tariffs. My only disappointment with the plan (besides the failure to recommend the cancellation of all of Africa's debt) is the fact that its call for reform is one-sided. It does not demand the reform of Western financial institutions and global capital transfer practices, a reform which would make it difficult or impossible for corrupt African leaders to bilk the continent of aid money, which are then used to finance and lubricate investments and accounts overseas in a destructive cycle of corruption and hypocrisy.

POSTSCRIPT

The debate surrounding debt relief inevitably veers toward deeper issues surrounding the prescription for underdevelopment in marginalized countries. For every developing country that succeeds in improving governance along the lines set out by multilateral lending agencies another is unable or unwilling to pay the political and social costs. While improvements in the stability of governing institutions in places such as Nigeria and Liberia have contributed to a great deal of optimism, the descent of Zimbabwe into virtual economic chaos has dealt a blow to optimism for other parts of Africa.

There is no question that longstanding debt servicing has held back many parts of the developing world for decades. In the most marginalized countries of Africa and other reaches of the developing world, it stands as an insurmountable burden with or without improvements in governance. Efforts at debt forgiveness are therefore only the tip of the iceberg when it comes to addressing the broader problems of underdevelopment and poverty.

Suggested Additional Readings

Easterly, William. "Think Again: Debt Relief," *Foreign Policy* (November/ December 2001). plato.acadiau.ca/COURSES/POLS/Grieve/Debt%20relief %20easterly.html

Hjertholm, Peter. "Theoretical and Empirical Foundations of HIPC Debt Sustainability Targets," *Journal of Development Studies,* 39, no. 6 (August 2003): 67–101.

Leech, Garry. "Economic Sovereignty: A Prerequisite to Broad-Based Development," *Colombia Journal Online.* www.colombiajournal.org/ colombia204.htm

Rodino, Virginia. "African Debt, War and Imperialism are Linked," *Global Research* (August 2, 2005). globalresearch.ca/index.php?context= viewArticle&code=ROD20050802&articleId=787

Rowden, Rick. "A World of Debt," *The American Prospect,* 12, no. 12 (July 2001): 29–32.

Schmitz, Andrea. "Generous Gestures: What Is the Point of G8 Debt Cancellation?" *SWP Comments* (July 2005). www.swp-berlin.org/en/ produkte/swp_aktuell_detail.php?id=4842&PHPSESSID=7d60ca023a8f9 93b40e9dcbc600e7de1

Thomas, Melissa A. "Getting Debt Relief Right," *Foreign Affairs,* 80, no. 5 (September–October 2001): 36–45.

InfoTrac® College Edition

Search for the following articles in the InfoTrac® database:

Brutus, Dennis. "Africa 2000 in the New Global Context: A Commentary," *Africa Today,* 44, no. 4 (October–December 1997): 379–383.

Fosu, Augustin Kwasi. "Mapping Growth into Economic Development: Has Elite Instability Mattered in Sub-Saharan Africa?" *The American Journal of Economics and Sociology,* 63, no. 5 (November 2004): 1173–1192.

For more articles, enter:
"debt relief," "African development," or "NEPAD" in the keyword search.

Web Resources

JUBILEE DEBT CAMPAIGN

www.jubileedebtcampaign.org.uk

Founded in the late 1990s, the Jubilee Debt Campaign was the early standard-bearer of a global movement for debt cancellation.

MAKE POVERTY HISTORY

www.makepovertyhistory.ca

The Make Poverty History campaign gathered celebrities and average citizens around the world in favour of a series of anti-poverty initiatives in the run-up to the Gleneagles G8 Summit of 2005.

HIGHLY INDEBTED POOR COUNTRY (HIPC) DEBT INITIATIVE

www.imf.org/external/np/hipc/index.asp

The HIPC debt initiative was launched by the World Bank and IMF in 1996 in order to relieve the poorest countries of debts that they could not service. Analytical reports of the most heavily indebted poor countries are searchable through the IMF site.

Are Property Titling Systems the Key to Increased Economic Growth?

✔ **YES**

HERNANDO DE SOTO, *The Mystery of Capital* (New York: Basic Books, 2000), pp. 39–67

✗ **NO**

ALAN GILBERT, "On the Mystery of Capital and the Myths of Hernando de Soto," *International Development Planning Review*, 24, no. 1 (2002): 1–16

Modernization theory held that societies moved in a linear fashion from backward economies with an undifferentiated division of labour toward modern industrialized economies with a complex division of labour. This suggested that most societies moved from the ancient feudal system through the Industrial Revolution toward urbanized and modern society. This process granted property rights to citizens in modern societies such that they might exchange their status as tenant farmers for status as the urban proletariat. Indeed, people in most developed societies have been able to use their labour to earn sufficient capital to purchase property of their own. The ability to buy and sell land as one form of capital has become second nature in most developed societies through the development of a universally accepted system of legal title and exchange of notes that represent ownership over land and other forms of capital.

However, the movement of developing countries from feudal systems to industrialized societies has been uneven. As industrialization took root in the West, poor peasant farmers in underdeveloped nations sought to bring about change through more revolutionary means. In some countries, such as China or Vietnam, wars were fought to overturn the quasi-feudal order of the past, promoting nationalization of all property as a means of redistributing its benefits to the peasantry. In most Latin American countries, similar attempts to overthrow colonial-era landed oligarchies met with strong established resistance over the years, contributing to a series of revolutionary measures designed to redistribute property from the landed classes to landless peasants. The limited success of governments in this region to redistribute property remains a complaint among rural farmers and is frequently cited as a reason for persistently high levels of income inequality in these countries. By the same token, states such as South Korea, Japan, and Taiwan, where feudalism was disrupted by war and foreign occupation, or areas of Africa and India, where feudalism had never taken root or took a different form, have not suffered from the same level of inequality.

For these reasons and others, many development theorists have focused upon patterns of land ownership as important predictors of the success or failure of a nation to develop properly. Likewise, many developing-nation governments have championed the cause of land reform as a means of promoting social justice and equity. In some cases, it motivates large-scale social disruptions and violence, such as in the case of the Mexican Zapatista revolt in the state of Chiapas during the mid-1990s. Socialist movements elsewhere in Latin America have come to power seeking to centralize and nationalize key assets in order to encourage redistribution. Others have embraced land tenure reforms so that poor farmers can take possession of land that they have tilled for decades and pass the land down to their progeny. In addition to promoting economic incentives and prosperity in the countryside, it is hoped that rural land reform will help to prevent rapid urbanization, which has largely overwhelmed the abilities of developing states to respond with construction and services for the burgeoning populations of Third World cities.

The growth of these cities has illuminated new problems of land usage and economic management. The masses of urban poor in developing countries have clustered in large and growing shantytowns, living in makeshift dwellings known as "spontaneous" or "informal" housing. Many of these homes are built by squatters either on privately held land or land that has been essentially nationalized in response to the political demands of its inhabitants. However, for most of these city dwellers, there are no legal titles to the land that they occupy or building permits for the homes in which they live. What is more, a large proportion of the people living in these communities engage in under-the-table employment and business that operates outside government sanction in the "informal" economy. In many cases, this is because the strictures of government licensing and permission are beyond the means of the urban poor or run by corrupt political systems that make it extremely difficult for the poor to conduct their business or build their homes legally.

Writing in the 1980s and 1990s, Peruvian economist Hernando de Soto took an interest in these informal settlements and the economy that had arisen with them. In his groundbreaking 1986 work, *The Other Path,* de Soto argued that the entrepreneurial spirit was ripe among the urban poor of the developing world but stifled through overregulation and patronage that forced people into the informal economy. In 2000, the English edition of his much-discussed work *The Mystery of Capital* appeared. Here he provides the essentials of his argument about the importance of formalized legal title to capital in the developing world. Since the publication of *The Mystery of Capital*, many have criticized the practical necessity and significance of land ownership. In this vein, Alan Gilbert argues that land reforms of the sort championed by Hernando de Soto are not proving to be the sort of remarkable solution to world poverty that de Soto believes them to be.

✔ YES
The Mystery of Capital
HERNANDO DE SOTO

The sense of the world must lie outside the world. In the world everything is as it is and happens as it does happen. In it there is no value—and if there were, it would be of no value.

If there is a value which is of value, it must lie outside all happening and being-so. For all happening and being-so is accidental.

What makes it non-accidental cannot lie in the world, for otherwise this would again be accidental.

It must lie outside the world.

—Ludwig Wittgenstein, *Tractatus Logico-Philosophicus*

Walk down most roads in the Middle East, the former Soviet Union, or Latin America, and you will see many things: houses used for shelter, parcels of land being tilled, sowed, and harvested, merchandise being bought and sold. Assets in developing and former communist countries primarily serve these immediate physical purposes. In the West, however, the same assets also lead a parallel life as capital outside the physical world. They can be used to put in motion more production by securing the interests of other parties as "collateral" for a mortgage, for example, or by assuring the supply of other forms of credit and public utilities.

Why can't buildings and land elsewhere in the world also lead this parallel life? Why can't $9.3 trillion of dead capital produce value beyond their "natural" state? My reply is, Dead capital exists because we have forgotten (or perhaps never realized) that converting a physical asset to generate capital—using your house to borrow money to finance an enterprise, for example—requires a very complex process. It is not unlike the process that Einstein taught us whereby a single brick can be made to release a huge amount of energy in the form of an atomic explosion. By analogy, capital is the result of discovering and unleashing potential energy from the trillions of bricks that the poor have accumulated in their buildings.

There is, however, one crucial difference between unleashing energy from a brick and unleashing capital from brick buildings: Although humanity (or at least a large group of scientists) has mastered the process of obtaining energy from matter, we seem to have forgotten the process that allows us to obtain capital from assets. The result is that 80 percent of the world is undercapitalized; people cannot draw economic life from their buildings (or any other asset) to generate capital. Worse, the advanced nations seem unable to reach them. Why assets can be made to produce abundant capital in the West but very little in the rest of the world is a mystery.

CLUES FROM THE PAST (FROM SMITH TO MARX)

[...]

Great classical economists such as Adam Smith and Karl Marx believed that capital was the engine that powered the market economy. Capital was considered to be the principal part of the economic whole—the preeminent factor (as the capital issues in such phrases as *capital* importance, *capital* punishment, the *capital* city of a country). What they wanted to understand was what capital is and how it is produced and accumulated. Whether you agree with the classical economists or not, or perhaps view them as irrelevant (maybe Smith never understood that the Industrial Revolution was under way; maybe Marx's labor theory of value has no practical application), there is no doubt that these thinkers built the towering edifices of thought on which we can now stand and try to find out what capital is, what produces it, and why non-Western nations generate so little of it.

For Smith, economic specialization—the division of labor and the subsequent exchange of products in the market—was the source of increasing productivity and therefore "the wealth of nations." What made this specialization and exchange possible was capital, which Smith defined as the stock of assets accumulated for productive purposes. Entrepreneurs could use their accumulated resources to support specialized enterprises until they could exchange their products for the other things they needed. The more capital was accumulated, the more specialization became possible, and the higher society's productivity would be. Marx agreed; for him, the wealth that capitalism produces presents itself as an immense pile of commodities.

[...]

Smith emphasized one point that is at the very heart of the mystery we are trying to solve. For accumulated assets to become active capital and put additional production in motion, they must be *fixed and realized in some particular subject* "which lasts for some time at least after that labour is past. It is, as it were, a certain quantity of labour stocked and stored up to be employed, if necessary, upon some other occasion." Smith warned that labor invested in the production of assets would not leave any trace or value if not properly *fixed*.

What Smith really meant may be the subject of legitimate debate. What I take from him, however, is that capital is not the accumulated stock of assets but the *potential* it holds to deploy new production. This potential is, of course, abstract. It must be processed and fixed into a tangible form before we can release it—just like the potential nuclear energy in Einstein's brick. Without a conversion process—one that draws out and fixes the potential energy contained in the brick—there is no explosion; a brick is just a brick. Creating capital also requires a conversion process.

[...]

This essential meaning of capital has been lost to history. Capital is now confused with money, which is only one of the many forms in which it travels. It is always easier to remember a difficult concept in one of its tangible manifestations than in its essence. The mind wraps itself around "money" more easily than "capital."

But it is a mistake to assume that money is what finally fixes capital. As Adam Smith pointed out, money is the "great wheel of circulation," but it is *not* capital because value "cannot consist in those metal pieces." In other words, money facilitates transactions, allowing us to buy and sell things, but it is not itself the progenitor of additional production. As Smith insisted, "the gold and silver money, which circulates in any country, may very properly be compared to a highway, which, while it circulates and carries to market all the grass and corn of the country, produces itself not a single pile of either."

[...]

THE POTENTIAL ENERGY IN ASSETS

[...]

Capital, like energy, is also a dormant value. Bringing it to life requires us to go beyond *looking* at our assets as they are to actively *thinking* about them as they could be. It requires a process for fixing an asset's economic potential into a form that can be used to initiate additional production.

Although the process that converts the potential energy in the water into electricity is well known, the one that gives assets the form required to put in motion more production is not known. In other words, while we know that it is the penstock, turbines, generators, transformers, and wires of the hydroelectric energy system that convert the potential energy of the lake until it is fixed in an accessible form, we do not know where to find the key process that converts the economic potential of a house into capital.

This is because that key process was not deliberately set up to create capital but for the more mundane process of protecting property ownership. As the property systems of Western nations grew, they developed, imperceptibly, a variety of mechanisms that gradually combined into a process that churned out capital as never before. Although we use these mechanisms all the time, we do not realize that they have capital-generating functions because they do not wear that label. We view them as parts of the system that protects property, not as interlocking mechanisms for fixing the economic potential of an asset in such a way that it can be converted into capital. What creates capital in the West, in other words, is an implicit process buried in the intricacies of its formal property systems.

THE HIDDEN CONVERSION PROCESS OF THE WEST

[...]

For some time now I have been looking at the law from an extralegal point of view, to better understand how it functions and what effects it produces. This is not as crazy as it seems. As the French philosopher Michel Foucault has argued, it may be easier to discover what something means by looking at it from the opposite side of the bridge. "To find out what our society means by sanity,"

Foucault has written, "perhaps we should investigate what is happening in the field of insanity. And what we mean by legality in the field of illegality." Moreover, property, like energy, is a concept; it cannot be experienced directly. Pure energy has never been seen or touched. And no one can see property. One can only experience energy and property by their effects.

From my viewpoint in the extralegal sector, I have seen that the formal property systems of the West produce six effects that allow their citizens to generate capital. The incapacity elsewhere in the world to deploy capital stems from the fact that most of the people in the Third World and in former communist countries are cut off from these essential effects.

Property Effect No. 1: Fixing the Economic Potential of Assets

The potential value locked up in a house can be revealed and transformed into active capital in the same way that potential energy is identified in a mountain lake and then transformed into actual energy. In both cases, the transition from one state to another requires a process that transposes the physical object into a man-made representative universe where we can disengage the resource from its burdensome material constraints and concentrate on its potential.

Capital is born by representing in writing—in a title, a security, a contract, and in other such records—the most economically and socially useful qualities *about* the asset as opposed to the visually more striking aspects *of* the asset. This is where potential value is first described and registered. The moment you focus your attention on the title of a house, for example, and not on the house itself, you have automatically stepped from the material world into the conceptual universe where capital lives. You are reading a representation that focuses your attention on the economic potential of the house by filtering out all the confusing lights and shadows of its physical aspects and its local surroundings. Formal property forces you to think about the house as an economic and social concept. It invites you to go beyond viewing the house as mere shelter—and thus a dead asset—and to see it as live capital.

[...]

Legal property thus gave the West the tools to produce surplus value over and above its physical assets. Property representations enabled people to think about assets not only through physical acquaintance but also through the description of their latent economic and social qualities. Whether anyone intended it or not, the legal property system became the staircase that took these nations from the universe of assets in their natural state to the conceptual universe of capital where assets can be viewed in their full productive potential.

With legal property, the advanced nations of the West had the key to modern development; their citizens now had the means to discover, with great facility and on an ongoing basis, the most potentially productive qualities of their resources. As Aristotle discovered 2,300 years ago, what you can do with things increases infinitely when you focus your thinking on their potential. By learning to fix the economic potential of their assets through property records, Westerners created a fast track to explore the most productive aspects of their possessions. Formal property became the staircase to the conceptual realm where the economic meaning of things can be discovered and where capital is born.

Property Effect No. 2: Integrating Dispersed Information into One System

[...] Most people in developing and former communist nations cannot get into the legal property system, such as it is, no matter how hard they try. Because they cannot insert their assets into the legal property system, they end up holding them extralegally. The reason capitalism has triumphed in the West and sputtered in the rest of the world is because most of the assets in Western nations have been integrated into one formal representational system.

This integration did not happen casually. Over decades in the nineteenth century, politicians, legislators, and judges pulled together the scattered facts and rules that had governed property throughout cities, villages, buildings, and farms and integrated them into one system. This "pulling together" of property representations, a revolutionary moment in the history of developed nations, deposited all the information and rules governing the accumulated wealth of their citizens into one knowledge base. Before that moment, information about assets was far less accessible. Every farm or settlement recorded its assets and the rules governing them in rudimentary ledgers, symbols, or oral testimony. But the information was atomized, dispersed, and not available to any one agent at any given moment. As we know too well today, an abundance of facts is not necessarily an abundance of knowledge. For knowledge to be functional, advanced nations had to integrate into one comprehensive system all their loose and isolated data about property.

Developing and former communist nations have not done this. In all the countries I have studied, I have never found just one legal system but dozens or even hundreds, managed by all sorts of organizations, some legal, others extralegal, ranging from small entrepreneurial groups to housing organizations. Consequently, what people in those countries can do with their property is limited to the imagination of the owners and their acquaintances. In Western countries, where property information is standardized and universally available, what owners can do with their assets benefits from the collective imagination of a larger network of people.
[...]

Property Effect No. 3: Making People Accountable

The integration of all property systems under one formal property law shifted the legitimacy of the rights of owners from the politicized context of local communities to the impersonal context of law. Releasing owners from restrictive local arrangements and bringing them into a more integrated legal system facilitated their accountability.

By transforming people with property interests into accountable individuals, formal property created individuals from masses. People no longer needed to rely on neighbourhood relationships or make local arrangements to protect their rights to assets. Freed from primitive economic activities and burdensome parochial constraints, they could explore how to generate surplus value from their own assets. But there was a price to pay: Once inside a formal property system, owners lost their anonymity. By becoming inextricably linked to real estate and businesses that could be easily identified and located, people forfeited the ability to lose themselves in the masses. This anonymity has practically disappeared in the West, while individual accountability has been reinforced. People who do not pay for goods or services they have consumed can be identified, charged interest penalties, fined, embargoed, and have their credit ratings downgraded. Authorities are able to learn about legal infractions and dishonored contracts; they can suspend services, place liens against property, and withdraw some or all of the privileges of legal property.

Respect in Western nations for property and transactions is hardly encoded in their citizens' DNA; it is rather the result of having enforceable formal property systems. Formal property's role in protecting not only ownership but the security of transactions encourages citizens in advanced countries to respect titles, honor contracts, and obey the law. When any citizen fails to act honorably, his breach is recorded in the system, jeopardizing his reputation as a trustworthy party to his neighbors, utilities, banks, telephone companies, insurance firms, and the rest of the network that property ties him to.

[...]

Property Effect No. 4: Making Assets Fungible

One of the most important things a formal property system does is transform assets from a less accessible condition to a more accessible condition, so that they can do additional work. Unlike physical assets, representations are easily combined, divided, mobilized, and used to stimulate business deals. By uncoupling the economic features of an asset from their rigid, physical state, a representation makes the asset "fungible"—able to be fashioned to suit practically any transaction.

By describing all assets in standard categories, an integrated formal property system enables the comparison of two architecturally different buildings constructed for the same purpose. This allows one to discriminate quickly and inexpensively between similarities and differences without having to deal with each asset as if it were unique.

Standard property descriptions in the West are also written to facilitate the combination of assets. Formal property rules require assets to be described and characterized in a way that not only outlines their singularity but also points out their similarity to other assets, thus making potential combinations more obvious. Through the use of standardized records, one can determine (on the basis of zoning restrictions, who the neighbors are and what they are doing, the square footage of the buildings, whether they can be joined, etc.) how to exploit a particular piece of real estate most profitably, whether as office space, hotel rooms, a bookshop, or racquetball courts and a sauna.

Representations also enable the division of assets without touching them. Whereas an asset such as a factory may be an indivisible unit in the real world, in the conceptual universe of formal property representation it can be subdivided into any number of portions. Citizens of advanced nations are thus able to split most of their assets into shares, each of which can be owned by different persons, with different rights, to carry out different functions. Thanks to formal property, a single factory can be held by countless investors, who can divest themselves of their property without affecting the integrity of the physical asset.

[...]

Once assets are in a formal property system, they endow their owners with an enormous advantage in that they can be split up and combined in more ways than an Erector set. Westerners can adapt their assets to any economic circumstance to produce continually higher valued mixtures, whereas their Third World counterparts remain trapped in the physical world of rigid, non-fungible forms.

Property Effect No. 5: Networking People

By making assets fungible, by attaching owners to assets, assets to addresses, and ownership to enforcement, and by making information on the history of assets and owners easily accessible, formal property systems converted the citizens of the West into a network of individually identifiable and accountable business agents. The formal property process created a whole infrastructure of connecting devices that, like a railway switchyard, allowed the assets (trains) to run safely between people (stations). Formal property's contribution to mankind is not the protection of ownership; squatters, housing organizations, mafias, and even primitive tribes manage to protect their assets quite efficiently. Property's real breakthrough is that it radically improved the flow of communications about assets and their potential. It also enhanced the status of their owners, who became economic agents able to transform assets within a broader network.

This explains how legal property encourages the suppliers of such utilities as electricity and water to invest in production and distribution facilities to service buildings. By legally attaching the buildings where the services will be delivered to their owners, who will be suing and paying for the services, a formal property system reduces the risk of theft of services. It also reduces the financial losses from bill collecting among people hard to locate, as well as technical losses from incorrectly estimating the electricity needs of areas where businesses and residents are clandestine and not recorded. Without knowing who has the rights to what, and without an integrated legal system where the ability to enforce obligations has been transferred from extralegal groups to government, utilities would be hard-pressed to deliver services profitably. On what other basis could they identify subscribers, create utility subscription contracts, establish service connections, and ensure access to parcels and buildings? How would they implement billing systems, meter readings, collection mechanisms, loss control, fraud control, delinquent charging procedures, and enforcement services such as meter shutoffs?

Buildings are always the terminals of public utilities. What transforms them into *accountable* and *responsible* terminals is legal property. Anyone who doubts this need only look at the utility situation outside the West, where technical and financial losses plus theft of services account for 30 to 50 percent of all available utilities.

Western legal property also provides businesses with information about assets and their owners, verifiable addresses, and objective records of property value, all of which lead to credit records. This information and the existence of integrated law make risk more manageable by spreading it through insurance-type devices as well as by pooling property to secure debts.

Property Effect No. 6: Protecting Transactions

One important reason why the Western formal property system works like a network is that all the property records (titles, deeds, securities, and contracts that describe the economically significant aspects of assets) are continually tracked and protected as they travel through time and space. Their first stop is the public agencies that are the stewards of an advanced nation's representations. Public record keepers administer the files that contain all the economically useful descriptions of assets, whether land, buildings, chattels, ships, industries, mines, or airplanes. These files will alert anyone eager to use an asset about things that may restrict or enhance its realization, such as encumbrances, easements, leases, arrears, bankruptcies, and mortgages. The agencies also ensure that assets are adequately and accurately represented in appropriate formats that can be updated and easily accessed.

In addition to public record-keeping systems, many other private services have evolved to assist parties in fixing, moving, and tracking representations so that they can easily and securely produce surplus value. These include private entities that record transactions, escrow and closings organizations, abstractors, appraisers, title and fidelity insurance firms, mortgage brokers, trust services, and private custodians of documents. In the United States, title insurance companies further help the mobilization of representations by issuing policies to cover parties for specified risks, ranging from defects on titles to unenforceability on mortgages and unmarketability of title. By law, all these entities have to follow strict operating standards that govern their document-tracking capabilities, physical storage facilities, and staffing.

Although they are established to protect both the security of ownership and that of transactions, it is obvious that Western systems emphasize the latter. Security is principally focused on producing trust in transactions so that people can more easily make their assets lead a parallel life as capital.

In most developing countries, by contrast, the law and official agencies are trapped by early colonial and Roman law, which tilt toward protecting ownership. They have become custodians of the wishes of the dead. This may explain why the creation of capital in Western property happens so easily, and why most of the assets in developing and former communist countries have slipped out of the formal legal system in search of mobility.

The Western emphasis on the security of transactions allows citizens to move large amounts of assets with very few transactions. How else can we explain that in developing and former communist nations people are still taking their pigs to market and trading them one at a time, as they have done for thousands of years, whereas in the West, traders take representations of their rights over pigs to the market? Traders at the Chicago commodities exchange, for example, deal through representations, which give them more information about the pigs they are trading than if they could physically examine each pig. They are able to make deals for huge quantities of pigs with little concern about the security of transactions.

CAPITAL AND MONEY

The six effects of an integrated property process mean that Westerners' houses no longer merely keep the rain and cold out. Endowed with representational existence, these houses can now lead a parallel life, doing *economic* things they could not have done before. A well-integrated legal property system in essence does two things: First, it tremendously reduces the costs of knowing the economic qualities of assets by representing them in a way that our senses can pick up quickly; and second, it facilitates the capacity to agree on how to use assets to create further production and increase the division of labor. The genius of the West was to have created a system that allowed people to grasp with the mind values that human eyes could never see and to manipulate things that hands could never touch.

[...]

Property, then, is not mere paper but a mediating device that captures and stores most of the stuff required to make a market economy run. Property seeds the system by making people accountable and assets fungible, by tracking transactions, and so providing all the mechanisms required for the monetary and banking system to work and for investment to function. The connection between capital and modern money runs through property.

[...]

Capital, as I argued earlier, is therefore not created by money; it is created by people whose property systems help them to cooperate and think about how they can get the assets they accumulate to deploy additional production. The substantial increase of capital in the West over the past two centuries is the consequence of gradually improving property systems, which allowed economic agents to discover and realize the potential in their assets, and thus to be in a position to produce the noninflationary money with which to finance and generate additional production.

So, we are more than squirrels who store food for winter and engage in deferred consumption. We know, through the sophisticated use of property institutions, how to give the things we accumulate a parallel life. When advanced nations pulled together all the information and rules about their known assets and established property systems that tracked their economic evolution, they gathered into one order the whole institutional process that underpins the creation of capital. If capitalism had a mind, it would be located in the legal property system. But like most things pertaining to the mind, much of "capitalism" today operates at a subconscious level.

Why did the classical economists, who knew capital was abstract and had to be fixed, not make the connection between capital and property? One explanation may be that in Adam Smith's or even Marx's day property systems were still restricted and undeveloped, and their importance was difficult to gauge. Perhaps more significantly, the battle for the future of capitalism shifted from the book-lined studies of theoreticians into a vast web of entrepreneurs, financiers, politicians, and jurists. The attention of the world turned from theories to the real deals being made on the ground, day by day, fiscal year after fiscal year.

Once the vast machine of capitalism was firmly in place and its masters were busy creating wealth, the question of how it all came into being lost its urgency. Like people living in the rich and fertile delta of a long river, the advocates of capitalism had no pressing need to explore upstream for the source of their prosperity. Why bother? With the end of the Cold War, however, capitalism became the only serious option for development. So the rest of the world turned to the West for help and was advised to imitate the conditions of life on the delta: stable currencies, open markets, and private businesses, the objectives of so-called macroeconomic and structural adjustment reforms. Everyone forgot that the reason for the delta's rich life lay far upriver, in its unexplored headwaters. Widely accessible legal property systems are the silt from upriver that permits modern capital to flourish.

This is one of the principal reasons macroeconomic reforms are not working. Imitating capitalism at the level of the delta, by importing McDonald's and Blockbuster franchises, is not enough to create wealth. What is needed is capital, and this requires a complex and mighty system of legal property that we have all taken for granted.

[...]

✘ NO
On the Mystery of Capital and the Myths of Hernando de Soto
ALAN GILBERT

Hernando de Soto's bestseller, *The Mystery of Capital* (2000), attributes the failure of capitalism in the Third World to the lack of property titles. While this is hardly a new argument, it is likely to acquire renewed momentum because his is a very influential voice in Washington. Latin American governments, which have long been active in distributing title deeds, will continue to implement this policy on an even larger scale.

The question addressed in this paper is: what difference does the 'gift' of a title deed actually make to the lives of the poor? Do title deeds enable them to borrow money from the formal sector, as de Soto and the World Bank claim? Do they open up a new world of capital accumulation to the poor because property may be transferred legally from one 'owner' to another? Or do they, in fact, make so little difference that most of the so-called advantages of legalisation are a sham?

Using data gathered in the now legalised self-help settlements of Botogá, I will question the main benefits of legalisation. I will show how sales are sometimes more frequent when people do not have legal titles, how informal finance is available from the initial information of an illegal settlement, and how little formal finance is forthcoming after legalisation. Most importantly, I will show that there is not much indication of secondary housing markets developing in legalised settlements. It is hard for the poor to make money from ownership when they are unable to sell their houses.
[...]

THE 'NEW' CONVENTIONAL WISDOM ABOUT LEGAL TITLE

According to de Soto, very little needs to be done to make capitalism work well in Africa, Asia and Latin America. Because the poor save money and have developed a variety of business skills, all they need is the means to increase their turnover. The key element required to turn them into successful businesspeople is access to formal credit. The legal title to their property will enable them to gain entry into the world of formal banking. If they can use their capital assets as collateral, the world will be their oyster.
[...]

THE NEED FOR A LAND TITLE

De Soto is undoubtedly correct in his belief that the lack of legal titles can inconvenience the poor. The occupants of newly formed settlements often feel insecure; even in long-established neighbourhoods, female-headed households, immigrant communities and minority groups may feel insecure without formal title. The absence of legal titles may complicate the process of buying and selling property and obtaining credit. No doubt this partly explains why so many Latin American governments have staged massive land-titling programmes.

However, it is widely recognised that security of tenure does not require the issue of full legal title (Durand-Lasserve, 1986; McAuslan, 1985; Fernandes and Varley, 1998). In practice, the vulnerability of informal settlements varies considerably. It depends on many factors including the identity of the original owner, the location of the land, alternative uses for the land, the nature of the government and the date of the next election.

As such, many argue that massive titling programmes are being conducted for reasons that have nothing to do with helping the poor. Such programmes are popular because they are cheap; it is much less expensive to issue property titles than to provide settlements with services. In addition, the authorities and international agencies can actually make money from titling programmes. The World Bank has long recognised that the profits made by a government agency may be used to finance upgrading programmes elsewhere (McAuslan, 1985, 62). Indeed, many people in Washington argue that issuing legal titles on a large scale can only be justified in the beneficiaries are prepared to pay the full cost of the process.

[...]

LEGAL TITLE AND HOUSING IMPROVEMENT

Does the issue of legal titles accelerate the process of housing improvement? In practice, there is plenty of evidence that settlers improve their homes even when they do not possess anything resembling a title deed (Gilbert and Ward, 1985; Payne, 1989; Razzaz, 1993; Varley, 1987; Riley, 2001). As Payne (1989, 44) puts it:

> perceived security of tenure is more critical in releasing investment for housing consolidation than legal status as such, and clearly the provision of public utilities is regarded by residents as strong evidence that they are officially accepted and enjoy de facto security tenure.

The perception of security is the key. Razzaz (1993, 349) argues that:

> empirical evidence points to a continuum of security in illegal settlements that depends less on the exact legal status and more on occupants' perceptions of the probability of eviction and demolition (enforcement), as well as the availability of services and passage of time.

In Guayaquil, Lanjouw and Levy (1998, 1) 'find the informal sources of property rights confer many of the same advantages as formal rights'. Even in the *barriadas* of Peru, legal tenure does not seem to be critical: 'Tenure matters, but for the average squatter with 10.4 years at a site, the chance of eviction around Lima was known to be low' (Strassmann, 1984, 747).

In settlements that are not threatened with removal, illegality seems to have little effect on the willingness of poor people to build (Varley, 1987; Skinner et al., 1987, 236). Riley (2001, 5) observes that in a *favela* close to Copacabana, 'illegality of tenure has not acted as a barrier to residents investing in their homes over time'. In the pirate urbanisation of Bogotá, security of tenure seems to be assumed from the start; settlers build homes as soon as they have receipts for their payments for plots of land. Most are prepared to build without titles to their land. Insofar as they have doubts, they are reassured when the authorities provide services to the settlements. Once water and electricity are available, there is no real barrier to self-help construction. Two- or three-storey buildings appear despite the absence of legal titles. Although there is no doubt that legalisation is sometimes necessary to provide assurance to particularly insecure settlers, the direction of causality if often reversed. Not infrequently, it is housing investment that brings out the granting of legal titles (Hirschman, 1984; Razzaz, 1993, 350).

Even where legal title has been granted, complementary measures are required to bring forth investment. Service provision has unleashed housing investment in Cartagena and Medellin (Columbia), Lima, Lusaka, Nairobi, Rawalpindi and Tunis (Strassmann, 1984, 751).

DOES LEGAL TITLING IMPROVE THE FUNCTIONING OF THE HOUSING MARKET?

According to de Soto (2000, 47), 'any asset whose economic and social aspects are not fixed in a formal property system is extremely hard to move in the market'. In my experience, this is simply wrong. In Latin America, informal and illegal markets function effectively for a wide range of products, including invaded land, contraband imports, stolen goods and drugs. Illegality rarely stops a market developing; it merely affects the prices in that market. In the case of drugs, illegality increases the transaction price; in the case of low-income land, it reduces it.

In Bogotá, an active market for plots of land exists despite the lack of legal titles, and similar markets have developed in most poor countries. In Mexico, *ejido* land is sold despite the threat of legal sanctions (Azuela, 1989; Gilbert and Ward, 1985; Varley, 1987). Even in settlements founded by invasions, land transactions occur. In Valencia (Venezuela), for example, most of the inhabitants of two invasion settlements had bought into the settlement: 23 per cent of the total settlers had bought a house, 32 per cent had bought a plot with a shack, and 11 per cent had bought an empty plot (Gilbert and Healey, 1985, 122).

In his customarily contradictory way, de Soto recognises this fact. Why is a formal property title so important? Because with 'no property to lose', sellers 'are taken seriously as contracting parties only by their immediate family and neighbours. People with nothing to lose are trapped in the grubby basement of the pre-capitalist world' (de Soto, 2000, 56). They can buy and sell, but only at reduced prices. Despite these low prices, 'the total value of the real estate held but not legally owned by the poor of the Third World and former communist nations in at least US$8.3 trillion' (2000, 35).[1] If a property market of such importance already exists, what is the point of title deeds?

[...]

Despite poor home-owners possessing the title deeds, the self-help housing market is extremely flat and possibly dead. This is true even in cities in which land and housing markets are very buoyant in high-income or commercial areas. You cannot accumulate capital if there is no market in which to trade your asset. If title deeds are not the problem, what is?

DO LEGAL TITLES IMPROVE POOR PEOPLES' ACCESS TO FORMAL FINANCE?

The sale of property in self-help settlements is quite common, even when the 'owners' do not have legal titles and have 'stolen' the land. The problem with the self-help settlements is not the lack of a market, but its limits. Many people buy and sell plots of land, shacks and even two-room houses. However, it is uncommon to find sale of two- or three-storey homes. You don't need much money to buy a shack, but you need a lot to buy a well-constructed house. In the low-income areas of Bogotá, owners of such homes were asking between US$20,000 and US$50,000 in the summer of 1997. There were few sales because no one could afford to buy them. Self-help home-owners can sell quality homes only with great difficulty, and/or at a very low price (Gilbert, 1999).

According to de Soto, the possession of legal title would remove this problem by unleashing a flood of formal financing. Support for this belief comes from experience in the US, where 'the single most important source of funds for new businesses ... is a mortgage on the entrepreneur's house' (de Soto, 2000, 6). Banks will lend to the poor in these circumstances because the property title may be used as a security against the loan, and the banks have something that they can repossess in the case of default. Lanjouw and Levy (1998, 45) agree: 'just as transfer uncertainty limits a household's ability to sell its property, it limits a bank's ability to repossess property, lowering the value of property as a collateral asset'.

Bankers and Slums

My evidence from Bogotá, fully supported by studies from other parts of the worlds, suggests that the possession of a legal title makes little or no difference to the availability of formal finance. In Turkey, Ozuekren (1998, 11) recognises that 'there are very few opportunities for households to obtain home-owner loans from financing institutions'. Mexico's 'sophisticated housing finance system' also has a poor track record in terms of progressive options and community-based finance (Siembieda and López Moerno, 1998, 22), and experience in recent years in South Africa has been very similar (Bond and Tait, 1997; Goodlad, 1996; Tomlinson, 1998). Even the

World Bank and the IADB recognise how difficult it is to reach poor families (Rojas, 1995; World Bank, 1993, 121). Government efforts to lend to the poor have often proved an embarrassing failure; most of the funds end up in the hands of middle-income groups or favoured labour groups (Bhattacharya, 1990; Daniere, 1999; Laun, 1976; Persaud, 1992; Rakodi, 1995; Struyk, 1989; Datta and Jones, 1998). Formal financial systems face various difficulties in reaching the poor:

> Regulations governing mortgage lending are usually biased towards completed owner-occupied housing, making it unattractive or impossible for financial institutions to lend for the purchase of rental or condominium housing, or for house improvements or unfinished core houses on serviced sites. (World Bank, 1993, 118)

> Individual freehold titles are the tenure solution favoured by many international agencies and national governments. However, even in situations in which they are the most appropriate option, they are unlikely to increase access to formal credit significantly, since it is low incomes that deter finance institutions from lending to the poor. (Balamir and Payne, 2001, 9)

Even when incomes are adequate, 'mortgage lenders have difficulty verifying self-employed income and developing an accurate estimate of self-employed income from analysis of tax returns' (Ferguson, 1999, 187). In Bogotá, few lending institutions have rules that can deal with independent workers. Lending procedures are based on the ability of potential borrowers to demonstrate that they have a regular income. Of course, few independent workers are able to do this. In addition, lenders lack confidence in the ability of poor people to repay their loans, and the final straw is the low profitability of lending to the poor (UNCHS, 1996, 370).
[...]
Micro-finance programmes have also failed to make much impression on the poor's need for housing finance (Almeyda, 1996). Micro-finance institutions have tended to follow the practice of Bangladesh's Grameen Bank, building up their lending portfolios on the basis of frequent small loans. This approach presents difficulties in the housing field, which requires much greater sums of money. Even when cooperatives are prepared to finance low-income housing, their programmes are severely limited by financial constraints and by their preference for funding housing construction (Avila, 1995, 26).[2] They do not provide loans for upgrading or for the purchase of used housing, and this seems to be a worldwide problem (Ferguson, 1999).

Do the Poor Want to Borrow?

If the banks are reluctant to lend to the poor, the latter seem reluctant to borrow. Among the recipients of housing subsidies in South Africa, those 'who said they did not want a mortgage loan outnumber those who did by three to one'

(Tomlinson, 1999, 1357). Perhaps, as the World Bank admits (2000, 74–5): 'Poor people are often discouraged and simply do not seek loans since they believe that they will be denied credit or will not be able to fulfil bank requirements'. However, this reluctance may be due primarily to anxiety about the consequences of failing to repay the loan. For very poor families, a loan is a burden that may endanger the whole household's financial viability. As Rogaly and Johnson (1997, 119) put it, lending 'can harm as well as enable poor people. Financial relationships, especially those of debt, are one way in which the powerlessness of groups of poor people is entrenched'. In Bogotá, few low-income families borrow against the title of their home, and lending agencies seem to be less convinced of the virtues of land title (Gilbert, 2000).

Most poor families build and improve their homes using personal savings and loans from informal sources (Boleat, 1985; Calderón, 2001; Renaud, 1987; World Bank, 1993; Macaloo, 1994; Napier, 1999; Ozuekren, 1998; UNCHS, 1996). These sources include:

> individual and group savings, windfalls, fabrication of their own building materials, sweat equity, small loans from neighbourhood money lenders, barter arrangements and communal self-help, and remittances from family living abroad. These funding sources share a common problem. They dribble in unevenly and, often, slowly because they remain unconnected to formal institutions and markets. The overall result is that much of the built environment in cities improves unevenly and slowly. (Ferguson, 1999, 189)

Ironically, the largest property loans made in Bogotá's low-income areas are those provided for the purchase of land. These are unsupported by any sort of collateral or property title, and are provided by illegal subdividers. Subdividers tend to sell plots on the basis of a down-payment of 10 per cent, the remainder being payable in monthly instalments over three or four years (Gilbert and Ward, 1985). In a survey in four older settlements that I conducted in 1997, most families that had occupied an empty plot received informal financing through an illegal subdivider. 33 buyers of empty plots participated in the survey, and very few had paid the full amount in cash. Of the 29 who provided details, 75 per cent paid an initial deposit and provided the rest of the sum in instalments. Of the remainder, only three had paid the whole sum in one payment.

[...]

In short, the largest loans in low-income settlements in Bogotá are received from illegal subdividers when there is no semblance of legal title. When families have acquired title deeds they borrow little or nothing through formal financial institutions. Their sources of credit would be much the same without title deeds.

[...]

CONCLUSION

Most poor urban families are glad to receive title deeds. This explains why so many governments have taken up this housing option. No doubt governments are also attracted to this approach because it is cheap, particularly when the poor are prepared to pay the costs or will start to pay property taxes as soon as they receive their deeds.

I do not believe that title deeds hold many dangers for poor families. There is unlikely to be much downward-raiding and, even if there was, some poor families would appreciate being given the opportunity to make capital gains. In Africa, parts of Asia and the Latin American countryside, the situation may be different, particularly when customary rights are overridden by a new commercial logic. However, in most cities title deeds cannot do a great deal of harm beyond accelerating the introduction of taxes on land and housing in poor settlements.

However, I am worried about the rhetoric of Hernando de Soto and his advocacy of the supposed advantages of legalisation. In Bogotá's self-help settlements, property titles have not resulted in a healthy housing market or a regular supply of formal credit. The uncomfortable truth is that, in practice, the granting of legal title has made very little difference.

If this is so, why should we worry about de Soto? He is dangerous because he is conjuring up a myth about popular capitalism. He is encouraging the delusion that anyone, anywhere, can become a fully fledged capitalist. Although he offers little or no empirical evidence in support of this assertion, that has not stopped Washington from rallying to his call. The danger is that his views will persuade policy makers that all they have to do is offer title deeds, and that they can leave the market to do everything else—providing services and infrastructure, offering formal credit and administering the booming property market. In the process, every householder will be able to own his or her own home and even make money from it.

It is my belief that, even in the unlikely event of a flourishing property market, there is little reason to believe that the poor will be major beneficiaries. Successful estate agents always claim that the secret of high property values in 'location, location, location'. The consolidation self-help settlements of the poor are rarely thought of as desirable locations. The promise of property wealth is as mythical to them as it is to the low-income families of the US (Edel et al., 1984; Rohe et al., 2000). Those who make money from property are likely to be drawn mainly from the ranks of the middle class; those who make the real money tend to be affluent already.

Thus, without wishing to deny the advantages that the poor can derive from home-ownership in a self-help suburb, de Soto's argument is dangerously flawed. Had anyone else proposed the same argument, it might have been better to ignore it. However, because de Soto is a big name, his message will be taken up by some powerful people. As such, the argument needs to be shown up for what it is. Instead of offering an answer to the mystery of capital, he is in danger of generating a myth about capitalism based on a populist dream.

NOTES

1. How does de Soto know that property is worth so much? Because it is easy to work out the real estate value of informal property: 'You can ascertain [its] value simply by surveying the cost of the building materials and observing the selling prices of comparable buildings' (de Soto, 2000, 31).

2. In Bogotá, institutions such as FENAVIP (National Federation of Popular Housing), SERVIVIENDA, Association for Popular Housing (AVP), Compartir and FEDEVIVIENDA operate in the housing field and were responsible for the production of around 30,000 housing units between 1990 and 1996 (Vejarano-Alvarado, 1997).

POSTSCRIPT

The premise that provision of capital is an important part of stimulating the latent entrepreneurial spirit of the poor in developing nations has become reigning wisdom among most development agencies. In addition to the land titling programs championed by Hernando de Soto, several initiatives have been designed to provide stimulus capital to the masses. Perhaps the highest profile of these has been the micro-credit scheme pioneered by Nobel Peace Prize winner Muhammed Yunus at the Grameen Bank in Bangladesh. The provision of small-scale loans to the poor for the development of entrepreneurial projects is widely held to be one of the most effective approaches to stimulating development and self-sufficiency. Given the massive popularity of the model, other programs aimed at putting capital to work in developing areas seem likely to come in the future.

Several scholars listed in the Suggested Additional Readings have engaged in studying the effects of land titling on development in the Third World. For the most part, their findings have been positive or neutral. Yet the land titling programs and expansion of capital availability for the use of the poor relies as much upon the security and stability of a society as any other major development strategy. It remains difficult if not impossible to create modern capitalist systems in countries beset by civil war or widespread internal conflict. Further, many countries remain affected by the political demands of patronage and clientelism that hinder widespread changes to land titling and reform. If anything, land titling is not a unique "magic bullet" to achieve higher levels of development so much as one of many tools that might be used.

Suggested Additional Readings

Agarwal, Bina. *A Field of One's Own: Gender and Land Rights in South Asia* (Cambridge: Cambridge University Press, 1995).

————. "Gender and Land Rights Revisited: Exploring New Prospects via the State, Family, and Market," *Journal of Agrarian Change,* 3, no. 1–2 (2003): 184–224.

Arrunada, Benito, and Nuno Garoupa. "The Choice of Titling System in Land," *Journal of Law and Economics,* 48 (2005): 709–727.

Boucher, Stephen R., Bradford L. Barham, and Michael R. Carter. "The Impact of 'Market-Friendly' Reforms on Credit and Land Markets in Honduras and Nicaragua," *World Development,* 33, no. 1 (January 2005): 107–128.

Deininger, Klaus, and Juan Sebastian Chamorro. "Investment and Income Effects of Land Regularization: The Case of Nicaragua," *World Bank Policy Research Working Paper No. 2752* (1999).

Dowall, David E., and Michael Leaf. "The Price of Land for Housing in Jakarta," *Urban Studies,* 28, no. 5 (October 1991): 707–722.

Feder, Gershon, and David Feeny. "Land Tenure and Property Rights: Theory and Implications for Development Policy," *The World Bank Economic Review*, 5, no. 1 (1991): 135–153.

Galiani, Sebastian, and Ernesto Schargrodsky. "Property Rights for the Poor: Effects of Land Titling" (2005). www.utdt.edu/Upload/CIF_wp/wpcif-062005.pdf

Gavian, Sarah, and Marcel Fafchamps. "Land Tenure and Allocative Efficiency in Niger," *American Journal of Agricultural Economics*, 78, no. 2 (May 1996): 460–471.

Gravois, John. "The De Soto Delusion," *Slate* [online] (29 January 2005). www.slate.com/id/2112792

Macours, Karen. "Insecurity of Property Rights and Matching in the Tenancy Market" (August 2004). www.sais-jhu.edu/faculty/kmacours/pdf_research/Matching_WP.pdf

Miceli, Thomas, C.F. Sirmans, and Joseph Kieyah. "The Demand for Land Title Registration: Theory with Evidence from Kenya," *American Law and Economics Review*, 3, no. 2 (2001): 275–287.

Migot-Adholla, Shem, et al. "Indigenous Land Rights Systems in Sub-Saharan Africa: A Constraint on Productivity?" *The World Bank Economic Review*, 5, no. 1 (1991): 155–175.

Smets, Peer. "The Market Does Not Work for All; and Not Just Because of Lacking Property Titles," *Focaal–European Journal of Anthropology*, 41 (2003): 193–196.

Skidelsky, Robert. "The Wealth of (Some) Nations," *New York Times* (24 December 2000).

InfoTrac® College Edition

Search for the following articles in the InfoTrac® database:

Field, Erica. "Property Rights, Community Public Goods, and Household Time Allocation in Urban Squatter Communities: Evidence from Peru," *William and Mary Law Review*, 45, no. 3 (February 2004): 837–887.

Lanjouw, Jean O., and Philip Levy. "A Difficult Question in Deed: A Cost-Benefit Framework for Titling Programs," *William and Mary Law Review*, 45, no. 3 (February 2004): 889–951.

Ondetti, Gabriel. "Landing Votes: Representation and Land Reform in Latin America," *Political Science Quarterly*, 120, no. 3 (Fall 2005): 544–545.

For more articles, enter:
"land tenure," "informal economy," or "mystery of capital" in the keyword search.

Web Resources

THE INSTITUTE FOR LIBERTY AND DEMOCRACY

www.ild.org.pe

Since 1981, Hernando de Soto's research team has been researching the informal economy and the challenges of achieving legal status in developing countries. This research team has developed into the Institute for Liberty and Democracy.

THE WORLD ECONOMIC FORUM

www.weforum.org

The World Economic Forum is a Swiss-based non-profit organization that brings together leaders in corporate, charitable, and governmental capacities to discuss the problems of economic development. Under the motto of "entrepreneurship in the global public interest," it seeks business-friendly solutions to problems of world development.

CENTER FOR GLOBAL LIBERTY AND PROSPERITY

www.cato.org/economicliberty

The Cato Institute provides pro-market liberal policy solutions to a wide array of policy areas. Its Center for Global Liberty and Prosperity provides resources aimed at the expansion of liberal market-friendly solutions in the developing world.

PART THREE

DEVELOPMENT AND INTERNATIONAL INSTITUTIONS

Do current World Bank and IMF lending and aid models alleviate poverty?

Do Canadian government foreign aid programs help to alleviate poverty?

Are the Millennium Development Goals achievable?

Has the adoption of a rights-based approach to development failed?

Has gender mainstreaming been effective?

Do Current World Bank and IMF Lending and Aid Models Alleviate Poverty?

✔ **YES**
BRIAN AMES, WARD BROWN, SHANTA DEVARAJAN, AND ALEJANDRO
IZQUIERDO, *Macroeconomic Policy and Poverty Reduction*. Prepared by
the International Monetary Fund and World Bank, August 2001

✗ **NO**
ADAM DAVIDSON-HARDEN, "An 'Empty Glass': How the Bretton Woods
Institutions Sustain and Exacerbate Poverty"

In the 1990s, major international lending agencies began a fundamental re-examination of how grants and loans are delivered, particularly to the poorest of the developing countries. The impetus for this review was the ongoing criticism of the lending policies of the International Monetary Fund (IMF) and the World Bank undertaken within the framework of their "structural adjustment programs" (SAPs), which many argued had failed to adequately address the needs of the poorest populations. Evaluation of the SAPs had shown that they had produced only limited results in terms of promoting sustained growth of the economy, while poverty and social inequalities often increased as a result of their implementation. Critics suggested that there needed to be greater attention to social reforms that made a more coherent linkage between macroeconomic, structural changes, and more equitable social policies. In addition, studies had shown that the conventional poverty reduction strategies pursued by many development countries have produced disappointing results because of their failure to adequately engage civil society actors and allow for more participatory forms of governance.

As a result of these discussions, in 1999 the World Bank and IMF adopted a new set of policies and procedures to guide their lending to developing countries. This approach, known as the Poverty Reduction Strategy Paper (PRSP), set out a process that very poor countries would need to follow in order to access any of the concessionary lending facilities of either of the agencies, including debt relief under the Highly Indebted Poor Countries Initiative (HIPC). IMF and the Bank saw these changes as constituting a significant departure from their previous way of dealing with low-income countries.

According to the new procedures, each country wishing to receive assistance from the World Bank and IMF is expected to develop a Poverty Reduction Strategy Paper (PRSP). This document sets out a national strategy for integrating poverty reduction into the macroeconomic policymaking of recipient governments. In preparing this document, the recipient government confers with a broad base of stakeholders in the civil society and private sectors in regards to the formulation, implementation, and monitoring of the PRSP. The hope is that this will give the recipient country a greater sense of ownership and legitimacy of the reforms measures that are agreed to. By fostering a stronger ownership of the strategy and participation among a broader range of stakeholders, it is hoped that a more successful and sustained implementation will occur than was the case for the previous Structural Adjustment Programs.

Proponents of the PRSP also contend that the new approach will enable a shift away from the SAP's top-down approach to a more bottom-up approach that would more successfully include the poor. In explaining the new approach, the World Bank argued that by increasing the voice and participation of the poor in decision-making, not only would the new poverty reduction policies be given more legitimacy, but also the popular input would actually improve the quality and the policies and services provided. Such popular participation would ensure that a stronger political basis for the pursuit a "pro-poor growth strategy" would be built.

Both the Bank and IMF have been careful to emphasize that they are not proposing a single template for a PRSP, a common criticism of the former SAP agreements. Rather, they suggest that each nation should develop its own unique PRSP around the following five core principles. Each PRSP must be:

- country-driven and owned, founded on broad-based participatory processes for formulation, implementation, and outcome-based monitoring;

- results-oriented, focusing on outcomes that would benefit the poor;

- comprehensive in scope, recognizing the multidimensional nature of the causes of poverty and measures to attack it;

- partnership-oriented, providing a basis for the active, coordinated participation of development partners (bilateral, multilateral, non-governmental) in supporting country strategies; and

- based on a medium- and long-term perspective for poverty reduction, recognizing that sustained poverty reduction cannot be achieved overnight.

Each recipient country is expected to take the lead in designing and implementing its own development strategies. A broad level of consultation and participation among civil society and private sectors is intended to ensure both a wide consensus on policies and a more effective integration of local values into the policy initiatives. A well prepared PRSP would lay out a plan to both reduce poverty and increase sustainable economic growth. Rather than just addressing macroeconomic and structural changes designed to produce economic growth, the PRSP would address improvement in participatory governance, sectoral policies for reducing poverty, and realistic and appropriate funding levels for social programs.

Both the World Bank and IMF claim that the PRSP approach represents a radical departure to their previous lending policies. In particular, they argue that the new approach demonstrates their sensitivity to criticism and ability to adapt to demands to make their programs more focused on poverty reduction and the fostering of popular participation.

But to what extent do the current lending policies represent a new and radical departure from the past? In the first reading, a group of economists from IMF and the World Bank set out the case for the new Poverty Reduction Strategy approach. In the second reading, Adam Davidson-Harden provides a careful reading and critique of this approach. He argues that elements of the neoliberal focus on economic growth, which typified the era of structural adjustment, still undergirds the new approach. As a result, he suggests that the PRSP should be seen as more of an effort at "rebranding" of old policies that have already been called into question rather than a radically new departure.

✔ YES
Macroeconomic Policy and Poverty Reduction
BRIAN AMES, WARD BROWN, SHANTA DEVARAJAN,
AND ALEJANDRO IZQUIERDO

1. INTRODUCTION

Poverty is a multidimensional problem that goes beyond economics to include, among other things, social, political, and cultural issues (see Box 7.1). Therefore, solutions to poverty cannot be based exclusively on economic policies, but require a comprehensive set of well-coordinated measures. Indeed, this is the foundation for the rationale underlying comprehensive poverty reduction strategies. So why focus on macroeconomic issues? Because economic growth is the single most important factor influencing poverty, and macroeconomic stability is essential for high and sustainable rates of growth. Hence, macroeconomic stability should be a key component of any poverty reduction strategy.

Macroeconomic stability by itself, however, does not ensure high rates of economic growth. In most cases, sustained high rates of growth also depend upon key structural measures, such as regulatory reform, privatization, civil service reform, improved governance, trade liberalization, and banking sector reform, many of which are discussed at length in the *Poverty Reduction Strategy Sourcebook*, published by the World Bank. Moreover, growth alone is not sufficient for poverty reduction.

BOX 7.1
DEFINITION AND MEASUREMENT OF POVERTY

The World Bank's 2000 World Development Report defines poverty as an unacceptable deprivation in human well-being that can comprise both physiological and social deprivation. Physiological deprivation involves the non-fulfillment of basic material or biological needs, including inadequate nutrition, health, education, and shelter. A person can be considered poor if he or she is unable to secure the goods and services to meet these basic material needs. The concept of physiological deprivation is thus closely related to, but can extend beyond, low monetary income and consumption levels. Social deprivation widens the concept of deprivation to include risk, vulnerability, lack of autonomy, powerlessness, and lack of self-respect. Given that countries' definitions of deprivation often go beyond physiological deprivation and sometimes give greater weight to social deprivation, local populations (including poor communities) should be engaged in the dialogue that leads to the most appropriate definition of poverty in a country.

Growth associated with progressive distributional changes will have a greater impact on poverty than growth that leaves distribution unchanged. Hence, policies that improve the distribution of income and assets within a society, such as land tenure reform, pro-poor public expenditure, and measures to increase the poor's access to financial markets, will also form essential elements of a country's poverty reduction strategy.

To safeguard macroeconomic stability, the government budget, including the country's poverty reduction strategies, must be financed in a sustainable, noninflationary manner. The formulation and integration of a country's macroeconomic policy and poverty reduction strategy are iterative processes. Poverty reduction strategies need first to be articulated (i.e., objectives and policies specified), then costed, and finally financed within the overall budget in a noninflationary manner. The amount of finance, much of which will be on concessional terms, is, however, not necessarily fixed during this process: if credible poverty reduction strategies cannot be financed from available resources, World Bank and IMF staff should and will actively assist countries in their efforts to raise additional financial support from the donor community. Nonetheless, in situations where financing gaps remain, a country would have to revisit the intermediate objectives of their strategy and reexamine their priorities. Except in cases where macroeconomic imbalances are severe, there will usually be some scope for flexibility in setting short-term macroeconomic targets. However, the objective of macroeconomic stability should not be compromised.

2. THE LINKS BETWEEN MACROECONOMIC POLICY AND POVERTY REDUCTION: GROWTH MATTERS

Economic growth is the *single most important factor* influencing poverty. Numerous statistical studies have found a strong association between national per capita income and national poverty indicators, using both income and nonincome measures of poverty. One recent study consisting of 80 countries covering four decades found that, on average, the income of the bottom one-fifth of the population rose one-for-one with the overall growth of the economy as defined by per capita GDP (Dollar and Kraay, 2000). Moreover, the study found that the effect of growth on the income of the poor was on average no different in poor countries than in rich countries, that the poverty–growth relationship had not changed in recent years, and that policy-induced growth was as good for the poor as it was for the overall population. Another study that looked at 143 growth episodes also found that the "growth effect" dominated, with the "distribution effect" being important in only a minority of cases (White and Anderson, forthcoming). These studies, however, establish association, but not causation. In fact, the causality could well go the other way. In such cases, poverty reduction could in fact be necessary to implement stable macroeconomic policies or to achieve higher growth.

Studies show that capital accumulation by the private sector drives growth. Therefore, a key objective of a country's poverty reduction strategy should be to establish conditions that facilitate private sector investment. No magic bullet can guarantee increased rates of private sector investment. Instead, in addition to a sustainable and stable set of macroeconomic policies, a country's poverty reduction policy agenda should, in most cases, extend across a variety of policy areas, including privatization, trade liberalization, banking and financial sector reforms, labor markets, the regulatory environment, and the judicial system. The agenda will certainly include increased and more efficient public investment in a country's health, education, and other priority social service sectors.

Macroeconomic Stability Is Necessary for Growth

Macroeconomic stability is the cornerstone of any successful effort to increase private sector development and economic growth. Cross-country regressions using a large sample of countries suggest that growth, investment, and productivity are positively correlated with macroeconomic stability (Easterly and Kraay, 1999). Although it is difficult to prove the direction of causation, these results confirm that *macroeconomic instability has generally been associated with poor growth performance.* Without macroeconomic stability, domestic and foreign investors will stay away and resources will be diverted elsewhere. In fact, econometric evidence of investment behavior indicates that in addition to conventional factors (i.e., past growth of economic activity, real interest rates, and private sector credit), private investment is significantly and negatively influenced by uncertainty and macroeconomic instability (see, for example, Ramey and Ramey, 1995).

[...]

Macroeconomic Instability Hurts the Poor

In addition to low (and sometimes even negative) growth rates, other aspects of macroeconomic instability can place a heavy burden on the poor. Inflation, for example, is a regressive and arbitrary tax, the burden of which is typically borne disproportionately by those in lower income brackets. The reason is twofold. First, the poor tend to hold most of their financial assets in the form of cash rather than in interest-bearing assets. Second, they are generally less able than are the better off to protect the real value of their incomes and assets from inflation. In consequence, price jumps generally erode the real wages and assets of the poor more than those of the non-poor. Moreover, beyond certain thresholds, inflation also curbs output growth, an effect that will impact even those among the poor who infrequently use money for economic transactions. In addition, low output growth that is typically associated with instability can have a longer-term impact on poverty (a phenomenon known as "hysteresis"). This phenomenon typically operates through shocks to the human capital of the poor. In Africa, for instance, there is evidence that children from poor families drop out of school during crises. Similarly, studies for Latin American countries suggest that adverse terms-of-trade shocks explain part of the decline of schooling attainment (see, for example, Behrman, Duryea, and Szeleky, 1999).

Composition and Distribution of Growth Also Matter

Although economic growth is the engine of poverty reduction, it works more effectively in some situations than in others. Two key factors that appear to determine the impact of growth on poverty are the *distributional patterns* and the *sectoral composition* of growth.

If the benefits of growth are translated into poverty reduction through the existing distribution of income, then more equal societies will be *more efficient transformers of growth into poverty reduction.* A number of empirical studies have found that the responsiveness of income poverty to growth increases significantly as inequality is lowered. This is also supported by a recent cross-country study that found that the more equal the distribution of income in a country, the greater the impact of growth on the number of people in poverty (Ravallion, 1997). Others have suggested that greater equity comes at the expense of lower growth and that there is a trade-off between growth and equity when it comes to poverty reduction. A large number of recent empirical studies, however, have found that there is not necessarily such a trade-off and that equity in its various dimensions is growth enhancing.

The *sectoral composition* of growth can determine the impact that growth will have on poverty. Conventional wisdom has been that growth in sectors of the economy where the poor are concentrated will have a greater impact on reducing poverty than growth in other sectors—indeed, this is almost a tautology. For example, it is often argued that in countries where most of the poor live in rural areas, agricultural growth reduces poverty because it generates income for poor farmers and increases the demand for goods and services that can easily be produced by the poor. Various country-specific and cross-country studies have shown that growth in the agricultural and tertiary sectors has had a major effect on reducing poverty, while growth in manufacturing has not. This reinforces the case for duty-free access to industrial country markets for agricultural exports from low-income countries. The links may be more complex over the long run, however. While faster growth in agriculture may address rural poverty in the short-term, reliance on agricultural activity may also intensify output variability, which, in turn, would contribute to increasing rather than decreasing poverty. A more diversified economy with a vibrant manufacturing sector might offer the best chances for a sustainable improvement in living standards in the long run.

What are the implications of these empirical findings for macroeconomic policy? First, in light of the importance of growth for poverty reduction, and of macroeconomic stability for growth, the broad objective of macroeconomic policy should be the establishment, or strengthening, of macroeconomic stability. Policymakers should therefore define a set of attainable macroeconomic targets (i.e., growth, inflation, external debt, and net international reserves) with the objective of maintaining macroeconomic stability, and pursue macroeconomic policies (fiscal, monetary, and exchange rate) consistent with those targets. In cases where macroeconomic imbalances are less severe, a range of possible targets may be consistent with the objective of stabilization. Precise targets can then be set within that range, in accordance with the goals and priorities in the country's poverty reduction strategy (see the section on fiscal policy later in this [essay]).

Second, most developing countries will likely have substantial scope for enhancing the quality of growth, that is, the degree to which the poor share in the fruits of such growth, through policies aimed at improving income distribution. These policies (e.g., land tenure reform, changes in marginal and average tax rates, increases in pro-poor social spending, etc.) often are politically charged, and usually require supporting structural and governance reforms that would empower the poor to demand resources and/or ensure that resources intended for them are not diverted to other groups of the population. As these topics pertain more broadly to political economy, rather than exclusively to macroeconomics, they are beyond the scope of this [essay]. But they reinforce the point that economic growth alone is not sufficient for poverty reduction and that complementary redistributional policies may be needed to ensure that the poor benefit from growth.

Finally, while issues regarding the composition of growth also go beyond strict macroeconomics, several general policy observations can be made. There is a general consensus that policies that introduce distortions in order to influence growth in a particular sector can hamper overall growth. The industrial policies pursued by many African developing countries in the 1960s have long been discredited (World Bank, 1982). Instead, strategies for sector specific growth should focus on removing distortions that impede growth in a particular sector. In addition, policymakers should implement policies that will empower the poor and create the conditions that would permit them to move into new as well as existing areas of opportunity, thereby allowing them to better share in the fruits of economic growth. The objectives of such policies should include creating a stable environment and level playing field conducive to private sector investment and broad-based economic growth; removing the cultural, social, and economic constraints that prevent the poor from making full use of their existing asset base and accessing markets; and increasing the human capital base of the poor through the provision of basic health and education services. Using these policies, and the redistributive policies described above, policymakers can target "pro-poor" growth—that is, they can attempt to maximize the beneficial impact of sustained economic growth on poverty reduction.

[...]

Sources of Instability

There are two main sources of economic instability, namely exogenous shocks and inappropriate policies. Exogenous shocks (e.g., terms of trade shocks, natural disasters, reversals in capital flows, etc.) can throw an economy into disequilibrium and require compensatory action. For example, many low income countries have a narrow export base, often centered on one or two key commodities. Shocks to the world price of these commodities can therefore have a strong impact on the country's income. Even diversified economies, however, are routinely hit by exogenous shocks, although, reflecting their greater diversification, shocks usually need to be particularly large or long-lasting to destabilize such an economy. Alternatively, a disequilibrium can be "self-induced" by poor macroeconomic management. For example, an excessively loose fiscal stance can increase aggregate demand for goods and services, which places pressure on the country's external balance of payments as well as on the domestic price level. At times, economic crises are the result of both external shocks and poor management.

Stabilization

In most cases, addressing instability (i.e., stabilization) will require policy *adjustment*; whereby a government introduces new measures (possibly combined with new policy targets) in response to the change in circumstances. Adjustment will typically be necessary if the source of instability is a permanent (i.e., systemic) external shock or the result of earlier, inappropriate macroeconomic policies. However, if the source of instability can be clearly identified as a temporary shock (e.g., a one-time event) then it may be appropriate for a country to accommodate it. Identifying whether a particular shock is temporary or is likely to persist is easier said than done. Since there is often a considerable degree of uncertainty surrounding such a judgment, it is usually wise to err somewhat on the side of caution by assuming that the shock will largely persist and by basing the corresponding policy response on the appropriate adjustment.

In most circumstances where adjustment is necessary, both monetary (or exchange rate) and fiscal instruments will have to be used. In particular, successful adjustment to a permanent unfavorable shock that worsens the balance of payments will often require a sustained tightening of the fiscal stance, as this is the most immediate and effective way to increase domestic savings and to reduce domestic demand—two objectives typically at the center of stabilization programs.

Adjustment policies may contribute to a temporary contraction of economic activity, but this contingency should not be used to argue against implementing adjustment policies altogether, as the alternative may be worse. Attempting to sustain aggregate demand through unsustainable policies will almost certainly aggravate the long-run cost of a shock, and could even fail in the short run to the extent that it undermines confidence. In the long run, greater benefits to the poor are to be had as a result of the restoration of macroeconomic stability. The appropriate policies to protect the poor during adjustment are to maintain, or even increase, social expenditures and to adopt, where feasible, compensatory measures that would insulate or offset temporary adverse impacts to the fullest extent possible. This is best done by devoting resources to the establishment of effective social safety nets, as an enduring part of a country's poverty reduction strategy, rather than as a response to crisis. Countries that lack such resources/safety nets could be forced to either subject their poor to the short-term adverse effects of stabilization or to delay the pace with which macroeconomic adjustment proceeds (and put off the corresponding long-term benefits to economic growth and poverty reduction).

Countries in macroeconomic crisis typically have little choice but to stabilize quickly, but for countries in the "gray" area of partial stability, finding the right pace may prove difficult. In some cases, a lack of financing will drive the pace of stabilization. Where financing is not a constraint, however, policymakers will need to assess and carefully weigh various factors on a case-by-case basis in choosing the most appropriate pace of stabilization.

Elements of Macroeconomic Stability

Macroeconomic policies influence and contribute to the attainment of rapid, sustainable economic growth aimed at poverty reduction in a variety of ways. By pursuing sound economic policies, policymakers send clear signals to the private sector. The extent to which policymakers are able to establish a *track record of policy implementation* will influence private sector confidence, which will, in turn, impact upon investment, economic growth, and poverty outcomes.

Prudent macroeconomic policies can result in *low and stable inflation.* Inflation hurts the poor by lowering growth and by redistributing real incomes and wealth to the detriment of those in society least able to defend their economic interests. High inflation can also introduce high volatility in relative prices and make investment a risky decision. Unless inflation starts at very high levels, rapid disinflation can also have short-run output costs, which need to be weighed against the costs of continuing inflation.

By moving toward *debt sustainability*, policymakers will help create the conditions for steady and continuous progress on growth and poverty reduction by removing uncertainty as to whether a government will be able to service new debt. By keeping domestic and external debt at levels that can be serviced in a sustainable manner without unduly squeezing nondebt expenditure, policymakers can also ensure that adequate domestic resources are available to finance essential social programs.

Inappropriate exchange rate policies distort the composition of growth by influencing the price of tradable versus nontradable goods. Household survey data for a number of countries indicate that the poor tend to consume higher amounts of nontradable goods while generating relatively more of their income from tradable goods (Sahn, Dorosh, and Younger, 1997). Hence, in addition to distorting trade and inhibiting growth, an overly appreciated exchange rate can impair the relative incomes and purchasing power of the poor.

By building and maintaining an *adequate level of net international reserves,* a country can weather a temporary shock without having to reduce essential pro-poor spending. External shocks can be particularly detrimental to the poor because they can lower real wages, increase unemployment, reduce nonlabor income, and limit private and net government transfers. The level of "adequate" reserves depends on the choice of exchange rate regime.

[...]

Fiscal Policy

Fiscal policy can have a direct impact on the poor, both through the government's overall fiscal stance and through the distributional implications of tax policy and public spending. Structural fiscal reforms in budget and treasury management, public administration, governance, transparency, and accountability can also benefit the poor in terms of more efficient and better targeted use of public resources. As indicated above, there is no rigid, pre-determined limit on what would be an appropriate fiscal deficit. An assessment would need to be based on the particular circumstances facing the country, its medium-term macroeconomic outlook, and the scope for external budgetary assistance. The terms on which external assistance is available are also important. There is a strong case, for instance, for allowing higher grants to translate into higher spending and deficits, to the extent that those grants can reasonably be expected to continue in the future, and provided that the resources can be used effectively.

With regard to the composition of public expenditure, policymakers will need to assess not only the appropriateness of the proposed poverty reduction spending program, but also of planned nondiscretionary, and discretionary nonpriority, spending. In so doing, they will need to take into particular consideration the distributional and growth impact of spending in each area and place due emphasis on spending programs that are pro-poor (e.g., certain programs in health, education, and infrastructure) and on the efficient delivery of essential public services (e.g., public health, public education, social welfare, etc.). In examining these expenditures, policymakers should evaluate the extent to which government intervention in general, and public spending in particular, can be justified on grounds of market failure and/or redistribution.

Policymakers must also ask themselves whether the envisaged public goods or services can be delivered efficiently (e.g., targeted at the intended beneficiaries) and, if not, whether appropriate mechanisms and/or incentives can be put in place to ensure such efficient delivery. Countries should begin by assessing in a frank manner their administrative capacity at both the national and subnational levels to deliver well-targeted, essential public services in support of poverty reduction. In this regard, policymakers should consider the extent to which both technical assistance and the private sector can play a role in improving the delivery of these services.

In the context of medium-term budget planning, policymakers should consider the scope for reallocating existing government spending into priority areas and away from nonproductive spending, including areas where a rationale for public intervention does not exist. Operation and maintenance expenditure tied to capital spending should also be reviewed with a critical eye. The quality of public expenditure could be assessed in the context of a public expenditure review with the assistance of multilateral and/or bilateral donors. Policymakers could then assess the new poverty reduction projects and activities that have been identified in the context of the poverty reduction strategy and integrate them into the preliminary spending program. In so doing, they should attempt to rank the poverty programs in order of relative importance in line with the country's social and economic priorities, the market failure/redistribution criteria identified above, and the country's absorptive capacity in the light of existing institutional and administrative constraints. If spending cuts are deemed necessary in the context of the integrated poverty reduction/macroeconomic framework, policymakers should refer back to the ranking of the spending program based on the relative importance and priority assigned to each activity.

A key aspect of any poverty reduction strategy will be an assessment of the impact of the present tax and nontax system on the poor. An important medium-term objective for many developing countries will be to raise domestic revenue levels with a view to providing additional revenue in support of their poverty reduction strategies. The existing revenue base should be reviewed relative to its capacity to provide for the poverty spending requirements from nonbank domestic financing. Revenues should be raised in as economically neutral a manner as possible, while taking into consideration equity concerns and administrative capacities.

In a developing country, taking account of allocational effects means that the tax system in particular should not attempt to affect savings and investment—experience indicates that aggregate savings and investment tend to be insensitive to taxes, with the result that the tax system typically only affects the allocation of those aggregates across alternative forms. As regards equity, the tax system should be assessed with respect to its direct and indirect impact on the poor. It is difficult to have a tax system that is both efficient and progressive, particularly in those countries without a well-developed tax administration. Therefore, governments should seek to determine a distribution of tax burdens seen as broadly fair rather than use the tax system to achieve a drastic income redistribution.

[...]

The scope for domestic budgetary financing will depend on a number of factors, including the sustainable rate of monetary growth, the credit requirements of the private sector, the relative productivity of public investment, and the desired target for net international reserves. Sacrificing low inflation (through faster monetary growth) to finance additional expenditure is generally not an effective means to reduce poverty because the poor are most vulnerable to price increases. At the same time, since private sector development stands at the center of any poverty reduction strategy, governments need to take into account the extent to which public sector borrowing "crowds out" the private sector's access to credit, thereby undermining the country's growth and inflation objectives. At times, public sector borrowing can also "crowd in" private sector investment by putting in place critical infrastructure necessary for private enterprise to flourish. Given that at any point in time there is a finite amount of credit available in an economy, policymakers must therefore assess the relative productivity of public investment versus private investment and determine the amount of domestic budgetary financing that would be consistent with the need to maintain low inflation and support sustainable economic growth.

The amount and type of available external resources to finance the budget will vary depending on the particular circumstances facing the country. Countries that have access to external grants need to consider what amount is available and sustainable under the present circumstances. The same is true in the case of external debt, but policymakers also need to determine whether the terms on such borrowing are appropriate and whether the added debt burden is sustainable. To the extent that a country is benefiting from, or may benefit from, external debt relief under the enhanced Heavily Indebted Poor Countries (HIPC) Initiative, net resource flows—flows that are predictable over the medium term—will be freed up to finance poverty-related budgetary expenditure. Domestic debt reduction could also represent a viable use of additional concessional foreign assistance, since it would both free up government resources to be directed at priority poverty expenditure, as well as free up additional domestic credit for use by the private sector.

There may be a limit to the amount of additional external financing that a country would deem to be appropriate, however. For example, there may be absorptive capacity constraints that could drive up domestic wages and prices, as well as appreciate the exchange rate and render the country's exports less competitive, thereby threatening both stability and growth. The extent of such pressures will depend on how much of the additional aid is spent on imports versus domestic nontraded goods and services. There may also be uncertainty regarding aid flows, especially over the medium term, as well as considerations regarding long-term dependency on external official aid. In the absence of medium-term commitments of aid, policymakers may therefore wish to be cautious in assuming what levels of assistance would be forthcoming in the future.

[...]

External Shocks and the Choice of Exchange Rate Regime The choice of exchange rate regime—fixed or flexible—depends crucially on the nature of the economic shocks that affect the economy, as well as the structural features of the economy, which may either mitigate or amplify these shocks. Choosing a fixed exchange rate regime when these underlying features of the economy are not supportive leaves a country more exposed to the possibility of an external crisis, which can result in the ultimate abandonment of the peg. In addition, shocks to output can have a strong impact on the poor. Since different exchange rate regimes have different insulating properties vis-à-vis certain types of shocks, choosing the regime that best insulates the economy will serve to moderate fluctuations in output, and thereby best serve the poor.

For example, if the predominant source of disturbance to an economy is shocks to the terms of trade, a flexible exchange rate regime may be best because the nominal exchange rate is free to adjust in response to the shock and bring the real exchange rate to its new equilibrium (see, for example, Devarajan and Rodrik, 1992). Alternatively, if domestic monetary shocks predominate, such as shocks to the demand for money, output may be best insulated by a fixed exchange rate that allows these shocks to be absorbed by fluctuations in international reserves. Of course, one of the challenges facing the policymaker is to identify which shocks are in fact predominant in a particular economy.

The structural features of the economy may also affect the impact a particular shock has on the economy, as well as the insulating properties of exchange rate regimes. For example, if an economy is characterized by a significant degree of nominal wage rigidity, wages will not fully adjust (at least in the short run) in response to small real shocks, and hence the effect of those shocks on output will be amplified. In these circumstances, even if domestic monetary shocks are important, a flexible exchange rate regime may well be preferable (in contrast to the conclusions above). Another important structural feature is the degree of an economy's openness. Typically the more open an economy is, the greater is its exposure to external shocks. This would argue generally in favor of a flexible exchange rate regime. However, if an open economy is sufficiently diversified (i.e., it trades a wide range of goods and services) and if its prices are sufficiently flexible, then a fixed exchange rate may be preferable because the volatility of flexible exchange rates may impede international trade, and thus lower external demand (although the evidence on this is mixed). In conclusion, these various pros and cons of fixed versus flexible exchange rate regimes need to be carefully assessed and weighed on a case-by-case basis—again, there is no universal "right answer."

Policies to Insulate the Poor Against Shocks

Given that the poor are adversely affected by macroeconomic shocks, what should governments do about it? The question can be divided into two parts: How should economic policy be designed to cushion the impact of shocks on the poor, in particular during times of crisis and/or adjustment? What specific policies can governments undertake to insulate the poor from the consequences of shocks by removing existing distortive policies?

Social Safety Nets Sound macroeconomic policies will help a country to reduce its exposure to macroeconomic shocks, but there is no cost-effective policy that will insure against *all* possible shocks. It is therefore crucial to have *social safety nets* in place to ensure that poor households are able to maintain minimum consumption levels and access to basic social services during periods of crisis. Social safety net measures are also necessary to protect the poor from shocks imposed on them during periods of economic reform and adjustment. Safety nets include public work programs, limited food subsidies, transfers to compensate for income loss, social funds, fee waivers, and scholarships for essential services such as education and health. The specific mix of measures will depend on the particular characteristics of the poor and their vulnerability to shocks and should be well-targeted and designed in most cases to provide temporary support.

Equally important, the resources allocated to social safety nets should be protected during economic crises and/or adjustment, when fiscal tightening may be necessary. Governments should have budgetary guidelines approved by their legislatures that prioritize and protect poverty-related programs during periods of crisis and provide a clear course of action that ensures access of the poor to basic social services during periods of austerity (see Lustig, forthcoming). As will be discussed below, countercyclical fiscal policies can also ensure the availability of funds for financing safety nets during crises.

Another important factor to consider is that safety nets should already be operating before economies get hit by shocks so that they can be effective in times of distress (for a more detailed account, see World Bank, 2000). However, if a shock occurs before appropriate safety nets have been developed, then "second-best" social protection policies may be necessary. For instance, food subsidies have been found to be inefficient and often benefiting the non-poor, and most reform programs call for their reduction or even elimination. However, after a severe shock such as the 1997–98 East Asian financial crisis, when countries like Indonesia lacked comprehensive safety nets, existing food subsidies were probably the only means of preventing widespread malnutrition and starvation. In the context of a country's reform process, however, these subsidies should be replaced with better targeted and less distorting transfers to the poor.

[...]

Finally, and most important, governments can do a lot to reduce the pro-cyclical nature of their fiscal policies by saving rather than spending windfalls following positive shocks and ideally using those savings as a buffer for expenditures against negative shocks. A cautious approach would be for the government to "treat every favorable shock as temporary and every adverse one as permanent," although judgment would also depend on, among other things, the availability of financing (Little, and others, 1993). However, even this rule of thumb may not be enough. Governments need to find ways of "tying their hands" to resist the pressure to spend windfall revenues (Devarajan, 1999). For example, when the source of revenue is publicly owned, such as oil or other natural resource, it may be appropriate to save the windfall revenues abroad, with strict rules on how much of it can be repatriated. Countries such as Colombia, Chile, and Botswana have tried variants of this strategy, with benefits not just for overall macroeconomic management, but also for protecting the poor during adverse shocks, since saved funds during good times can be applied to financing of safety nets during crisis.

✘ NO

An "Empty Glass": How the Bretton Woods Institutions Sustain and Exacerbate Poverty*
ADAM DAVIDSON-HARDEN

INTRODUCTION

As the international community continues in a project of seemingly earnest self-scrutiny concerning the feasibility of reaching the modest targets reflected in the Millennium Development Goals (MDGs)—the successor to earlier, failed benchmarks—citizens of both the global South and North remain the principal witnesses to the track record of the Bretton Woods Institutions (BWIs), the World Bank and International Monetary Fund (herein referred to as the Bank and Fund), in their stated intentions and associated efforts to alleviate global poverty. The outstanding question casting a long shadow on these institutions is whether the proverbial glass is seen as "half-full" or "half-empty" in this regard. With respect to the track record of these international financial institutions (IFIs) as arbiters of development finance and policy, culpability of the Bank and Fund for their failures in helping to address global poverty has been routinely dismissed along with promulgated visions of progress "around the next bend" or "over the next hill". With only that further commitment to initiatives of trade liberalization, privatization, or investment deregulation, it is argued by the BWIs that paradise is seemingly around the corner. Skeptics question both the earnestness and truthfulness of the Bank and Fund (as well as the northern economic and political powers behind them), however, and see these institutions' potential for development as an either nearly or completely "empty glass," to follow the saying.

In particular, the term "structural adjustment" stands as a damning icon for the destructive social impact and legacy of the BWIs in the global South. With increasing global recognition—including within the BWIs themselves—that structural adjustment policies have hurt rather than helped the world's poor, the turn of the 21st century has seen a momentous "re-branding" of the way the Bank and Fund seek to manage the odious debts of the global South and its beleaguered citizens. The term "poverty reduction" is now as ubiquitous as "structural adjustment" once was in the lexicon of the BWIs, and its use as a mantra to help legitimate and justify the current modus operandi of these institutions has been well established. Though ever-eager to take advantage of any meagre concessions in terms of debt relief and allowance for social policy shifts favouring investment in crucial social services such as health and education, both observers of and participants in the deliberately inclusive Poverty Reduction Strategy Paper (PRSP) processes in heavily indebted countries continue to grapple with a set of core conditions that act as an unalterable foundation for the Bank and Fund, rooted in policies and economic ideologies of "free trade" or global economic integration, as well as financial liberalization, privatization, deregulation, and restrictive regimes for social spending (a policy recipe known to critics and proponents as economic neoliberalism, or colloquially, the "Washington Consensus"[1]). This set of prescriptions—known among insiders as "structural conditionalities" on loans and aid—remain consistent with the policy-based lending formulas stubbornly adhered to by the BWIs throughout the "era" of structural adjustment. This regime of conditionality, referred to as the "Washington Consensus," is very much alive and continues to act as a frustrating barrier toward effective models of human development. Through the ideological furtherance of unfair rules and systems of debt, aid, and trade, the Bank and Fund work to sustain and exacerbate global poverty, particularly in the countries that are most susceptible to imposed conditionalities. This article will briefly touch upon two essential characteristics of the BWIs' ideological framework, which, if unchanged, will continue to be responsible for the immiseration of a substantial portion of humanity into the 21st century. These are a) the proffering of false arguments concerning the state of global poverty and the role of the BWIs' preferred policies in alleviating it; and b) the ongoing entrenchment of market-based or "neoliberal" solutions for development as conditions for loans and aid within current BWI frameworks for "poverty reduction," in the context of an unfair global trade system.

COMING TO TERMS WITH THE NUMBERS ON POVERTY AND THE BWIs' CULPABILITY

The approach to development finance espoused by the BWIs remains rooted in essentially myopic approaches to measuring "success" with respect to outcomes related to poverty. Despite musings and discussions about more holistic measures, the Bank and Fund remain committed to more simplistic economic definitions of poverty as opposed to multidimensional and comprehensive interpretations. In addition, the principal criterion underlying all of the BWIs' methodology in evaluating poverty reduction programs remains the consideration of aggregate economic growth as a precondition for addressing poverty. Consequently, a standard set of macroeconomic adjustment policies are assumed to be the only means of achieving such growth by the BWIs, policies that themselves are contributors to poverty and inequality, as this article will endeavour to show. A principal paradox of this stubborn approach to development economics is evident in the fact that economic growth measures themselves are insufficient, indeed incapable, of constituting any valid measure of social or ecological progress, because of the simple fact that economic growth rates (whether measured through changes in Gross National [or Domestic] Income/Product) only take into account aggregate economic output. Indeed, this is their only purpose. However, inequality, poverty, or ecological degradation may all increase along with positive economic growth.[2] Measures of aggregate economic growth are at best an extremely limited means of measuring progress in development, and at worst, a completely misrepresentative tool for this goal, one continually taken for granted by the BWIs in current strategies and planning around policies for "poverty reduction".[3] Consequently, the piece by Bank and Fund authors included in this volume, "Macroeconomic Policy and Poverty Reduction,"[4] is an excellent example of how the discourse of the BWIs concerning poverty remains rooted in disingenuous arguments about the effectiveness of these institutions' policies in the global South.

Associated with an ongoing, drawn-out debate surrounding economic growth and its relationship to global poverty, a sharp, detailed, and comprehensive critique of the BWIs' proffered numbers and statistics suggesting a decline in global poverty rates has surfaced in recent years.[5] Through pointing out the fact that data used to calculate rates of poverty by the Bank and Fund are insufficient, inaccurate, and based on incommensurable sources and datasets, it has been suggested that the BWIs consistently obtain lower global poverty rates than could be expected from more effective, comprehensive, and comparable measurements. For instance, accepting an arbitrarily low international poverty line based on a crude figure of U.S. dollars per day, per capita income, Pogge and Reddy effectively argue that the purchasing power of those in poorer countries is erroneously conflated with that of citizens of richer countries by the Bank and Fund. One example of this error is evidenced by the necessity of the global poor to rely on purchases of basic necessities such as food and water to survive, whereas aggregate measures conflate more expensive commodities and services—which only the comparatively wealthy can afford—along with commodities necessary for survival, thus making poverty as measured by crude income seem less prevalent.[6] An alternative measure of poverty might focus, it is suggested, on attempts to measure for multiple dimensions through more qualitative rather than economic and purely quantitative tools. For instance, multidimensional conceptions of poverty can focus on levels of human deprivation seen through the lenses of lack of access to basic needs (shelter, food, water, health services, education, a clean environment), or lack of fulfillment of basic human "capabilities" (in terms of malnutrition, life expectancy, literacy rates, etc.).[7] Economistic conceptions of poverty preferred by the BWIs in the main focus myopically on inaccurate measures of income in dollars per day, per capita, and as such paint a much too optimistic appraisal of the state of global poverty today.[8] Still more accurate measures come from consultation with those affected by BWI programs and policies; one important example of such research will be discussed below.

Considering that the deficiency of the IFIs' predominant method of measuring poverty relates to essential dynamics of global inequality (for instance, in terms of purchasing power), it is perhaps unsurprising that other researchers have forcefully argued that the BWIs employ a related "glass mostly full" approach when it comes to assessing purported progress in levels of within- and between-country inequality during the period of their growing ascendancy in financing development in the global South. Branko Milanovic, himself a Bank researcher, argues in this case that contrary to the dominant discourses of the BWIs, in fact global inequality has been on the rise in the past three decades.[9] In both cases of numbers around poverty and inequality, data from India and China serve to skew the global picture somewhat, which, along with the methodological deficiencies touched on here, lead to a far more sober and grim picture of the reinforcing effects growing global poverty and inequality. A 2006 study undertaken by the World Institute for Development Economics Research (WIDER, affiliated with the United Nations University) confirmed—using comprehensive household survey methods—that 2 percent of the world's wealthy own more than half of all global household wealth, and that the richest 1 percent on their own hold 40 percent of global assets, while the poorer half of the global adult population owns not even 1 percent of household wealth.[10] The phenomenon of such vast social polarization on a global scale accompanied with trends toward worsening poverty is deplorable on its own, even without the evidence linking such trends with increased vulnerability and incidence of violent conflict.[11]

THE TERMS OF THE "DEBT SENTENCE": UNFAIR TRADE, ODIOUS DEBTS, AND A RE-BRANDED NEOLIBERAL "TOOLKIT" FOR "POVERTY REDUCTION"

The previous discussion of the debate around numbers lacks a concrete social or historical context to make the reality of growing poverty and inequality apparent to the reader. However, even this general body of evidence facing us prompts a natural line of questioning concerning how the BWIs—institutions with a stated commitment to alleviating poverty—could be culpable for a precipitous deterioration of the global situation during the same time in which their influence in development agendas has become all the more pronounced. The key to understanding frustration and regression in achieving even modest levels of adequate and ecologically sustainable human development—understood through essential indicators such as health, education, employment and livelihoods, food security, access to safe water, preservation of biodiversity, etc.—lies in appreciating the fact that uneven development today is an outgrowth of a continually uneven and asymmetrical world system with colonial roots. The massive, disproportionately unequal distribution of wealth and attendant severe discrepancies in quality of life in the world today are reflected in the politics of the "debt sentence" that continue to immiserate a substantial portion of humanity. The politics of the debt of the global South have been directly responsible for the imposition of a set of failed, destructive, and still-preferred economic policies that continue to sustain and exacerbate poverty today.

At the same time, the debts themselves are questioned by many as being illegitimate or "odious."[12] The BWIs themselves were initially intended to solve short-term balance of payments problems in the post-WWII context.[13] With the U.S. dominating lending to post-war Europe under the Marshall Plan, the Bank and Fund, particularly beginning under Robert McNamara in the 1970s, began a program of lending to poorer countries. Several exogenous economic shocks, however, contributed to the precipitous ballooning of the debts of these new recipient countries—among which the oil shock of 1973 and the interest rate fluctuations of the early 1980s deserve special credit, raising the level of total external debt among developing countries from $70 billion U.S. in 1973 to approximately $540 billion by 1982. Today, the figure has mushroomed to approximately $2.8 trillion U.S.[14] As a consequence, the estimated $100 billion (an optimistic figure) in debt relief that has been disbursed to recipient countries during the years 1989–2005 does not even equal half of the amount hemorrhaged from sub-Saharan African countries alone in the form of debt service payments between 1980 and 2000, an estimated $240 billion U.S.[15] When one considers—as does a recent report[16]—that the "odiousness" and illegitimacy of such transfers and debts not only stems from unpredictable exogenous shocks but also from the actions of occasional money-hoarding, corrupt dictators (from Galtieri to Mobutu or Marcos, and many others who enjoyed support from the BWIs in their time[17]), the validity of these debts in the eyes of the publics of affected countries can be roundly called into question. In the meantime, the Fund and particularly the Bank have continued to use a discourse of anti-corruption and governance reform as important justifiers for their particular approach to poverty reduction strategies, helping to entrench, as is argued here, the same dynamics that have worsened the situation of poverty in poorer countries.[18]

The reality of the disjuncture between BWI promises of development and the effects of their preferred policies on the ground began to become apparent as the "lost decade" of the 1980s took its cruel course in the global South. Under a neoliberal ideological policy cookie cutter, a "one-size-fits-all" recipe emphasizing trade liberalization in all sectors, currency devaluation, financial liberalization, privatization and deregulation (there are privatization "toolkits" for a variety of sectors, including water and sanitation), and austere and restrictive regimes of social spending in public services such as health and education, countries of the global South watched as structural adjustment took its toll. With the advent of the "strict fiscal discipline" of the BWIs, domestic manufacturing industries suffered and collapsed, domestic finance and investment in critical small- and medium-sized businesses languished,[19] economies were restructured toward export of primary agricultural and natural resource commodities whose value steadily plummeted, and the vital—if meagre—social safety nets in vulnerable states were either emaciated, destroyed, or left to stagnate for lack of funding. In addition, the position of workers was made more tenuous with "flexibilization" of the workforce through changes and relaxations in labour laws. In all cases, women, as the principal caretakers of households in the global South, were disproportionately affected, and the precarious position of indigenous peoples was made even more so. There are obviously regional variations in these trends, though, in the main, the pattern holds. Ironically, the developing states that are most often held up to be contemporary success stories are those which adhered the least to the prescriptions on offer from the BWIs, countries such as China, India, and Singapore, for example (though we must take "success" with a grain of salt here beyond simple economistic terms).[20] Meanwhile, in the unfortunate, debt-ridden countries that had no choice but to accept the strings attached to loans and aid brokered by the Bank and Fund, a fundamental transformation of the state's role in the economy gained pace, one that oriented the state toward facilitation of the market as a principal role, with involvement in service provision (from water, to health and education) also mediated through market mechanisms. In health and education, this neoliberal transformation meant (and continues to mean) the encouragement and demand of the use of "cost-recovery" methods and "demand-side financing" (or user fees, in every day terms) in service provision, while in water, transportation, and other infrastructure (that existed) privatization was (and is) the preferred vehicle for delivering "efficiencies" to "public expenditure management".[21]

Civil society actors and organizations have helped to track and document the impact of these reforms, and their contribution to deepening effects of poverty and inequality as structural adjustment took its course. One such path-breaking and comprehensive research project was the Structural Adjustment Participatory Review Initiative (SAPRI) (SAPRIN, 2004). SAPRI tracked experiences of structural adjustment from the perspective of a large constituency of citizen-driven, participatory review exercises in conjunction with civil society organizations in 12 countries subject to BWI programs. Many core themes emerged from this research, although they coalesced significantly around the shared experience that the standard prescriptions of structural adjustment—and the core conditionalities on loans and aid that enforce it—were directly culpable for increased poverty and inequality in the countries studied (chapter 9, SAPRIN, 2004). Initially undertaken in cooperation with the Bank in the late 1990s under then-President James Wolfensohn, the SAPRI report produced damning evidence of the ongoing and lasting legacy of an ideological adherence to a set of development policies that continues to sustain and exacerbate the poverty affecting the most vulnerable among us.

Of course, given the effects of adjustment as described in brief above, it seems logical that poverty and inequality would be worsened as a result. One need not see too much evidence to realize that increases in fees for access to critical and life-sustaining public services and human needs—from water to health and education—increasingly dictated that access to these goods would be stratified according to one's ability to pay for them in the absence of state investment in providing subsidized or free access. In tandem with these more stark effects of structural adjustment were the more insidious effects in economic terms in sectors such as agriculture, for instance, which—as alluded to above—saw steadily falling prices for primary export goods such as coffee (a staple export of many African and Latin American countries), making small-scale farmers unable to eke out a livelihood in a global market dominated by large-scale, often corporate producers and distributors from the North who enjoy heavy subsidies and advantages that the BWIs refuse domestic small-scale agricultural producers in the South. Nevertheless, debtor countries remain beholden in this context to continued policies of maintaining an economy predicated on exports of primary commodities that can earn sufficient foreign exchange to service debts. In India—a country not looked at in the context of SAPRI—these globally unfair terms of trade have marginalized small-scale farmers to the extent that suicide rates among rural farmers have skyrocketed in recent years, along with enforced global trade rules entrenching below-living wage rates of return to small-scale producers for staple crops such as rice, and related trade rules that make traditionally saved and harvested seed the intellectual property of northern corporations, a trend described as "biopiracy".[22] Such trends and related questions have led more observers to wonder whether the BWIs are simply acting as the latest arbiter of a politics of (neo)colonial dependency economics, as both cheap raw materials and commodities as well as debt interest payments are continually siphoned from the global South for the good of the global North and its consumers.[23]

Ironically, just as the Bank began to distance itself from the findings of SAPRI report, the evidence and bad PR of the "era of structural adjustment" had finally, it seems, sunk in. At the turn of the 21st century Bank President James Wolfensohn would introduce the new discursive wrapping or "re-branding" of structural adjustment in the new emphasis on "poverty reduction," along with a re-branded and deliberately inclusive and participatory process for mediating BWI-sanctioned development plans, in the form of Poverty Reduction Strategy Papers (PRSPs). PRSP processes sport several positive attributes relative to their predecessors in the National Development Plans—namely in the direct mandate of incorporating elements of a debtor country's civil society in consultation processes around what poverty reduction strategies should entail. However, a significant number of organizations in affected countries have cited difficulties in becoming engaged in the process,[24] while other observers note that the essential "veto power" remains with the BWIs to vet and authorize the policy directions inherent in PRSPs through various mechanisms.[25] Finally and most damning is the necessity for PRSP countries (HIPC countries must complete the process to qualify) to adhere to previous neoliberal conditionalities attached to existing debt commitments, as well as new sets of neoliberal conditions for further debt relief or cancellation.[26] A report by the World Development Movement sums up this dilemma in terms of conditionalities emphasizing water privatization attached to existing loans brokered by the BWIs:

> There are three reasons why it has been extremely difficult, if not impossible, for the poorest countries to truly determine their own development strategies. First, the content of PRSPs is influenced by pre-existing World Bank and IMF programme conditions. Rather than start afresh, these IFI determined policies are generally 'cut-and-pasted' into the PRSP with no further analysis or scrutiny. For example, in the Gambia, Ghana, Guinea, Malawi, Mali, Mozambique, Nicaragua, Sierra Leone and Yemen, water privatisation was already a condition of a Bank and/or Fund programme *before* being included in the PRSP. These countries had little choice but to include water privatisation within the document. In theory then, IMF and World Bank policy conditions are determined by the content of PRSPs, but in practice, in many cases the PRSP content is determined by already existing IMF and World Bank conditions. (Hardstaff & Jones, 2006, p. 43)

These effects of a self-sustaining mode of re-branded structural adjustment remain a critical area of concern when it comes to the BWIs' present tactic of advocating, requiring, and brokering the privatization of water, a basic necessity for life in a world characterized by severely unequal access.[27] Across all areas of crucial social services, the Bank, for instance, retains the status of its "private sector development strategy" by requiring and advocating for various forms of privatization of social services such as health and education and other infrastructure.[28] User fees remain a rampant and evident feature of social systems across the heavily indebted world, despite public assertions on the part of the Bank and Fund that user fees in education, for example, are not preferred. Years of starvation-level financing for social services in Africa, southeast Asia, and Latin American poorer countries has entailed a continued reliance on user fees of various kinds to help support public services such as health and education (or other types of infrastructure, including water), making the situation all the more pressing, and all of this in spite of the assertion within countless human rights instruments and conventions that such services should be free.[29] Terry McKinley of the United Nations Development Programme suggests that the replication of neoliberal conditionalities constitutes more of a form of continuous economic imperialism than an attempt to address poverty (McKinley), particularly in the context of obvious challenges and frustrations toward achieving modest—and critical—development targets such as the MDGs. Though the IMF's Independent Evaluations Office produced a review of conditionality in IMF programs in 2005,[30] the focus of this report and the continued operational mandate remain focused on core tenets of neoliberal conditionality, albeit carefully phrased through a discursive wrapping of country "ownership" of "poverty reduction strategies".

REVISITING PRIORITIES OF DEVELOPMENT AND HOLDING THE BWIs ACCOUNTABLE

In the context of an unfair global trade system premised on maintaining the advantage of northern (and now southern) capitalists[31] to continue exploiting the resources of the poorer global South, the ongoing debt crisis has served to further impoverish the world's poor rather than lift them out of poverty as per the mantra of "poverty reduction" repeated by the BWIs. Given the fact that the debts of the nations in which the most impoverished peoples of the world are citizens are arguably odious and/or illegitimate, and that so much of the wealth of the South has already flowed into the coffers of Northern banks and corporations at the behest of the BWIs, it seems patently unjust, for example, that debt servicing obligations represented 417 percent of health care outlays in Angola in 2003, and 352 percent in the Democratic Republic of the Congo in the same year.[32] These are the consequences of a drastic misalignment in priorities on the part of the institutions that wield so much influence and power with respect to the development agenda impacting the world's poorest and most vulnerable people.

Ironically and even pitifully, despite the change in public relations strategies on the part of the BWIs, they still cling to the same core conditions of neoliberal macroeconomic policy that have served to sustain and exacerbate the problems of inequality and poverty that persist today. Current poverty reduction strategies endorsed by the Bank and Fund have been roundly criticized for furthering immiseration in sub-Saharan Africa[33] and the world over. Announcements regarding full multilateral/BWI-related debt cancellation for the 18 HIPCs (heavily indebted poor countries, according to the BWIs' criteria) are an important precedent, but exclude 40 other countries that are heavily indebted while maintaining a stubborn affinity for policies of neoliberal conditionality. With soft-edged internal review processes having been undertaken at the BWIs, recently the U.K. has joined a chorus of critical voices calling for an end to these conditions, although a threat of cancelling funding because of the issue fizzled (see endnote 18 for further discussion). Recently at the time of writing, a conference in Norway reviewing policy conditionality attracted representatives from several countries as well as the dedicated critical civil society organizations that have helped to keep these issues on the public radar.[34] A global call for action against poverty from global civil society organizations and citizen movements (GCAP), rooted in a confrontation of unfair systems of debt, trade, and aid, has garnered incredible global support from global citizens across the planet,[35] and another global call for action against the IFIs points a finger more concertedly at where a good share of the blame lies for the present crisis.[36] This author wholeheartedly endorses both campaigns and particularly the latter for its specific demands of the BWIs. The time is long past due for a thoroughly critical revisitation of the role, mandate, structure, and operation of these institutions[37] and a re-orientation of development away from the benefit of the creditors of odious debts, northern corporations, and the wealthy toward the betterment of all.

NOTES

* I am indebted to both Fraser Reilly-King, co-ordinator of the Halifax Initiative, Ottawa, Ontario, Canada, and Patrick Bond, Director of the Centre for Civil Society, University of KwaZulu-Natal, Durban, South Africa, for their useful comments on this work.

1. Cf. George (1999); Demartino (2000). This neoliberal "toolkit" or policy recipe is well evidenced in a 2005 speech by Danny Leipziger, the Vice-President, Poverty Reduction and Economic Management, of the Bank, to the sixth session of the World Trade Organization Ministerial meeting in Hong Kong in December of that year.

2. For one exploration of this seeming contradiction, see Woodward & Simms (2006).

3. One particularly vicious example of this incapability of aggregate economic growth to measure anything related to progress against poverty can be found in Angola. A civil society organization report put the case of Angola in the following way: "... there is the problem that even if an economy grows—something that you can measure by looking at its gross domestic product (GDP)—that doesn't mean that poor people within it are better off. GDP doesn't account for distribution of wealth within an economy. GDP can grow if an economy sells arms or requires the clean up of a major environmental disaster. GDP will also grow if a few companies generate high profits, but these factors don't mean that the economy's poor people are benefiting. Angola is a perfect example of this dichotomy. Thanks to oil and diamonds, Angola's economy has grown significantly in 2000. Yet a third of Angolan children still die before their fifth birthday; the Human Development Index rates the country 160th [161st as of 2006] of a possible 171, and UNICEF considers it "the worst place in the world to be a child." Angola's GDP is growing even as most of its people derive no benefit from oil or diamonds. Indeed, it is growing even as many people are further impoverished. (CCIC, 2001, p. 6). The most recent World Bank Independent Evaluations Group review of development effectiveness (2006) acknowledges that growth remains uneven and untied to any substantial reductions in poverty apart from the crude income changes in the rapidly growing "emerging markets" of China and India.

4. Ames et al. (2001).

5. Pogge & Reddy (2006).

6. The Bank reproduces these critical flaws and limitations in depicting supposed progress in declining poverty rates in a recently updated website portraying poverty issues "at a glance": http://web.worldbank.org/WBSITE/EXTERNAL/NEWS/0,,contentMDK: 20040961~pagePK:64257043~piPK:437376~theSitePK:4607,00.html.

7. This work will operationalize a more multidimensional approach to poverty as deprivation of basic needs and capabilities. These types of measurements are employed in the construction of the United Nations Development Programme (UNDP)'s Human Development Reports (http://hdr.undp.org/). Two papers, one by Boltvinik (1998) and another by Lok-Dessalien (1998) of the UNDP, offer an accessible introduction to

different approaches to conceptualizing and measuring poverty. A more in-depth study is offered by Laderchi et al. (2003), who compare four approaches and the weaknesses of each along with methodological issues and difficulties.

8. Pogge & Reddy, *op cit.*

9. Milanovic's (2005) analysis of ways of measuring inequality is comprehensive in its scope and a good introduction to methodological controversies in this area.

10. UNU-WIDER (2006). This picture of a massive global gap between rich and poor is complemented by a broader perspective that takes into account the lack of progress in ameliorating inequality since the 1970s. Developing countries have 80 percent of the world's people but share in only a fifth of global GDP. Meanwhile, global GDP has increased in the past 30 years from $3 trillion to $30 trillion. The richest 20 percent of the world's people control 82 percent of world export trade and 68 percent of world foreign direct investment, while the bottom poorest 20 percent share barely more than 1 percent of these categories. Continuing a two-century trend, the same 20 percent of the world's richest people in OECD countries in 1997 had 74 times the income of the poorest 20 percent, up from a 30:1 ration in 1960. Astonishingly, the world's richest 200 people's net worth increased to $1 trillion from $440 billion between 1994 and 1998, and the assets of the world's three richest people totalled to an excess of the GNP of the world's 43 poorest or "least-developed" countries combined. This information is adapted from the United Nations Development Programme's Human Development Report for 1999, pp. 25–37.

11. Kofi Annan affirmed this line of research and its implications for the conception and policy model of "human security" in his report, *A more secure world* (UN, 2004).

12. Mandel (2006); see also Mutasa (2005).

13. Interestingly, John Maynard Keynes had a rival vision of an institution not tied directly to the U.S. dollar but instead to a neutral currency, a proposal which was trumped by the U.S. For an accessible introduction to this historical contextualization of the BWIs, see the World Development Movement (WDM) "Out of time: The case for replacing the World Bank and IMF" (2006).

14. Ferraro & Rosser (1994); CETIM et al. (2006, p. 5). See also the data from the most recent *Global Development Finance* report of the Bank (2006), at http://web.worldbank.org/ WBSITE/EXTERNAL/DATASTATISTICS/EXTGLODEVFINVOL2/0,,contentMDK:20915314~ menuPK:2459328~pagePK:64168445~piPK:64168309~theSitePK:2459286,00.html.
    Current total external debt for developing countries in Africa amounted to 91.2 percent of the value of trade in goods and services in 2005. For "net debtor" countries according to the IMF's criteria, this statistic is more than 166 percent, while debt service payments constitute over a fifth of the value of traded goods and services in these countries (IMF, 2006, pp. 251–253).

15. Dembele (2005, p. 390). For a post-mortem analysis on the comparatively meagre promises of debt relief at the much-vaunted Gleneagles G8 summit in 2005, see a recent report by the European Network on Debt and Development (2006).

16. Mandel, *op cit.*

17. Cf. Mandel, *op cit;* another notable example of a power-hungry regime that enjoyed the full support of the BWIs is that of Habyarimana's in Rwanda up until 1993; see Storey (2001).

18. Tensions flared in September 2006 as the U.K.'s Department for International Development, under Hilary Benn, threatened to withhold £50 million in protest of the Bank's "aggressive agenda" concerning anti-corruption strategies under current

President Paul Wolfowitz. Joseph Stiglitz, for one, draws attention to the fact that anti-corruption strategies can be but one more potentially blunt "stick" for cutting aid where it is desperately needed (http://www.globalpolicy.org/socecon/bwi-wto/critics/2006/1027stiglitzcorruption.htm); while at the same time not enough attention is paid to transnational corporations and other business who may benefit from corruption, bribery, and "kickback" schemes associated with neoliberal privatization and trade liberalization reforms. Transparency International (http://www.transparency.org/) is a global civil society organization that attempts to track these, and related trends.

The U.K. backed down on its threat in December of the same year, although not before the Bank moved to withhold funds from Chad, India, Argentina, Congo, Kenya, Ethiopia, and Bangladesh under its new guidelines purportedly aimed at combating corruption. The U.K. has, in 2005-6, begun to join a chorus of international civil society voices in decrying the BWIs' persistent focus on certain forms of neoliberal policy conditionality. This stated focus, however, rings somewhat hollow while U.K. Trade and Investment continues a strong push for trade liberalization and neoliberal policies in the developing world (cf. http://www.ukinvest.gov.uk/10415/en_GB/0.pdf). Meanwhile, Wolfowitz—an architect of the 2003 war on Iraq—embodies a critical fusion of neoliberal and neoconservative politics for the Bank's leadership. For a synopsis of the debates around corruption and the BWIs, see http://www.globalpolicy.org/socecon/bwi-wto/bankind.htm.

19. Estimates concerning levels of short-term, speculative international currency and other forms of trading are up to 2 trillion dollars per *day* today, severely dwarfing "productive" forms of global, regional, and local investment. Liberalization of finance has meant the freer movement of speculative capital and its disconnection from productive investment. Social movements have arisen around the possibility of a "transaction tax" on the massive amounts of speculative capital criss-crossing the world daily; one prominent advocate was the late Nobel Prize for Economics winner James Tobin, a Canadian. See the website for ATTAC, a global social movement based in France pushing for a transaction tax to provide development funds (http://www.attac.org/), the Halifax Initiative (http://www.halifaxinitiative.org), as well as Tobin (1996) and Haq et al. (1996). The U.S. has historically opposed this kind of move, representing the interests of powerful finance capitalists.

20. Cf. Kiely (2004). Kiely's study also instructively points out that "globalizing" countries—those which most faithfully implemented BWI prescriptions for trade liberalization and integration with global markets—show poorer rates of productivity than do countries that protect domestic industries and sectors.

21. This topic comes up below and other useful works are referenced. Cf. Mehrotra & Delamonica (2005).

22. Shiva (2005). See also a documentary and resources produced by the U.S. Public Broadcasting Service entitled "Seeds of Suicide," available at http://www.pbs.org/frontlineworld/rough/2005/07/seeds_of_suicid.html. For one among many other critics and observers, Shiva also contends that implication of poorer countries in the global agricultural trade exacerbates poverty by turning attention away from food security on a local and regional basis, or "food sovereignty" (2002).

23. In addition to sector-specific effects of an unfair global trade system, international trade regimes acting in tandem with the neoliberal orientation of the BWIs—such as the World Trade Organization and its sub-agreements, and many Regional Trade Agreements as well as bilateral agreements—serve to reinforce patterns of entrenchment of neoliberal social and economic policy from a supranational

basis. The General Agreement on Trade in Services (GATS) of the WTO is an interesting case in point in this regard, used as a lever by richer states in demanding market access into services relating to water, education, and health, for example.

24. Wood (2004).

25. Alexander (2004); Hardstaff & Jones (2006).

26. World Development Movement (2005); McKinley (2004). These represent a mere sample of a pattern of criticism that has emerged along with the evolution and observation of the PRSP processes at work. Many civil society organizations agree that the rhetoric surrounding "country ownership" in the end seems but a façade for an edifice of neoliberal conditionalities in a different guise.

27. There are several adequate primers on the topic of the global water crisis and problems of equity of access for proper nourishment and survival, *vis-à-vis* unlimited access by corporations and industry at little to no cost, for profit. See Barlow and Clarke (2005) for one such critical introduction. The UNDP's Human Development Report for 2006 is built around a theme of the global water crisis (UNDP, 2006), although Bond and Ruiters (2006) argue that even the UNDP remains mired in a neoliberal approach to water management that serves to frustrate progress toward ameliorating poverty through improving access. For a primer on the Bank's involvement in water privatization schemes in developing countries, see a resource developed by the Halifax Initiative (2004).

28. cf. World Bank (2004).

29. For a discussion of the prevalence of user fees in global education systems as of August 2006 as a form of "human rights violation," see the work of Tomasevski (2003; 2006). Tomasevski was UN Special Rapporteur on the Right to Education from 1998–2004. For a sampling of literature on how user fees persist in health care systems—including those in heavily indebted countries—see Homedes & Ugalde (2005), van Doorslaer et al. (2005), as well as Gilson & McIntyre (2005).

30. IMF Independent Evaluations Office (2005).

31. Increasingly in Africa, for example, the interests of "southern capitalists" in the form of Chinese interests in oil and other commodities has also taken centre stage, highlighting ongoing structural problems in indebted countries vulnerable to whatever form of foreign direct investment chooses to look their way. The cases of Sudan, the Democratic Republic of the Congo, and Zambia, for example, are germane in this regard. Each are the source of invaluable commodities in global markets, and both nations' citizens have been caught in a literal and figurative crossfire between competitors seeking to exploit valuable resources such as oil, gold, coltan, tin, and timber among others, while poverty continues to worsen. Angola's dependence on oil "resource rents" from American TNCs are another example; Africa abounds with examples of these dynamics. These points highlight the fact that BWI encouragement and imposition of neoliberalism comes in tandem with unfair and unaccountable trade dynamics involving capital in the North and South.

32. These statistics and related analyses can be found at the website of the International Debt Observatory: http://www.oid-ido.org/en.ratio.php3?id_article=96. IDO compiles ratios of debt servicing obligations relative to various other expenditure categories, including health and education, in the most indebted countries.

33. Lewis (2005); Bond & Dor (2003); Bond (2004).

34. Cf. http://www.eurodad.org/articles/default.aspx?id=747; with the tensions raised through critics from global civil society and now government quarters, however, many acknowledge that outwardly, at least, the stance on conditionality has softened; the roots and operationalization of conditionality, however, remain firmly in place. For a recent synopsis of the BWIs shape-shifting in this respect, see Bull et al. (2006).

35. http://www.whiteband.org. The four goals of the global campaign are "just governance, accountable to the general public, and the fulfilment of human rights; trade justice; a substantial increase in the quantity—and quality—of aid, and financing for development; and debt cancellation".

36. http://www.cadtm.org/article.php3?id_article=1893. The goals of this campaign are more specific than those of the GCAP:

    1. Immediate and 100% cancellation of multilateral debts as part of the total cancellation of debts claimed from the South, without externally imposed conditionalities.
    2. Open, transparent and participatory External Audit of the lending operations and related policies of the International Financial Institutions, beginning with the World Bank and IMF.
    3. Stop the imposition of conditions and the promotion of neoliberal policies and projects.
        a. In this 50th anniversary year of the International Finance Corporation (IFC), the IFIs must end the promotion of privatization of public services and the use of public resources to support private profits.
        b. Stop IFI funding and involvement in environmentally destructive projects beginning with big dams, oil, gas and mining and implement the major recommendations of the Extractive Industries Review.
        c. Immediately stop imposing conditions that exacerbate health crises like the AIDS pandemic and make restitution for past practices such as requiring user fees for public education and health care services.

37. As another program for action, I also support the essential restructuring of the BWIs along the lines suggested by both the World Development Movement (in Hardstaff & Jones, 2006) and the Halifax Initiative (http://www.halifaxinitiative.org). Although this work has limited itself to probing the effect of the Bank and Fund on poverty in a broad sense, cross-cutting issues with respect to the BWIs like their domination by the U.S. and U.K. under current voting rights, their lack of transparency to those affected most by related programs, and the fundamental links between northern capitalist interests and the modus operandi of the Bank and Fund are issues that require systematic attention in any attempt to come to terms with unfair systems of debt, trade, and aid. Finally, with respect to the future of the Bank and Fund, the current and ongoing debate in global civil society revolves around whether to reform or reject the BWIs, to "fix" or "nix" them. This author gravitates substantially toward the latter in favouring a complete re-tooling of the uneven and hyper-liberalized global financial architecture that continues to ensnare the globally poor. Two works that may assist the reader in formulating their own opinion are those of the WDM (2006) and another paper by Bond (2006). Soederberg's (2006) book puts these matters in the context of controversies surrounding the BWIs and related institutions of "global governance".

POSTSCRIPT

For several decades, development NGOs have worked at building stronger transnational advocacy networks for holding the major development funding agencies like the International Monetary Fund and the World Bank more accountable. Clearly, there have been shifts in the development discourse coming from these two agencies. The adoption of the PRSPs approach, they argue, shows that the Bank and IMF have been sensitive to criticism from the development community. The two agencies claim to have moved away from the standard "cookie cutter" approach of their previous SAPs and have instead adopted an approach that is both more sensitive to the specific needs of each country and more encouraging of national participation and ownership of the planning process.

Does this mean that the years of lobbying by the NGO sector paid off? In light of Professor Davidson-Harden's critique, have the World Bank and International Monetary Fund conditionality really significantly changed? Or, has this simply been a "rebranding" exercise that leaves the same fundamental assumptions in place? Given the G8 Summit commitments to significantly increase aid in order to meet the UN Millennium Development Goals, the PRSP process will ensure that the World Bank and IMF continue to function as the primary gatekeepers to development aid and debt relief for some years to come. In light of this, what strategy should NGOs now take to ensure great accountability of these two critically important agencies?

Suggested Additional Readings

Cornwall, Andrea, and Karen Brock. "What Do Buzzwords Do for Development Policy? A Critical Look at 'Participation,' 'Empowerment' and 'Poverty Reduction,'" *Third World Quarterly,* 26, no. 7 (2005): 1043–1060.

Craig, David, and Doug Porter. "Poverty Reduction Strategy Papers: A New Convergence," *World Development,* 31, no. 1 (2003): 53.

Fraser, A. "Poverty Reduction Strategy Papers: Now Who Calls the Shots?" *Review of African Political Economy,* 32 (2005): 317–340.

Gore, Charles. "MDGs and PRSPs: Are Poor Countries Enmeshed in a Global-Local Double Bind?" *Global Social Policy,* 4, no. 3 (2004): 277–283.

Gottschalk, Ricardo. "The Macro Content of PRSPs: Assessing the Need for a More Flexible Macroeconomic Policy Framework," *Development Policy Review,* 23, no. 4 (2005): 419–442.

Gould, Jeremy. *The New Conditionality: The Politics of Poverty Reduction Strategies* (London: Zed Books, 2005).

Hanley, Eric. "Thinking and Doing Things about Poverty II: The Poverty Reduction Strategy Process in Africa," *Progress in Development Studies,* 2, no. 1 (2002): 47–51.

International Monetary Fund. *Independent Evaluation of the PRSPs* (Washington, DC: IMF, 2004).

Maxwell, S. "Heaven or Hubris: Reflections on the New 'New Poverty Agenda,'" *Development Policy Review,* 21, no. 1 (2003): 5–25.

"Old Battle; New Strategy," *Economist,* 354, no. 8152 (2000): 74–75.

Onis, Z., and F. Senses. "Rethinking the Emerging Post-Washington Consensus," *Development and Change,* 36, no. 2 (2005): 263–290.

Weber, Heloise. "Reconstituting the 'Third World'? Poverty Reduction and Territoriality in the Global Politics of Development," *Third World Quarterly,* 25, no. 1 (2004): 187–206.

Whitfield, Lindsay. "Trustees of Development from Conditionality to Governance: Poverty Reduction Strategy Papers in Ghana," *Journal of Modern African Studies,* 43, no. 4 (2005): 641–664.

World Bank. *The Poverty Reduction Strategy Initiative. An Independent Evaluation of the World Bank's Support Through 2003* (Washington, DC: World Bank, 2004).

InfoTrac® College Edition

Search for the following articles in the InfoTrac® database:

"Poverty-Reduction Strategy for IMF, World Bank," *United Press International* (April 14, 2000): 1.

Sandstrom, Sven. "Poverty Reduction: Learning the Lessons of Experience," *Finance & Development,* 31, no. 3 (September 1994): 30–33.

Welch, Carol. "Structural Adjustment Programs & Poverty Reduction Strategy," *Foreign Policy in Focus,* 5, no. 14 (April 24, 2000): 1.

For more articles, enter:
"poverty reduction strategy," "World Bank," and "International Monetary Fund" in the keyword search.

Web Resources

ELDIS WORLD BANK AND IMF RESOURCE GUIDE

www.eldis.org/wbimf/index.htm

This guide provides access to a range of full-text documents dealing with various dimensions of World Bank and IMF policies.

IMF POVERTY REDUCTION STRATEGY PAPERS

www.imf.org/external/np/prsp/prsp.asp

This official IMF site contains both a number of IMF reports in PRSPs and the full text of the PRSPs that various countries have submitted to date.

POVERTYNET

www.worldbank.org/prsp

This World Bank–operated site provides extensive materials on the Bank's approach to PRSPs. You can find full-text reports as well as an extensive collective of data and some papers written produced by other agencies and researchers.

OVERSEAS DEVELOPMENT INSTITUTE

www.odi.org.uk/publications/

The ODI is the leading research institute on development issues in the United Kingdom. Under the publication section of their website, you will find a number of working papers on the PRSP approach, including a number of country case studies.

EURODAD

www.eurodad.org/uploadstore/cms/docs/SwedishPRSPRapporteng.pdf

EURODAD is a network of European-based development NGOs. Their website contains a section of papers and report on PRSPs. The link above will take you to a paper by a group of Swedish NGOs entitled, "Reducing Poverty or Repeating Mistakes: A Civil Society Critique of the Poverty Reduction Strategy Papers."

TROCAIRE

trocaire.org/policyandadvocacy/prsp.php

Trocaire is the official overseas development agency of the Catholic Church in Ireland. At this site they have a list of papers analyzing their experience in working on PRSPs in various countries.

Do Canadian Government Foreign Aid Programs Help to Alleviate Poverty?

✔ **YES**

CANADIAN INTERNATIONAL DEVELOPMENT AGENCY, *CIDA Annual Report 2004–05* (excerpts). www.tbs-sct.gc.ca/rma/dpr1/04-05/CIDA-ACDI/CIDA-ACDId45_e.asp

✗ **NO**

DEXTER SAMIDA, "A Hand Out Instead of a Hand Up: Where Foreign Aid Fails," *Public Policy Sources,* no. 30 (1999), Fraser Institute Occasional Papers Series

Overseas development assistance or ODA is the name typically given to funds set aside by developed countries to promote development in the nations of the South so as to eliminate poverty and achieve higher levels of human development. ODA is committed by Western industrialized nations through a set of key development agencies and financial institutions. Among these must be included the intergovernmental agencies known as multilateral aid agencies, such as the UN Development Programme (UNDP), the World Food Programme (WFP), and the United Nations High Commissioner for Refugees (UNHCR). International financial institutions such as the World Bank and International Monetary Fund also each have a special role to play in supporting the primary sources of financing among developing nations. These multilateral agencies receive funding from member governments that in turn is allocated and distributed to various countries based on the mandate of the agency and the assessment of worldwide need. Multilateral aid agencies are important in setting the tone of world development efforts and in providing the backbone of relief efforts in the midst of humanitarian emergencies.

A second class of development agencies are the bilateral aid agencies set up by individual governments to deliver aid funding directly from the donor government to projects established in the developing world. These organizations engage in transfers to foreign governments (government-to-government transfers), to voluntary organizations, and in other forms of relief and development assistance. They also channel development funds toward the multilateral agencies. Most of the larger Western capitalist countries have set up their own bilateral development agencies, such as the United States Agency for International Development (USAID), the British Department for International Development (DFID), and the Swedish International Development Agency. Others distribute ODA directly through their ministries of foreign affairs.

To the multilateral and bilateral aid agencies must be added the array of non-governmental organizations (NGOs) involved in delivering relief and development assistance throughout the world. Many of these organizations raise funds independently among average citizens and philanthropic networks and deliver their services in nations around the world. Some of the most prominent of these include the International Red Cross/Red Crescent, World Vision, and Oxfam. Over the years, multilateral and bilateral aid organizations have come to use NGOs as a primary method of delivery of front-line services to developing countries.

Canada's bilateral aid agency, the Canadian International Development Agency, or CIDA, oversees most of the development assistance that Canada provides to areas of the developing world. CIDA has its origins in the early Cold War period. During the 1950 Colombo Conference, Canada was one of many countries to commit to ongoing development assistance to less developed countries. Canada's ODA was first primarily devoted to other Commonwealth countries in Asia and Africa. In 1968, CIDA was created to administer the bulk of the development assistance. Responding to the Pearson Commission on International Development of 1969, most Canadian governments have pledged with other bilateral aid donors to work toward committing 0.7 percent of Canada's Gross Domestic Product (GDP) toward ODA. Although frequently reiterated as a goal by successive governments, Canada has never actually met this target. The closest Canada came to the target was in 1988, when the Canadian government gave the equivalent of 0.5 percent of GDP. Over the course of the 1990s in the midst of a prolonged government budgetary crisis, aid spending was reduced significantly. In spite of the reduced commitments to ODA, the concluding years of the Jean Chrétien and Paul Martin administrations saw a renewed rhetorical commitment to alleviating poverty through aid spending. However, the proportion of Canada's commitment has continued to slide, reaching 0.28 percent of GDP in 2005.

That same year, the Canadian government embarked on an international policy review that sought to renew its commitment to the so-called "three Ds": defence, diplomacy, and development. Since that time, CIDA has reassessed and refocused its efforts, as laid out in the following report of CIDA themes and priorities. However, there are those who question the very wisdom of development assistance as a means of enhancing development. In the second reading, Dexter Samida of the Fraser Institute elaborates on a series of objections to development assistance as a means of reinforcing the very problems of poor governance that leads to underdevelopment in the first place.

✔ **YES**
CIDA Annual Report 2004–05
CANADIAN INTERNATIONAL DEVELOPMENT AGENCY

The Development Challenge

"The world must advance the causes of security, development and human rights together, otherwise none will succeed. Humanity will not enjoy security without development, it will not enjoy development without security, and it will not enjoy either without respect for human rights."[1]

−Kofi Annan

INTRODUCTION: MAKING GOOD ON A PLEDGE

In the fall of 2000, Canada, along with the rest of the international community, endorsed the historic Millennium Declaration and the Millennium Development Goals (MDGs)[2], which reflect a global consensus on what needs to be done to make the world a better, safer, and fairer place for all its citizens by 2015. Five years later, in September 2005, the countries of the world gathered at the United Nations (UN) World Summit to assess progress on that pledge. The MDGs set out critical goals such as eradicating poverty and hunger, achieving universal primary education, promoting gender equality, reducing child and maternal mortality, combating HIV/AIDS and other devastating diseases, ensuring environmental sustainability, and strengthening the global partnerships that make sustainable human development possible.

This global consensus is more than a statement of good intentions. At the UN International Conference on Financing for Development in Monterrey in 2002, world leaders agreed that aid was not enough if developing countries were to reduce poverty—they needed markets for their products, investment in their economies, debt relief, and other financial resources. This broadened understanding of the requirements for sustainable development called for greater coherence and synergy between trade, diplomacy, foreign investment, and other financial, commercial and institutional relationships.

This "new development compact" articulated a new partnership of mutual benefits and obligations for developing and industrialized countries alike. It was grounded in the principle that developing countries bear the primary responsibility for their own development, with the support of the international community. The 2003 Rome High Level Forum on Harmonization, and the subsequent 2005 Paris High Level Forum on Aid Effectiveness, introduced to the international community the principles by which international assistance is governed today. Canada's commitment to the Rome Declaration was confirmed by the launch in September 2004 of CIDA's *Action Plan to Promote Harmonization*. As a member of the Organisation for Economic Co-operation and Development's (OECD) Development Assistance Committee (DAC), Canada is now finalizing its targets and indicators to support the implementation of the 2005 Paris Declaration. Taken together, these international agreements reflect a new consensus on the goals, resources, and conditions necessary to achieve sustainable development and poverty reduction.

THE GLOBAL PICTURE

In 2005, as the international community takes stock of achievements in relation to the MDGs, the global development picture is one of both important progress and daunting challenges.

In just over a generation, developing countries have advanced in several key areas, including infant and child health, education and literacy, income and access to clean water and sanitation, and decent housing and other social services. Between 1990 and 2002, average incomes increased by some 21 percent; child mortality rates dropped from 103 per 1,000 live births a year to 88; and, despite population growth, the actual number of people living in poverty declined by 130 million.[3]

Notwithstanding this progress, however, concern remains that if present trends continue, many of the MDG targets will not be met by 2015. Some targets, such as poverty reduction in Africa, may not be met until well into the next century. Serious challenges remain in such areas as gender equality, the development of the private sector, the protection of children from exploitation and abuse, sanitation and quality of life in urban slums. Areas of particularly pressing concern—where progress is limited and human costs are mounting—include maternal mortality, HIV/AIDS, and environmental degradation. [...]

CIDA's MANDATE AND OBJECTIVES

CIDA[4] was established in 1968 to administer the bulk of Canada's Official Development Assistance (ODA). CIDA's programming contributes to Canada's broader foreign policy objectives—to promote prosperity, to protect Canadian and global security, and to project Canadian values.

As set out in Canada's foreign policy statement, *Canada in the World* (1995), CIDA's mandate was defined as follows:

- support sustainable development in order to reduce poverty and contribute to a more secure, equitable, and prosperous world;

- support democratic development and economic liberalization in countries in transition in Eastern Europe and the former Soviet Union; and

- support international efforts to reduce threats to international and Canadian security.

To deliver on this mandate, CIDA has measured its progress in terms of the following development goals: economic well-being, social development, governance, and environmental sustainability. These goals are an integral component of CIDA's Key Agency Results (KARs). They reflect the fundamental development results or "strategic outcomes" that CIDA seeks to achieve through delivery of Canada's aid program. Working in cooperation with the international community, CIDA aims to ensure that Canada's development assistance program contributes to the achievement of the MDGs.

In 2004–2005, CIDA participated in a comprehensive review of Canada's international policy framework. Through the International Policy Review, the Agency worked with other departments involved in international affairs to develop a more integrated and effective international agenda for Canada. The Review culminated with the issuance by the Government of Canada of the International Policy Statement (IPS) in April 2005.[5] The IPS sets out key principles, directions, and priorities that will underpin Canada's aid program in coming years. [...]

BENEFITS FOR CANADIANS

Canada's development cooperation program reflects values cherished by Canadians: humanitarianism, justice, equity, peace, and security. However, Canadians' support for aid goes beyond the desire to help people and countries in need. It also brings a wide range of benefits:

1. It gives Canada a voice on the world stage. Participation in donor groups, dialogue with developing countries, support to emerging donors, and membership in multilateral organizations such as the UN and the World Bank, allow Canada to advocate for policies that are important to Canadians, for example in the areas of health, governance and human rights, basic education, private sector development, environmental sustainability and gender equality.

2. It helps build long-term relationships with emerging economies. Some of the world's fastest-growing economies, such as China, India, and Brazil, are developing nations with which Canada has worked for many years. These countries are also our economic partners, with trade, travel, and institutional linkages growing every year. Through support to developing countries' own efforts to strengthen their private sectors, Canadians are helping to build the engine for economic growth.

3. It contributes to global peace and security. Security and development are inextricably linked. Canada's aid program directly addresses such challenges as environmental disaster, human rights violations, and economic and social exclusion that provoke conflict and create conditions that terrorists and criminals can exploit. Building the capacity of developing countries to deal with these threats, and also others such as health crises reduces pressures not only locally, but also regionally and globally.

Canadians recognize that their future is intertwined with that of people around the world, and that the failure to achieve significant political, economic, social and environmental progress in the developing world will have an impact on Canada in terms of long-term security and prosperity. In 2004–2005, the massive response to the Indian Ocean tsunami was a compelling reflection of Canadians' global perspective and their abiding commitment to generosity and humanitarianism. This generosity has resulted in many achievements over the years, not only in emergency assistance, but also in long-term development. [...]

STRATEGIC OUTCOMES: ACHIEVING RESULTS

Economic Well-Being

In the area of economic well-being, planned spending for 2004–2005 totalled $734.4 million, and actual disbursements totalled $804 million.

Poverty reduction is the cornerstone of CIDA's development cooperation program. Because economic growth is essential to reducing poverty, Canada's aid programming includes a focus on investments aimed at stimulating such growth and improving standards of living.

Building a dynamic, growth-oriented private sector that benefits all members of society is critical to the achievement of all the Millennium Development Goals (MDGs). In 2004–2005, CIDA's work in this area continued to be guided by its policy, *Expanding Opportunities Through Private Sector Development*, released in 2003. It also remained guided by the directions set out in Unleashing Entrepreneurship: Making Business Work for the Poor, the 2004 Report of the UN Commission on the Private Sector and Development, which had been co-chaired by Prime Minister Paul Martin and by the former President of Mexico, Ernesto Zedillo. With Canadian support and advocacy, Canada's multilateral partners and other donors, as well as developing country partners, are integrating private sector development into institutional policies and strategies. CIDA has also maintained its leadership in supporting microfinance, building local institutions, and targeting women microentrepreneurs.

In developing countries, where many of the poor live in rural areas, private sector development often revolves around agriculture. In 2004–2005, CIDA's support for agriculture continued to be informed by its policy *Promoting Sustainable Rural Development Through Agriculture*, released in 2003. As a result of a re-balancing of priorities within the Agency, in 2004–2005 CIDA did not meet its original spending target of $225 million, as set out in the 2003 policy. However, the Agency's investment in agriculture did continue to grow during the fiscal year, reaching a substantial $178 million. CIDA remains committed to programming in this area. The 2004–2005 International Policy Review and resulting IPS have identified priority sectors of activity (e.g. private sector development; health, including food security; environmental sustainability) under which continued investments in agriculture and rural development will remain important.

Finally, in addition to support for private sector development and agriculture, in 2004–2005 CIDA also placed continued emphasis on initiatives to create an enabling environment for economic growth as well as increase opportunities for the poor, including through improved legislation and policies. CIDA's work in this area further included initiatives to enhance the capacity of governments and entrepreneurs in the developing world to participate effectively in international trade and investment. [...]

Social Development

In the area of social development, planned spending for 2004–2005 totalled $1,190.2 million, and actual disbursements totalled $1,593.2 million.

Development is first and foremost about people. People care for the human and natural resources, create the institutions and processes, and drive the productivity and commerce upon which development depends. Education, health care and other basic needs are the foundations of human progress. Investment in these sectors has proven to be the single most effective contribution to poverty reduction and sustainable development that a country can make, provided that it is undertaken in an environmentally sustainable manner.

In September 2000, the Minister for International Cooperation launched CIDA's *Social Development Priorities: A Framework for Action*. The framework outlined four priority areas for CIDA: education, health and nutrition, HIV/AIDS, and child protection. The Agency's objective was to strategically invest in these Social Development Priorities (SDPs) in order to make a stronger contribution to social and economic well-being and to accelerate progress toward achieving the MDGs. In 2004–2005, CIDA successfully met its commitments to double spending on the SDPs between 2000 and 2005. The cumulative investment target for the five-year period was set at $2.8 billion; by the end of 2004–2005, CIDA had surpassed this target and had invested $3.2 billion.

In addition to CIDA's success in meeting the SDP targets, the Agency also accomplished significant results in the areas of health and nutrition, HIV/AIDS, and humanitarian assistance, where the Agency's performance exceeded expectations. Important progress was also achieved in child protection and the promotion of gender equality. [...]

Governance

For CIDA programming related to governance, planned spending for 2004–2005 totalled $430.5 million, and actual disbursements totalled $426.4 million.

Developing and industrialized countries alike agree that peace and good governance are essential conditions for achieving the MDGs. However, many developing countries are new democracies, still struggling to build their institutions, update their public services, enforce the rule of law, and establish peace and stability. Countries in crisis, where governance has failed, or is at risk of failing, require special attention. It is often in these countries where the challenge of meeting the MDGs is most profound.

Building sound governance and security requires support in a wide range of areas. In 2004–2005, CIDA's programming in support of good governance focused on strengthening democratization, human rights, rule of law, and public sector institutions, as well as on conflict prevention and peacebuilding efforts. A major event during the period under review was the launch by CIDA of Canada Corps, now a key focal point for Canadian governance-related assistance. [...]

Environmental Sustainability

For CIDA programming related to environmental sustainability, planned spending for 2004–2005 totalled $177.2 million, and actual disbursements totalled $147.7 million.

Economic growth, public health, and social peace all depend on a stable and functioning ecosystem. Developing countries are struggling with a number of major challenges to the sustainability of their natural resource base, including desertification, climate change, deforestation, vulnerability to natural disasters, and the unregulated exploitation of resources. For the poor, whose livelihoods often depend directly on soil, water, and air, environmental damage can be disastrous.

In 2004–2005, CIDA continued to support a range of initiatives in support of environmental sustainability, and accomplished particular progress through measures aimed at ensuring CIDA's compliance with the *Canadian Environmental Assessment Act* (CEAA) and the *Cabinet Directive on the Environmental Assessment of Policy, Plan and Program Proposals*. CIDA's strengthened performance in the area of environmental sustainability provides a good example where CIDA took active and significant steps to respond to the findings of an external audit, conducted in 2004 by the Commissioner of the Environment and Sustainable Development, which had found weaknesses in CIDA's existing approaches. [...]

Learning from Experience: Challenges, Risks, and Future Directions

The preceding review of CIDA's performance in 2004–2005 indicates that, overall, the Agency succeeded in meeting the commitments set out in its 2004–2005 RPP. At the same time, while the Agency enjoyed considerable achievements, it also experienced challenges and continued to benefit from lessons learned—many of which have been highlighted throughout this DPR. Reviewing the year's activities in a balanced manner, and reflecting on how risks can be managed and lessons incorporated into day-to-day operations, is essential to improving the future performance of Canada's aid program.

The following section, although not exhaustive, highlights a few key areas that were relevant to CIDA's performance and experience in 2004–2005, and that will inform future directions for the Agency.

Implementing program-based approaches and shared funding modalities In 2004–2005, CIDA continued to learn from its experience with implementing [Problem-Based Approaches (PBAs)]. Although CIDA has made tremendous progress with PBAs, particularly in Africa, it has also recognized that participating in large, multi-donor programs requires time for intensive negotiations between partners, revisions to the administrative and accountability systems of all players, new skills and expertise, enhanced field capacity, and due diligence to ensure that risks are managed at acceptable levels.

During the period under review CIDA's administrative, accountability, and approval requirements—not yet fully adapted to PBAs—in some cases contributed to delays in the implementation of some projects, giving rise to concerns about the potential impact on CIDA's credibility in the field. Lessons from CIDA's experience with PBAs include the recognition that predictability of resources, and timeliness and flexibility of approaches, are increasingly important conditions for aid effectiveness. A 2004 donor survey indicated that CIDA needs to improve aligning disbursements to correspond with partner countries' planning cycles, and disbursing on time.

CIDA's first progress report on harmonization identified a number of additional challenges for coming years, which included the complexity of promoting alignment; the need to develop harmonization and alignment mechanisms in crisis countries; the need to continue enhancing field presence, decision-making, and financial authority; and the need to develop benchmarks to assess when a country's capacity for increased financial authority (i.e. shift toward PBAs and budget support) is sufficient to allow for alignment of aid programming with its systems. Other challenges will include attention to addressing crosscutting issues such as gender and environmental sustainability, particularly where programs are large and donors play a more limited role in managing aid. Monitoring also remains an important challenge, particularly when larger programs are established.

Implementation of PBAs and joint funding modalities will continue to require due diligence. CIDA continues to strengthen its risk management framework generally, and recognizes that risk analysis and management play an important role in respect of PBAs. CIDA is already implementing numerous measures, including the development of risk mitigation strategies (e.g. risk-based audit frameworks, results-based management and accountability frameworks, and other practical tools), to ensure the proper use of aid funds. CIDA will continue to work closely with other donors and partner countries to exchange lessons learned and to strengthen local capacities and accountability systems, where required. The Agency will also continue to work with TBS on approaches which support both effective aid programming in the new context, and also provide assurances that public funds are being well spent.

Responding to humanitarian emergencies and other crises   In 2004–2005, CIDA continued to work in dangerous and unstable environments, including areas of conflict, poor governance, extreme poverty, and social marginalization. The Agency has a well-developed risk assessment framework that addresses these factors. However, unforeseen political, security, economic, or natural events can add to overall levels of risk.

During the year under review, drought in East and Southern Africa, the collapse of the Haitian government, hurricanes in the Caribbean, and the Indian Ocean tsunami all took a terrible human toll and put development gains at risk. Although CIDA responded effectively, these events nonetheless had an impact on CIDA's programming context. The need to undertake rapid and large-scale responses to some crises required the re-allocation of human and financial resources away from other areas, resulting in some instances in the delay or cancellation of activities. For example, to address the priority of the government's commitment to Haiti, Americas Branch re-allocated $8 million (6 percent) of its own resources. While this strategy was appropriate, it also meant that projected aid increases for Honduras and Bolivia, two of CIDA's countries of focus, did not take place.

Despite these challenges, CIDA continued to learn from its experience in working in these contexts, and to develop effective risk management strategies. For example, in Haiti, collaboration within the donor community and the flexible use of programming mechanisms were key to implementing reconstruction efforts. In Nepal, the absence of elected officials has meant that CIDA has delivered aid through multilateral institutions or NGOs, rather than through local government channels. CIDA's work in countries such as Sudan and Iraq further underlined the need for conflict analysis, strong risk management, and close donor collaboration in fragile or conflict-affected countries. The Agency will continue to bring these lessons to future programming. In addition, during the year under review, the tsunami, the hurricanes in the Caribbean, a food crisis in Niger and the ongoing conflict in Darfur revealed weaknesses in the international humanitarian response system. CIDA will be pursuing efforts to strengthen this system as part of Canada's UN reform agenda.

Reforming approaches to planning, measuring and reporting on performance The 2004–2005 fiscal year saw the Agency focus systematically on the review of its frameworks for planning, performance measurement, and reporting to Parliament and Canadians. In relation to the introduction by the TBS in April 2005 of the new MRRS, the Agency undertook an intensive effort to develop an initial PAA. This undertaking was a complex and time consuming process, which will ultimately require a full realignment of the Agency's financial systems and performance measurement strategies, tools, and indicators.

While it is expected that the development of CIDA's PAA will benefit the Agency, by supplying *inter alia* a more rigorous methodological framework for planning and monitoring performance, a period of transition will be required before it is finalized and fully integrated by the Agency. Moving forward, the Agency will need to consider the implications not only of its KARs (presently at the heart of the Agency's accountability framework), but also of the new directions set out in the IPS, for the design of its PAA.

Implementing outcomes from government-wide initiatives During 2004–2005, CIDA participated in two significant government-wide initiatives—the International Policy Review and the Expenditure Review exercise—both of which will result in benefits for Canada's aid program, but which also had implications for the Agency during the year and for its future directions.

In respect of the Expenditure Review initiative, the Agency undertook a systematic evaluation of its programs to identify resources which were supporting priorities that were less effective at achieving Canada's development goals. CIDA identified reductions amounting to over $458 million over five years ($40.9 million in 2005–2006; $74.0 million in 2006–2007; and $114.4 million in 2007–2008 and ongoing). Because these reductions will only begin to take effect in 2005–2006, the full impact of the Expenditure Review on the Agency's operations is not yet entirely clear. That said, savings generated through the process were achieved in relation to the anticipated elimination of some country programs (through graduation strategies), some operational savings, and anticipated reduction of funding to selected smaller regional programs and funding initiatives assessed to have more limited impact.

The International Policy Review also had significant implications for CIDA operations in 2004–2005. As might be expected with any significant change management initiative, development of the IPS led to some delays in program delivery, and also increases in workload as the Agency reconsidered aid priorities and its overall direction. The negotiation of the IPS also led to uncertainties amongst CIDA's partners, both at home and abroad. Many concerns were resolved with the release of the IPS, or will be addressed shortly as the process of IPS implementation unfolds.

FUTURE DIRECTIONS: IMPLEMENTING THE IPS

In coming years, implementation of the IPS will be the major focus of CIDA's work. The IPS builds on the past several years' reforms, confirms CIDA's overall sustainable development strategy and provides a 21st century context within which the aid program will operate.

At the same time, challenges associated with implementation of the IPS, and CIDA's role as manager of the "development pool" of the IAE will be numerous. The implications for resource re-allocation, organizational structure, staffing and training, and administrative systems will need to be addressed. Ensuring a balance between the alignment of CIDA's geographic and sectoral priorities with the IPS on the one hand, and a continued responsiveness to developing country needs and Canadian ideas, innovations, and investments in international development on the other, will also be a challenge. Moving forward, CIDA will also need to focus on deepening and strengthening its interdepartmental relationships to support a whole-of-government approach to IPS implementation and IAE management, as well as a coherent Canadian approach to poverty reduction and achievement of the MDGs.

NOTES

1. In *Larger Freedom: Towards Development, Security and Human Rights for All*, United Nations, New York, 2004. Kofi Annan is Secretary-General of the UN.

2. http://www.un.org/milleniumgoals/

3. Sachs, Jeffrey D., *Investing in Development: A Practical Plan to Achieve the Millennium Development Goals*, Millennium Project, New York, 2005.

4. http://www.acdi-cida.gc.ca

5. http://www.acdi-cida.gc.ca/ips

✗ NO

A Hand Out Instead of a Hand Up: Where Foreign Aid Fails

DEXTER SAMIDA

The alleviation of misery among the least fortunate of the world's citizens is an objective beyond reproach. Foreign aid is often uncritically presumed to further this goal. The fact that money transferred from domestic taxpayers to foreign governments is referred to as *aid* implies that these expenditures are indeed beneficial. Indeed, the organization that distributes these transfers in Canada is called the Canadian International Development Agency, a title that simultaneously prejudges the effects of the aid and helps to disarm critics (Bauer 1981: 86, 141).

Public policy should not be based on the *assumed* virtue of a program, or be judged solely by the warm feelings it generates. We should rather investigate whether the program accomplishes what it intends. Thus, foreign aid should be evaluated on whether and to what extent it benefits people within recipient countries. More broadly, the question should be whether aid facilitates the creation of an institutional environment that allows those in the recipient countries to better provide for themselves. If aid is successful, it should encourage economic growth and its associated benefits (e.g., lower infant mortality).

The purpose of this study is to evaluate critically the role Canadian foreign aid has played in the development of targeted countries. Since the object of foreign aid should be the creation of economic growth (for reasons explained below), we examine research that looks at the effects of aid on growth and specific standard-of-living indicators. An extension of this research suggests that we take a different approach to those countries with good governance than to those with bad governance. In this context, we examine the Canadian foreign aid record. Finally, this study examines the appropriate role of aid in different institutional environments and how to best assist less developed countries.

THE PURPOSE OF AID

Many nations exist in seemingly perpetual states of poverty. In Bangladesh, 68 percent of the children under age five are malnourished. In Zambia, only 43 percent of the population has access to safe drinking water. In Pakistan, 76 percent of females over age 15 are illiterate (World Bank 1998). In the Sudan, 60 percent of local telephone calls fail. In Ghana, 61 percent of the main paved roads are in poor condition (Canning 1998). These countries share two characteristics. They are poor, and they have been recipients of massive amounts of foreign aid.[1] Contrast these countries with Japan, South Korea, and Chile, all former, less developed countries which have received very little aid, yet have produced superior results. The natural question is whether aid facilitates or deters development.

The Department of Foreign Affairs and International Trade has stated that "Canadians want to be sure that their aid dollars are being used effectively, that their help is making a difference in the lives of people benefitting from Canadian assistance by increasing their *self-reliance*" (DFAIT 1998, emphasis added). If self-reliance is its ultimate goal, foreign aid should seek to increase the self-generated incomes of those in developing countries, and must involve the eventual elimination of aid flows.

The only possible way to ensure the affluence of less developed countries without continuous aid transfers is through economic growth.[2] Since economic growth benefits all members of society (not just those at higher initial starting points), economic growth can, with time, vastly improve the lives of those within growing societies (Dollar et al. 1998: 38). Within one generation, even modest economic growth can double the average income of an economy. If foreign aid is intended to make a "difference in the lives of people" and "increase their self reliance," clearly it can only do so if it elicits economic growth.

ECONOMIC GROWTH

Economic growth can be thought of as the additional goods and services produced in an economy over the previous year due to improvements in the efficiency and quantities of labour and capital. When economic growth outpaces population growth, standards of living improve. When countries have divergent levels of growth, living standards diverge as well. In this way, past economic growth is an important factor that separates a country like Canada from a country like Chad. Thus, future economic growth is critical in bringing the standard of living of poor countries to the level found in places such as Canada. If aid is to have any long-term significance, it must foster conditions that result in economic growth.

Too often, the analysis of growth has focused on specific quantities of inputs, such as the amount of capital, while ignoring the importance of entrepreneurship, institutions, and technological change. This has had detrimental effects on the disbursement of aid, and on the policy recommendations offered to developing countries.[3]

AID AND GROWTH

Research examining foreign aid and growth has typically found that aid does not influence economic growth. A study of 97 countries from 1971 to 1990 found that "in all countries there was no significant correlation between aid and growth" (Boone 1995: 4). There was also little evidence that aid helps reform tax structures or change distortionary policies; rather, it tends to increase the size of government. In addition, aid did not improve infant mortality rates, primary school enrolment, or life expectancy. Rather "aid flows primarily benefit a wealth political elite," and thus aid "does not benefit the poor" (Boone 1995: 5, 26).

Another study of 73 countries from 1971 to 1995 found that neither aid per capita nor aid as a percentage of GDP was positively correlated with economic growth (Vásquez 1998: 276). Similarly, an analysis that examined the source of aid found no positive relationship between aid and growth. Thus, programs with different approaches to aid disbursement have had a similar lack of success, even though they share the common goal of promoting growth (Vásquez 1998: 276).

To date, foreign aid has failed to increase growth.[4] Furthermore, aid has typically focused on two areas believed to be critical to economic development: education and health care. In these areas, too, aid has failed to make a difference.

AID AND EDUCATION

Education is often thought to be an important development lever, and the implication that follows is that financial resources should flow to impoverished nations to increase education spending. Proponents of this view often point to the success of the Asian countries in expanding the skills of their citizens and their purportedly consequent future rapid development. They conclude, incorrectly, that the devotion of large amounts of money to education in other less-developed countries would have a similar effect. While these Asian nations were, at the time, less developed countries, it is seldom noted that these countries were not, in fact, dedicating large resources to education. If one measures education spending as a percent of GDP, or by physical inputs such as student-teacher ratios, these countries were unexceptional (Dollar et al. 1998: 77). Moreover, research that examined a large sample of countries found that "standard measures of schooling quality such as pupil-teacher ratio, class size, and teacher characteristics do not effectively explain student cognitive achievement" (Hanushek et al. 1995: 3). Thus, simply increasing foreign aid is unlikely to significantly improve a country's human capital.

Also, aid may not be directed to improving the educational attainment of everyone in a country. Côte d'Ivoire was one of the world's biggest spenders on education when measured as a percent of the government's budget, but 40 percent of the children aged 6 to 12 were not enroled in school in 1985. Studies also show that 50 to 80 percent of education spending went to higher education, and the cost per university student was among the highest in the world. This spending mainly benefited the rich, as university students were typically drawn from the richest families (Wick et al. 1998: 14-5). Quantity of spending, in this case as in many others, is no certain indication of quality.

AID AND HEALTH CARE

Health care is often a development priority, but health outcomes are rarely related to the level of health expenditures. Infant mortality is an example. The ten countries with the worst infant mortality rates (rates 40 percent higher than demographics justify), spend more as a share of GDP on health care than the top 10 countries

(Dollar et al. 1981: 76). How institutions are organized and run is more important than the amount of money that is put into the system. This is true even in the developed world. A recent analysis found that additional funds devoted to health care are unlikely to substantially reduce patient waiting times in Canada (Zelder 1999).

The developed world also foists unrealistic goals on developing countries. Free universal health care is often touted as a goal, even while Canada's own attempts at this enterprise are failing and care is being rationed by using waiting lists (Ramsay et al. 1998). In the developing world, resources are spread even thinner, and health care providers often do not have access to the drugs or supplies needed to provide adequate care. When clinics in Cameroon began charging user fees in order to secure a reliable drug supply, use of these clinics actually increased. The increase consisted of a disproportionate number of low-income users, who were for the first time given access to a reliable source of drugs. Previous attempts to provide universal care meant that resources were simply spread too thinly, leading to even low-income earners shunning these clinics (Dollar et al. 1998: 95).

Similarly, some governments that receive aid have no intention of directing this spending towards helping the poor. In the Cote d'Ivoire, for example, rural populations received only 11 percent of health spending, while accounting for 50 percent of the population. Much of the budget was spent on "highly sophisticated treatments not suited to the needs of the majority of the population, who needed low-cost preventive care" (Wick et al. 1998: 15). Clearly, aid directed to health care systems in this manner will be unlikely to improve the quality of life for a majority of the population.

WHY AID DOESN'T HELP

Government-directed aid tends to be ineffective for two reasons. First, such aid alters the political structure of a country by being a force of centralization and politicization. Second, a lack of appropriate evaluation techniques by donor governments has led to an uninformed selection of recipient countries, creating disappointing results. The following paragraphs describe how these factors have contributed to foreign aid's ineffectiveness.

Aid Is Centralizing

Aid can be a powerful force of centralization. Aid dollars often flow directly to the central government of a recipient country, where decisions on how to allocate this money are made. This is often not the best way to make expenditure decisions. Rather, in an efficient political system, decisions are made at the lowest level that has the capacity to make them. Local governments have more information about the needs, concerns, and goals of the local populace, and are also more accountable to them than are centralized governments with their larger constituencies. To the extent that aid discourages appropriate local decision-making, it reduces its effectiveness (Dollar et al. 1998: 22).

Aid also increases the returns to being involved in politics, diverting resources from productive activities. Because of their size, the flow of aid to some countries can be greater than their central governments' expenditures (World Bank 1998). This can have a distorting effect on the country, as the power and prestige of those in government and those who have domestic control over the aid dollars increases. Individuals previously involved in productive activities become more concerned about the workings of the political process. This encourages them to lobby, bribe, or even join the bureaucracy. Consequently, the effectiveness of business is reduced due to the lowered level of available talent for the private sector, which has adverse consequences for the whole economy. When a country's best and brightest workers dream of jobs with the government, the private sector must necessarily suffer (Bauer 1981:104).

Aid Is Improperly Evaluated

Common aid evaluation techniques also reduce aid's effectiveness by ignoring crucial determinants of success. These evaluations focus instead on the quantity of disbursements, or on narrow project-specific measures. The reason these evaluation methods fail to generate effective aid is because they do not give donor countries adequate guidance on who should get aid. The importance of this will be discussed in the next section.

The first problem with typical aid evaluation is that it is often quantity-based. This assessment method arises from the belief that if some aid is good, more aid is better. The Canadian government is often criticized by lobby groups, church organizations and others because the percentage of Canadian GDP devoted to foreign aid is low in comparison to other countries, or some unknown socially optimal level. Even sophisticated magazines like the *Economist* have espoused this dubious argument (*Economist*, January 9–15, 1999). However, measuring only the dollar cost of foreign aid is not a satisfactory way to evaluate it.[5] This common view that more is always better has also affected aid agencies who "have too often focused on how much money they disburse" rather than the results of the aid (Dollar et al. 1998: 6). Clearly this is unsatisfactory.

The second problem is that aid's success is often judged on a project-by-project basis. Despite the intuitive appeal of this standard, the counter-intuitive truth is that in many circumstances the return to the recipient country is not the return to the project funded, but is rather influenced by the reactions of the recipient government to the aid. Indeed, much of aid's success or failure depends on how the institutions in a country transform revenue into public expenditures. The following example illustrates this point.[6]

Before aid enters a country, the government has its own priorities and objectives. Money given does not flow into a vacuum. Suppose a country has eleven potential projects, each costing $10 million, that it is considering. The quality of these projects range from excellent (Project 1: 100% return on investment) to poor (Project 11: 0% return). Each of projects 2 through 10 have returns successively

10 percent less than the project immediately preceding it. If we imagine a foreign government with a budget of $50 million without aid, the government may choose to fund five projects, for example, projects 1 through 5.

A donor selecting a project in this country has a number of options. If the donor funds project 1, the apparent rate-of-return of the aid-financed project is 100 percent. This looks good for the aid-giving organization but does not represent the true effect of the aid. The true effect of the aid is the additional benefit beyond what would have happened without the foreign aid. Recall that the foreign government had planned, before the aid, to fund projects 1 through 5. If the country uses the $10 million of freed resources to fund project 6, the true effect of the aid is a return on investment of 40 percent. It is also possible that the resources freed are spent on project 11, which could have a high political return for the recipient government, but a financial return of 0 percent. Finally, the $10 million could finance tax reductions, which would have an unknown effect depending on how distortionary the prior tax regime was. If the donor country finances project 6, the apparent and actual return to the project is 40 percent. For the aid organization, this is a less favourable result than financing project 1; the effect on the country is however, similar.[7]

While this example is hypothetical, the real world consequences are not. Recent research shows that recipients of aid treat aid income exactly as they treat an additional dollar of domestically derived revenue. While a significant portion of foreign aid is *targeted* towards investment spending, "estimates suggest that the net effect of a dollar of aid is to increase public investment by only 29 cents—exactly the amount by which any dollar of government revenue would have raised investment. Similarly, an aid dollar used to finance projects in education tends to increase government spending in all sectors to the same extent as a dollar of government revenue from any source" (Dollar et al. 1998: 19). Aid is used by recipient governments as is money collected any other way (Feyzioglu et al. 1998: 54).[8]

THE IMPORTANCE OF GOVERNANCE

Governance is important because of the effect that governance can have on economic growth, standards of living, and the effectiveness of aid. Bad government policy puts constraints on growth by thwarting private incentives and distorting choices. Research clearly shows that countries with extensive restrictions on economic activity grow more slowly than those that do not. Recent work also shows that governance plays a role in determining the success of aid in generating growth. If aid evaluation methods do not take governance into account, poor country selection may occur.

Research shows that the quality of governance is an important determinant of economic growth. Burnside and Dollar (1997) conclude that better-managed countries have higher levels of growth. They estimate that changes in policy would enable some countries to increase their yearly economic growth by 2 to 3 percentage points. For example, "the difference in management between, say,

Thailand and Tanzania may have been worth about 4 percentage points of growth" per year (Dollar et al. 1998: 33). Similarly, the Economic Freedom of the World project (1996, 1997, 1998) indicates that from 1985 to 1996 the countries with the greatest restrictions on economic activity shrank at a rate of 1.9 percent per year, while those with the least government interference grew at an average rate of 2.9 percent (Gwartney et al. 1997: 34). Another study notes that "the large differences in per capita income across countries cannot be explained by differences in access to the world's stock of productive knowledge or to its capital markets, by differences in the ratio of population to land or natural resources, or by differences in the quality of marketable human capital or personal culture.... The only remaining plausible explanation is that the great differences in the wealth of nations are mainly due to differences in the quality of their institutions and economic policies" (Olson 1996: 19).

The effectiveness of aid is also influenced by the quality of governance, since aid is used as if it were regular budgetary revenue. As noted previously, a number of studies have found no evidence that aid increases economic growth. An extension of this research is a recent World Bank report that examined the influence of governance on the effectiveness of aid. The effect of aid on countries with a poor score on the economic management index created for this study is negligible, and perhaps even negative. This implies that aid sent to foreign countries with poor governance has been a waste of resources, or even a detriment to the receiving country.[9] Only aid flowing to better-governed jurisdictions was found to be beneficial (Dollar et al. 1998: 36).

THE CANADIAN EXPERIENCE

Since only aid distributed to well-governed nations fulfils aid's objective of increasing growth, the quality of governance in recipient countries provides us with a good criterion with which to judge Canadian aid. While the economic management index created for the World Bank research is useful, there exists a better measure of the quality of governance. The Economic Freedom of the World project, published by 53 research organizations worldwide, uses 25 indicators to measure the extent to which governments impinge on the economic freedoms of their citizens. The economic freedom index shares a number of variables with the economic management index of the World Bank, as well as the objective of differentiating between good and bad governance. [...]

Poorly governed nations are the world's poorest, and their governments receive large inflows of aid. [...]

Ironically, these flows, which represent a significant portion of the nation's resources, protect the policies that made the nation poor in the first place. Foreign aid, unlike domestic revenue, is sheltered from the ups and downs of the domestic economy. Since those within the political apparatus are in part subsidized and protected from the negative consequences of their own policies, these high levels of dependency serve to dampen the incentives and even the grassroots support for widespread programs of liberalization. Prudent aid should strive to encourage reform and lessen the effects of this subsidization of bad governance.

There are two ways to mitigate these effects. The first option, discussed below, is to condition aid expenditures on legitimate reform. The second option is to counterbalance some of the concentrated power of the government by directing aid expenditures to groups outside of the government in the hope that better governance might ensue.[10] In this regard, the Canadian record is disappointing.

CANADA AND BAD GOVERNMENTS

The World Bank study indicates that when a country is poorly managed, aid is not a sufficient ingredient for economic growth, but that good institutions and policies are. This supports what the Economic Freedom of the World project has already shown. Economic freedom (or good economic management, to use the World Bank terminology) produces economic growth. This research also shows that aid flowing to governments with poor economic management (or limited economic freedoms) is not helpful to development: there is no increase in economic growth, no lessening of poverty, and no increase in living standards. If aid is meant to fund development, its use cannot be justified for countries with low levels of economic freedom.

If aid is not the answer, what is? First, if one can identify reformers and elements of change within the government or country, public policy research and technical knowledge shared with these groups could go a long way toward encouraging change. By disseminating and discussing this knowledge, support for extensive programs of liberalization can accumulate. Public education projects in countries unfamiliar with western concepts of democracy and governance may also be fruitful. These options are unlikely to produce immediate results, yet long-run changes may be substantial.

Second, linking aid expenditures to reform will provide the incentive to make meaningful changes. This option, however, is fraught with potential difficulties. In the past, aid-granting organizations have had too much incentive to give out promised monies and too little incentive to ensure that the conditions of the grant were indeed upheld. A study of a particular subset of conditional loans found that although only 53 percent of loan conditions were met, almost all promised funds were distributed. Research suggests, however, that adjustment lending given to countries committed to reform helps ensure that the reforms are carried out (Dollar et al. 1998: 50–2). If Canada wishes to pursue this option, aid must actually be conditional. Third party information should be used to judge policy reform in order to prevent internal biases from creeping in, and aid must be withheld from governments failing to meet expectations.

[...]

ALLOCATING AID

The fact that aid is only beneficial in countries with higher levels of economic freedom indicates some guiding principles for the allocation of aid. There should be a shift of aid money from countries with low levels of economic freedom towards countries with more economic freedom. Public choice theory suggests, however, that it is questionable whether a political process can reach this perceived optimal allocation.[11] As noted before, research by Vásquez (1998) indicates that there has not been a system used by any government agency that has been able to distribute aid in a way that enhances economic growth. It is unlikely that government will be able to improve on this poor record.[12]

Voluntary organizations and action tend to move towards optimality without prompting. Investment naturally flows to countries that are well-managed and where the economic freedoms of citizens are secure. In countries with repressive regimes, voluntary organizations typically work with the poor themselves rather than with government bureaucrats. There are also organizations that exclusively focus on political and economic education in developing countries. This sharing of knowledge and the development of contacts between the developed and developing world can only prove to be fruitful. While research has only recently shown us an 'optimal' policy for distributing government aid, for some time, private actions on the part of individuals have distributed assistance more effectively than governments.[13]

Since private investment tends to gravitate toward well-managed countries, this lessens the need for foreign aid. If a country is well-managed, aid is not as greatly needed, due to the country's ability to attract private foreign capital.[14] Research indicates that if a country is mismanaged, aid does not help development. What, then, is the appropriate role for government foreign aid? We should encourage the development of institutions that protect the rule of law and private property,[15] and policies that move the country towards greater economic freedom such as freer trade, low and stable inflation, and the ability to exchange domestic currency for foreign currency;[16] after that, foreign aid has little role to play, since "developing countries are to a large extent masters of their own fate" (Dollar et al. 1998: 23).

RECOMMENDATIONS

Enhanced understanding of the consequences of government foreign aid, as this paper has provided, gives rise to a number of basic recommendations.

- *Immediately stop foreign aid to countries with low levels of economic freedom.* The World Bank research noted above shows that aid to these countries does not foster development. Without development, poverty is not alleviated, and standards of living do not improve. There are no rational arguments in favour of funding these countries.

- *Slowly cut back aid to countries with higher levels of economic freedom.* Research does indicate that aid can play a role in the development of countries with better economic management. However, private investment in well-managed countries lessens the need for aid. If aid is given, it should focus on helping to build the infrastructure and institutions necessary to encourage private investment and to secure self-sufficient sources of domestic financing. Aid should be given cautiously, and for a limited number of years, in order to encourage independence. Aid must be stopped if there are large reversals in economic freedom.

- *Economic freedom should be promoted in the developing world.* The research is clear: greater economic freedom means greater economic prosperity. Increasing economic freedom in developing countries has been shown to increase the standards of living, whereas foreign aid has been, for the most part, ineffective. If aid can induce governments to give their citizens more economic freedom, it should be used for these purposes.

- *Tariffs, agricultural subsidies, and other trade restrictions should be eliminated.* If we are concerned with reducing global poverty, freer trade is essential. Removing trade restrictions imposed by the developed world could significantly improve growth prospects in the developing world (Mihlar 1997).

- *The role of voluntary action should be highlighted.* Voluntary organizations and investment flows have always tended to distribute financial and non-financial resources more effectively than government. As the level of aid from the government is decreased, the role that these organizations can play should be emphasized to Canadians.

NOTES

1. These nations rank in the top 20 recipients of aid from 1975–95 in nominal terms (Chang et al. 1998).

2. It is doubtful that even continuous transfers can increase the incomes of anyone but a political elite; see Boone (1995).

3. For example, aid was sometimes conditional on the creation of economic plans, or directed toward massive capital expenditures.

4. A review of the literature on foreign aid and economic growth done for the Congressional Budget Office (1997) also found no evidence of a positive relationship between aid and growth.

5. Consumers, for example, do not evaluate the quality of goods by simply examining their price tags.

6. This example is taken from Dollar et al. 1998, pages 72–4.

7. The impact is equivalent to the government funding project 6, given that foreign aid funded project 1. The impact is better if the government funds project 11, and indeterminate if the government funds the lessening of tax distortions.

8. This does not mean that the money is by assumption wasted, but rather that the recipient government uses it like it would use any other funding, regardless of the donor country's intentions.

9. Tornell et al. (1999) offer additional support for this view. In their paper, the authors create an economic model of countries with powerful special interest groups and weak institutional structures. Their model predicts that windfall gains (such as foreign aid) will provide little benefit to this type of country due to the interaction of these groups. Their view is supported by the empirical evidence they represent.

10. This, however, is only a second best solution. Countries with low economic freedom will have lower levels of economic growth even if all aid expenditures are directed to organizations outside of all the government.

11. Special interest groups may have vested interests in funding particular countries in spite of a lack of economic freedom. For example, a recent *Vancouver Sun* editorial recounted how aid dollars were used in a foreign country to 'educate' foreign engineers about Canada's nuclear technology. Essentially, this activity was a marketing program for Candu reactors (Cassels 1999). See also Alesina et al. (1998) for a description of the political/strategic considerations entering into aid allocation decisions.

12. Governments around the world, for example, maintain minimum wage legislation even though its detrimental effect has long since been shown (Law 1999). Clearly, governments do not always do that which is in the best interest of the whole population.

13. Voluntary organizations should be mindful of this research, however, in selecting countries to receive aid.

14. Alesina et al. (1999) and Alesina et al. (1998), for example, show that foreign direct investment (money *not* from governments) is greater in less corrupt nations, as well as in nations with good economic policy and respect for the rule of law.

15. This role may not be a financial one, rather one of simply sharing technical knowledge.

16. Since these options are not cost-free and it may be impossible for a country to reform all policies simultaneously, we need to be able to choose among the various dimensions of economic freedom.

POSTSCRIPT

A continuing decline in the proportion of Canadian aid expenditures has arisen in the past decade thanks to sustained levels of economic growth and the low priority given to ODA spending. While recent governments have made strong statements in favour of increased ODA and Canadians consistently register high levels of support for the ideals of international development, Canada continues to lag behind several other international donors. Skepticism over the effectiveness of aid as well as the feeling that aid is spread too thinly to be of any use may have some influence over government policy.

However, CIDA's part in the international policy review, as reflected above, displays a willingness to respond to common criticisms and seek to maintain a strategic focus to Canadian development spending. These are aimed at achieving the Millennium Development Goals. Aid advocates also stress that aid can be tailored to improving governance and competitiveness while addressing the problems of the poorest of the poor. Time will tell whether political commitments will favour increasing or at least maintaining the current levels of spending.

Suggested Additional Readings

Addison, Tony, George Mavrotas, and Mark McGillivray. "Aid, Debt Relief, and New Sources of Finance for Meeting the Millennium Development Goals," *Journal of International Affairs*, 58, no. 2 (Spring 2005): 113–128.

Axworthy, Lloyd. *Navigating a New World: Canada's Global Future* (Toronto: Vintage Canada, 2004).

Bhagwati, Jagdish. "Development Aid—Getting it Right," *OECD Observer*, 249 (2005): 27–30.

Crosswell, Michael. "The Development Record and the Effectiveness of Foreign Aid," *Praxis: The Fletcher Journal of Development Studies*, 15 (1999): 1–23.

Gibson, Clark C., Krister Anderson, Elinor Ostrom, and Sujai Shivakumar, eds. *The Samaritan's Dilemma* (Oxford: Oxford University Press, 2005).

Hancock, Graham. *Lords of Poverty: The Power, Prestige, and Corruption of the International Aid Business* (New York: The Atlantic Monthly Press, 1989).

Morrison, David R. *Aid and Ebb Tide: A History of CIDA and Canadian Development Assistance* (Waterloo: Wilfrid Laurier University Press, 1998).

Nossal, Kim Richard. "Mixed Motives Revisited: Canada's Interest in Development Assistance," *Canadian Journal of Political Science*, 21, no. 1 (March 1988): 35–56.

Pratt, Cranford, ed. *Canadian International Development Assistance Politicies: An Appraisal* (Montreal & Kingston: McGill-Queen's University Press, 1994).

Rath, Amitav. "Canada and Development Cooperation," *International Journal*, 59, no. 4 (Fall 2004): 853–871.

Welsh, Jennifer. *At Home in the World: Canada's Global Vision for the 21st Century* (Toronto: Harper Collins Canada, 2005).

InfoTrac® College Edition

Search for the following articles in the InfoTrac® database:

Powell-Jackson, Timothy, et al. "Countdown to 2015: Tracking Donor Assistance to Maternal, Newborn, and Child Health," *Lancet*, 368, no. 9541 (23 September 2006): 1077–1088.

Wenar, Leif. "Accountability in International Development Aid," *Ethics & International Affairs*, 20, no. 1 (April 2006): 1–24.

For more articles, enter:
"development aid" or "Third World development" in the keyword search.

Web Resources

CANADIAN INTERNATIONAL DEVELOPMENT AGENCY (CIDA)

www.acdi-cida.gc.ca

CIDA is Canada's overseas development agency, involved in distributing resources to development partners throughout the world. Key information about CIDA and its strategies is available on its webpage.

UNITED STATES AGENCY FOR INTERNATIONAL DEVELOPMENT (USAID)

www.usaid.gov

The world's largest state-based international development agency, USAID is the American equivalent of Canada's CIDA.

THE NORTH-SOUTH INSTITUTE

www.nsi-ins.ca

Described as Canada's first independent, non-governmental, and non-partisan research institute focused on international development, the North-South Institute is an influential voice in the study of Canadian overseas development assistance.

THE INTERNATIONAL DEVELOPMENT RESEARCH CENTRE (IDRC)

www.idrc.ca

The IDRC is a Canadian institute dedicated to research into understanding and ameliorating problems of development in partnership with prominent researchers from the developing world.

Are the Millennium Development Goals Achievable?

✔ **YES**
SAKIKO FUKUDA-PARR, "Millennium Development Goals: Why They Matter," *Global Governance*, 10 (2004): 395–402

✘ **NO**
MICHAEL CLEMENS AND TODD MOSS, "What's Wrong with the Millennium Development Goals?" *Centre for Global Development*, 2004

In 2000, the members of the United Nations adopted a set of goals intended to cut poverty around the world by half by the year 2015. Since then, these goals, commonly referred to as the Millennium Development Goals (MDGs), have been a dominant focus for discussions regarding development assistance strategies and global awareness campaigns, such as "Make Poverty History".

The end of setting global development goals is not new. Rather the adoption of the MDGs is really the end product of a number of UN development initiatives dating back to the 1960s. The United Nations sponsored three consecutive UN Development Decades in the 1960s, '70s, and '80s, each of which focused on achieving economic growth.

In the 1990s, the attention on development shifted to issues relating to "getting policies right". As result, issues of macroeconomic adjustments, establishing good governance policies, and institutional reforms became the central theme. At the same time, the growing international human rights movement focused increased attention on social and economic rights, including the right to food, health care, education, and a decent standard of living.

As the decade of the 1990s drew to a close and a new millennium was about to begin, many members of the United Nations began to call for both a renewal of political will to tackle the challenges of development and poverty and a broader, more comprehensive approach than had been taken in previous decades. In 1998, the United Nation's General Assembly voted to create a Millennium Summit of the UN. This summit was held in September 6–8, 2000. Based on the deliberations of this gathering, the 189 members of the UN General Assembly subsequently voted unanimously to adopt the Millennium Declaration. As a follow-up to this, the Secretary-General, all UN specialized agencies, and other institutions such as the International Monetary Fund (IMF), the World Bank, and the Organization of Economic Cooperation and Development (OECD) were asked to develop a plan for achieving the objectives of the Millennium Declaration. The result was the establishment of 8 goals, 18 specific targets, and a total of 48 indicators. Collectively these became known as the Millennium Development Goals (MDGs). The aim of this process was to establish goals that would be both measurable and time bound—that is, they would have a specific target date for their achievement.

The overall aim of the MDGs is to reduce global poverty by half by the year 2015. Achievement of the goals assumed a global collective effort by both rich and poor nations, as well as a coordinated endeavour by all the major economic and social development agencies. The eight principal MDGs are: (i) the eradication of extreme poverty and hunger; (ii) the achievement of universal primary education; (iii) the promotion of gender equality and empowerment of women; (iv) the reduction of child mortality; (v) the improvement of maternal health; (vi) the combating of HIV/AIDS, malaria, and other debilitating diseases; (vii) the establishment of environmental sustainability; and (viii) the development of a global partnership for development (see table on page 218).

Each of the first seven goals is intended to be measurable and they are mutually reinforcing in their collectively tackling various dimensions of the global problem of poverty. The United Nations has set specific targets for each of these goals as well as established indicators by which progress toward their achievement can be measured. Goal 8 is more of an aspirational goal needed to achieve the other seven goals.

What is unique about the development of the MDGs, in contrast to previous UN development targets, is that they are specifically expressed in human rights language. The MDGs are premised on six fundamental values that find expression in the Universal Declaration of Human Rights (articles 22, 24, 25, and 26): freedom, equality, solidarity, respect for nature, and shared responsibility. The purpose of this was to emphasize the point that these goals were not just vague economic aspirations which nations could ignore, but rather fundamental obligations for which all nations and leaders should be held accountable.

In order to ensure that the MDGs were not just an exercise in idealistic dreaming, the UN called on each development agency and every member country to adopt the MDGs and carefully review their policies to ensure that their programs incorporate these goals. Clearly, success in achieving these goals was dependent on a mutual, self-reinforcing progress in each of the goals. No single one can be focused on alone. In addition, the achievement of goals 1–7 will depend heavily on the success of goal 8. In particular, the richer countries must be willing to adapt their development assistance policies, debt relief programs, and trade and technology transfers in ways the facilitate achievement of the goals. To encourage this, subsequent UN meetings such as the Monterrey International Conference on Financing for Development in March 2002, the Johannesburg World Summit on Sustainable Development in September 2002, the G8 Summit in Gleneagles, Scotland, and the 2005 World Summit in New York have provided opportunities to both measure the progress being made and to renew commitments. In addition, the UN publishes an annual Millennium Development Goals Report to chart the progress made to date in achieving the goals, and to keep up the pressure to work harder for their achievement.

But how useful are such efforts at setting global development targets? Is this an effective means of collectively rallying global cooperation and ensuring progress? Or, is this a futile public relations exercise by the United Nations likely to breed further aid fatigue and cynicism by setting unrealistic goals that UN decision-makers know from the outset are unachievable? In the first reading, Sakiko Fukuda-Parr discusses why the focus on the MDGs is an important exercise. In response, Michael Clemens and Todd Moss explain some of the weaknesses and failings of the MDG campaign.

✔ YES
Millennium Development Goals: Why They Matter
SAKIKO FUKUDA-PARR

Many development goals have been set by the United Nations since the first "development decade" of the 1960s. What is new about the Millennium Development Goals (MDGs)? First, an unprecedented assembly of the world's heads of state generated them when they met in September 2000. Second, the goals put human development—poverty and people and their lives—at the center of the global development agenda for the new millennium, a shift away from growth as the central objective of development. Third, MDGs are not just aspirations but provide a framework for accountability; they do not simply state ideals but go on to define concrete goals that can be monitored. Fourth, they address not only development outcomes but also inputs from rich countries, thus forming a compact that holds both rich and poor governments accountable for opening markets, giving more aid and debt relief, and transferring technology.

MDGs ARE A HUMAN DEVELOPMENT AGENDA

The eight MDGs—poverty, education, gender equality, child mortality, maternal health, HIV/AIDS and other diseases, environment, and global partnership—have been areas of concern for some time, but they have not been at the center of the UN's development agenda. The first, second, and third UN development decades (1960s, 1970s, and 1980s) were more involved in economic transformation and growth, especially industrialization. The adoption of the MDGs reflects an important endorsement of the central objectives of poverty and human well-being. The MDGs speak directly to improving human lives.

In the development debates of the past four decades, the debate has shifted among economists and policymakers about how much attention should be paid to economic growth, to people, and to poverty. Although almost everyone would agree that all three objectives are important, some assume that economic growth is primary. Human needs are often overshadowed by the preoccupation with the growth of the gross domestic product (GDP). Economic expansion is critical to human flourishing, but it is a means, not an end in itself. Economic development can be ruthless, by benefiting some at the expense of others; voiceless, by excluding the voice of people; jobless, by creating wealth but not jobs; futureless, by exhausting the next generation's resources; and rootless, by destroying cultural traditions and identities.

Many economists have developed alternative frameworks or approaches. In the 1970s, the International Labour Organization (ILO) and economists such as Hans Singer and Richard Jolly argued for the importance of employment. In the 1980s, Paul Streeten, Frances Stewart, and others argued that the priority of development was to meet basic needs. Starting in the 1980s, Amartya Sen began to define development as expanding people's capabilities to lead lives that they value. Building on these ideas, Mahbub ul Haq launched the concept of human development, which defines development as a process of creating an environment in which all people can lead full, creative lives. He launched the annual *Human Development Reports* in 1990 to track the progress of countries according to measures of human well-being rather than economic growth. The Human Development Index (HDI) was introduced to reflect capabilities in three critical areas: to survive, to be knowledgeable, and to enjoy a decent standard of living. These reports have applied this conceptual framework to explore different capabilities, such as being educated and healthy, but they also investigate areas such as political freedoms and cultural liberties and suggest policy tools to promote expansion of these capabilities. Over the years, a human development approach or paradigm has evolved.[1]

The Millennium Declaration and human development share a common vision, guided by the values of freedom, dignity, solidarity, tolerance, and equity among people and nations. These principles are also fundamental human rights, and the MDGs set standards for the "progressive realization" of economic and social rights. They are part of a multidimensional vision that integrates political factors such as civil rights and democratic representation, social factors such as education and health, and economic factors such as growth and employment. This vision considers people not only as the beneficiaries of progress but also as the key agents of change. The MDGs address some of the most critical areas of human development, although they do not deal with participation, democracy, and human rights.[2] MDGs are not in themselves a paradigm, but they are benchmark indicators of how we are progressing in human development and social and economic rights.

MDGs AS A FRAMEWORK OF ACCOUNTABILITY

The MDGs are not a new strategy but a new instrument for mobilizing action. The MDGs are not a technocratically defined set of goals that emerged from an analysis of development constraints accompanied by a finely tuned set of policy prescriptions. Rather, the MDGs are a global commitment and a framework of accountability.

The MDGs' newness is not attributable to their content but to how they have mustered political consensus on common objectives. They also explicitly commit world leaders to a collective responsibility for all people irrespective of national borders. The MDGs were not formulated overnight. They build on a global consensus reached in the 1990s among governments—a dialogue to which many civil society groups actively contributed.[3] All but two of the eight MDGs are outlined in the agendas negotiated and adopted at various UN conferences during the 1990s. The MDGs also draw on goals proposed by rich countries; the Organization for Economic Cooperation and Development (OECD) had earlier drawn up its own development goals.[4]

The MDGs are more powerful tools than mere UN declarations because time limits and quantifiable outcomes, by which progress can be objectively measured and monitored, are specified. They provide a framework for accountability at local, national, and international levels.

The most divisive element in negotiating the MDGs has been the eighth goal—global partnership—which includes trade, debt, aid, and technology transfer. This goal is important for the developing countries, but it is weak on accountability; it is the only MDG without quantified and time-bound indicators. Developing countries are not interested in opening themselves up to global scrutiny unless there is a real commitment to joint accountability.

An accountability framework is useful only if it is based on evidence. The UN system is mounting a systematic procedure for global monitoring and support. MDGs are monitored by specialized agencies that report annually to the UN General Assembly. The Statistical Division of the UN Department of Social and Economic Affairs consolidates information into an integrated data system. At the country level, the UN Development Programme (UNDP) is helping countries develop progress reports based on national data.

Many UN resolutions have been passed, only to be left with no follow-up. Other proposals succeeded in mobilizing massive action and effectively realized their objectives, such as achieving universal coverage in child immunization. The leadership role of the UN Children's Fund (UNICEF) in advocating and monitoring progress was key to the success of those important goals.[5]

The UN secretary-general's personal leadership has helped energize and activate the entire UN system, including the World Bank and the International Monetary Fund (IMF). The UN has established a special project with three components: support for countries in defining national strategies and monitoring progress; a campaign to advocate for MDG priorities and for the mobilization of all stakeholders; and a research program to identify an agenda for action.

Unlike other UN goals that have been inconsistent with one another or ignored by the Bretton Woods institutions, international cooperation is gradually being aligned with MDG priorities. Although still not implemented fully, the Washington-based financial institutions are committed to including the MDGs in their Poverty Reduction Strategy Papers (PRSPs). These are national policy frameworks being prepared in the world's poorest aid-dependent countries; they define poverty-reducing targets, priorities, and measures on which donors can agree. As shown in the *Human Development Report 2003,* development should accelerate dramatically to achieve the MDGs in most of the world's poorest countries. The PRSPs then should be first to reflect such ambitious goals and targets. But much more needs to be done.[6]

MDGs AS A COMPACT

The MDGs differ from previous international goals in another politically significant way. For the first time, rich countries' inputs are considered alongside the objectives of poor countries. Of the eight MDGs, the eighth—global partnership—is the most significant departure. It commits rich countries to do more in the areas of access to trade, aid, debt relief, and technology transfer. If this goal had not been included, developing countries would not have agreed to the MDG package.

The MDGs have been followed by the Monterrey Consensus, adopted at the International Conference on Financing for Development held in March 2002.[7] Again, responsibility and accountability are shared. Recipient countries should do more to improve the effective use of resources by employing measures such as combating corruption and strengthening institutions, and donor countries should provide greater support in return.

However, like other international compacts, the MDGs suffer two related weaknesses: asymmetry and noncompliance. Accountability of developed country performance is weak because goal eight has neither timetable nor quantified targets. Moreover, there is little pressure to even report efforts. Sweden has taken the lead in presenting a self-assessment to the Economic and Social Council, but this is not required. Attempts to make reporting a requirement in the UN have failed.

THE IMPORTANCE OF NATIONAL OWNERSHIP

The MDGs are not without critics and skeptics. Some academics, social activists, and government officials have argued that the MDGs create false incentives and distortions. The most incisive voices have suggested the following:[8]

- They leave out many objectives such as employment, reproductive health, human rights, and many other issues that developing countries and civil society groups have been advocating.

- They do not go far enough on global partnership: they leave targets vague and neglect institutional reform. Issues such as the decision-making processes of the World Trade Organization (WTO), the governance of multilateral institutions, and the restructuring of the global financial architecture are excluded.

- They impose a large data collection and reporting burden on underresourced government offices.

- They could lead to top-down planning and implementation, thereby promoting a donor-led agenda at the expense of a participatory approach in which communities and countries set their own priorities.

- They could distort priorities by focusing on issues that appear arbitrary. For example, certain diseases are singled out (e.g., malaria, HIV/AIDS, and other communicable diseases), but other emerging issues (e.g., tobacco) are ignored.

- They could weaken the bargaining position of developing countries because the MDGs can be hijacked by the World Bank to create opportunities for further conditionality.

- They could lead to a preoccupation with quantitative rather than qualitative achievement, such as the number of children enrolled in schools rather than the quality of the education.
- They could encourage excessive optimism and lead to discouragement and cynicism if the goals are not achieved.

Although these legitimate concerns do not challenge the fundamental usefulness of the MDGs, they do indicate the need for critical choices. MDGs can be meaningful only if they are "nationally owned." Governments and communities bear responsibility for achieving the MDGs, and civil society has an essential watchdog role at both the national and the global level. As the guardian of collective responsibility, the UN must use its leadership to maintain and mobilize global political commitment. Donor support and inputs need to be aligned with national priorities, not vice versa. Integrating the MDGs in the PRSP process, for example, is therefore essential.[9]

The MDGs should not be interpreted mechanistically. The success and failure of a goal should not be judged simply by the achievement of a numerical target, but by whether it has galvanized political will to shift priorities and to accelerate progress. As critical benchmarks of progress, the MDGs make sense only when they are properly embedded in national strategies for development. Each country has specific challenges and shortcomings; adaptability to national priorities is of the essence. For example, for many countries, the threshold of U.S. $1 of earnings per day is not meaningful; a $2 per day threshold may be more helpful for identifying people living in poverty.

CONCLUSION

The MDGs show promise as an effective framework for holding key actors accountable for their commitment to eradicating global poverty in the twenty-first century. If we fast-forwarded to 2015, what would we see?

Only two targets would be met: access to clean water and the reduction of income poverty rates by half—mostly due to China's economic prosperity. In Africa, Latin America, and the Arab world, although the proportion of the poor would barely decline, the absolute numbers of those living in poverty would increase. The 1990s was a decade of dramatic growth in countries such as China and Vietnam. But it was also a decade when development stagnated or even declined in many countries. The *Human Development Report 2003* revealed a decline in the HDI for twenty-one countries; such a decline is unprecedented. Other indicators also show reversals. Primary school enrollment declined in twelve countries. Hunger rates increased in twenty-one countries. Child mortality rates worsened in fourteen countries. Per capita income was lower in 2000 than in 1990 in fifty-four countries. In thirty-seven out of sixty-seven countries with trend data, the proportion of people living on less than $1 a day declined in thirty-seven countries. At the current rate, it would take until nearly the twenty-second century to achieve primary education for all children. For lagging countries and regions, improvement would take even longer—for example, it would take Africa until 2169 to reduce child mortality rates by two-thirds.[10]

The MDGs are thus a clarion call to tackle the enduring failures of human development. Has it been heard? Too many people around the world still cannot meet their most basic survival needs, let alone lead free and creative lives. Every year some 10 million children die of preventable causes, 15 percent of the world's people are hungry, and about a quarter of primary school age children are not in school. Some 1.2 billion people, about a fifth of the world's population, live on less than $1 a day. The gap between those for whom opportunities for a creative life are ever expanding and those for whom even the basic options are denied is becoming wider and starker.

Should world leaders who sought to establish lasting peace and uphold the principles of human dignity, equality, and equity be taken seriously? Is the ambition to rid the world of poverty in the new century realistic? The answer is yes. The achievements of the twentieth century demonstrate that leaps are feasible in just one generation. Sri Lanka raised life expectancy at birth by twelve years in just seven years following its independence in 1946. From 1994 to 2001, South Africa cut in half the numbers who lived without access to clean water. China cut the percentage of its people living in extreme income poverty in the 1990s from 33 to 18 percent. In Botswana, primary school enrollment nearly doubled after independence in 1970, from 46 to 89 percent in just fifteen years. Actions during the last half of the twentieth century did more to reduce poverty than actions in the previous 500 years, all but eliminating extreme poverty in Europe, North America, Japan, Australia, and New Zealand. In the developing world, life expectancy has increased by twenty years, about as much as was achieved in previous human history. Illiteracy has been cut nearly in half, from 47 percent to 25 percent over the past thirty years. And in East Asia in the past decade, the number of people living on less than $1 a day was halved. In the state of Kerala, India, universal schooling has been achieved. In a generation, Singapore transformed itself from a disease ridden, ethnically divided, and uneducated society to one that has achieved levels of education and life expectancy that rival those of Western Europe.

The MDGs are realistic targets that call on both rich and poor governments, on civil society and international organizations, and on ordinary people to ask: What needs to be done to achieve the goals by 2015? At this moment, the goal that is farthest from being met is the one calling for a global partnership—rich countries simply must do more to facilitate trade, aid, access to technology, and debt relief.

NOTES

1. See Sakiko Fukuda-Parr and A. K. Shiva Kumar, eds., *Readings in Human Development: Concepts, Measures, and Policies for a Development Paradigm* (New York: Oxford University Press, 2003).

2. Millennium Declaration, United Nations, September 2000, UN Doc. A/RES/55/2.

3. See Louis Emmerij, Richard Jolly, and Thomas G. Weiss, *Ahead of the Curve? UN Ideas and Challenges* (Bloomington: Indiana University Press, 2001), chap. 4.

4. *Shaping the 21st Century: The Contribution of Development Cooperation* (Paris: OECD, 1996).

5. Richard Jolly, "Do UN Goals Make a Difference?" Background paper for *Human Development Report 2003*. See also Richard Jolly, Louis Emmerij, Dharam Ghai, and Frédéric Lapeyre, *UN Contributions to Development Thinking and Practice* (Bloomington: Indiana University Press, 2004), chap. 10.

6. Makiko Harrison, Jeni Klugman, and Eric Swanson, "Are Poverty Reduction Strategy Papers Undercutting the Millennium Development Goals?" Draft mimeograph, 17 September 2003.

7. The consensus can be found on the UN Economic and Social Development website at www.un.org/esa/ffd/aconf198-11.pdf.

8. See John Foster, *The Millennium Declaration: Engaging Civil Society Organisations* (New York: World Federation of United Nations Associations, 2002), available online at www.wfuna.org; Roberto Bissio, *Civil Society and the MDGs* (Montevideo: Instituto del Tercer Mundo, 2003); Howard White and Richard Black, eds., *Targeting Development: Critical Perspectives on Millennium Development Goals and International Development Targets* (London: Routledge, 2002).

9. David Booth and Henry Lucas, "Monitoring Progress Towards the Millennium Development Goals at the Country Level," in White and Black, *Targeting Development*.

10. UNDP, *Human Development Report 2003: A Compact Among Nations to End Human Poverty* (New York: Oxford University Press, 2003).

✗ NO

What's Wrong with the Millennium Development Goals?

MICHAEL CLEMENS AND TODD MOSS

In mid-September international leaders will gather for a Summit at the United Nations to consider how well the world has kept its promises made five years earlier. In September 2000 at the UN, the largest ever gathering of heads-of-state unanimously adopted the Millennium Declaration, committing to reach eight goals by 2015. Known as the MDGs (Table 9.1), these are the yardstick by which current international development efforts are to be judged. A flurry of studies also estimated that, if the MDGs were to be reached, global aid levels would have to rise by $50 billion per year.

The first message from the Summit will no doubt be grim. Despite gains by many countries (especially India and China), much of the world is off track and will not reach the MDGs. Sub-Saharan Africa will probably miss them by a wide margin. Indeed, if things do not change radically, the number of Africans living in poverty may actually increase, while more than two dozen African countries may not even reach 50% primary school completion in time.

TABLE 9.1

THE MILLENNIUM DEVELOPMENT GOALS

Goal	Targets for 2015 (from 1990 level)
1 Poverty	Halve the fraction of those with income <$1/day
	Halve fraction of people who suffer from hunger
2 Education	Universal primary schooling completion
3 Gender equality	Eliminate gender disparity in schooling (preferably by 2005)
4 Child mortality	Reduce the under-five mortality rate by 2/3
5 Maternal health	Reduce the maternal mortality rate by 3/4
6 Disease	Halt and begin to reverse spread of HIV/AIDS, malaria and other major diseases
7 Environment	Halve the ratio of people without access to safe drinking water and basic sanitation
8 Global partnership	7 targets related to: trade, debt, youth, technology, drugs affordability, and special needs

This apparently bleak state of affairs will lead to the second message from the Summit: that more aid is needed. Even though global aid rose from $53 billion in 2000 to $79 billion in 2004, the increases have been slow in coming and less than the hoped-for doubling. In fact, the lack of progress in meeting the MDGs will be used to demand more aid sooner and possibly to justify implementing proposals to tax international airline tickets or to borrow from private capital markets. But are the goals really achievable? Are the expectations of what more aid can do realistic? If not, is the aid community setting up Africa, and themselves, for failure?

ARE THE MDGs PRACTICAL TARGETS?

The MDGs are laudable and undoubtedly well-intentioned. But that does not mean they are realistic for all countries. Based on the actual rates of progress for both rich and poor countries in the past, the MDGs are now asking many countries to perform at the top end of historical experience. Indeed, in a few cases the bar for the world's poorest countries is now set well above any historical experience. To take just a few examples:

Goal 1: Halving poverty. African economies must grow at about 7% per year over 2000–2015 in order to halve the number of people living below the poverty line. Just seven out of 153 countries for which we have data accomplished this feat in the preceding 15 years (Figure 9.1). Of those seven, only two were African: Botswana and Equatorial Guinea, neither of which are easily replicable.

Goal 2: Universal primary school completion. Many countries are starting from such a low level that they must now attain in about a decade what rich countries took nearly a century to complete. At least 20 African countries have primary school enrollment of 70% or less, but to reach 100% by 2015 is enormously ambitious if history is any guide (Figure 9.2).

Goal 4: Decrease child mortality by two thirds. If the same goal had been set in 1975, only one poor country in the world (Indonesia) would have met the goal (Figure 9.3).

CAN MORE AID ACHIEVE THEM?

The studies suggesting $50 billion more is needed each year are frequently misinterpreted and contribute to an excessive—and unhelpful—focus on aid. All of the studies have significant problems with the methods used to arrive at the bottom line. The more careful ones come with caveats, but these tend to get lost once advocates or the media get hold of them. More importantly, by putting a price tag on outcomes, cost estimates inadvertently create an illusion that any goal can be met, if only the right amount of money can be mobilized. Among development experts, however, it is widely accepted that resources are not the sole—and perhaps not even the most important—constraint to meeting the MDGs.

FIGURE 9.1
GROWTH GOAL VS. PERFORMANCE

Each dot represents one country. Only a handful of countries on Earth, in the best of circumstances, grew recently at the rate all of Sub-Saharan Africa would need to grow in order to halve poverty by 2015.

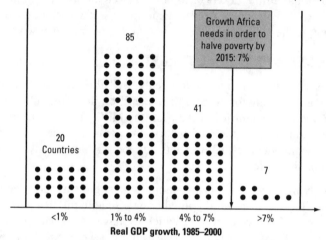

Includes all 153 countries for which the World Bank's World Development Indicators 2005 lists constant-price GDP.

FIGURE 9.2
EDUCATION GOAL VS. PERFORMANCE

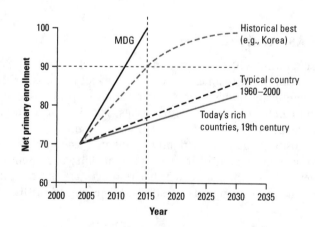

FIGURE 9.3

CHILD MORTALITY GOAL VS. 1975–2000 PERFORMANCE

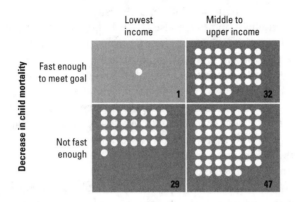

No amount of aid will make Africa grow at 7%. A huge literature looks at the link between aid and economic growth, and the results are not overly promising. Even those studies that do show aid can cause growth (for example, certain kinds of aid or that given to countries with good policies), also show very steep diminishing returns to additional aid. That is, even if aid boosts growth a little, more aid cannot make Africa grow like China.

In the social sectors it is also already well known that more money often does not translate into results; more health spending does not necessarily mean better health. This is because of deep structural problems in local health and education systems that aid projects have a poor record of rapidly removing. The effectiveness of aid is at times also undermined by the way donors operate.

Most importantly, the weak link between spending and services exists also because health and education do not occur in a vacuum, but rather in a broader economic environment. It may be an uncomfortable truth, but even something as basic as primary education still has a demand side. The desire of parents to keep their children in school is affected not only by the availability and quality of schools, but also by a range of incentives linked to cultural preferences, family circumstances, and wider changes in the economy. Knowing the cost of putting several million children through school may be useful, but it is not the same as knowing how to actually get them in school.

WHAT MIGHT BE THE DOWNSIDE?

A literal interpretation of the MDGs accepts the goals as real targets. A more nuanced view might see the MDGs as a symbol of the kinds of outcomes toward which the world should strive. This view takes the MDGs as a tool, not a practical target. Goals generate discussion, focus attention, and help assign accountability. The MDGs have doubtlessly served these purposes to some degree.

But there is a long history of setting international development goals. In the 1960s the UN set its sights on universal primary education by 1980, and in 1980 it committed to 6.5% economic growth throughout the developing world by 1990—among many, many others. Through the 1980s and 1990s there was growth, poverty reduction, improved schooling, and much else to celebrate throughout the large majority of the developing world, but did anyone notice? These impossible goals focused attention far away from what was accomplished through sound domestic policies, aid, and other forms of cooperation. The latest round of unattainable goals will do so again. That's bad for poor people and bad for the development community.

Indeed, there is a real risk that the MDGs, as currently conceived and promoted, could turn real development successes into imaginary failures. Creating targets such as the MDGs may help to rejuvenate the aid debate and energize the development community. But there is also a danger that the MDGs, by creating utopian expectations of what can be achieved quickly, will create unnecessary impressions of failure.

Burkina Faso, for instance, has net primary school enrollment of around 40 to 45%. Should it be termed success or failure if wise governance, aid, and other types of engagement allow the country to reach only 60% enrollment by 2015? Such a feat would be extraordinary by historical standards, but a patent failure according to the MDGs. It took the United States over a century to make the transition from Burkina Faso's current enrollment rate to universal primary schooling. Would it not energize the development community more to celebrate Burkina Faso's performance than to condemn it as disaster?

The excessive focus on aid is also potentially risky. Aid can and will play a role in improving the lives of the world's poor. But another $50 billion or even $100 billion more, cannot achieve the MDGs. If lots more money does appear, unrealistic promises will undercut much of the rationale for aid and bolster those who claim aid is a waste. If huge increases in aid do not materialize, then poor countries will complain that rich countries have not lived up to their end of the MDG bargain.

WHAT NOW?

The MDGs, despite these risks, are not going away. The UN, its members governments, and the donor community should:

- Accept that it is not feasible for most countries to reach most of the MDGs, especially in Africa;

- Stop misusing costing studies as evidence that we can purchase outcomes with more aid (the studies themselves explicitly make no such claim);

- Consider new ways of recognizing real success at the country level rather than in global targets;

- Avoid these problems with the next round of goals—yes, there will be more—by basing them on where countries are and on reasonable expectations of performance.

CONCLUSION

The vast majority of developing countries will miss most of the MDG targets in 2015. Nearly all African countries will miss most of them. But this will not be a sign that poor countries have failed, or that aid has been a waste. Nor will it primarily be because donors did not spend the right amount of money.

At the same time, many of the world's poorest countries will in all likelihood make great progress in improving the quality of life of their people—and aid will almost certainly have played a crucial part. It would be a shame if the MDGs, in trying to make the case that the world can and should help the world's poor, wound up undermining the cause by over-reaching on the targets and overselling the efficacy of aid.

What poor countries need from rich ones is broad-based, sustained, moderate engagement—not emotional, moralistic, centralized big bangs. Aid can work, but it must be dramatically improved. Innovations like the Global Health Fund or the Millennium Challenge Account are a great start, but we need much more such experimentation and evaluation before "scaling up" makes any sense. And we need to go far beyond aid, investing in key technologies (such as vaccines), opening our markets, finding creative arrangements for win-win labor mobility, and many other avenues to support ongoing efforts by poor countries themselves.

But development is a marathon, not a sprint. In a democratic society, the only way to build support for the long haul is to nurture a constituency by showing the public that good things happen in Africa and other very poor places. The MDGs simply will not do this. They were designed, in fact, to do the opposite.

POSTSCRIPT

The UN's Millennium project has been taken seriously by the international development community. The major UN multilateral agencies, donor governments, and developing countries have all drawn up plans to achieve the MDGs. Certainly it has been a valuable means of focusing the world's attention on the progress being made in development and mobilizing support for development efforts.

At the time of the adoption of the MDGs, critics pointed out that the plan did not include specific commitments by donor countries for the provision of adequate resources to meet these targets. Although some progress has been made, many now suggest that only a massive infusion of new aid funding will ensure that the goals are met. But is an infusion of more money all that is needed to meet the MDGs?

While it is possible that many, or even most, of the goals may be met at the global level, few would suggest that each country will achieve this at the national level. In fact, a large number of developing countries will fail in meeting the majority of their national targets. Some analysts suggest that goals have been unrealistic at the national level since meeting them would require rates of improvement in economic growth and development that are at the outer edges of historical precedent. Thus, the simple infusion of more funds will be insufficient in itself. What then is the value of the MDGs? Is there a danger that, if not fully met, they will simply foster greater cynicism about target setting and future aid-giving? Or will they serve as a symbol of hoping for mobilizing an even greater global collective effort?

Suggested Additional Readings

Attaran, Amir. "An Immeasurable Crisis? A Criticism of the Millennium Development Goals and Why They Cannot Be Measured," *PLoS Medicine*, 2, no. 10 (2005): 955–961.

Atkinson, A.B. "Funding the Millennium Development Goals: A Challenge for Global Public Finance," *European Review*, 14, no. 4 (2006): 555–564.

Bond, Patrick. "Global Governance Campaigning and MDGs: From Top-down to Bottom-up Anti-poverty Work," *Third World Quarterly*, 27, no. 2 (2006): 339–354.

Bosman, M. Martin, and M. Mark Amen. "Recasting Neo-liberalism in the Americas: A Critique of the Preliminary Needs Assessment of the Millennium Development Goals in the Dominican Republic," *Globalizations*, 3, no. 2 (2006): 227–236.

Davey, Gail, Daniel Fekade, and Eldryd Parry. "Must Aid Hinder Attempts to Reach the Millennium Development Goal," *Lancet*, 367, no. 9511 (2006): 629–631.

Grown, Caren. "Answering the Skeptics: Achieving Gender Equality and the Millennium Development Goals," *Development,* 48, no. 3 (2005): 82–86.

Mestrum, Francine. "Global Poverty Reduction: A New Social Paradigm?" *Development,* 49, no. 2 (2006): 62–66.

Mistry, Percy S. "Reasons for Sub-Saharan Africa's Development Deficit that the Commission for Africa Did Not Consider," *African Affairs,* 104, no. 417 (2005): 665–678.

"The Millennium Development Goals: How Are We Doing?" *Scientific American,* 293, no. 3 (2005): 62–63.

Soederberg, Susanne. "Recasting Neoliberal Dominance in the Global South? A Critique of the Monterrey Consensus," *Alternatives: Global, Local, Political,* 30, no. 3 (2005): 325–364.

Taylor, Ian. "The Millennium Development Goals and Africa: Challenges Facing the Commonwealth," *Round Table,* 95, no. 385 (2006): 365–382.

InfoTrac® College Edition

Search for the following articles in the InfoTrac® database:

"Aid Must Be Better Targeted for MDGs," *Finance & Development,* 43, no. 2 (June 2006): 2.

Sachs, Jeffrey. "A Practical Plan to Achieve the MDGs," *UN Chronicle,* 42, no. 2 (June–August 2005): 5–6.

Wai-Poi, Matthew. "Financing the Millennium Development Goals," *Journal of International Affairs,* 58, 2 (Spring 2005): 285–290.

For more articles, enter:
"millennium development goals" and "MDGs" in the keyword search.

Web Resources

UN MILLENNIUM DEVELOPMENT GOALS

www.un.org/millenniumgoals/

This official site of the UN's campaign to support achievement of the Millennium Development Goals contains the annual report of the Secretary-General on the global progress in meeting the goals. It also contains a number of other UN documents relating to the MDGs.

WORLD BANK & MILLENNIUM DEVELOPMENT GOALS

ddp-ext.worldbank.org/ext/GMIS/home.do?siteId=2

The is the World Bank's official page for tracking progress in achieving the MDGs. It contains a number of maps, charts, and tables reporting on the achievement of these goals in various parts of the world.

UNDP MILLENNIUM DEVELOPMENT GOALS

www.undp.org/mdg/

This United Nations Development Programme provides a number of resources for tracking the achievement of the goals and discussions of the strategies being employed.

MILLENNIUM CAMPAIGN

www.millenniumcampaign.org

This is the site of the UN-supported Millennium Campaign. You will find a number of reports of the activities of NGOs and other civil society groups supporting the MDGs.

MAKE POVERTY HISTORY

www.makepovertyhistory.org

One of the larger transnational advocacy efforts that has promoted the achievement of the MDGs, along with other goals, is the Make Poverty History campaign. This site has a number of resources available as well as links to other campaigns.

Has the Adoption of a Rights-based Approach to Development Failed?

✔ **YES**

PETER UVIN, "On High Moral Ground: The Incorporation of Human Rights by the Development Enterprise," *Praxis: The Fletcher Journal of Development Studies*, XVII (2002)

✘ **NO**

HUGO SLIM, "Making Moral Low Ground: Rights as the Struggle for Justice and the Abolition of Development," *Praxis: The Fletcher Journal of Development Studies*, XVII (2002)

Following the Second World War, the discourses on human rights and development emerged simultaneously but largely independent of each other. Development discourse focused on the notion of development as a problem of promoting economic growth. Whether this meant increases in the Gross National Product, meeting "basic needs," or promoting "structural adjustment policies," human rights were largely absent from the equation.

Within the human rights field, debates focused on the appropriate balance between traditional civil and political rights and the more collectivist-oriented economic, social, and cultural rights. The dichotomy between these two sets of rights was formally institutionalized by the adoption in 1966 of two separate international agreements—the International Covenant on Civil and Political Rights and the International Covenant on Economic, Social, and Cultural Rights.

During the Cold War, debates on the appropriate balance between these two sets of rights were largely shaped by the ideological divisions of the Cold War. Western nations, led by the United States, argued that civil and political rights should always be given priority and that true development could be achieved only when civil and political rights are first recognized. Many developing states, led by China, argued that social, economic, and cultural rights needed to take precedence. If someone is starving, what good does a guarantee of freedom of speech do? Some pointed to the so-called Asian Tigers—South Korea, Taiwan, Malaysia, and Singapore—as examples where authoritarian governments were successful in promoting development. Human rights might have to take a secondary place until economic development and growth is achieved.

The artificial distinction between these two sets of rights came under increased challenge in the 1980s. The first significant step in this process was the 1986 adoption by the United Nations General Assembly of the Declaration of the Right to

Development. True development, it was argued, ensures that all human rights are realized—civil, political, economic, social, and cultural. According to this concept, the two sets of rights formed an integral whole.

Acceptance of this notion gained momentum with the end of the Cold War. The 1993 UN Conference on Human Rights in Vienna made the case that all human rights form an undivided, interdependent, and non-hierarchical whole. This theme was picked up in subsequent UN meetings, such as the Copenhagen Summit on Social Development in 1995, which focused attention on the importance of human rights in meeting the goals of social development. A growing number of UN agencies began identifying the promotion of human rights as a part of their development agenda. For example, UNICEF takes the UN Convention on the Right of the Child and the UN Convention on the Elimination of All Forms of Discrimination Against Women as the reference point for all their programming. The United Nations Development Programme (UNDP) has promoted the development agenda, but focused its *Human Development Report 2000* on "Human Rights and Human Development." As its report noted: "Human rights and development share a common vision and a common purpose—to secure the freedom, well-being and dignity of all people everywhere" (p. 1). As noted in the discussion on Issue 9, the adoption of the Millennium Goals was also framed in the context of human rights commitments to ensure the establishment of a development process through which all humans could reach their full capacities.

As a result of these developments, a growing number of both official government development agencies and non-governmental organizations have integrated human rights discourse into their development programming. Proponents of a "rights-based" approach to development argue that this helps to establish a clearer normative framework for orienting development cooperation. It links development efforts to an internationally agreed set of norms that are backed by international law. As a result, citizens have a stronger basis for making claims against their own states, and civil society groups can more effectively hold states accountable for their actions and policies.

In addition, a rights-based approach marks an improvement in the "basic needs" strategies that many advocated a decade ago. Needs-based approaches tend to focus on the securing of new or additional resources for delivering services to the identified "needy" groups. Such an approach can be driven primarily by charitable or even paternalistic concerns which may overlook some more fundamental issues of social justice. Instead, rights-based approaches shift the focus to a more equitable sharing and distribution of existing resources, with greater attention to those groups and individuals who are particularly marginalized and vulnerable. As a result, some feel that the adoption of rights-based approaches give legitimacy to more progressive, even radical, approaches to development rather than the technocratic, managerial approaches that dominated in the past. Many of the quantifiable measures of development used in the past are no longer relevant. Instead, development success may now be measured in terms of the empowerment of people and communities to take greater control of their futures.

A growing number of intergovernmental development organizations, governmental development assistance agencies, and non-governmental organizations have adopted the discourse of human rights in their development programming. But, is all this just new window dressing? Has the fundamental way in which development agencies operate been significantly altered? In the following essay, Peter Uvin raises several questions regarding the widespread adoption of rights-based approaches. While he applauds the intentions, he is ultimately fearful that the changes have been primarily rhetorical and amount to not much more than "fluff." Hugo Slim responds by acknowledging some problems with the concept, while arguing that Uvin should not underestimate the importance of the "prophetic" use that many NGOs make of human rights discourse to hold governments and development agencies accountable.

✔ YES
On High Moral Ground: The Incorporation of Human Rights by the Development Enterprise
PETER UVIN

Until quite recently, the development enterprise operated in perfect isolation, if not ignorance, of the human rights community.[1] This does not mean that all development practitioners are undemocratic people or lack personal interest in human rights. Rather, it means that development practitioners did not consider human rights issues as part of their professional domain: they neither weighed the implications of their own work on human rights outcomes, nor sought explicitly to affect human rights through their work. This tendency continued until well into the 1990s, allowing the organizers of a prestigious UN-sponsored 1999 Conference on Nutrition and Human Rights to state that "the human rights approach to nutrition is not even on the radar screen"[2] and that "interaction between the [UN human rights machinery] and the UN development agencies has been essentially non-existent."[3]

This intellectual and operational gap began to close slowly from the early 1990s onwards. There is nowadays a significant and growing literature, mainly of the 'gray' kind, on the relationship between development and human rights: policy declarations and exhortations of the need for further integration, mainstreaming, collaboration, and analysis are commonplace.

While much of this is to be applauded—at the very least, a major departure from the previous policy of complete blindness and acquiescence seemed overdue—there is still much to worry about in this context. Two issues stand out: 1) much of this work risks being little more than rhetorical, feel-good change, further legitimizing historically created inequalities and injustices in this world, and 2) the many faces of power reveal themselves, as they always do, when the powerful and the rich voluntarily set out to collaborate and redefine the conditions of misery and exploitation for the rest of the world, and fund the resulting solutions.

I intend to critique some of the typical ways in which human rights have made their way into the development agenda. Specifically, I will discuss three levels that are part of a continuum from the most status-quo oriented approach to the most radical. At the lowest level, I will describe the incorporation of human rights terminology into classical development discourse. As this is purely rhetorical, the traditional discourse is not challenged at all. On the contrary, it is validated by its occupation of yet another plane of high moral ground. At a second level, human rights objectives are added to a range of goals and criteria for development agencies, thus allowing for the establishment of new programs with specific human rights aims. A perfect example thereof is the fashionable good governance agenda. At the third and highest level, the mandate of development itself may be redefined in human rights terms, potentially bringing about a fundamental rethinking of the development paradigm itself—a so-called "human rights approach to development." In this context, the work of Amartya Sen stands out. The following discussion investigates each of these approaches in greater detail.

THE RHETORICAL-FORMULAIC INCORPORATION

During the 1990s, bilateral and multilateral aid agencies published a slew of policy statements, guidelines and documents on the incorporation of human rights in their mandate. An enormous amount of this work was little more than thinly disguised repackaging of old wine in new bottles. As Frankovits rightly states:

> With an increasing demand for economic and social rights to be a major factor in development assistance, donors have tended to reformulate their terminology. Beginning with the World Bank's statement at the 1993 Conference on Human Rights in Vienna, followed by frequently heard assertions by individual donor agencies, the claim is made that all development assistance contributes to economic and social rights. Thus agricultural projects—whatever their nature—are claimed to contribute directly to the fulfillment of the right to food.[4]

A few additional quotes on the issue will get my point across nicely. There is the World Bank, claiming that its "lending over the past 50 years for education, health care, nutrition, sanitation, housing, environmental protection and agriculture have helped turn rights into reality for millions."[5] Or UNDP, declaring that it "already plays an important role in the protection and promotion of human rights.... Its program is an application of the right to development."[6] Essentially, these statements colonize the human rights discourse, arguing—as Moliere's character, who discovered he had always been speaking prose—that human rights has been the focus of these development agencies all along. Case closed; high moral ground safely established.[7]

Interpreted more benignly, this wordplay constitutes the first step towards a true shift in vision. Indeed, much scholarship argues that discourse changes have real-world impacts: they slowly reshape the margins of acceptable action, create opportunities for redefining reputations and naming and shaming, change incentive structures and the way interests and preferences are defined, and influence expectations. This is, after all, a key proposition of all international law: even in the absence of enforcement mechanisms, international law does matter by affecting actors' perceptions, calculations, reputations, and norms. The same insight is also a key tenet in so-called sociological, institutionalist, and social-constructivist schools of thought in the academic discipline of international relations. Hence, the kind of rhetorical incorporation discussed in this section, while it may change few of the immediate actions undertaken, may make a real difference in the longer run. How much of a change this will amount to is a matter of time.

There are, however, some serious problems with this habit of rhetorically incorporating human rights. Typically, until now, what this approach has produced is not only a simple sleight-of-hand; it is also wrong, for it overlooks the tensions between the logics of human rights and development.[8] As Donnelly convincingly argues, referring to the UNDP's new work on human development:

> Human rights and sustainable human development "are inextricably linked" only if development is defined to make this relationship tautological. "Sustainable human development" simply redefines human rights, along with democracy, peace, and justice, as subsets of development. Aside from the fact that neither most ordinary people nor governments use the term in this way, such a definition fails to address the relationship between economic development and human rights. Tensions between these objectives cannot be evaded by stipulative definitions.[9]

Working out the relationship between development and human rights requires more than simply stating that one automatically implies, equals, or subsumes the other. Michael Windfuhr, founder of Food First Information and Action Network, one of the world's foremost human rights organizations devoted to an economic right (the right to food), correctly adds:

> Besides the general misconceptions related to ESC-Rights[10]—that they are costly to implement, that implementation can only be done progressively and that they are therefore not rights at all but rather political objectives— one additional basic misunderstanding often comes up in discussions on how to integrate ESC-Rights into development cooperation, the concept that development cooperation automatically implements ESC-Rights because it is oriented to improve health or food situations of groups of the population. A rights-based approach means foremost to talk about the relationship between a state and its citizens.[11]

There is a real danger in this kind of rhetorical discourse. Far from constituting the first step towards a fundamental re-conceptualization of the practice of development cooperation, it seems merely to provide a fig leaf for the continuation of the status quo. By postulating that development projects and programs by definition constitute an implementation of human rights, the important distinction between a service-based and a rights-based approach to development is obscured.

Another pernicious tendency to manipulate words exists as well. In the previous paragraphs, the rhetorical sleight of hand consisted of arguing that the development community has always—automatically and axiomatically—furthered human rights, and everything is thus fine and dandy. The exact opposite rhetorical trick is sometimes employed as well. It consists of suggesting that major, epochal changes are now underway in the development enterprise, and they follow directly from the blinding realization of the crucial importance of human rights in development practice. The key human rights contribution to development practice, as repeated in countless documents, is the need for the engagement and participation of the poor in the processes that affect their lives.[12] This argument is breathlessly presented as a major breakthrough that we all ought to feel truly pleased about, as if development practitioners have not been proposing exactly the same thing for decades now, with very little to show for it. When human rights specialists, most of whom are lawyers, write this kind of nonsense, one can forgive them on the grounds of their ignorance. When development practitioners write such things, however, it amounts to deliberate misrepresentation.

The prime reason why development agencies adopt such language with its deliberate obfuscations is, of course, to benefit from the moral authority and political appeal of the human rights discourse. The development community is in constant need of regaining the high moral ground in order to fend off criticism and mobilize resources. As the development community faces a deep crisis of legitimacy among both insiders and outsiders, the act of cloaking itself in the human rights mantle may make sense, especially if it does not force anyone to think or act differently.

GOOD GOVERNANCE

At a second level we find the concept of good governance, developed by the World Bank in the early 1990s. The Bank identified "four areas of governance that are consistent with [its] mandate: public sector management, accountability, the legal framework, and information and transparency."[13] The good governance notion was an extension and deepening of the Bank's economic conditionality agenda, contained in the structural adjustment programs of the 1980s. It was widely perceived that these programs had not lived up to expectations and this failure was seen as a result of political factors. Economic conditionality had not worked as expected. Governments signed structural adjustment agreements but subsequently failed to implement them correctly, if at all. If only the workings of Third World governments were more transparent and accountable, the thought went, then surely other social groups would demand the right policies and a domestic basis for a stable and liberal policy environment would be laid. As such, the good governance agenda was explicitly designed to be the complement, the political extension, of structural adjustment programs.

The good governance agenda also fulfilled a rhetorical-political function. It allowed the World Bank to discuss the reforms that it proposed as economic and not political matters. In short, it constituted an attempt to de-politicize the concepts of democracy (and *a fortiori* human rights) in order to avoid allegations of undermining state sovereignty, as well as to benefit from the widespread acceptance that economic thinking enjoys in the development community. As the Human Rights Council of Australia puts it: "The use of 'good governance' arises from a perception that governments in developing countries will prove less resistant to such euphemisms than to talk of 'corruption' or 'human rights.'"[14] This apolitical nature is crucial for the survival of international organizations in a world of *de jure*, if not *de facto*, sovereignty.

In some ways the good governance agenda, being defined in a more restrictive fashion, is less politically interventionist than that of democracy and human rights. In other ways, it extends the reach of the international community, for it has almost no backing in international law. Unlike human rights (and some would even argue democracy), not a single international treaty or legal instrument commits governments to transparency, accountability of civil servants, or 'good' public sector management, however defined. State practice, for that matter, differs dramatically even among the rich countries.

The access to public information that U.S. citizens enjoy under the Freedom of Information Act is absolutely unthinkable in most of Europe. Then again, the degree of financial clout exerted by Wall Street on the U.S. Department of Treasury, or by large corporations on the U.S. Department of Commerce, if not on the entire political system in the United States, would be unacceptable to most European citizens. Yet the extent to which French foreign policy, especially towards Africa, is a private presidential matter beyond democratic scrutiny is unimaginable in most other countries. Moreover, the broad-based coalition governments underpinned by corporatist institutions reaching deep into society, characteristic of a number of European countries, are inconceivable in the United States. Indeed, profound differences in the way public institutions are accountable or transparent to citizens, or the way the public sector is managed, exist between rich countries. None of these matters are governed by international legal standards. Although good governance is defined as a technical matter, essentially another term for liberal public sector management, it is a strong extension and imposition of the liberal ideology of its promoters and is also totally unsupported by international legal standards.

More recently, the World Bank has officially converted to 'real' human rights, and its discourse on governance has subsequently become much less technical, at least in documents meant for human rights activists. This produces interesting results. According to the Bank itself, "By helping to fight corruption, improve transparency, and accountability in governance, strengthen judicial systems, and modernize financial sectors, the Bank contributes to building environments in which people are better able to pursue a broader range of human rights."[15] As this quote suggests, and as I have already discussed, much of the human rights conversation still amounts to little more than rhetorical repackaging. Policies that were once justified by their promise to improve investor confidence are now justified for their human rights potential.

Nothing else has changed. It takes more than a few ideological leaps to see how strengthening financial systems is a human rights activity. Certainly the framers of the Universal Declaration and the two Covenants were not thinking of shoring up banking reserve requirements, improving accounting standards, or liberalizing current accounts when they constructed the original human rights edifice.

In such statements, the many faces of power and their associated discourses come together. Human rights, free trade, or the willingness to let multinational corporations (MNCs) buy national assets become conflated, amounting to restatements of the 'good world' as the powerful see it. They are decreed from above, morally self-satisfying and compatible with the status quo in the centers of power. Rich countries remain immune to criticism. Over-consumption in the north, a history of colonialism, environmental degradation, protectionism, the dumping of arms in the Third World, the history of shoring up past dictators, the wisdom of structural adjustment, and globalization are not on the table for discussion. No wonder so many people resent the human rights agenda.

SEN AND FREEDOM AS DEVELOPMENT

At a third level, a new paradigm of rights-based development is emerging in which development and rights become different aspects of the same dynamic. The boundaries between human rights and development disappear, and both become conceptually and operationally inseparable parts of the same processes of social change. Development comes to be redefined in terms that include human rights as a constitutive part: all worthwhile processes of social change are simultaneously rights-based and economically grounded, and should be conceived in such terms. This makes intuitive sense, because at the level of human experience these dimensions *are* indeed inseparable.[16]

Amartya Sen has produced significant and often-quoted reflections on this new paradigm. His latest book, *Development as Freedom,* synthesizes many of his earlier insights. He defines development as the expansion of capabilities or substantive human freedoms for each person, "the capacity to lead the kind of life he or she has reason to value."[17] He rightly adds, "despite unprecedented increases in overall opulence, the contemporary world denies elementary freedoms to vast numbers—perhaps even the majority—of people." He argues for the removal of major factors that limit freedom, defining them as "poverty as well as tyranny, poor economic opportunities as well as systematic social deprivation, neglect of public facilities as well as intolerance or over-activity of repressive states."[18]

An interesting part of Sen's work is his treatment of freedom as simultaneously instrumental, constitutive, and constructive for development. This goes beyond arguing that both development and freedom are nice (so why don't we call them something else altogether). Rather, it sets out the deep and mutually constitutive links that exist between these two concepts and domains in ways that make their inseparability clear for all. As he states:

> There is the often asked rhetoric: What should come first—removing poverty and misery, or guaranteeing political liberty and civil rights, for which poor people have little use anyway? Is this a sensible way of approaching the problem of economic needs and political freedoms—in terms of a basic

dichotomy that appears to undermine the relevance of political freedoms because the economic needs are so urgent? I would argue, no, this is altogether the wrong way to see the force of economic needs, or to understand the salience of political freedoms. The real issues that have to be addressed lie elsewhere, and they involve taking note of extensive interconnections between political freedoms and the understanding and fulfillment of economic needs. The connections are not only instrumental (political freedoms can have a major role in providing incentives and information in the solution of acute economic needs), but also constructive ... I shall argue that the intensity of economic needs *adds* to–rather than subtracts from–the urgency of political freedoms. There are three different considerations that take us in the direction of a general preeminence of basic political and liberal rights:

1. Their *direct* importance in human living associated with basic capabilities (including that of social and political participation);
2. Their *instrumental* role in enhancing the hearing that people get in expressing and supporting their claims to political attention (including the claims of economic needs);
3. Their *constructive* role in the conceptualization of "needs" (including the understanding of "economic needs" in a social context).[19]

Such ideas have made great inroads in international development discourse. Take this statement, for example, from the UN Secretary-General's *Agenda for Development*, which clearly discusses the first two types of relations between development and human rights:

Democracy and development are linked in fundamental ways. They are linked because democracy provides the only long-term basis for managing competing ethnic, religious, and cultural interests in a way that minimizes the risk of violent internal conflict. They are linked because democracy is inherently attached to the question of governance, which has an impact on all aspects of development efforts. They are linked because democracy is a fundamental human right, the advancement of which is itself an important measure of development. They are linked because people's participation in the decision-making processes which affect their lives is a basic tenet of development.[20]

This was written five years before Amartya Sen's book, by an institution that is not exactly the hotbed of philosophical innovation. And we can go back further in time as well: cannot Wilson's four freedoms be seen as direct precursors of exactly the same ideas? Hence, we have to acknowledge that these concepts have been around a long time in the development field. Rather than congratulating ourselves on how smart and insightful we have become since we all read and talk about Sen's work, we ought to ask why we have not acted on these ideas before.

And this is where we encounter the limits of Sen's major contribution to development. There is no politically grounded analysis of what stands in the way of his approach. In addition, Sen does not even try to move beyond the level of broad paradigmatic insight. This is hardly a cause for discarding Sen's major contribution: no man is obliged to do everything. What it does mean, though, is that agencies, by signing up to Sen's vision, remain committed to little more than improved discourse.

Why then the barrage of praise for Sen's seminal contributions to development? The reason is deeply linked to the constant search for high moral ground that preoccupies so many in a field where competition for scarce resources is intense. In the development enterprise money is never made, only spent. The voices of those who receive the services supplied are hardly heard, actions are rarely evaluated, and product quality measures are almost totally unknown. In that world, the creation of attractive visions is a prime mechanism to ensure survival and growth. Such visions combine the appeal of science with the high moral ground of 'doing good.' Indeed, their essential function is just that—providing visions of oneself, markers of identity, trademarks of progressiveness. Many of the ideological changes that the development community goes through are traceable to this imperative, and the glorification of Sen's fine work is no exception. With insightful and stimulating conceptual formulations, but zero practical guidelines or obligations, there is little to disagree with in Sen's thinking: adopting it costs nothing. Aid agencies are left with a pure win-win situation.

In addition, Sen has been able to restate well-known concepts intelligently in *economic-sounding language.* He is an economist by profession, and a good one. Over the years, he has constructed a body of work that is deeply erudite, methodologically and theoretically sound, and empirically rich, as well as—a rarity in his profession—multidisciplinary and informed by a strong ethical vision.[21] Because he is an economist employed by prestigious universities such as Harvard and Cambridge and is therefore certifiably authoritative, the fact that he speaks the language of the dominant ideology of "economism" simply adds to his appeal—an appeal that has come to border on beatification since he received the Nobel Prize. We, the do-gooders working in the margins, need every economist who comes our way! Nevertheless, there are a few limitations in his work that should be discussed.

Specifically, if we believe Amartya Sen is right, what do we do differently when we redefine development along his path? It is interesting here to look at the institution whose discourse has most taken over Sen's ideas: UNDP. Their excellent 2001 *Human Development Report* deals with human rights, human development, and the relations between the two. This report is chocked-full of interesting insights, and has a distinctly different intellectual feeling to it than, for example, a typical World Bank report or even UNDP work a decade ago. Yet the most remarkable finding comes from the section that describes the practical implications of "promoting rights in development."[22] According to the Report, there are five concrete things to be done in the new approach:

1. Launch independent national assessments of human rights;

2. Align national laws with international human rights standards and commitments;

3. Promote human rights norms;

4. Strengthen a network of human rights organizations; and

5. Promote a rights-enabling economic environment.

Four out of the five implications—ensure that governments make references to human rights in their constitutions and remove contrary laws; educate, sensitize, or mobilize people in human rights; create national human rights commissions or ombudsmen—are largely legalistic and technical and will not challenge anyone. These are all potentially useful activities, but they do not reflect any mainstreaming of human rights into development practice. They are simply small, technical add-ons. Only the fifth seems to offer the potential of going further. Allow me to quote from it at more length from the same report:

> How to create an enabling environment in which public policy can most effectively provide resources for advancing human rights? First, the public sector must focus on what it can do and leave for others what it should not do ... Second, with this division of labor, the state can focus on the direct provision of many economic, social, and civil rights.... Third, the major economic ministries, such as finance and planning, need to integrate rights into the economic policy-making process ... Fourth, the private sector also has responsibilities in creating an enabling economic environment. Chambers of commerce and other business organizations should contribute to efforts to further improve human rights ...

This is all the new approach amounts to: a standard repetition of the late 1990s liberal dogma of the sanctity of economic growth combined with a measure of human resource development and pious statements that ministries and corporations ought to think about human rights. Vagueness dominates. Are UNDP's suggestions different from what the World Bank's *World Development Report* would allow? If so, how would they be operationalized? What would the role of external aid agencies be? Not a word on any of these questions. In addition, none of the human rights objectives relate to UNDP, the aid enterprise, or the international community itself. All of them are to be implemented out there, in this separate place called the Third World, but do not require any critique of the global system and our place in it.

CONCLUSION

As could be expected, there is less to the emerging human rights approach in the development regime than meets the eye. Much of it is about the quest for moral high ground: draping oneself in the mantle of human rights to cover the fat belly of the development community while avoiding challenging the status quo too much, cross-examining oneself, or questioning the international system. One can see power at work here, which is to be expected. Most of this rethinking constitutes a voluntary act by people in New York, Washington, London, or Geneva (not to forget Medford, Massachusetts). Smart and well intended, most of them, but not exactly people in great need to overthrow the established order or second-guess themselves. The people in whose name the innovations are adopted did not fight for this change. It is not part of a fundamental reshuffling of the cards of power or a redistribution of resources worldwide: no such dynamic has occurred. As a result, one could expect little more than fluff, self-congratulation, and more or less hidden transcripts of power.

I am aware that I am painting a particularly negative picture in these pages. As someone who has strongly argued that the old development paradigm and associated practice was in need of profound repair,[23] I am certainly not making the case that we should simply leave things alone, or that any alteration of the development mandate in the direction of a greater attention to human rights is by definition a bad idea. I also appreciate how major change always starts small, and how even rhetorical gains sometimes turn out to be the snowballs that set in motion fresh avalanches. I even realize that there are organizations and people, in both rich and poor countries, who are courageously rethinking long-held ideologies and practices in human rights terms. That said, for this paper, I have chosen the uppercut approach to argumentation: pricking through a few balloons in the hope that when they burst, the noise will be enough to rouse academics, policymakers, and practitioners from the comfortable sleep of the just.

NOTES

1. Katarina Tomasevski, *Development Aid and Human Rights Revisited* (New York: Pinter, 1993) and Hans-Otto Sano, "Development and Human Rights: The Necessary, but Partial Integration of Human Rights and Development," *Human Rights Quarterly* 22, no. 3 (2000), 742.

2. Lawrence Haddad, "Symposium Synthesis and Overview," *SCN News*, no. 18 (July 1999), 14.

3. Urban Jonsson, "Historical Summary on the SCN Working Group on Nutrition, Ethics, and Human Rights," *SCN News*, no. 18 (July 1999), 49; David P. Forsythe, "The United Nations, Human Rights, and Development," *Human Rights Quarterly* 19, no. 2 (1997), 334. Note that the right to food is probably the most well developed of all economic, social, and cultural rights; hence, the situation is even worse in all other fields of development!

4. André Frankovits, "Rejoinder: The Rights Way to Development," *Food Policy* 21, no. 1 (1996), 126; see also Human Rights Council of Australia, "Inquiry into the Link

between Aid and Human Rights," Submission to the Joint Standing Committee on Foreign Affairs, Defense and Trade, February 2001, sections 2 and 3.

5. James C. Lovelace, "Will Rights Cure Malnutrition? Reflections on Human Rights, Nutrition, and Developments," *SCN News,* no. 18 (July 1999), 27; World Bank, *Development and Human Rights: The Role of the World Bank,* (Washington DC: World Bank, 1999), 3–4.

6. "Integrating Human Rights with Sustainable Development," *UNDP Policy Document* 2 (1998), 6.

7. See also Katarina Tomasevski, "International Development Finance Agencies," *Economic, Social and Cultural Rights: A Textbook,* eds. Asbjorn Eide, Catarina Krause, and Allan Rosas (Dordrecht: Martinus Nijhoff, 1995), 409.

8. Sano, "Development and Human Rights," 744.

9. Jack Donnelly, "Human Rights, Democracy and Development," *Human Rights Quarterly* 21, no. 2 (August 1999), 611.

10. Economic, social and cultural rights.

11. Michael Windfuhr, "Economic, Social and Cultural Rights and Development Cooperation," in *Working Together: The Human Rights Based Approach to Development Cooperation–Report of the NGO Workshop,* eds. Andre Frankovits and Patrick Earle (Stockholm: October 16-19, 2000), 25.

12. DFDID, *Realizing Human Rights for Poor People* (London: DFID Strategy Paper, 2000), 5; Stella Mukasa and Florence Butegwa, *An Overview of Approaches to Economic and Social Rights in Development in Uganda–Draft report for DANIDA* (Kampala: Nordic Consulting Group, June 2001), 40; Arjun Sengupta, *Study on the Current State of Progress in the Implementation of the Rights to Development,* Commission on Human Rights, 56th sess., July 1999; Arjun Sengupta, "Realizing the Right to Development," *Development and Change,* 31 (2000a), 553–578; Note by the Secretary-General for the 55th session. A/55/306. Aug. 2000b. E/CN.4/1999/WG.18/2.

13. World Bank, *Governance and Development* (Washington DC: World Bank, 1992), *passim.*

14. HRCA 2001.

15. World Bank, *Development and Human Rights,* 3.

16. Craig Scott, "Reaching Beyond (Without Abandoning) the Category of 'Economic, Social and Cultural Rights,'" *Human Rights Quarterly* 21, no. 3 (1999), 635–6.

17. Amartya Sen, *Development as Freedom* (New York: Alfred A. Knopf, 1999), 87.

18. *Ibid.,* 1; see also UNDP, *Human Development Report 2001* (New York: Oxford University Press, 2001), 19.

19. Sen, *Development as Freedom,* 147–8.

20. United Nations, *An Agenda for Development: Report of the Secretary-General* (New York: UN, A/48/935, 6 May 1994), par. 120.

21. Please note that, in the community of his economist peers, the latter qualifiers—all the ones that follow the words "methodologically and theoretically," in fact—are much less appreciated. As a colleague recently remarked: "Sen couldn't get tenure in any good American economics department on the basis of his famous work."

22. UNDP, *Human Development Report 2001,* 112.

23. Peter Uvin, *Aiding Violence: The Development Enterprise in Rwanda* (West Hartford: Kumarian Press, 1998).

✗ **NO**
Making Moral Low Ground: Rights as the Struggle for Justice and the Abolition of Development
HUGO SLIM

It is always a pleasure to reply to the exciting, broad-brush strokes of a scholar like Peter Uvin. He paints an expressive and important picture of the adoption of human rights speak by powerful sectors of the international development establishment—or "enterprise," as he usefully describes it. Not surprisingly, I find myself agreeing with much of what he says and admiring the way in which he says it. There is indeed "much to worry about" when the powers-that-be adopt the liberationist language of the oppressed and drape their projects in revolutionary garb. Peter Uvin is right to be concerned that much of the new rights agenda in international development circles is really about "fluff and power." In this reply, I would like to amplify some of his main themes. But, above all, I would like to take them further and think about what happens when people other than the development establishment use human rights to talk about poverty.

But first, there are a couple of things that might be usefully added to Uvin's piece. It is slightly inaccurate to say that the development enterprise has lived "in perfect isolation, if not ignorance, of the human rights community." This is partly but not entirely true. Assuming that "the development enterprise" includes NGOs, churches, and community-based organizations (CBOs), then this statement is not correct. For those of us whose work is primarily concerned with Africa, it is easy to forget the experience of Latin America, South Asia, and even South Africa.

In these societies and their polities, the idea of human rights has played a central part in the struggle for development, social justice, and peace. In conflicts and political repression in Latin America, Freireans and liberation theologians conceived of development as a popular movement for social justice. While their analysis was essentially Marxist in many of its aspects, most of them were not averse to the political philosophy of human rights and framed their struggle for land, livelihood, democracy, and peace in rights terms. In this process they radicalized many European and North American NGOs. The highly conflictual experience of the Roman Catholic Church in Latin American politics played an equally major part in the Church's determination to reach a conclusion about the ideology of human rights and to endorse them as an important and acceptable aspect of Catholic teaching. Similar processes took place in South Asia around land and gender rights and in South Africa around the struggle against apartheid.

In reality, therefore, there are perhaps two development traditions—a Latin American–style one and a more paternalistic and scientific one. In NGOs that I know best, people have tended to stay in one tradition and seldom move between the two. One exciting possibility is that the introduction of human rights into development might mean that we see a more Latin American flavor to development struggles in future.

Another topic that may have been overlooked in Uvin's piece is the way in which human rights ideology is (perhaps increasingly) contested. This can take three main forms. Particular rights, around gender or childhood for example, can be contested at the periphery of a majority of rights that are generally accepted. In this way, states or groups can argue moral relativism on particular rights. More fundamentally, however, and in a way which Uvin himself comes close to doing, states, societies, or groups can reject the whole way the human rights regime functions as simply a bossy and superior aspect of Western hegemony serving Western interests. In other words, while societies may share many of the values expressed in human rights ideology, they will reject the human rights regime. Finally, of course, others will take cover under both these objections to use them as a means of ignoring international law and opinion while they deliberately violate human rights.

The fact that human rights ideology is contested is important when it comes to rights-based development because inevitably such contest will lead to conflicts that might not arise if a less legal and political discourse were pursued to focus on public goods. So, for example, one could envisage a government refusing to work with UNICEF on a child health program because it cannot tolerate the particular politics of child rights and state obligation that accompanies the program. Such a government could just as likely be a right wing U.S. donor government as well as an aid recipient government. Development pragmatists might argue that using the idea of rights in such situations is a sure way to ensure that nothing gets done for poor people. Thus, rhetoric or not, rights-talk can simply be a bad tactic in certain situations.

But enough about what Peter Uvin may have overlooked in his wide-ranging sketch. Let us now focus on his main point, that the adoption of rights-based development is really all about "fluff and power" and the taking of moral high ground without changing one's practice in any meaningful way. For this is a serious charge and one which is pretty well on target as things stand. In many NGOs advocating a rights-based approach, there is as much confusion as excitement. While most development people have got their hearts around a rights-based approach, they have not yet got their heads around it. Many feel that rights are important, but they may also have a hunch that Peter Uvin is onto something and that reading Sen and talking rights makes for little more than an "improved discourse" which may not be of much use to people enduring poverty around the world.

So, what about rights as fluff? Much of the breathless adrenalin rush of the new rights talk does indeed seem to offer a new way of feeling good. I began to embrace the political philosophy of human rights three years ago and have always noticed how passionate I can become when talking about rights and what a warm glow it leaves me with after lecturing on the subject. Peter Uvin is right. Simply talking about human rights quite literally makes me feel virtuous. At last, rights-talk seems to give the dry, quasi-scientific theory of development a moral and political vision. It can really make one quite excited. Such is the sad life of a British academic! This aspect of rights-talk is a bit like prayer. One mouths escha-tological ideas about human dignity and the coming of heaven on earth. One prays and feels good but has very little idea of its power and effect. It does indeed allow one to walk the "moral high ground" and makes one feel self-righteous.

But human rights don't only do this. They can act socially as well as piously. And rights-talk can function differently from different mouths. Human rights can sound and act very differently when they are spoken from what Gustavo Gutierrez calls "the underside of history"—the muddy side where people pay the price for those walking along the top. The same language of rights that may be rhetorical fluff in one place may be words of extreme courage and radical change in another. The power of speech is the power to name and define things. Rights-talk in Washington or Paris might be used piously as new words for the same old liturgy in the cathedrals of international trade and development. This might indeed be "repackaging" of old wine in new bottles as Peter Uvin suggests. It represents the power of re-dressing rather than power of redress. But from another place (a slum or the scene of a rigged election) and spoken from another voice (that of a poor man or a woman land rights lawyer) the same words of rights-talk could function prophetically as a demand for redress to change and challenge power.

So, I think the shift of development talk from previous discourses of philan-thropy, charity, modernization, and progress to one of human rights can be made to be extremely significant. Most importantly, rights-talk has the ability to finally politicize development between the muddy low ground and the moral high ground. Human rights give a language of political contract to matters of poverty, injustice, and armed violence. Rights-talk stops people being perceived as 'needy,' as 'victims,' and as 'beneficiaries.' Instead, it enables these same people to know and present themselves as rightful and dignified people who can make just demands of power and spell out the duties of power in terms of moral and polit-ical goods. In grammatical terms, it moves them from being the objects in some-body else's sentence to being the subject of their own free speech. This requires courage, knowledge, and organization but it has often happened and it will happen again. Human rights can fire people up. It is a political philosophy that can have deep meaning to people—meaning deep enough for them to risk their lives and die for. This is what happened in Boston in the 18th century. It has hap-pened many times since and is happening somewhere every day.

But does this mean that I have only moved from an idea of rights as fluff to one of rights as prophetic fluff? I hope not! But to be sure it is necessary to look at Peter Uvin's second point about rights-based development talk as simply serving Western power. Power certainly does tend to use ideas to serve its own interests and there is a serious risk that this is happening with rights ideology. As Uvin suggests, neo-liberal economic and political projects of "good governance" are simply being re-packaged in rights terms. There is little evidence that the structural violence and injustice of global power systems are being truly challenged by the philosophy of equal rights now mouthed by power itself. The traffic of change-talk still really flows in one direction only. Human rights in the mouths of OECD governments send a predominant message to the effect that "human rights demand that you—poor countries—must change." As Uvin observes, rights-talk has engendered very little revolutionary analysis of the structures of poverty or serious consideration of the demands these same human rights make for powerful countries to change their ways.

Yet I would like to suggest that the situation is not quite as simple or as bad as Uvin presents it. There may well be a way in which the fact that Western power continues to talk a discourse of rights may increasingly make it accountable to those rights. In welcoming human rights into the citadel of development, I have a hunch that rights ideology may function as something of a Trojan horse for those who really mean what they say about human rights. Peter Uvin's analysis focuses on governments, multilateral agencies, and transnational corporations as the adopters of the new rights talk. But, as noted above, there are others using human rights in a different and prophetic way down in the muddy lowlands. And, there is also a group of international NGOs who straddle the middle hill country between the moral highlands and the muddy lowlands who are also using human rights talk in a slightly different way to mainstream power. While these NGOs can be more pious than most on occasion, they can also challenge Western power extremely effectively from time to time. Between them, the lowlanders and the NGOs might make up an important group who, like the Greeks before them, may be able to leap out of the Trojan Horse and take the real struggle for rights to the heart of politics and policy-making in governments, corporations, and public opinion. Once inside, they may also find that the citadel contains many others who are sympathetic. For, dare I say it, government departments, political parties, and transnational corporations contain people who benefit from living on the powerful upper side of history but who would also like to change the world in pursuit of human rights. Uvin is right to claim that—in the main—the move to rights has not resulted in a thorough analysis of the construction of poverty and a system-wide strategy for its transformation. But some organizations among the powerful are making some connections. For example, the British Government's Department for International Development (DFID) has important policies that see the links between global trade and poverty, arms exports and violence, and energy consumption and ecological crisis.

The challenge for people using human rights prophetically rather than piously is to organize and create a counter-veiling force to the complacency and oppression of those on the moral high ground. (This is the part of the paper where Uvin's feel-good law kicks in as using rights-talk starts to make me feel virtuous again!) In practice, this means producing the analysis that Uvin notes is lacking and making the connections between global power structures and poverty. It means having the courage to build local, national, and global movements that argue for specific duties to be met by governments, corporations, and individuals that will enable all people to enjoy their rights. Above all, it involves abolishing the development enterprise as a neo-colonial program of correction administered from rich to poor and replacing it with a common political project that recognizes everyone's equal rights and judges the behavior of all on the basis of how they realize or violate these rights. This would involve all involved looking in the mirror as well as looking down from the moral high ground.

Then, finally perhaps, we could also do away with the very word 'development.' The common struggle for human rights and social justice would at last bring the end of the era of development. We could begin to talk a proper moral and political language of equality, fairness, social justice, right, and responsibility. This would be an equal discourse that has no notion of some people being whole (developed) and other people being inadequate (under-developed). Rather, everyone would be sharing responsibility and working towards common goals. This would be heaven. But we are encouraged to start making it here on earth or, at the very least, to continue to ensure that the basic moral goods involved in such a vision are struggled for each day. In doing so, rich and poor alike would have to meet on the muddy low ground where they all really live, and make it moral.

POSTSCRIPT

The growing acceptance of "rights-based" approaches to development has been applauded by many working in the field of international development. What it does, they argue, is to put discussions of politics, power, and social justice back into development planning, which too often focuses exclusively on technical and utilitarian economic calculations. Injecting rights talk into development discourse restores a sense of passion and justice and mobilizes people in a way that technocratic economic models of development cannot.

But, is there a danger, as Peter Uvin suggests, that simply shifting the discourse toward human rights will have little effect on the day-to-day operations of development agencies? Is rights talk mere "fluff" as Uvin claims? Is there a need for a greater "mainstreaming" of human rights into development agencies themselves? If so, what changes would this necessitate? How would development agencies operate differently if human rights were more fully integrated into development planning?

Hugo Slim reminds of us of the useful "prophetic" role that rights language provides for critiquing development policies. At the same time, the definition of many of these rights remains highly contested. For example, within many Western countries themselves, the appropriate balance between political/civil rights and social/economic/cultural rights is still subject to considerable debate. What is the appropriate balance between individual and collective rights? If these issues are still contested in donor countries, how can the appropriate balance of rights be incorporated into the policies of development agencies?

Suggested Additional Readings

Cornwall, Andrea, and Celestine Nyamu-Musembi. "Putting the 'Rights-based Approach' to Development into Perspective," *Third World Quarterly,* 25, no. 8 (2004): 1415–1437.

Eade, D. *Development and Rights* (Oxford, UK: Oxfam Great Britain, 1998).

Forsythe, David P. "The United Nations, Human Rights, and Development," *Human Rights Quarterly,* 19, no. 2 (1997): 334–349.

Hoehn, Sabine. "Reinventing Development? Translating Rights-based Approaches from Theory into Practice/Legitimizing Human Rights NGOs: Lessons from Nigeria," *African Affairs,* 105, no. 420 (2006): 488–490.

Korey, W. *NGOs and the Universal Declaration of Human Rights: A Curious Grapevine* (New York: Palgrave, 2001).

Jochnick, C. *The Human Rights Challenge to Global Poverty* (New York: Center for Economic and Social Rights, February 1999). http://www.cesr.org/

Rosalin, Eyen. "The Rise of Rights: Rights-based Approaches to International Development," *IDS Policy Briefing,* Issue 17 (May 2003).

Sano, Hans-Otto. "Development and Human Rights: The Necessary, but Partial Integration of Human Rights and Development," *Human Rights Quarterly,* 22, 3 (2000): 734–752.

Sen, Amartya. *Development as Freedom* (New York: Knopf, 1999).

Tomalin, Emma. "Religion and a Rights-based Approach to Development," *Progress in Development Studies,* 6, no. 2 (2006): 93–108.

Tomasevski, Katarina. *Development Aid and Human Rights Revisited* (New York: Pinter, 1993).

Uvin, Peter. *Human Rights and Development* (Bloomfield: Kumarian Press, 2004).

InfoTrac® College Edition

Search for the following articles in the InfoTrac® database:

Donchin, Anne. "Converging Concerns: Feminist Bioethics, Development Theory, and Human Rights," *Signs,* 29, no. 2 (Winter 2004): 299–325.

Singh, Anita Inder. "Human Right and Development," *UN Chronical,* 39, no. 1 (March–May 2002): 30–31.

Speth, James Gustave. "Poverty: A Denial of Human Rights," *Journal of International Affairs,* 52, no. 1 (Fall 1998): 277.

For more articles, enter:
"rights based approaches to development" and "human rights and development" in the keyword search.

Web Resources

UNITED NATIONS HIGH COMMISSION ON REFUGEES

www.unhchr.ch/development/approaches.html

This section of the UNHCR's website contains a number of documents relating to the relationship between human rights and development, including the text of the Declaration on the Right to Development passed by the United Nation's General Assembly in December 1986.

DEVELOPMENT RESEARCH CENTRE

www.drc-citizenship.org

The Development Research Centre on Citizenship, Participation and Accountability (Citizenship DRC) is a network of international partners working on the concepts of rights and citizenship in a variety of developing countries.

ASSOCIATION FOR WOMEN'S RIGHTS IN DEVELOPMENT

www.awid.org

AWID is an association promoting the enhancement of women's rights in development programs. Look here for a primer on "A Rights Based Approach to Development."

INTERACTION

interaction.org/rba/about.html

The official website for the American Council for Voluntary International Action contains an InterAction 2003 paper on "An Introduction to the Concept of a Rights Based Approach to Development."

HUMAN RIGHTS TOOLS

www.humanrightstools.org

This site is primarily designed for human rights activists. It contains information of relationship of human rights to humanitarian assistance and development.

RIGHTS AND ACCOUNTABILITY IN DEVELOPMENT (RAID)

www.raid-uk.org

Rights and Accountability in Development (RAID) was founded specifically to promote a rights-based approach to development.

INTERNATIONAL HUMAN RIGHTS NETWORK

www.ihrnetwork.org

The International Human Rights Network is a non-governmental organization supporting other agencies in applying rights-based approaches in their work. Their site contains considerable background material as well as links to other human rights–oriented websites.

Has Gender Mainstreaming Been Effective?

✔ **YES**
ARUNA RAO, "Making Institutions Work for Women," *Development,* 4, no. 1 (2006): 63–67

✗ **NO**
REBECCA TIESSEN, "What's New about Gender Mainstreaming? Three Decades of Policy Creation and Development Strategies," *Canadian Journal of Development Strategies,* XXVI, Special Issue (2005): 705–728

The question of how gender concerns should be addressed within development policy has been the subject of considerable debate and analysis over the past several decades. In the 1970s and the 1980s, advocates of the "women in development" (WID) approach argued for the need to "integrate women into development." As a result, development agencies tried to become more aware of the needs of women and give more attention to projects designed specifically to improve the incomes or production of women. The WID approach sought to integrate women into existing development processes by ensuring that women-specific activities were included in the list of projects being undertaken.

However, some analysts soon argued that the WID approach did not go far enough. Since the approach tended to be rather narrow, such as improving health services to women or improving women's incomes, more fundamental relationships of inequality were not addressed. As a result, WID projects often were unsustainable and often treated women as only passive recipients of "women's aid." Critics suggested that because development planners did not engage in a more comprehensive gender analysis of the situation, WID projects often were blind to the roles and responsibilities that men played in contributing to the ongoing disempowerment of women.

As a result, a shift to a "gender and development" (GAD) focus has taken place in order to address the more fundamental issues of unequal gender relations and to ensure that women are given full participation with the development process. Each development program, and specific projects within it, should be subjected to comprehensive gender and development analysis that examines related social, political, and economic structures and development policies from the perspective of gender inequalities. Projects are then designed not to just address immediate objectives such as increases in food production, but also to take into account the impact of the project on gender imbalances.

Although the GAD approach gained increased popularity, concerns were raised that this new approach too did not go far enough. Hoping for more gender-sensitive projects that addressed fundamental inequalities is insufficient if the policies and processes that give rise to them are themselves "gendered." Thus, in the 1990s, the emphasis shifted toward the problem of institutionalizing gender issues into development policy and planning. This approach, commonly referred to as "gender mainstreaming," argues that unless institutions themselves, including development agencies, are changed to better reflect women's interests, the real goal of gender equality will not be attained.

Unlike previous approaches, which focused on the gender aspects of development projects themselves, gender mainstreaming addresses the organizational cultures and ways of thinking within development agencies themselves. Perhaps the most common definition of what is meant by gender mainstreaming was set out by the UN Economic and Social Council in 1997. According to this definition, gender mainstreaming is:

> ... the process of assessing the implications for women and men of any planned action, including legislation, policies or programmes, in all areas and at all levels. It is a strategy for making women's as well as men's concerns and experiences an integral dimension of the design, implementation, monitoring and evaluation of policies and programmes in all political, economic and societal spheres so that women and men benefit equally and inequality is not perpetuated.

This means going beyond just adding a "gender component" to existing activities or practices and reforming the institutions and processes by which development projects are designed and implemented. Rather, gender mainstreaming seeks to overcome the limitations of previous approaches which still see gender equality as a "separate issue" that could be dealt with by distinctive projects. Instead, gender mainstreaming makes a gender dimension explicit in all sectors and phases of the policy planning and implementation process. It does not look at women in isolation, but looks at women and men—both as actors in the development process and as its beneficiaries. This does not necessarily mean that specific policies, programs, or projects on gender equality are obsolete. Rather, it ensures that the organizational environment in which policies and programs are developed and implemented do not themselves contribute to perpetuating gender inequalities. Thus, gender mainstreaming addresses the issue of gender inequality at a much more fundamental level and seeks to identify how current planning systems and structures themselves can sometimes create an institutional framework that contributes to the inequalities in the first place.

In the following essays, we find two somewhat different perspectives on gender mainstreaming. In the first essay, Aruna Rao, a former president of the Association for Women's Rights in Development (AWID), sets out that argument in favour of gender mainstreaming and outlines some of its benefits. In the second essay, Rebecca Tiessen of Dalhousie University evaluates the progress that gender mainstreaming has made so far. She argues that, from a feminist perspective, gender mainstreaming in many instances still falls short of its stated goals. Relying on a number of case studies that she has examined, Professor Tiessen argues that gender mainstreaming at times has focused on more technical and managerial problems and has not really altered fundamental imbalances in power.

✔ **YES**
Making Institutions Work for Women
ARUNA RAO

INTRODUCTION

The danger of insidious insider/outsider stereotyping undermines potential for making organizations work for women—and men. In one fairytale, gender equality activists working in cramped institutional spaces to make change happen for women are cast as the ugly stepsisters to the sexy, kick-ass, glamour girls of the global feminist movement. The flip side of this story is that of capable, dedicated feminists making a real difference inside institutions while strident ideologues do nothing but criticize what's wrong, alienating rather than building, and never lifting a finger to practice what they preach. Neither image is fair; both are damaging. Insiders need outsiders to create pressure for change. Outsiders need insiders to make real progress for gender equality.

Internal activists live in gender units, women's cells, programme and project offices in ministries, trade unions, international agencies, and a range of civil society organizations. They forage for resources amidst bureaucracies that make money disappear into vaguely formulated policy goals. They termite their way into organizational agendas. They are under threat of burial under mountains of paper requiring them to gender mainstream using a rights-based approach and show measurable results in neat little boxes. They try to entice higher profile colleagues to take gender mainstreaming seriously but they lose precious time in endless coordination meetings. Armed with the conviction that they know what makes a difference and that they can make a difference, the best of them fight the long hard battles from the trenches while quietly strengthening women to organize and demand their rights. Yet they get little airtime and even less support. Instead, they are denigrated as sell-outs by the radical feminist fringe.[1]

UNSUNG HEROINES MAKING NOISE

No wonder that these unsung heroines (and some heroes), mainstreaming divas, and ostensible institutional sell-outs, gathered in unexpected numbers at the first session at the AWID Forum on gender mainstreaming to share both their contents and discontents. They are the first to acknowledge that what has *not* been achieved is remarkable despite some real gains for women in education, employment, and governance. While the intention of gender mainstreaming is transformation, it has been chewed up and spit out by development bureaucracies in forms that feminists would barely recognize. We have long known that development bureaucracies excel in reductionism and control, not in promoting revolution and creativity, so that should not surprise us. What is particularly worrying, however, is the pernicious misunderstanding that gender mainstreaming is different from women's empowerment work resulting in the withdrawal of funds for the latter in the name of mainstreaming. In a discouraging example of this confusion, Kusakabe notes that provincial gender focal points in the Cambodian Ministry of Women's Affairs are not very clear about what they should do *vis-à-vis* their colleagues in other government ministries regarding gender mainstreaming but their most successful work—direct projects addressing violence against women and anti-trafficking—is considered least important by their own Women's Ministry (Kusakabe, 2005).

Much of the current re-think in feminist circles is focused on questions such as what is the contribution of feminism to justice and social change in a context shaped by economic orthodoxies, religious fundamentalism, unilateral political action, and terrorism. That is the right political question, but we are also concerned with the more down-to-earth unfinished business of making systems work for women now.

MAKING IT WORK

In an overview on gender mainstreaming in international development institutions, Moser points out that while most institutions have put gender mainstreaming policies in place, implementation is inconsistent and most importantly the outcomes in terms of gender equality remain largely unknown (Moser and Moser, 2005). This speaks both to the fuzziness of our analysis and intentions and to the lack of adequate ways of measuring progress. As we have stated elsewhere (Rao and Kelleher, 2005), there are different levels to this, starting with difficulties on obtaining sex-disaggregated data to a lack of tracking mechanisms that can notice relative contributions to different goals in a particular project. But more fundamentally we need to find better ways to measure the intangibles that are at the root of social change of any sort—the change in consciousness of women and men, the change in community norms, or the change in attitudes. Incremental change must be perceived and understood as valued results knowing that gender equality is a long-term goal.[2]

Understanding that a key dimension of the feminist project is redesigning the architecture of human relationships helps us understand why this work is so difficult and why it takes so much time. Radical feminists would say that working on women's empowerment within institutions simply tinkers at the margins of patriarchy and dulls the political edge of the movement. There is of course truth in that. But if we are tinkering, can we at least get that right? Can we gender mainstreaming divas explain the persistent neglect of addressing systemic change to deliver development benefits to women by practitioners, policy makers, and donors alike? Poor implementation and lack of accountability consistently sink the good intentions of gender equality policies. It is commonly known for example, that when ordinary women go to get services from public, private, or informal systems they are often ignored or worse, they are abused. These persistent deficits operate across sectors and issues ranging from land registration and fair policing to securing maintenance payments, healthcare delivery, decent teaching in schools, or access to water. And yet, when we talk of social contracts or cultural change we do not extend the conversation to the systems and mechanisms that translate intention to outcomes. Even the minimalist and mundane MDGs require effective institutional delivery systems. At best we call for more committed leadership and resources and more of whatever did not work too well the last time, most often better analysis and planning. Moreover, even if the intention and focus is there, often the devil is in the institutional details. In the Indian state of Karnataka, the NGO Grama Vikas is working with families to register land in the name of women. The stumbling block is not men's attitudes; it is that changing land registration is made both difficult and expensive by the state. So, while families have co-registered homesteads in women's names—a far less expensive transaction—the land re-registration is pending. The budgetary allocation by the state to fund land registration in women's name was discovered by the NGO after considerable digging but by then the officer in charge had sent back the allocation unannounced and therefore unspent.

BUILDING AN ENABLING ENVIRONMENT

Policies are statements of intent, they are not reflections of reality. States and governmental delivery systems do not make change happen. They can, however, build an enabling environment for justice and equity. But even then, they have to be prodded, negotiated with, and held accountable. That is the job of civil society organizations. If that job is not done, even the most progressive of intentions will falter on the bedrock of patriarchy, and business as usual. In Bolivia, the Law of Popular Participation rolled out in 1994 instituted democratic municipal government on a nationwide basis for the first time and devolved 20 per cent of the national tax revenue to the local level. For women, the real gain is that the LPP gives explicit legislative entitlement to participate in decision-making processes. As Clisby (2005) explains, where it worked such as in Entre Rios, it did so because a dynamic was created by women's organizations, a powerful indigenous people's organization, and gender specialists from the Ministry of Human Development working at the municipal or sub-secretariat level together with NGOs whereby many traditional relationships of ethnic and gender oppression were seriously publicly questioned and human rights work carried out. However, in many other places, 'the preexisting structures which deprived women on *de facto* political power' were not changed.

We need to focus on reform of existing institutional structures and developing alternatives to those that now exist. This means making public and private service delivery systems work for women and finding new institutional solutions for systems that cannot be fixed and for new issues that defy traditional solutions. This requires institutional change that drives equitable resource allocation, catalyses new means of monitoring and measuring the performance of service providers, produces attitudinal and behavioural change in service providers, and results in concrete benefits for women. How do incentive systems change? What is the impact of an empowered and vocal clientele demanding accountability? How do complaints mechanisms put in place by committed leaders change behaviour? How do gender-sensitive performance measures work? What is making services available for women in ways that do not abuse them, do not exclude them, and do not reinforce gender-biased norms? How are things done when they are done well?

MOVING FORWARD

A key element in changing institutions involves strengthening external constituencies' ability to hold institutions to account. One example of this is popular auditing of public accounts—an experiment started by MKSS (a non-party political movement in Rajasthan, India), which focused on public works projects. The MKSS spearheaded a national right to information campaign enabling citizens' access to most non-defense-related documents held by the government including records of expenditures. The main tools of spending analysis and audit used by MKSS are public hearings held in villages. Meticulous and extensive work happens before these public hearings comparing stated expenditure with evidence of actual spending. At the hearings held in the village squares and town markets, relevant details of questionable work are raised by the assembly. Relevant testimony is invited by MKSS to tell people if their experience fits with the official recorded version or not. For example, mainly the female workers on public works programmes are asked if they were paid rupees 50 per day as stated in the employment register signed by the foreman. Local officials are invited to attend and defend themselves or account for discrepancies. The MKSS had also successfully campaigned for state laws to create mandatory legal procedures for investigating corruption and institutionalizing the public hearing audit method at the village assembly level.

SOME TRICKY QUESTIONS

But holding up the mirror to institutions is only part of the picture. We must also hold up the mirror to ourselves. Civil society organizations including women's organizations that claim to be at the forefront of the equality and justice struggle are sometimes themselves some of the worst examples of institutionalized patriarchy and inequity. How can such civil society organizations talk of citizenship and democracy and be allies in the struggle for social justice for men *and* women? How can women's and feminist organizations that have few alternative models of effective organizing and leadership models to offer expect to lead this fight?[3]

A focus on making systems work for women is particularly timely now in the context of the MDGs combined with increased aid levels often packaged through new aid modalities that can easily obscure a specific focus on gender equality and women's rights even while they specify greater governance conditionalities of better aid effectiveness, accountability, and service delivery efficiency. To achieve basic development objectives, we need both better delivery and better accountability for a range of services to women—not just education and health, but also agricultural extension, land registration and property protection, regulation of labour markets, and safety.

The complex process of turning policy into practice and intentions into outcomes requires both effective institutional insiders and strategic external critics. From the inside out, it requires shifting opportunity structures in institutional environments toward equality of women's agency, changing incentives and capacity in global, state, and community agencies to respond to women including delivering on services and on rights. From the outside in, it requires strengthening women's awareness of their own agency, voice and mobilization, and their influence over institutions, and their ability to hold them to account. However, neither the top-down process of changing the opportunity structure nor the bottom-up process of mobilization and empowerment happen in a vacuum. This struggle happens within a context where civil society organizations, political parties, and trade unions operate in ways that are crucial to mobilization, but often less than helpful when it comes to *women's* rights, and where informal institutions—ideology and culture maintained by unequal power relations—also operate in ways that constrain some actions and make others possible. Thus, to move from tinkering to making significant change happen, we need to understand the confluence of the opportunity structure provided by the state, the empowerment of women and their organizations, and formal and informal institutions that mediate both access and benefits. And we need to both support institutional insiders and hold them to account not only for changing systems but also for gender equality. Neither the feminist glamour girls nor the mainstreaming divas can make sustainable change happen on their own. If we can find ways to support each other and build on each others' strengths and energies, we will have found the fulcrum that will upset the *status quo.*

NOTES

1. For an insightful analysis of the need to support these agents see Goetz (2004). For a scathing critique of gender mainstreaming see McFadden (2004).

2. For conceptual tools to aid in designing measuring instruments and processes, see Rao and Kelleher (2005); and Making the Case produced by the Women's Funding Network.

3. Tools to aid in building strong organizations exist such as Smart Growth that is aimed at enabling women's organizations to benchmark overall life stage and key organizational capacities over time and plan strategically for moving forward.

✗ NO

What's New about Gender Mainstreaming? Three Decades of Policy Creation and Development Strategies
REBECCA TIESSEN

INTRODUCTION

Gender mainstreaming policies have been adopted by multilateral agencies, government departments, and NGOs alike as a strategy to promote gender equality and women's empowerment. Policies promoting gender mainstreaming, however, do not necessarily translate into practical solutions or political change. The UNDP, in their 2004 report *Transforming the Mainstream*, noted, "In no area of international development is the gap between stated intentions and operational reality as wide as it is in the promotion of equality between men and women" (UNDP 2004, 3). Building on this critique, I explore the gap between rhetoric and reality by examining the wide range of gender mainstreaming activities employed by development agencies. Gender mainstreaming strategies rely heavily on technical solutions and create an illusion that gender equality is taken seriously in development agencies. Feminist research, including my own findings, demonstrates how technical solutions for gender mainstreaming (such as hiring more women in the organization, sending NGO staff for gender awareness training, or appointing a staff member to oversee gender-related activities within the organization) do not necessarily translate into political change, gender equality, or women's empowerment. Technical solutions and a focus on procedures for gender mainstreaming facilitate the appearance of change without transforming the gendered power structures of society (Ferguson 1984; True 2005). Given the limited impact of the technical solutions, I argue that gender mainstreaming is not an especially "new" approach to gender and development planning.

Feminist scholars have contributed important critiques highlighting the successes and limitations of gender mainstreaming (see Kabeer 2004; Prugl 2004; Rai 2003; True 2005). In this article, I build on this literature with examples from grounded research on the lived experiences of individuals attempting to promote gender mainstreaming in development agencies. In so doing, I examine the process of gender mainstreaming and adopt a feminist critical perspective of this important development approach. The grounded research facilitates a much more nuanced analysis of the subtle strategies as well as agency, power, and gender relations operating within development organizations.

Subtle strategies (including resistance, silence, and subversion) can tell us much more about agency and the potential for shifting power. Resistance and subversion are examples of the day-to-day strategies adopted as a way to challenge gendered social relations and negotiate power. All development agency staff hold some form of positional power that enable them to exert influence or subvert daily routines (Rao, Stuart, and Kelleher 1999). Subtle strategies (such as withholding the boss's phone messages), however, are unlikely to lead to empowerment or long-term changes in organizational practices. Rather, they are reactive and short-term responses and are frequently targeted at individuals rather than organizational structures and norms. Networking, coalition-building, and leadership initiatives off a much longer-term strategy for promoting gender equality and empowerment.

I. GENDER MAINSTREAMING AND ORGANIZATIONAL CHANGE

Gender mainstreaming is both a technical and political process (Kardam 1997) involving changes in the cultures, values, and practices of organizations for the purpose of confronting gender inequality. Strategies for mainstreaming gender cannot sacrifice long-term political change for short-term technical solutions. Rather, technical solutions and long-term structural changes go hand in hand. Overall, gender mainstreaming is intended to make gender sensitive practices routine in all aspects of an organization's work and activities. Gender mainstreaming should not be confined to the work of certain staff or to specific project interventions. Rather, it should inform all aspects of the organization's mandate (Akpalu, Okei-Abougye, and Derbyshire 2000). In addition, gender mainstreaming goes beyond what an organization does to examine the institution itself: how it operates and the norms and attitudes toward gender that are prevalent.

In her book *The Elusive Agenda: Mainstreaming Women in Development,* Rounaq Jahan (1995) makes the case for building the institutional capacity of organizations as a key step in addressing gender inequality both for immediate and long-term change. Evaluating gender issues within development agencies therefore requires an understanding of the "deep structure of organizations" (Rao, Stuart, and Kelleher 1999) whereby values, behaviours, and attitudes of individuals and their everyday practices entrench gender stereotypes and reinforce gender inequality despite the gender mainstreaming strategies employed (Tiessen 2004). Gender and organizational development literature draws attention to a patriarchal culture that undervalues women's work because it is done by women (Mies 1986; Walby 1985). Organizational ideologies, value systems, structures, and management styles promote masculine cultures (Macdonald, Sprenger, Dubel 1997) at the expense of other norms and practices. In the final analysis, an organization's mainstream approach is one in which certain attitudes and behaviours are deemed appropriate and specific practices are considered the norm. Gender mainstreaming is an approach designed to alter mainstream thinking and to shift the status quo in such a way that alternative or marginalized perspectives are taken into consideration. Thus, gender mainstreaming entails challenging "the formal and informal norms, rules, attitudes and behaviours that institutionalize inequalities within an organization" (Kabeer 2004, 228). Feminists and gender experts make a strong case for gender mainstreaming as a tool for challenging gender inequality and promoting institutional and organizational change while highlighting the need for both technical and political change. Further to this research, I examine case studies in which gender mainstreaming has been implemented with an emphasis on the ways in which gender (mainstreaming policies translate (or fail to translate) into practice.

[...]

II. GENDER MAINSTREAMING AS AN APPROACH FOR DEVELOPMENT PLANNING

Gender mainstreaming was popularized at the 1995 United Nations World Conference on Women in Beijing and appears in the document emerging from this conference: the *Beijing Platform for Action*. Specifically, the *Platform for Action* recognizes that "many Governments have enacted legislation to promote equality between women and men and have established national machineries to ensure the mainstreaming of gender perspectives in all spheres of society" (UN 1995). The *Platform* calls for the promotion of gender mainstreaming policy by stating that "... Governments and other actors should promote an active and visible policy of mainstreaming a gender perspective in all policies and programs, so that, before decisions are taken, an analysis is made of the effects on women and men, respectively" (UN 1995).

The United Nations Economics and Social Council (ECESOC) later defined gender mainstreaming as:

> ... the process of assessing the implications for women and men of any planned action, including legislation, policies or programmes, in all areas and at all levels. It is a strategy for making women's as well as men's concerns and experiences an integral dimension of the design, implementation, monitoring and evaluation of policies and programmes in all political, economic and society spheres so that women and men benefit equally and inequality is not perpetuated. The ultimate goal is to achieve gender equality. (ECEOSOC 1997, second session, quoted in UN 2002)

More specifically, gender mainstreaming is concerned with concrete strategies to address gender inequality at the policy, program, and organizational levels. In this article, I am especially interested in the organizational level where gender mainstreaming is expected to provide a space for organizational learning and change that can benefit women and men equally (UNDP 2001). In order to achieve this, women and men need to examine their own attitudes and cultural norms surrounding gender issues, a process expected to affect both the public and private lives of individuals (UNDP 2001).

The origins of the term can be traced back to the 1st World Conference on Women held in Mexico City in 1975. References to gender mainstreaming can also be found in other early conferences and policy documents including the 1985 3rd World Conference on Women in Nairobi, Kenya (Pollack and Hafner-Burton 2000). The document that emerged from this conference, the *Nairobi Forward-looking Strategies for the Advancement of Women,* argues for the full and equal integration of women in all development activities.

Other conventions have also been adopted in an effort to ensure gender equality in access to and control over resources and to end gender-based discrimination. For example, the *Convention on the Elimination of All Forms of Discrimination against Women* (CEDAW) was adopted by the UN General Assembly in 1979 and provides a bill of rights for women. Many countries, having ratifies the CEDAW and, more recently, having adopted the gender mainstreaming approach, are working to create models for its delivery by developing national level *Platforms for Action.* International policy documents such as the *Beijing Platform for Action* act as guides to national level policies. Most countries that participated in the 4th World Conference on Women in 1995 have since designed national policy documents to demonstrate their commitment to gender equality. *Platforms for Action* contain important commitments to addressing gender equality and recommendations for gender mainstreaming. For example, the *Beijing Platform for Action* identified 12 critical areas of concern and urged governments to devise strategies to address each of these concerns.

The following section examines some of the ways that gender mainstreaming recommendations have translated into practice. Three categories of gender mainstreaming activities emerged in the research: technical solutions, subtle strategies, and networking. I elaborate on these categories using examples from the grounded research with development agencies.

III. TECHNICAL SOLUTIONS FOR GENDER MAINSTREAMING

Technical solutions for gender mainstreaming entail a set of operational guidelines involving hiring more women staff, training staff about gender concepts and issues, reporting on gender-related findings, budgeting for gender-related activities, and targeting women for specific "women appropriate" development projects. Gender-related activities are mandated by senior staff members and often by international donor agencies. Technical solutions are expected to ensure accountability to the people development organizations represent, to promote gender equality within and outside their organizations, and to offer gender-sensitive strategies for development planning. While technical solutions may not have a direct impact on attitudes or political change, they are expected to offer entry points for discussions and new approaches for gender equality. The technicality of these operational guidelines is apparent in the lack of reflection and analysis of the staff members as they perform these tasks. Many gender mainstreaming strategies have been adopted with superficial attention to the purpose and value of such activities. Two specific examples of technical solutions for gender mainstreaming are discussed here: hiring gender focal point officers and providing gender training. These examples represent two of the most common technical solutions to gender mainstreaming in development agencies. The grounded analysis of these practices provides a rich evaluation of gender mainstreaming in practice that moves beyond policy analysis.

A. Hiring Gender Focal Point Officers

Hiring or appointing a staff member to oversee all gender-related activities is a common approach in development agencies. The position often comes with a title such as "gender focal point officer" or "gender projects officer." The responsibilities of the gender personnel vary from organization to organization. These responsibilities include coordinating and mainstreaming gender within the organization, programs, and projects; representing the organization at gender meetings and networking; encouraging the participation of men and women in projects; reporting, monitoring, and evaluating gender activities within the organization; and sensitizing or training staff on gender issues.

In Malawi, for example, most of the development NGOs surveyed had a gender focal point officer designated to oversee gender-related activities. Of the 23 NGOs involved in the Malawi case study, 17 of these NGOs had assigned a staff member to gender-related tasks or had appointed a gender focal point officer. A similar approach has been adopted in most development agencies around the world. In Ghana, for example, the majority of government ministries, NGOs, and donor organizations have expressed their commitment to gender mainstreaming by appointing gender focal point staff members. These staff members are to "act as catalysts support and promoting gender related skills and approaches among their professional colleagues" (Akpalu, Okei-Abougye, and Derbyshire 2000, 26).

Female staff members (usually in low-paying jobs) are most often given the task of responding to gender-related demands by virtue of the fact that they are women and gender issues are (wrongly) considered women's issues by male staff members. Gender focal point officers say they lack formal training in gender and development issues; have few resources to fulfill the tasks involved in sharing gender-related information about the organization; and usually do not participate in management meetings. Therefore, these staff members argue they have little impact on the decision-making processes of the organization. Many of the women appointed to gender focal point positions considered themselves further marginalized within the organization since they now hold positions that are considered by male colleagues as "women's work." Work labelled as such is generally undervalued. During an interview, one NGO staff member in Malawi said that her male colleagues teased her for her new responsibilities looking after "ladies' affairs." One organization operating out of a house rented in the city physically marginalized the gender focal point officer by putting her desk in a separate building behind the main office in a space normally referred to as the "servant's quarters." For women who find it difficult to communicate with male colleagues on organizational or project matters, these same women now found their colleagues even less likely to discuss their work with them. When asked why they felt further marginalized, some gender focal point officers said male colleagues thought they could no longer speak freely around them for fear they may be reported for making sexist comments. Other gender focal point officers noted that their work was not taken seriously and therefore they were not treated as valuable staff members. These findings echoed those of Jahan (1995) who argue that the "image of WID [women in development] positions being 'women's jobs' made them appear less professional" (41).

When discussing lack of support from male colleagues, one gender focal point officer expressed her concerns that she was perceived by her male colleagues as a "watchdog." Gender mainstreaming involves overseeing a variety of activities carried out within an organization. As such, gender focal point officers are often required to review project proposals. Male staff members may feel threatened by their female colleagues if they perceive these women in supervisory roles, especially if the gender focal point staff members are in junior positions.

Development agencies frequently lack the resources to create a new position for a gender focal point officer. Therefore, these organizations rely on the (often voluntary) services of an existing staff member. The additional work is voluntary to the extent that the new responsibilities do not get remunerated. Women in these positions agree to the additional work because they fear they will be fired if they refuse. When forced to choose between their different sets of responsibilities, these staff members usually ignored the work required of a gender focal point officer. Also, the gender focal point staff often know little or nothing about gender.

The above examples demonstrate how a technical solution such as appointing a gender focal point officer may offer no real strategic or political change. Assigning gender officers or creating a gender office within the organization can result in little more than superficial titles used to create the appearance of important gender-related work. These activities often do nothing to promote political and behavioural change especially if the staff members appointed to do this work are too busy fulfilling other tasks within the organization, are unsympathetic, and/or lack the skills to foster gender equality.

Research on staff representatives from Canadian-based international NGOs uncovered similar challenges to gender mainstreaming. In one international NGO, a gender focal point officer commented that much has been done to research gender issues in their work and to provide reports to the decision-makers and supervisors in the organization. She added, however, that none of the supervisors read any of the reports. This example reflects the deeply held biases against gender equality. What results then is a lot of rhetoric around promoting gender equality and women in leadership but that this is a one-way direction of information feeding up to senior management with no meaningful development of programs to ensure policies translate into practice. The challenge for gender mainstreaming is to move beyond rhetoric or "window dressing" (Krizsan and Zentai 2004) and to pay attention to the ways in which gender mainstreaming policies do (or do not) translate into action. The proliferation in the adoption of gender mainstreaming raises concerns that the concept may be stretched too thin to have any real meaning. The theme of rhetoric re-emerges in the case of multilateral agencies whereby the language of feminism is co-opted and manifests itself in the use of words such as "participation" and "empowerment;" however, the disclosure obscures any meaningful change in practice.

Multilateral organizations also face problems in terms of the status and location of gender units and gender focal point staff. For example, gender units are frequently given low organizational status and therefore lack authority to advise other program staff. While the appointment of gender focal point officers in many multilateral organizations has been mandatory, these gender focal officers are usually junior staff members and most often women. In fact, some organizational staff considered the position of gender focal point undesirable, noting concerns that the position lacked the resources and respect it requires. These examples underscore the prevalence of patriarchal values and structures operating in development agencies.

[...]

Appointing a gender focal point officer in development agencies remains a prominent gender mainstreaming strategy despite the limitations experienced to date. Attempt at gender mainstreaming are thus thwarted by the lack of resources available to these staff members. Also, gender officers expressed resentment for this new workload and/or for the jokes their colleagues made about their new responsibilities. Uncovering the barriers to gender mainstreaming further requires a commitment to addressing negative attitudes toward gender issues more broadly and to women staff members in particular. Development agencies are not gender-neutral spaces. Rather, they reproduce and reinforce the broader societal gender norms through male privilege and patriarchal structures. The following section highlights a second technical solution for gender mainstreaming gender awareness training.

B. Gender Awareness Training

Most of the gender focal point officers interviewed identified gender training workshops as one of their primary responsibilities in the organization. Throughout the early 1990s, gender awareness training workshops were considered an important technical solution for addressing gender inequality because they introduced NGO staff to the key concepts and strategies for gender mainstreaming. However, mere attendance at a gender training session does not guarantee this information will translate into new and improved attitudes toward women and/or gender mainstreaming. Many development practitioners have attended gender awareness and analysis training and say the introduction to gender issues informed them about gender awareness and analysis training and say the introduction to gender issues informed them about gender concepts and clarified questions and concerns. However, not all staff members are receptive to this new information. Some gender focal point officers commented on the challenges of providing in-house gender training sessions including male staff members ridiculing their female colleagues for bothering them with this "nonsense" information. In one case when an in-house was set up, male staff members came late to the meeting, claiming their other, "more important" work kept them from attending the session on time. This example revealed reluctance on the part of some staff members to learn from the gender focal point officers and demonstrated the power of patriarchal practices and assumptions.

On the issue of gender training, a Canadian-based NGO staff member commented that gender training was a popular activity 10 years ago but since then nothing new has been done to promote widespread understanding of gender issues in the organization. Some development organizations are committed to using the skills learned in gender training sessions and promote the collection of gender-based data. However, gender officers claim the gender-disaggregated data are not used to develop or revise programs or projects. Furthermore, gender mainstreaming is frequently carried out "sideways," or as a secondary consideration. To expand on this comment, the Canadian-based NGO staff member noted that gender awareness is attached to other programmatic areas such as HIV/AIDS. The effect of "sideways" attention to gender issues is that gender inequality never becomes the primary concern and is more easily ignored or sidelines. Gender mainstreaming therefore runs the risk of being a strategy to achieve other goals without addressing gender inequality itself.

One of the major challenges ahead for NGO staff and, more broadly, development practitioners is recognizing that development agencies have the potential to mirror societal gender relations, thereby reinforcing gender inequality within the organizations and in the programs these organizations deliver. The perception of gender neutrality within organizations "is a great obstacle to sensitivity, and produces gendered consequences" (Heiskanen and Rantalaiho 1997, 196). Unless gender neutrality in the organization is challenged, even technical solutions for gender mainstreaming will yield limited successes. In some cases in which technical solutions have been employed (such as assigning individuals to specific gender-related responsibilities and sending staff to gender sensitization workshops), these technical strategies can actually mask the problem of male privilege and prevent political changes necessary for gender mainstreaming. The example of appointing one individual in the organization to be responsible for gender-related activities is especially poignant as it demonstrates how gender mainstreaming becomes someone else's problem rather than the responsibility of all staff members.

In theory, the technical solutions for gender mainstreaming provide entry points for development agency staff to address gender inequality and to adjust their policies, projects, and attitudes accordingly. However, the problems facing gender mainstreaming summarized above reveal the limitations of technical "solutions." Examples of technical solutions tell us more about how gender equality is imposed from outside (from donors and international policy-makers) and from within the organization (by one or a few key gender experts). What happens within organizations as individuals demonstrate resistance to inequalities and negotiate power is also relevant to this examination. Building on the work of Scheyvens (1998), I employ the term "subtle strategies" to describe those activities that demonstrate agency, resistance, and, in some cases, women's empowerment within development NGOs. Grounded research and thick description based on field research uncover important examples of struggles of power experienced in the day-to-day lives of organization staff. The following section on subtle strategies highlights some of these struggles with attention to how they shape organizational practices and facilitate gender mainstreaming.

IV. SUBTLE STRATEGIES FOR POLITICAL CHANGE AND EMPOWERMENT

The technical solutions for gender mainstreaming offer a glimpse of what takes place on the surface of development organization programming. Subtle strategies offer examples of deeper interactions, beliefs, and attitudes expressed in everyday practices. Scheyvens (1998) and Desai (2002) employed the term "subtle strategies" in their work to mean "actions that attempt to improve women's lives without stirring up wide-scale dissent" (Desai 2002, 219). Subtlety is necessary in many cases, especially when individuals are unable to change patriarchal attitudes and behaviours of colleagues. Nonetheless, many NGO staff opt to maintain the status quo as this is considered more secure and less threatening. Senior women in bureaucratic organizations are also known to promote the status quo to protect themselves and maintain their own personal power in relation to other women (Goetz 1992). Yet Desai (2002) maintains that organizational change is possible and that subtle and internal influences can sometimes provide the basis for that change.

In fact, women's empowerment relies on the creation of space within political structures where women are able to decide on—and design—strategies for organizational change. However, the extent to which these spaces translate into empowerment for women is unknown. What we need then is "much more careful, historically specific analyses of women's attempts to develop political strategies and networks which challenge male power structures" (Parpart, Rai, and Staudt 2002, 15). In the following section I highlight several strategies that are used to create this political space in an effort to design strategies for organizational change. These strategies can be deemed subtle to the extent that they often go undetected and are under-reported as important approaches for gender main-streaming. Some of the examples of subtle strategies discussed below reflect access to power. However, in most of these cases the power was short-lived, reactive, and limited to individuals or specific settings.

Day-to-day interactions with NGO staff in Malawi shed light on some of the strategies of resistance used by female staff to regain power within their hierarchical organizations. In one example, an NGO staff member (secretary) mentioned that she had been treated poorly that day by a senior staff member. Her response was to withhold his telephone messages for the rest of the day. This response enabled the secretary to demonstrate her power within the organization as she was able to control and withhold information. Her response highlighted her control of knowledge and communication within the organization, even if only temporarily.

Other forms of observed resistance tended to be even more subtle. Silence, for example, is frequently used to express dissatisfaction or disagreement. An example of silence was observed when staff members were discussing problems with the organization's leadership. In this example, silence was used to embarrass the organization's leader. The power of silence cannot be ignored as it sends an unmistakable message. The example of silence observed in this research, as well as the example of the secretary withholding phone messages, did not, however, lead to long-term changes to gender inequality patriarchal practices within the organization.

[...]

The findings from this research on gender mainstreaming in development agencies echo some of the realities of resistance and change examined in James Scott's *Weapons of the Weak* (1985). In Scott's analysis, resistance is a part of day-to-day realities and not a "revolutionary consciousness." Most of the examples of subtle strategies noted above (subversion, resistance, silence, and submission) are unlikely to foster long-term changes in the attitudes and behaviours of individuals and promote gender equality. Rather, they reveal stop-gap solutions to difficult situations. What is particularly interesting about each of these examples, however, is the dynamic set of activities and interactions taking place in the everyday lives of people as they negotiate power relations. What on the surface may appear powerlessness of some individuals is actually a much more complex exchange of power relations in which power is exerted in culturally relevant ways.

However, to truly reflect the essence of gender mainstreaming, subtle strategies must go beyond exposing how individuals navigate situations of conflict, to demonstrate how individuals can effect political change that promotes gender equality within the organization. Subtle strategies employed by organizational staff offer partial—but insufficient—insights into the potential for such change. Attention to subtle strategies fosters a better understanding of the barriers to gender equality and gender mainstreaming. At the same time, these strategies expose the possibilities for changing norms and practices through the agency of individuals fighting to create change in attitudes, beliefs, and practices. In the following section I highlight another avenue for gender mainstreaming with examples of networking and alliance-building among gender equality activists.

V. NETWORKING AND ALLIANCE-BUILDING

Many policies and action plans to address gender issues are now in place; however, new strategies are needed if gender mainstreaming rhetoric is to translate into reality. The technical solutions for gender mainstreaming offer entry points for individuals and organizations to initiate operational procedures for addressing gender inequality. Subtle strategies offer a deeper analysis of the ways in which power is negotiated within organizations and how attitudes toward gender mainstreaming may be addressed. However, these initiatives do not fully represent the extent of gender mainstreaming approaches in place. Networking and coalition-building are also important gender mainstreaming approaches.

United Nations agencies have developed their own strategies to build networks and coalitions around gender issues. Initiatives to promote a joint UN gender policy are promising as such a policy might force other agencies and organizations to be more pro-active on gender issues. The development of the UNGAD (United Nations Gender and Development Working Group), for example, pushes the gender mainstreaming agenda beyond the personal commitment of a few individuals to a more systemic approach to organizational commitment.

[...]

National machineries can also play an important role in gender mainstreaming (Rai 2003) by putting pressure on government to fund gender mainstreaming programs. The networking and alliances that have emerged around the world enable NGO and government staff members to share strategies and approaches for more effective gender mainstreaming. The interaction between individuals within these networks has also provided role models for many women who are empowered through the support and encouragement they receive from each other. Mentoring initiatives were considered important strategies by NGO workers in both national and international NGOs in both Canadian and Malawian organizations.

During an interview with an employee of an international NGO in Canada, the NGO staff member noted the importance of mentoring but expressed shame and regret that she, herself, lacked the time to do the mentoring necessary to spread awareness and tools within the organization to address gender inequality. "People need to be committed," she noted, and it is "a commitment that has to come with dogged determination. There are no shortcuts to gender equality." The NGO staff member went on to note that dogged determination too frequently is translated by male colleagues as women whining and complaining rather than as constructive, persistent, and relevant critiques of organizational performance. The strategy adopted by gender advocates and active women within the organization becomes that much more important because women need to find a way to make themselves heard without reinforcing stereotypes of "women complaining".[2] Many development practitioners continue to use language such as this despite the extensive training and awareness raising that has taken place with staff members. Male development practitioners will often resort to derogatory comments toward women in an effort to assert their own power and privilege within the organization. The challenges ahead for changing attitudes and behaviours, therefore, are enormous.

Support groups for women's issues within the organization can provide some opportunities to reflect on these changes; however, gender inequality remains a highly contested area laden with work/life issues. Several organizational features stand in the way of adopting a gender mainstreaming approach and these features include an action-oriented approach to development programming rather than a reflection-oriented approach. In one example, the staff member in the head office of an international NGO in Canada pointed to the way in which her organization was present in most humanitarian crises and the immediacy with which the organization acts. However, this approach precludes any meaningful reflection time as the crises are never-ending and there is always a new place to be doing development work. The lessons learned from one site are seldom evaluated and the information is not used to promote a better approach in new programs. Similar challenges were observed in relation to reflecting on issues of gender inequality.

International NGO staff members working in Canada, like those associated in organizations in Malawi, recognized the importance of wider connections to the women's movement. However, finding ways to be more involved in the wider women's movements is an ongoing challenge for those staff members who already face sacrifices of their personal time. Overall, development agencies located in Canada expressed much greater difficulty in networking than their southern partners. Networks and coalitions can facilitate gender mainstreaming by raising awareness about the strategies necessary to promote gender equality. Nonetheless, these coalitions cannot monitor progress nor can they enforce policies. Therefore, they offer no guarantee for gender mainstreaming.

CONCLUSION

Gender mainstreaming is an important goal for UN agencies, governments, and many NGOs around the world as reflected in the numerous policies and plans of action. After three decades of policy commitments to gender equality and a decade of explicit attempts to facilitate gender mainstreaming in development work, it is timely to evaluate the impact these policies are having in practice. To do this, we need detailed research on daily encounters during attempts to operationalize gender mainstreaming. My own research reveals a wide range of approaches used to translate gender mainstreaming policies into practice including technical solutions, subtle strategies, and networking. All three of these strategies provide opportunities for development practitioners to address gender inequality in their work and within their organizations. Technical solutions—or quick fixes—enable organizations and individuals to develop operational proce-dures for addressing gender inequality. However, technical solutions alone rarely address the political and attitudinal changes necessary for altering the status quo. For example, hiring or appointing a staff member to look after gender issues (i.e., a gender focal point officer) may offer few opportunities for addressing gender inequality if that staff member does not have the resources he or she needs to carry out the work.

Several subtle strategies of resistance or subversion were also uncovered through this research. Such approaches provide windows of opportunity for individuals to gain a small amount of power for a period of time. In some cases, subtle strategies may prove to be counterproductive if the actions prevent organizational progress (i.e., if such actions eliminate trust in the organization). Subtle strategies can facil-itate empowerment only when they move beyond passive resistance or subversive techniques and begin to tackle the institutional norms and personal beliefs that perpetuate inequality.

Networking provides opportunities for development workers to share examples of technical solutions and subtle strategies but also to find ways to ensure these operational procedures are linked to behavioural changes among staff members. The support received through networking was considered empowering for women who found role models and mentors through these initiatives. Networks and orga-nizations committed to addressing gender inequality provide spaces for reflection and analysis. The networks also foster communication between individuals and organizations and promote incentives to challenge gender inequality. Nonetheless, long-term goals of gender equality found in gender mainstreaming policies are frequently set aside in favour of quick fixes—or technical solutions—in an effort to meet short-term deadlines and supply progress reports to donors. It is not sur-prising, under these conditions, that gender mainstreaming has achieved limited and marginal success.

In order for gender mainstreaming to move from technical solutions to political change and women's empowerment, a range of commitments is required. At the societal level what is need is a set of legislative changes that will ensure that laws are put in place to promote gender equality and protect women's rights. The people who design the laws and all members of society must also be committed to the changes prescribed. Government ministries and development agencies (i.e., donors and NGOs) must work toward the design and implementation of gender-sensitive policies. The policies must also include action plans with realistic goals and the means to achieve them.

For development organizations, gender mainstreaming requires organizational and individual commitments to make gender-sensitive practices routine in all areas of the organization's work. Gender focal point staff can play an important role in providing training and feedback; however, they are not the only ones responsible for integrating gender into programs. All staff members need to reflect on the gender issues in their programs and design action plans to address gender imbalances. Gender training will be an essential first step for development practitioners, but ongoing gender sensitization and reflection on gender issues is crucial to maintaining the momentum. A long-term perspective will ensure that gender is mainstreamed over a period of time even if trained staff members leave and new people are hired. Senior level development administrators need to guarantee that financial resources are available to the gender focal point staff member(s) as well as all staff members who are responsible for gender mainstreaming. Finally, gender mainstreaming must involve both men and women. Asking sympathetic men to be champions of gender mainstreaming can be an effective strategy within development agencies. If men and women work as a team to promote gender equality, more staff members are likely to see the value in adopting a gender-sensitive approach. Thus, men need to be empowered in order to see themselves as part of the solution.

Gender mainstreaming, I argue in this paper, has not offered new solutions to gender inequality. What is new, however, is a commitment on the part of many development agencies (NGOs, governments, and UN agencies) to develop incentives for tackling gender inequality, and to create opportunities for communication and reflection in an effort to translate policy into practice. Despite these commitments, gender mainstreaming approaches face many of the same challenges that previous WID and GAD strategies experienced. Women continue to be targeted for specific tasks within organizations (i.e., gender focal point officers) and for certain jobs within development projects. Given the experiences of many development agencies and their work to date in this area, this "gender" approach may better be described as "mainstreaming women". In the case studies analysed here, it is clear that few attempts have been made to tackle the behaviours and attitudes that reinforce gender inequality. Gender mainstreaming has the potential to move beyond the technical solutions, subtle strategies, and policies highlighted in this paper. In order to make this transition, however, more emphasis in gender mainstreaming needs to be focused on organizational and individual commitments to promoting political change. The grounded research summarized here is an important first step to developing gender mainstreaming strategies as it highlights the masculinities, male privileges, and female subordination characteristic of development agencies and their practices.

POSTSCRIPT

The readings in this issue raise important questions regarding how changes in institutions take place. Since the 1970s, development analysts, aid donors, and NGOs have recognized the central role that women play in the development process. But how the issue of gender should be integrated into development practices has been the subject of ongoing debate. The development discourse has shifted from women in development (WID) to gender and development (GAD), with an emphasis more recently on the concept of gender mainstreaming. But, as Rebecca Tiessen argues, the creation of a gender officer in a development agency, or the creation of a gender unit, is no guarantee that the *status quo* will be altered. In fact, subtle practices or strategies may be employed that give the impression that gender issues have been addressed, while the more fundamental attitudes and culture of the organization has not really changed. As a result, she concludes that gender mainstreaming has "not offered new solutions to gender inequality". If this is true, what alternative strategies need to be employed? After three decades of effort, why has the achievement of gender inequality in development practices remained elusive?

Suggested Additional Readings

de Waal, Maretha. "Evaluating Gender Mainstreaming in Development Projects," *Development in Practice,* 16, no. 2 (2006): 209–214.

Grown, Caren. "Answering the Skeptics: Achieving Gender Equality and the Millennium Development Goals," *Development,* 48, no. 3 (2005): 82–86.

Jahan, Rounaq. *The Elusive Agenda: Mainstreaming Women in Development* (London: Zed Books, 1995).

Moser, Caroline, and Annalise Moser. "Gender Mainstreaming since Beijing: A Review of Success and Limitations in International Institutions," *Gender & Development,* 13, no. 2 (2005): 11–22.

Rao, Aruna, and David Kelleher. "Is There Life after Gender Mainstreaming?" *Gender & Development,* 13, no. 2 (2005): 57–69.

United Nations. *Gender Mainstreaming: An Overview* (New York: United Nations, 2003).

Wendoh, Senorina, and Tina Wallace. "Re-thinking Gender Mainstreaming in African NGOs and Communities," *Gender & Development,* 13, no. 2 (2005): 70–79.

InfoTrac® College Edition

Search for the following articles in the InfoTrac® database:

Angeles, Leonora. "Creating Social Spaces for Transnational Feminist Advocacy: The Canadian International Development Agency, the National

Commission on the Role of Filipino Women and Philippine Women's NGOs," *The Canadian Geographer*, 47, no. 3 (Autumn 2003): 283–302.

Child, Keith, and Saskia Tait. "Gender Mainstreaming the Tragedy of Property Rights: A Critical Assessment of the World Bank's Land Agenda," *Canadian Woman Studies*, 23, no. 1 (Fall–Winter 2003): 96–101.

For more articles, enter:
"gender mainstreaming" and "women and development" in the keyword search.

Web Resources

Association for Women's Rights in Development (AWID)

www.awid.org

AWID was founded to promote women's rights in development. Their site has a large collection of papers and articles by its members analyzing different dimensions of the gender and development issue.

Women's Empowerment, UNDP

www.undp.org/gender/

This is the official website of the United Nations Development Programme's Women's Empowerment program. The site contains a number of discussion papers and other resources that focus particularly in the UNDP's approach to gender mainstreaming.

Women's Human Rights Resources

www.law-lib.utoronto.ca/diana/

Housed at the University of Toronto's Faculty of Law, this online research and advocacy tool includes a number of NGO and UN reports dealings with women and human rights issues.

Gender (Commonwealth Secretariat)

www.thecommonwealth.org/subhomepage/34021/

This site provides information about the Commonwealth Secretariat's gender work, including gender mainstreaming.

Gender and Development, World Bank

www.worldbank.org/gender/

This site presents a variety of material reflecting the World Bank's approach to gender issues. It includes guides on how to incorporate gender in the design of development projects.

PART FOUR

CONFLICT AND POLITICAL DEVELOPMENT

Will the Post-Washington Consensus really benefit Africa?

Is ethnic diversity an inherent cause of conflict?

Is democratization conducive to development?

Will the Post-Washington Consensus Really Benefit Africa?

✔ **YES**
COMMISSION FOR AFRICA, *Our Common Interest, Report of the Commission on Africa,* "Executive Summary," pp. 13–17

✗ **NO**
RICHARD SANDBROOK, "Africa's Great Transformation?" *Journal of Development Studies,* 41, no. 6 (August 2005): 1118–1125

During the past several decades, there have been significant changes to the dominant paradigms governing international development policies. From the 1950s through the 1970s, a strategy of import-substitution industrialization (ISI) was commonly accepted by many developing nations. However, in the early 1980s, this approach came under increasing criticism and proposals for change. The impetus for this change arose out of the debt crises of the early 1980s, following the collapse of the second oil boom in 1981. Faced with accumulating debt burdens at a time when the world market prices for primary commodities were dropping sharply, international financial institutions, like the International Monetary Fund and the World Bank, increasingly demanded market-oriented reforms to as a condition for grants and loans. These "structural adjustment policies" (SAPs), rooted in a doctrine of neoclassical market liberalism, became the new establishment paradigm for the leading international development agencies.

Under what came to be known popularly as the Washington Consensus, the market was identified as the most efficient mechanism for promoting economic growth and redistributing scarce resources. As a result, international financial agencies pressured developing countries to dismantle market controls, liberalize trade, open their economies to foreign direct investment, privatize state enterprises, and abolish state subsidies. However, by the mid-1990s, strong criticism of the Washington Consensus emerged. Low-income countries in Latin America and Africa that had adopted the recommended policies failed to generate sustainable economic growth or significantly reduce poverty levels. The success stories in East Asia were called into question when several economies were plunged into a crisis in the late 1990s due to disruptions in regional financial markets.

As a result, the Washington Consensus has increasingly been replaced by a somewhat contrasting paradigm, sometimes referred to as the Post-Washington Consensus. The focus of this paradigm tended to rest on giving a great priority to poverty reduction, enhanced delivery of social services such as education and health care for the poor, and greater collaboration between governments and civil society sectors. Some have argued that this "new consensus" marks a significant move away from the neoliberal, market-oriented approach to one that places more emphasis on sustainable, egalitarian, and democratically oriented development. Others contend that the Post-Washington Consensus is basically the same old neoliberal agenda which simply tries to add on a social safety net to deal with "market failures".

These developments provide a useful background to ongoing debate over the most appropriate means for tackling contemporary development issues in a region such as Africa. In early 2004, Prime Minister Tony Blair called for the creation of a Commission for Africa, which would take a fresh look at Africa's needs and try to chart an appropriate development path for the future. The initiative was partially influenced by musician Bob Geldof and a group he is associated with, DATA (Debt, Aids, Trade, Africa). The establishment of the Commission was timely for Tony Blair since he was scheduled to chair the G8 Summit, and the Commission's report could become a centre piece for these meetings.

Launched in February 2004, the Commission for Africa established five formal objectives, including "to generate new ideas and action for a strong and prosperous Africa, using the 2005 British presidencies of the G8 and the European Union as a platform ... to help deliver implementation of existing international commitments towards Africa (and) ... to offer a fresh and positive perspective for Africa and its diverse culture in the 21st century." The Commission was asked to report in early 2005.

Calling Africa "the scar on the conscience of the world," Tony Blair felt that the time was right for a renewed focus on the development needs of the African continent. The United Kingdom was set to chair both the G8 and the European Union and could make Africa, along with climate change, the focus of both. In September 2005, the United Nations convened the first major summit to review implementation of the UN Millennium Development Goals (see Issue 9). It was becoming increasingly evident that the Millennium Goals for Africa would not be met by 2015 unless more vigorous actions were taken. In addition, 2005 marked the 20th anniversary of Live Aid and the 25th anniversary of the Brandt Commission's seminal report, North-South. Thus, 2005 seemed to be an opportune moment, both political and symbolically, to refocus development efforts in Africa.

After a series of meetings in 2004 and 2005, the Commission for Africa delivered its final report in March 2005. It had a significant impact on subsequent discussions regarding development policies towards Africa. Meeting in Scotland in July 2005, the G8 saw the Commission's report very much as a blueprint for future development in Africa. Members of the G8 pledged a doubling of aid to Africa and a significant increase in multilateral debt relief to the region. The G8 nations also agreed to adopt some 50 of the 90 total recommendations made by the Commission, although they shied away from some of those touching most deeply on their own interests, such as the elimination of agricultural export subsidies by industrialized nations.

It is clear that Tony Blair wanted to use the confluence of events in 2005 to generate both renewed political will and new ways of thinking about the development paradigm in Africa. But how successful was he? In the first reading, we present an excerpt from the Commission for Africa's report, which outlines in brief the main ideas that it set out. In the second reading, Richard Sandbrook, a political scientist from the University of Toronto and an African specialist, provides a critical reading of the report. While Professor Sandbrook is sympathetic with the goals of the report, he challenges us to think about the interface between economic reform and political and social realities. He argues that the Commission for Africa report does not sufficiently take into account the specific nature of the political and social systems in which their economies are embedded. In particular, he notes that the Commission's report still reflects the market-oriented assumptions of previous development paradigms which do not always sufficiently take into account the different "rationality" by which neopatrimonial societies operate.

✔ **YES**
Our Common Interest
COMMISSION FOR AFRICA

For its part, Africa must accelerate reform. And the developed world must increase and improve its aid, and stop doing those things which hinder Africa's progress. The developed world has a moral duty—as well as a powerful motive of self-interest—to assist Africa. We believe that now is the time when greater external support can have a major impact and this is a vital moment for the world to get behind Africa's efforts.

The actions proposed by the Commission constitute a coherent package for Africa. The problems they address are interlocking. They are vicious circles which reinforce one another. They must be tackled together. To do that Africa requires a comprehensive 'big push' on many fronts at once. Partners must work together to implement this package with commitment, perseverance and speed, each focusing on how they can make the most effective contribution.

GETTING SYSTEMS RIGHT: GOVERNANCE AND CAPACITY-BUILDING

Africa's history over the last fifty years has been blighted by two areas of weakness. These have been capacity—the ability to design and deliver policies; and accountability—how well a state answers to its people. Improvements in both are first and foremost the responsibility of African countries and people. But action by rich nations is essential too.

Building capacity takes time and commitment. Weak capacity is a matter of poor systems and incentives, poor information, technical inability, untrained staff and lack of money. We recommend that donors make a major investment to improve Africa's capacity, starting with its system of higher education, particularly in science and technology. They must help to build systems and staff in national and local governments, but also in pan-African and regional organisations, particularly the African Union and its NEPAD programme. Donors must change their behaviour and support the national priorities of African governments rather than allowing their own procedures and special enthusiasms to undermine the building of a country's own capacity.

Improving accountability is the job of African leaders. They can do that by broadening the participation of ordinary people in government processes, in part by strengthening institutions like parliaments, local authorities, trades unions, the justice system and the media. Donors can help with this. They can also help build accountable budgetary processes so that the people of Africa can see how money is raised and where it is going. That kind of transparency can help combat corruption, which African governments must root out. Developed nations can help in this too. Money and state assets stolen from the people of Africa by corrupt leaders must be repatriated. Foreign banks must be obliged by law to inform on suspicious accounts. Those who give bribes should be dealt with too; and foreign companies involved in oil, minerals and other extractive industries must make their payments much more open to public scrutiny. Firms who bribe should be refused export credits.

Without progress in governance, all other reforms will have limited impact.

THE NEED FOR PEACE AND SECURITY

The most extreme breakdown of governance is war. Africa has experienced more violent conflict than any other continent in the last four decades. In recent years things have improved in many countries, but in other places violent conflict is still the biggest single obstacle to development. Investing in development is investing in peace.

The most effective way to tackle conflict—to save both lives and money—is to build the capacity of African states and societies to prevent and manage conflict. That means using aid better to tackle the causes of conflict. It means improving the management of government incomes from natural resources and international agreements on how to control the 'conflict resources' which fuel or fund hostilities. It means controlling the trade in small arms.

African regional organisations and the UN can help prevent and resolve conflict when tensions cannot be managed at the national level, through, for example, effective early warning, mediation and peacekeeping. Donors can support this by providing flexible funding to the African Union and the continent's regional organisations; and supporting the creation of a UN Peacebuilding Commission. The co-ordination and financing of post-conflict peacebuilding and development must be improved to prevent states emerging from violent conflict from sliding back into it.

LEAVING NO-ONE OUT: INVESTING IN PEOPLE

Poverty is more than just a lack of material things. Poor people are excluded from decision-making and from the basic services the state ought to provide. Schools and clinics must be available to the poorest people in Africa. This is an urgent matter of basic human rights and social justice. But it is also sound economics: a healthy and skilled workforce is a more productive one, fulfilling their potential with dignity. Investing for economic growth means rebuilding African health and education systems, many of which are now on the point of collapse. This requires major funding, but it is not only a question of resources. It is also about delivery and results. These are powerfully strengthened when local communities are involved in decisions that affect them.

Properly funding the international community's commitment to Education for All will provide all girls and boys in sub-Saharan Africa with access to basic education to equip them with skills for contemporary Africa. Secondary, higher and vocational education, adult learning, and teacher training should also be supported within a balanced overall education system. Donors need to pay what is needed to deliver their promises—including the cost of removing primary school fees.

The elimination of preventable diseases in Africa depends above all on rebuilding systems to deliver public health services in order to tackle diseases such as TB and malaria effectively. This will involve major investment in staff, training, the development of new medicines, better sexual and reproductive health services and the removal of fees paid by patients, which should be paid for by donors until countries can afford it. Funding for water supply and sanitation should be immediately increased, reversing years of decline.

Top priority must be given to scaling up the services needed to deal with the catastrophe of HIV and AIDS which is killing more people in Africa than anywhere else in the world. But this must be done through existing systems, rather than parallel new ones. Governments should also be supported to protect orphans and vulnerable children and other groups who would otherwise be left out of the growth story. Around half of the extra aid we are recommending should be spent on health, education and HIV and AIDS.

GOING FOR GROWTH AND POVERTY REDUCTION

Africa is poor, ultimately, because its economy has not grown. The public and private sectors need to work together to create a climate which unleashes the entrepreneurship of the peoples of Africa, generates employment and encourages individuals and firms, domestic and foreign, to invest. Changes in governance are needed to make the investment climate stronger. The developed world must support the African Union's NEPAD programme to build public/private partnerships in order to create a stronger climate for growth, investment and jobs.

Growth will also require a massive investment in infrastructure to break down the internal barriers that hold Africa back. Donors should fund a doubling of spending on infrastructure—from rural roads and small-scale irrigation to regional highways, railways, larger power projects and Information & Communications Technology (ICT). That investment must include both rural development and slum upgrading, without which the poor people in Africa will not be able to participate in growth. And policies for growth must actively include—and take care not to exclude—the poorest groups. There should be particular emphasis on agriculture and on helping small enterprises, with a particular focus on women and young people. For growth to be sustainable, safeguarding the environment and addressing the risks of climate change should be integral to donor and government programmes. This programme for growth takes over a third of the total additional resources we propose.

MORE TRADE AND FAIRER TRADE

Africa faces two major constraints on trade. It does not produce enough goods, of the right quality or price, to enable it to break into world markets. And it faces indefensible trade barriers which, directly or indirectly, tax its goods as they enter the markets of developed countries.

To improve its capacity to trade Africa needs to make changes internally. It must improve its transport infrastructure to make goods cheaper to move. It must reduce and simplify the tariff systems between one African country and another. It must reform excessive bureaucracy, cumbersome customs procedures, and corruption by public servants, wherever these exist. It must make it easier to set up businesses. It must improve economic integration within the continent's regional economic communities. Donors can help fund these changes.

But the rich nations must also dismantle the barriers they have erected against African goods, particularly in agriculture. These barriers hurt citizens in both rich and poor countries. Rich countries must abolish trade-distorting subsidies to their agriculture and agribusiness which give them an unfair advantage over poor African farmers. They must lower tariffs and other non-tariff barriers to African products, including stopping the bureaucratic application of rules of origin which excludes African goods from preferences to which they are entitled. And they must show this ambition by completing the current Doha Round of world trade talks in a way which does not demand reciprocal concessions from poor African nations. Careful attention must be given to ensure that the poorest people are helped to take advantage of the new opportunities and to cope with the impacts of a more open system of world trade. Africa must be provided with the funds that can help it adjust to the new opportunities of a changed world trading regime.

WHERE WILL THE MONEY COME FROM: RESOURCES

To support the changes that have begun in Africa, we call for an additional US$25 billion per year in aid, to be implemented by 2010. Donor countries should commit immediately to provide their fair share of this. Subject to a review of progress then, there would be a second stage, with a further US$25 billion a year to be implemented by 2015. Ensuring the money is well spent will depend on two factors. First, good governance in Africa must continue to advance. But, second, donors must significantly improve the quality of aid and how it is delivered: that means more grants, more predictable and untied aid, and donor processes that are less burdensome on the already stretched administrations of African countries. It must also be better harmonised with the aid of other donors and better in line with the priorities, procedures and systems of African governments. Above all, it must be given in ways that make governments answerable primarily to their own people.

These changes are needed not just from individual donor nations but also from multilateral institutions—both African and global. The African Development Bank needs to be strengthened and the role of the Economic Commission for Africa enhanced. The IMF and World Bank need to give higher priority to Africa's development. They also need to become more accountable both to their shareholders and to their clients, and to give Africa a stronger voice in their decision-making.

Rich nations should commit to a timetable for giving 0.7 per cent of their annual income in aid. To provide the critical mass of aid which is needed now, the aid should be front-loaded through the immediate implementation of the International Finance Facility. Practical proposals should be developed for innovative financing methods such as international levies on aviation, which can help secure funding for the medium and longer term.

For poor countries in sub-Saharan Africa which need it, the objective must be 100 per cent debt cancellation as soon as possible. This must be part of a financing package for these countries—including those excluded from current debt schemes—to achieve the Millennium Development Goals to halve world poverty by 2015, as promised by the international community at meetings in Monterrey and Kananaskis.

CONCLUSION

Bold comprehensive action on a scale needed to meet the challenges can only be done through a new kind of partnership. In the past, contractual and conditional approaches were tried, and failed. What we are suggesting is a new kind of development, based on mutual respect and solidarity, and rooted in a sound analysis of what actually works. This can speed up progress, building on recent positive developments in Africa, towards a just world of which Africa is an integral part.

✗ NO
Africa's Great Transformation?
RICHARD SANDBROOK

'With shoes, one can walk on thorns.' This African proverb opens the section on 'The Argument' in the Commission for Africa's Report. Yet the report's major problem is that the shoes it offers do not fit. Hence, following the road to Africa's prosperity that the Commissioners survey will be more uncomfortable than they expect.

This report adheres to the Post-Washington Consensus. The Washington Consensus, which held sway in the 1980s and early 1990s, focused narrowly on achieving the goal of economic growth by means of macroeconomic stabilisation, economic liberalisation, external opening, deregulation, privatisation, and minor institutional reform. This narrow neoliberal approach did not work, even according to those employed by the World Bank *[Easterly 2001; Stiglitz 2002; Milanovic 2003]*. In response, the World Bank under James Wolfensohn designed a less orthodox and more complex strategy—designated by Wolfensohn a Comprehensive Development Framework—that has become known as the Post-Washington Consensus. At a minimum, this new consensus treats poverty reduction as a separate, or principal, goal of policy interventions, acknowledges that freeing markets and shrinking states are insufficient to trigger growth (let alone poverty reduction), but still holds that the best way forward involves embracing the private sector as the engine of development. To succeed, however, this strategy will require not only the liberalizing measures of the Washington Consensus, but also embedding the market in a facilitative framework of reformed institutions, and providing safety nets to ensure that the losers from reform, together with the chronic poor, remain quiescent. 'Ownership' and 'partnership' are further elements of the Post-Washington Consensus. Recovery plans will fail unless African governments, in consultation with their civil societies, are 'in the driver's seat', fully committed to their road maps. Yet, as good partners, donor countries and the international financial institutions will expedite the needed changes by offering tested knowledge and generous funding. The Commissioners succinctly echo this approach by suggesting that 'Africa's entrepreneurial energies can be released and that growth and poverty reduction will follow. The actions for release of these energies must originate in Africa and must start with much better governance. But everything will move so much faster if the developed world provides strong and sustained support' *[p. 117]*.

Accepting these assumptions, the report mainly makes good economic sense. Certainly, any worthwhile blueprint will tackle poverty (as this report proposes) not only by promoting rapid growth (with a target of 7 per cent per annum), but also by augmenting the participation of poor people in this growth. If this accelerated growth is to be achieved through a revitalised private sector, then this will surely require, as the report suggests, improving the 'investment climate'. Civil wars, insurgencies, and political unrest must be prevented or, where present, resolved through peacebuilding and post-conflict development. Poor governance must be rectified by enhancing governmental capacity and accountability to the people. Then the state will play its designated role as 'enabling' an efficient and reliable market economy (rather than sabotaging it). Physical and social infrastructure, especially healthcare and education, will need to be supplied. Agricultural productivity will be raised. Growth will also entail more trade (in diversified products) and fairer trade (requiring the EU and the USA to reduce their subsidies and import restrictions on African exports). Finally, donors must act generously to propel this multi-faceted programme forward. They must be willing to cancel (or is it just reduce?) the external debts of low-income countries, and double aid to Africa during the next three to five years (an increase of US$25 billion), with good performance precipitating a further US$25 billion increase.

To ensure that this growth benefits the poor, the latter must gain the capabilities to participate productively in an economy premised on private property. The report itemises the principal avenues for achieving this goal (see chapter 7). It is necessary to enhance the access of the poor to healthcare, skills, and education. They must also gain access to credit. Since a denuded natural environment perpetuates poverty, environmental protection will become a priority. Poor people without any assets will not thrive, so they will need to be provided with physical capital, especially land. (This potentially radical proposal is, unfortunately, not further elaborated.) To reduce the level of their risk and vulnerability, people entering into market relations will have access to 'social protection'. This protection might include pensions, disability allowances, assistance in finding work, and measures to enhance gender equity, in addition to free basic healthcare and education. The programme does not lack ambition.

Although bold thinking is to be applauded, the critic must register certain reservations. One reservation relates to the realism of the strategy. What is the likelihood that we will witness a doubling of aid to Africa over three to five years, with potentially a further increase of US$25 billion thereafter? The past experience of development assistance does not lead one to be sanguine. Another reservation concerns the ambiguity surrounding some of the key proposals. What, for instance, does the report actually propose to do about the heavy debt burdens of most sub-Saharan African countries? The proposals vary from '100 per cent debt cancellation as soon as possible' *[p. 60]* to 'cancellation of 100 per cent [of the debt] service falling due from [Heavily Indebted Poor Countries] that have passed their HIPC completion point [until] 2015' [Annex 9, Action 1, point 1(c)]. And what precisely is the report proposing when it mentions providing the poor with physical capital in the form of land? This needs to be spelled out. Third, the report, to its detriment, focuses heavily upon absolute poverty, but has relatively little to say about inequality or inequity. (In this respect, too, the report fits the mould of the current Post-Washington Consensus.) Not only can relative deprivation be as debilitating to its victims as absolute deprivation, but also the report's goal of igniting entrepreneurial spirits may lead to growing, new inequalities. These potentially destabilising trends deserve some reflection and response. It is unlikely that the proposed social protection schemes will be sufficient to offset these trends, in light of the fact that half or more of the population of these countries is poor. Finally, the technocratic cast of the report, though inevitable in light of its status as an official document, sharply diminishes its plausibility: what should be done, will be done. The report largely ignores or underplays the socio-political realities that will shape the success of this ambitious enterprise. Nor does it analyse several difficult dilemmas and trade-offs that will ensue.

Unleashing entrepreneurship in Africa—extending the sway of market exchange, in other words—involves nothing less than a Great Transformation in countries where, for many people, economic behaviour is governed by the institutions of redistribution and/or reciprocity rather than (or in addition to) market exchange.[1] Whereas neoliberals regard markets as a natural or spontaneous outgrowth of human societies, Karl Polanyi contended that the market is an 'instituted process'—one that is imposed on society. Market exchange involves a particular notion of rational behaviour, according to which individuals seek to maximise their material gain, in a context of scarcity, by treating land, labour and money as commodities. But in Africa, as in some other parts of the world, this notion of rationality coexists with two other, contradictory rationalities. One is the rationality of mutual support systems, in which economic activity is, in effect, embedded in a community—an extended family, a clan, a village, or increasingly in contemporary Africa, a religious association. Here, a complex set of mutual obligations governs economic roles and the distribution of the product.[2] Typically, neither land nor labour is regarded as a commodity. The other rationality is that of redistribution, in which a surplus is channeled to a political centre and then redistributed according to some religious or political principle. In neopatrimonialism, a contemporary form of redistribution, a central political elite captures resources from economic actors and redirects these to individuals and groups on the basis of political allegiance.[3] Insofar as all three rationalities—or institutional matrixes—coexist in the same country in dynamic tension, we may speak of a hybrid system. Any centralised attempt to displace reciprocity and redistribution in favour of market exchange will generally involve considerable conflict and disruption.

Disruption arises for two reasons. First, institutions reflect configurations of power and interests in a society; their attempted transformation, therefore, provokes intense opposition from the affected groups. For this reason, resistance from patrimonial rulers and communities to market reforms in hybrid societies sometimes converts the reforms into caricatures [Hibou 1999]: 'nothing is but what is not'. Second, institutions based on reciprocity and redistribution, though not ethically superior to market behaviour, do serve crucial societal functions. Hence, the ascent of possessive individualism may introduce unintended consequences as the integrative functions formerly served by the principles of reciprocity and redistribution deteriorate.

Although the report recognises the importance of mutual support networks (in chapter 3: 'Through African Eyes: Culture'), it fails to recognise that its goal of releasing entrepreneurial energies clashes with their continued vitality. The report marvels at the capacity of Africans 'to operate through an apparent anarchy' *[p. 127]*, identifying 'social networks' that, though 'invisible' to outsiders, are nonetheless crucial to the functioning of many communities *[p. 128]*. Indeed, the report acknowledges that 'Africa's strength lies in these networks' (of family, clan, tribe, etc.). 'Africans survive—and some prosper—in the face of low incomes and few formal economy jobs. The networks create social capital, which is crucial in [African] survival strategies' *[p. 127]*. A study of Sahelian cereal producers in Senegal succinctly notes the principle underpinning reciprocity: 'I receive, therefore I exist. I give, therefore I am respected'. The act of giving, a way of redistributing the surplus, thus 'confers respectability and prestige. What is determinant is the social context which legitimises the gift so that it is never an isolated act: the gift creates or reinforces the social ties; it calls for a counter-gift which is never spelt out, either for its content or for its expiry date' *[N'dione et al. 1997: 371]*. This principle, however, contradicts that of market exchange, a contractual relationship in which participants seek to maximise their personal gain. The danger is that this ethic will erode the ties of traditional solidarity that provide social protection in an unpredictable world, especially in a context where the AIDS pandemic has already imposed obligations that strain such ties.

Consider the clash between the norms of reciprocity and those of market exchange. Community solidarity may, for example, translate into nepotism and corruption, to the detriment of efficiency criteria in public bureaucracies and private firms. Also, norms of reciprocity often prescribe the expenditure of resources on lavish funerals. One's act of generosity reinforces social cohesion and enhances the likelihood of support from one's community in the event that one later encounters adversity. Market rationality, however, perceives such expenditures as a waste of resources that might otherwise have been directed into productivity-enhancing investments. 'It is no longer enough to be; to be more, it is necessary to have more and more, on pain of merely subsisting', as Senegalese peasants perceive it *[N'Dione et al. 1997: 372]*. The allure of personal gain may thus undermine norms of reciprocity. Land, too, is caught in this clash of rationalities. Market logic defines land as a commodity, and therefore prescribes that private ownership should override traditional land tenure arrangements. However, communal land tenure rules are important not only in preserving a degree of equality in the countryside, but also in underpinning reciprocal arrangements that tie peasant communities together, providing a safely net in times of trouble *[Mkandawire and Soludo, 1999: 112–14]*. If mutual support systems wither in the Great Transformation, will government-supported social protection schemes, as advocated by the Commission on Africa, be able to fill the breach? In light of the extensive poverty, one must be sceptical. This issue is one that the report needs to address.

Similar dilemmas surround the issue of neopatrimonialism, a form of redistribution. Again, the report acknowledges some of this complexity (under the rubric of culture). It notes that a '"big man" culture' exists in which powerful individuals are expected to offer patronage, and that 'it is not enough to dismiss patron–client relations simply as channels of corruption' *[p. 125]*. Yet, again, the report does not reconcile this observation with its strictures about good governance, which would seem to preclude such practices. Neopatrimonialism presents a dilemma that the report fails to address: it provides a basis of rule, albeit fragile, in weakly integrated peasant societies, but at a high cost in terms of economic development. Undercutting this system of rule, even with the best of intentions, can bring calamitous consequences. *The only thing worse than a poorly functioning neopatrimonial system is a collapsed state.*

An elective affinity between neopatrimonialism and the social and material conditions of many sub-Saharan countries accounts for the system's prevalence. Rulers face the challenge of governing poor, weakly integrated, and largely peasant societies.[4] Land and labour in the rural areas and the urban informal sector have, as yet, been only partially converted into commodities for sale on the market. Business classes and urban middle classes tend to be politically weak, as they are small in numbers, dependent on governmental largesse, and often poorly organised in representative associations. Patrimonial traditions retain deep roots in certain cultures *[Bayart 1993]*. The normative basis of central authority is weak or nonexistent. Rulers, in these circumstances, confront unpalatable options in maintaining their own positions and consolidating state power. One option—that favoured by the Commission on Africa and every other similar report—is that governments build their legitimacy by embracing economic development, the provision of improved services to all citizens, and democracy; but this strategy is long-term and uncertain, while leaders face immediate and insistent demands for tangible benefits on a personal, local, or ethnic basis. Hence, the imperatives of integrating a heterogeneous and divided society, building a political base, and cementing personal power and privilege push rulers toward subordinating market considerations (investment, efficiency) to short-term political expediency.

Though providing a precarious basis for rule, neopatrimonialism exacts a high price in missed opportunities. The resources channeled to political loyalists derive from various sources: from taxes and royalties on agricultural producers, exporters of natural resources, and importers; from foreign aid, loans and foreign investment; from the operations of state-owned corporations; and from appointments to the public sector. Officials feel under constant pressure to capture new resources to maintain the loyalty of subalterns. Production suffers as rulers invest scarce resources to realise these non-economic objectives. They divert resources from public investments in high-quality roads, schools, and health facilities in order to favour cronies and their cronies' clienteles. In addition, uncertainty and indiscipline, nurtured by patronage appointments to the civil service, unpunished corruption and fraud, and the insider manipulation of public-resource allocations, tax collection, licences, imports, and so on, further raise the risks to potential investors (including the rent-seekers with disposable incomes). Many potential entrepreneurs respond to these perverse incentives by pursuing state-derived rents or speculative activities, rather than creating new wealth through risky, long-term investments. Hence, this political–economic system fosters economic stagnation or, at best, modest growth.

What to do under these circumstances? The report predictably argues for reforming this system away through improved governance—creating more accountable, effective, and transparent government monitored by a revitalised and vigilant civil society (and by donors grimly holding on to their wallets). This refurbished public sector will then provide the enabling environment in which entrepreneurial energies can flourish. Would that life were so simple! In reality, the triumph of economic and political liberalism in many countries represents, not mere reform, but revolutionary change: a Great Transformation. The struggle between liberalism, on the one hand, and neopatrimonial redistribution and reciprocity, on the other, is an unresolved and ongoing struggle over basic institutions.

Will economic liberalism prevail, disembedding economy from society and thereby sweeping away Africa's hybrid systems? In a few countries, such as Mauritius, the Great Transformation occurred long ago—in this case, the absence of an indigenous population meant that the territory developed as a thoroughly capitalist society under colonial auspices.[5] Consequently, the structural adjustment programme that Mauritius adopted in the early 1980s quickly succeeded in re-igniting growth (about 6 per cent per annum since 1983). But elsewhere, as in Ghana, liberalism and neopatrimonialism coexist in uneasy tension, and a definitive defeat of the latter is neither imminent nor certain.[6] Structural adjustment, therefore, is a prolonged, halting process. The danger is that, as in Sierra Leone in the early 1990s, zealous external reformers will use the power of money to force neoliberal reforms on precarious neopatrimonial systems, thereby kicking away the remaining pillars of a faltering state system. Desperate to obtain external resources, Sierra Leone's rulers accepted all the conditionalities imposed by the international financial institutions and donors in exchange for loans. However, the policies designed to reduce waste, corruption and 'mismanagement', to shrink the state bureaucracy, and to privatise money-losing state corporations undermined existing clientele networks. Subaltern patrons, cut off from resource flows from the centre, turned to freelancing in their pursuit of resources to distribute.[7] Both governmental leaders and the emergent warlords then refashioned their clientele networks on the basis of external loans and alliances with private firms with interests in diamonds or timber. The pattern evolved into the deadly warlord politics that is only now, at tremendous cost, being contained. Hence, donors will need to employ both patience and a subtle recognition of underlying realities, if they are to help in Africa's complex circumstances.

In sum, the report provides a useful compendium of information about Africa and many positive proposals, but it lacks an acute sense of sociopolitical realities in that region. It advocates, in effect, a Great Transformation, but without calculating the costs and dangers of such a bold vision. It may well be that liberalism will prove to be a progressive force in Africa; in the meantime, something of value is lost as neoliberalism undermines mutual support systems and the precarious unity of neopatrimonial rule. It would help if we all recognised that development or poverty reduction is a double-edged sword, that history is fundamentally tragic.

NOTES

1. The distinction among these three principles that govern the integration of the economy in society is drawn from Karl Polanyi [2001].

2. Goran Hyden [1983: 8–22] deals at length with the nature and implications of this 'economy of affection'.

3. For an extensive treatment, see Sandbrook [1985].

4. Peasants, in this context, refer not only to smallholding households on the land, but also to the 'peasants in the cities'—that mélange of petty producers, hawkers, pedlars, helpers, and apprentices that throng the burgeoning informal sector.

5. For an analysis of the unusual historical origins of market society in Mauritius, see Sandbrook [2005].

6. For a dissection of this struggle in the 1990s, see Sandbrook [2000, chapter 5].

7. On this pattern in Sierra Leone, see Reno [1996]. For the pattern elsewhere in Africa, see Reno [1998].

POSTSCRIPT

The Commission for Africa as well as other reports—such as *Investing in Development*, a report of the UN Millennium Project—have called for a significant increase in aid transfers to Africa. If the suggested targets were met, it would mean that the budgets of developing countries would nearly triple. At the 2005 G8 Summit, governments pledged to double their aid giving to Africa in the next five years. This would mean a rise in Official Development Assistance (ODA) from $US 70 billion in 2003 to $US 130 billion in 2010. It is argued by some that such increases could easily be achieved without imposing too much of a burden on donor countries. In fact, it would only mean that spending on ODA would increase to 0.7 percent of national income, a longstanding commitment that donors have already made.

But, given the previous discussion, would such large increases of aid money be beneficial? Given the weak nature of many states in Africa and the neopatrimonial nature of their political and social systems, what impact would such infusions of capital have? Are the institutional mechanisms in place to effectively channel such large sums of money? Taking into account Professor Sandbrook's critique of the approach of the Commission for Africa, what alternatives should G8 members pursue in following up on their commitments made at Gleneagles in 2005?

Suggested Additional Readings

Booth, David. "The Africa Commission Report: What about the Politics?" *Development Policy Review,* 23, no. 4 (2005): 493–498.

Brown, William. "The Commission for Africa: Results and Prospects for the West's Africa Policy," *Journal of Modern African Studies,* 44, no. 3 (2006): 349–374.

Cammack, Paul. "Global Governance, State Agency and Competitiveness: The Political Economy of the Commission for Africa," *British Journal of Politics & International Relations,* 8, no. 3 (2006): 331–350.

Franks, Suzanne. "Our Common Interest: Report of the Commission for Africa," *Political Quarterly,* 76, no. 3 (2005): 446–450.

Gberie, Lansana. "A Common Cause? What Cause? A Commentary on Our Common Interest: An Argument," *Globalizations,* 3, no. 2 (2006): 245–247.

Jackson, Penny. "Briefing: The Commission for Africa, Gleneagles, Brussels and Beyond," *African Affairs,* 104, no. 417 (2005): 657–664.

Kayizzi-Mugerwa, Steve. "Report of the Commission for Africa: What Is New?" *Journal of Development Studies,* 41, no. 6 (2005): 1126–1132.

Kelsall, Tim. "African Solutions to African Problems? A Critique of Our Common Interest: An Argument." *Globalizations,* 3, no. 2 (2006): 248–250.

Maxwell, Simon. "Exhilarating, Exhausting, Intriguing: The Report of the Africa Commission," *Development Policy Review,* 23, no. 4 (2005): 483–492.

Mbiba, Beacon. "Untold Stories: The Commission for Africa and Zimbabwe," *Round Table,* 95, no. 384 (2006): 201–218.

Mistry, Percy S. "Reasons for Sub-Saharan Africa's Development Deficit that the Commission for Africa Did Not Consider," *African Affairs,* 104, no. 417 (2005): 665–678.

Morrissey, Oliver. "Imports and Implementation: Neglected Aspects of Trade in the Report of the Commission for Africa," *Journal of Development Studies,* 41, no. 6 (2005): 1133–1153.

Oguine, Ike. "The Trouble with Models," *New Internationalist,* 392 (2006): 29.

Verweij, Marco, and Dipak Gyawali. "Against More Aid," *Harvard International Review,* 27, no. 4 (2006): 26–30.

Williams, Paul D. "Blair's Commission for Africa: Problems and Prospects for UK Policy," *Political Quarterly,* 76, no. 4 (2005): 529–539.

InfoTrac® College Edition

Search for the following articles in the InfoTrac® database:

Humphreys, Macartan, and Robert Bates. "Political Institutions and Economic Policies: Lessons from Africa," *British Journal of Political Science,* 35, no. 3 (July 2005): 35–37.

Kiely, Sarah, Charles Abugre, Rachel Baggaley, and Anna Thomas. "The Commission for Africa: A Recipe for Success?" *The Lancet,* 365 (April 23, 2005): 1461–1462.

Manuel, Trevor A. "Finding the Right Path: Africa and the Washington Consensus," *Finance & Development,* 40, no. 3 (September 2003): 18–20.

For more articles, enter:
"Commission for Africa" and "Post-Washington Consensus" in the keyword search.

Web Resources

COMMISSION FOR AFRICA

www.commissionforafrica.org

The official website for the Commission for Africa, this site contains the full text for the report *Our Common Interest* as well as other information regarding the consultations that went into the making of the report.

G8 Summit Information Centre

www.g7.utoronto.ca/summit/2005gleneagles/africa_g8-vs-cfa.pdf

This website is part of a research project at the University of Toronto studying the G8 Summit diplomacy process. At this link you will find a document that compares the recommendations of the Commission for Africa report with the communiqué released at the end of the 2005 G8 Summit.

Learning Africa

www.learningafrica.org.uk/index.html

This website was established to assist teachers in teaching their students about the Commission for Africa report. While the material is directed toward a more elementary level, some useful information on Africa can be found here.

G8 Gleneagles 2005

www.g8.gov.uk

This is the official UK site for the 2005 Gleneagles Summit where the Commission for Africa's report was discussed. It contains background material on Africa.

Economic Commission for Africa

www.uneca.org

Not to be confused with Tony Blair's Commission for Africa, the UN Economic Commission for Africa has extensive data and reports on development issues on the African continent.

Is Ethnic Diversity an Inherent Cause of Conflict?

✔ **YES**

BARBARA HARFF AND TED ROBERT GURR, *Ethnic Conflict in World Politics* (Boulder: Westview Press, 2004): 1–17

✘ **NO**

JOHN MUELLER, "The Banality of 'Ethnic War,'" *International Security*, 25, no. 1 (Summer 2000): 42–70

In the wake of the Cold War, the dissolution of former communist regimes and the decline of ideological polarization gave way to the emergence of ethnic divisions as important political identifiers in many parts of the world. The eruption of conflict in the former Yugoslavia was the first in a series of very serious internal struggles that arose in the 1990s. In the developing world, a number of similarly vicious civil wars likewise stole the headlines. Ethnic divisions led to the separation of Eritrea from Ethiopia. In the wake of the 1991 Gulf War, Kurdish nationalists set up a functionally independent authority in northern Iraq. In Somalia, the state dissolved into factional and clan-based fighting. Elsewhere, the resurgence of ethnic awareness in the politics similarly seemed to suggest that Cold War proxies and ideological conflicts would give way instead to conflicts based on deep-seated identities. One particularly influential scholar of ethnic awareness, Benedict Anderson, argued that nationalism was a more persistent cultural form than ideological conflicts, that nations formed "imagined communities" which reinforced political boundaries as overriding cognitive tropes.

The largely unforeseen descent of Rwanda into civil conflict and genocide in mid-1994 brought particular attention to the relevance of ethnic conflict in the developing world. When Rwandan President Habyarimana's plane was shot down over the capital city of Kigali on April 9, 1994, the incident sparked a well-organized frenzy of violence aimed at eliminating an entire ethnic group: the minority Tutsi population of Rwanda. Over the ensuing 100 days, an estimated 800 000 Rwandans, from both the Tutsi minority and the Hutu majority, were killed in one of the most egregious acts of genocide in world history. In the midst of the fighting, the small United Nations–mandated peacekeeping force, the United Nations Assistance Mission in Rwanda (UNAMIR), was dismantled and reduced to a minimal detachment, unable to intervene as it was forced to bear witness to an orgy of killing. The genocide came to an end with the victory of rebel forces in July 1994 but refugee flows and contagion effects were felt in neighbouring Congo and elsewhere for several years afterward. The incident led to widespread concern over the inaction of the international community to respond to a human tragedy.

In the wake of the Rwandan genocide, many called for increased attention to ethnic tensions in the developing world. One common assertion was that the United Nations was not fully informed of the facts on the ground in Rwanda in the run-up to the conflict. UNAMIR had been poorly briefed on the political situation in Rwanda and the events unfolding in Rwanda took some time to be fully understood by outside observers. A large group of scholars led the call for systematic documentation of pending ethnic conflicts and minorities at risk of targeting for ethnic cleansing or genocide. The widespread view that a stronger United Nations intervention might well have contained the genocide motivated many to call for a more pre-emptive strategy for dealing with potential ethnic conflicts, and in many ways motivated a more active intervention in the case of Kosovo (1998–99).

The events of September 11, 2001 and ensuing US interventions in Afghanistan and Iraq, as well as the general subsiding of major ethnically based conflicts throughout the developing world, have diverted attention away from internal ethnic discord. Nonetheless, ethnic divisions continue to motivate widespread conflict in several areas. Despite promising signs of the renunciation of hostilities between the Northern Arab–dominated government of Sudan and Southern-based African rebels, war has persisted and worsened between the government and the black Africans of Darfur. Afghanistan has likewise descended into a civil conflict that could boil down to an ethnic divide between the majority Pashtun and minority populations. Elsewhere, long-running ethnic and religious rivalries threaten internal conflict or loom beneath the surface in many states, such as Burma, Nigeria, Lebanon, and Sri Lanka. Initial nationalist resistance to the American invasion and occupation of Iraq in 2003 has likewise devolved into a civil conflict pitting the large populations of Kurds, Arab Sunni, and Arab Shi'i against one another.

However widespread the phenomenon of ethnic conflict appears, scholars are by no means united in their assessment of the concept. Some point to the deep-seated and persistent nature of ethnic awareness as a particularly salient feature of division in developing societies, prone to prompt civil conflict. Others argue that ethnic awareness is little more than a convenient tool used by entrepreneurial leaders and local criminals for their own ends. In the first essay, Barbara Harff and Ted Robert Gurr, two scholars who have taken a central role in identifying the factors behind ethnic conflict, make the case for its persistence in developing areas. In the second essay, John Mueller argues instead that ethnic conflict is overstated, that in fact most ethnic conflicts, such as the genocide in Rwanda, are reflective not of widespread hatreds endemic to one ethnic group or another but of the ambitious and self-aggrandizing behaviour of small groups of criminals and thugs.

Ethnic Conflict in World Politics
BARBARA HARFF AND TED ROBERT GURR

Protracted conflicts over the rights and demands of ethnic and religious groups have caused more misery and loss of human life than has any other type of local, regional and international conflict since the end of World War II. They are also the source of most of the world's refugees. In 2002 about two-thirds of the world's 15 million international refugees were fleeing from ethnopolitical conflict and repression. At least twice as many others have been internally displaced by force and famine. At the beginning of the new millennium millions of people in impoverished countries are in need of assistance, hundreds of thousands of desperate emigrants from conflict-ridden states are knocking at the doors of Western countries, and, to make things worse, donor fatigue among rich states threatens to perpetuate inequalities and misery.

Ethnopolitcal conflicts are here to stay. Figure 13.1 shows that the number of countries with major ethnic wars increased steadily from a handful in the early 1950s to thirty-one countries in the early 1990s. We also know that between the

FIGURE 13.1

NUMBERS AND PROPORTIONS OF COUNTRIES WITH MAJOR ETHNIC WARS, 1946–2001

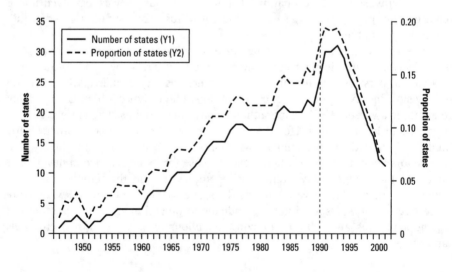

mid-1950s and 1990 the magnitude of all ethnopolitical conflicts increased nearly fourfold—an astonishing increase in light of what was hoped for in the aftermath of World War II.

The Holocaust should have enlightened us about what ethnic and religious hatred can do when used by unscrupulous leaders armed with exclusionary ideologies. Many people hoped that with the end of colonialism we could look forward to a better world in which nation-states would guarantee and protect the basic freedoms of their peoples. When the United Nations came into existence, were we wrong to believe that a new world order would emerge, one in which minimum standards of global justice would be observed and violators punished? Is it still possible that a civil society will emerge in which citizens eschew narrow ethnic interests in favor of global issues?

Instead we have witnessed more genocides and mass slaughters, an increase in ethnic consciousness leading to deadly ethnic conflicts, and religious fanaticism justifying the killing of innocent civilians in faraway lands. Some progress has been made to check ethnic wars since the mid-1990s, but we badly need more innovative ideas about how to fight the scourges that plague mankind. To top it off, the international political will to act has been waning in the wake of Somalia, Bosnia, Rwanda, Liberia, Burundi, the Democratic Republic of Congo, and other conflicts that need international attention. There is also the risk that, in the aftermath of the September 11 terrorist attacks on the World Trade Center in New York, the Western "war on terrorism" will divert international attention away from enduring problems.

[...]

DEFINING AND MAPPING THE WORLD OF ETHNIC GROUPS

Ethnic groups, like the Kurds, Miskitos of Central America, and the Turks in Germany are "psychological communities" whose members share a persisting sense of common interest and identity that is based on some combination of shared historical experience and valued cultural traits—beliefs, language, ways of life, a common homeland. They are often called **identity groups**. A few, like the Koreans and the Icelanders, have their own internationally recognized state or states. Most, however, do not have such recognition, and they must protect their identity and interests within existing states.

Some religious groups resemble ethnic groups insofar as they have a strong sense of identity based on culture, belief, and a shared history of discrimination. Examples are Jews and the various sects of Shi'i Islam. Politically active religious groups, such as offshoots of the Muslim Brotherhood, are motivated by grievances similar to ethnic groups.

Many ethnic groups coexist amicably with others within the boundaries of established states. The Swedish minority in Finland, for example, has its own cultural and local political institutions, which are guaranteed by a 1921 international agreement between Sweden and Finland. For eighty years the Swedish minority has had no serious disputes with the Finnish people or government. Since the 1960s the Netherlands has welcomed many immigrants from the Third World with relatively little of the social tension or **discrimination** aimed at immigrants in Britain, France, and Germany. Even in these tolerant countries the explosive growth of asylum seekers has led to some antiforeign political movements and xenophobic attacks.

If peaceful relations prevail among peoples for a long time, their separate identities may eventually weaken. For example, the Irish-Americans were a distinctive minority in mid-nineteenth-century North America because of their immigrant origins, their concentration in poor neighborhoods and low-status occupations, and the deep-rooted prejudice most Anglo-Americans had toward them. After a century of upward mobility and political incorporation, the Irish descent has little political or economic significance in Canada or the United States, although many Irish-Americans still honor their cultural origins.

The ethnic groups whose status is of greatest concern in international politics today are those that are the targets of discrimination and that have organized to take political action to promote or defend their interests. A recent study, directed by the second author, surveys politically active national peoples and ethnic minorities throughout the world. As of 2001, the project has identified and profile 275 sizable groups that have been targets of discrimination or are organized for political assertiveness or both.[1] Most larger countries have at least one such ethnic group, and in a few countries like South Africa and Bolivia, they comprise half of more of the population. Taken together the groups involve more than 1 billion people, or a sixth of the world's population. Figure 13.2 shows how these groups were distributed among the regions of the world in 2001. When the Soviet Union dissolved into fifteen independent republics at the end of 1991, the political demands of **ethnonationalists** like the Latvians, Ukrainians, and Armenians were met. Since then, however, at least thirty additional ethnic groups in the new republics have made new political demands.

The Minorities at Risk survey shows that about 80 percent of the politically active ethnic groups in the 1990s were disadvantaged because of historical or contemporary discrimination. Forty percent of these groups (111 out of 275) surveyed face discriminatory policies and practices harmful to their material well-being. For example, almost all indigenous peoples in the Americas have high infant mortality rates due in part to limited pre- and post-natal health care; Tamil youth in Sri Lanka have long been discriminated against by university admission policies that favor the majority Sinhalese. The survey also identified 135 minorities subjected to contemporary political discrimination. For example, Turkish governments have repeatedly banned and restricted political parties that sought to represent Kurdish interests; in Brazil people of African descent make up more than 40 percent of the country's population but hold less than 5 percent of seats in the national congress. Cultural restrictions also have been imposed on at least

FIGURE 13.2

POLITICALLY ACTIVE ETHNIC GROUPS BY REGION, 2001

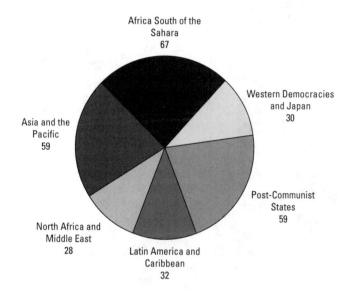

116 minorities. Muslim girls attending French secondary schools have been expelled for wearing head scarves; principals of Hungarian-language schools in Slovakia have been dismissed for not speaking Slovak at Hungarian teachers' meetings. Such restrictions may seem petty but symbolically their effects can be a painful and enduring reminder that the dominant society disvalues a minority's culture.

Ethnic groups that are treated unequally resent and usually attempt to improve their condition. Three-quarters of the groups in the survey were politically active in the 1990s. They did not necessarily use violence, however. On the contrary, most ethnic groups with a political agenda use the strategies and tactics of interest groups and social movements, especially if they live in democratic states. Figure 13.3 shows the highest level of political action among minorities in 1995. One-quarter were politically inactive (some of them had a history of intense activism), half were mobilizing for or carrying out political action, and only one-quarter used violent strategies of small-scale rebellion (including terrorism) or large-scale rebellion. The latter include the most serious and enduring of all conflicts within states, including ethnic wars between Hutus and Tutsis in Burundi and Rwanda, civil wars by southerners in Sudan and Muslim Kashmiris in India, and wars of independence by Kurds in Turkey and Iraq and by Palestinians in Gaza and the West Bank.

FIGURE 13.3

STRATEGIES OF POLITICAL ACTION USED BY ETHNOPOLITICAL MINORITIES IN 1995

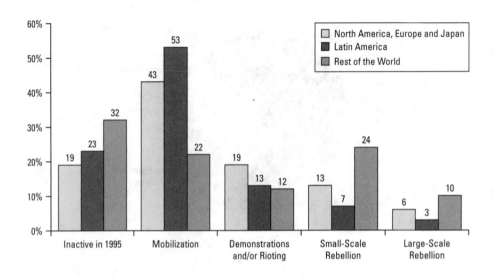

Figure 13.3 also shows the relative frequency of different kinds of political action among world regions. The highest level of mobilization in 1995 was in Latin America—mainly among indigenous peoples. Ethnic rebellions were uncommon in Europe and the Americas and when they did occur were mainly terrorist campaigns. Rebellions were much more numerous in Africa, Asia, and the Middle East. [...]

STATES OR PEOPLES?

Historically, ethnic groups, nations, states, empires, and other forms of large-scale social organization—for example, Islam and Christendom—have coexisted, but since the seventeenth century the dominant form of social organization has been the state system—the organization of the world's people into a system of independent and territorial states, some of which controlled overseas colonial empires.

Despite attempts to change the existing world order by insisting that the state was obsolete, as Marxists proclaimed, the state remains the key actor in international relations. Key, because the state at the very minimum controls the principle means of coercion. Ethnic groups rarely are equal in terms of power, legitimacy, or economic resources. But it is wrong to suggest that the state is a single monolithic enterprise. Instead, we may want to think of the state as a recognized territorial entity in flux. It is one thing to think of England as an established state since the Middle Ages, yet Germany in something like its present form has existed only since 1870. The new states that emerged in the Middle East, Asia, and Africa following the demise of empires were often just creations of the former colonizers, endowed with neither historical nor cultural continuity, nor boundaries that recognized the living space of ethnic groups. Thus for example, we have states such as Burundi and Rwanda in both of which a Tutsi minority rules a Hutu majority, which led to major conflicts and postindependence genocidal killings in both countries.

Some would argue that certain states should have no independent existence, either because the notion of territory was not part of their people's culture or because they would be better off within the boundaries of established states. Indeed, one could ask how viable, necessary, or rational is the division of the Arabian peninsula into many sheikdoms, some of which have emerged as independent states only since the 1960s. But, what are the alternatives? In tribal communities, local loyalties were very well developed, but rarely extended beyond the narrow boundaries of family or clan, thus leaving local communities at the mercy of would-be conquerors and usurpers. Necessity may have been the force that unified some warring tribes, laws and coercion are the means that have kept them together.

[...]

On the one side, states act independently of their constituent parts, such as peoples and institutions. After all, we talk about the economic viability or capabilities of states, not of the people who reside within the state. Today most states control capital through either public ownership or state-owned enterprises. But some theorists will see the state as passive, reacting mainly to pressures emanating from society. Though scholars disagree on the extent of cooperation and conflict between the state and society, it is still a fact that the state is a legally recognized sovereign entity in international law, endowed with rights and obligations vis-à-vis other states, groups, and its own citizens. Whatever the reasons that give birth to specific states, the nation-state is today the primary actor in international relations. It is the state that defines, provides, and controls the public good, through regulation and institutions. It is the state that enforces the rules through coercion and punishment.

Let us apply some of these arguments to the historical situation of the Kurds, whose situation is symptomatic of many other **ethnonationalists.** After the demise of the Ottoman Empire following World War I, they were the largest ethnic group within the former empire without a state of their own. Instead, Kurds came to live within five other states, the largest segment of them now citizens of the new Republic of Turkey. Ever since, the Turkish government has tried through incentives, coercion, discrimination, and punishment to undermine Kurdish ethnic consciousness, hoping to deter any attempts to secede. Here the state has become omnipotent, using all means at its disposal to subdue Kurdish national aspirations.

An essential question is whether or not a people have rights to a territory on which they resided for many centuries. International law today recognizes that it is inadmissible to acquire territory by waging an aggressive war, but the reality is somewhat different. International law, often invoked but seldom enforced, was used to bolster the legality of the Gulf War in 1990, ostensibly to free Kuwait from the Iraqi occupation, as well as U.S. intervention in Panama and Vietnam. Israel, invoking its defensive posture in the 1967 war, holds on to territory inhabited by Palestinians for centuries. The Abkhaz in Georgia have technically won an independence war, but are not recognized by the international community of nation-states. What does this mean for the rights of groups vis-à-vis states? It means that sometimes group rights are recognized by individual states and the international community and sometimes, depending on various power constellations, they are not. However, international law can provide the justification or the means to establish claims to specific territory. Let us look briefly at the state as arbiter, problem-solving agent, or restrictor or denier of the rights of collectivities.

Indeed, few states are able to unite a multitude of **ethnies** into a harmonious unit. Although long-established liberal democracies probably are more successful than autocracies in doing so, problems persist. Recall the situation of African-Americans prior to the Civil Rights movement and current issues ranging from outright discrimination to disenfranchisement. Consider that Native Americans are a people organized into a number of self-governing segments or "nations" within the greater American nation yet are economically and politically dependent on the United States.

One of the more heretical thoughts that comes to mind is whether the institutionalized state has a future, given the many ethnic groups that clamor for independence. The answer has to be yes, because what is it that these ethnic groups demand? They seek the right to govern their own territory, which they hope will become a sovereign, internationally recognized state. What this suggests is that the current international system may fragment into hundreds of mini-states unless ethnic demands can be satisfied within existing states. In fact more than a dozen ethnic wars were settled in the 1990s by granting autonomy to ethnonationalists within existing states. Successful settlements like these depend on the political system. Democracies are better able to accommodate ethnic demands than autocracies. But it is also true that in newly emerging democracies, ethnic demands may exceed the capacity of state structures, thus leading to failure of existing states.

The ascendance and expansion of the state system has meant that states are parties to most deadly conflicts: wars between states, civil wars within states, and **genocides** and political mass murders by states. But here we find a different phenomenon at work. States wage war, but people decide to make war. Here the collective can triumph over state structures. The collective will as exemplified by prevailing ideologies and political movements within the state system have dramatically influenced ethnic conflict. In the 1920s and 1930s, anti-Semitic doctrines in Germany and other European countries promoted ethnic polarization. They competed with Communist doctrine in the Soviet Union, which emphasized the common interests of all Soviet peoples and minimized the significance of ethnic and nationalist identities. In the 1940s and 1950s anti-colonialism emerged as a major form of resistance against European domination in Asia and Africa. With the help of liberation ideologies, nationalists were able to unite diverse ethnic groups in their efforts to replace colonial rule by European powers with their own independent states. And they succeeded beyond what was expected. By the early 1960s almost all European-ruled colonial territories had gained independence and become members of the state system. But the success came at a cost as tribal and ethnic consciousness soon re-emerged in a number of states. Congo immediately after its independence from Belgium in 1970 and Nigeria a decade later experienced major ethnic wars. More recently we have seen a new kind of resistance to the state system that has affected every world region except Latin America: It is an accelerating wave of self-determination movements.

But there are other trends. At times throughout the twentieth century, ethnic peoples have coalesced across boundaries to join in common causes—for example, by joining pan-Islamic, **pan-Arab**, and **indigenous peoples'** movements. In the Arab world such movements have been short-lived and have been characterized by constantly shifting coalitions. Despite paying lip service to equality of economic status, a shared religion, and the brotherhood of a common ancestry, Arabs have continued to fight fellow Arabs.

But rarely has a common ethnic or religious background been sufficient to cause peoples to subordinate the interests of states to a greater transnational identity or cause, even a limited one. This is especially true for peoples of countries with long-established boundaries who have developed identities beyond their immediate tribes and clans.

At present we witness two competing trends in human organization. At one extreme, we see a reemergence of xenophobia in long-established countries—for example, the increase in exclusive ethnic identity that motivates antiforeign excesses in Germany, France, and Great Britain. No less extreme are movements that demand ethnic purity in formerly heterogeneous federations, such as Serbian nationalism in the former Yugoslavia. At the other end of the continuum are oppressive leaders who defend existing boundaries at all costs, despite historically justified claims by national peoples, such as Palestinians in the Middle East and Kurds in Iraq, for internal autonomy or independence. Ironically, the new elites of former Asian and African colonies share with Saddam Hussein a willingness to fight to maintain existing boundaries and states, despite arbitrarily drawn borders that accommodated European interests but ignored demographic and cultural realities.

The End of the Cold War

The Cold War between the Soviet bloc and the U.S.-led Western alliance created, for better or worse, a sense of stability among most of the world population. Policymakers' calculations concerning conflict outcomes could be made with greater confidence in a more rigidly ordered world. The dissolution of the global system from a loose, bipolar world into an ethnically fragmented multipolar system left in its wake a greater sense of insecurity among the leaders of the established states. This is what U.S. President Bill Clinton alluded to when he told a journalist, "I even made a crack the other day ... 'Gosh, I miss the Cold War.'" How does one deal with hostile warlords in Somalia and respond to ethnic and nationalist unrest in the Soviet successor states? Finding a workable framework for this new era and defining the role of the United States, Clinton added, "could take years."[2] By the end of Clinton administration, no clear framework or consistent set of policies had emerged, though the administration had shifted toward more proactive engagement.

But events do not wait for policymakers to devise new frameworks. With the collapse of Soviet hegemony at the end of the Cold War, the citizens of the former Soviet Union and Eastern Europe were freed to act upon communal rivalries with a vengeance. The demise of communism in the former Soviet Union left a political and ideological vacuum that is only gradually being filled. It was ideology that bound historically hostile peoples together; now old rivalries have reemerged, and neighbors have again become antagonists fighting for power, status, and control of adjacent territories. Communist citizens' place in society was predictable, and their economic welfare was guaranteed at a basic level. Communism in its ideal form also instilled a sense of collective responsibility and solidarity that over came more parochial identities. The transformation of socialist societies into predatory capitalist societies has led to a sense of alienation and isolation and an increased emphasis on narrow group interests and self-interests. This increased sense of isolation has been circumvented by a heightened ethnic awareness and, in some states, a growth in intolerance toward members of other groups.

A decade after the end of the Cold War, the ethnic landscape of post-socialist states is remarkably diverse. The Russian Federation has been widely and justly criticized for fighting a dirty war against rebels in the breakaway republic of Chechnya. But during the 1990s it also successfully negotiated autonomy agreements with Tatarstan, Bashkiria, and some forty other regions of the Russian Federation, thus defusing a number of potentially violent conflicts. A new sense of common interest and identity is being built among most of the peoples of Russia. In East Central Europe, the civil wars that broke up the Yugoslav Federation contrast sharply with Czechoslovakia where ethnic conflict between the Czech and Slovak republics ended peacefully in a "velvet divorce" in 1993. Nationalist governments in Romania and Slovakia cracked down on the restive Hungarian minorities in the early 1990s, but the nationalists were ousted in democratic elections in the late 1990s and Hungarian politicians joined new coalition governments. And the new democratic government of Bulgaria, whose Communist regime had persecuted the country's large Turkish Muslim minority, granted the Turks full cultural, economic, and political rights. The Roma (gypsies) are a worrisome exception to these trends toward ethnic tolerance. They are disliked and discriminated against throughout Europe, East, and West.

CONTEMPORARY EXAMPLES OF ETHNOPOLITICAL CONFLICT

Since the 1960s increasing numbers of ethnic groups have begun to demand more rights and recognition, demands that are now recognized as the major source of domestic and international conflict in the post–Cold War world. The protagonists in the most intense ethnic conflicts want to establish their **autonomy** or independence, as is the case with many Kurds. Other ethnic conflicts arise from efforts by subordinate groups to improve their status within the existing boundaries of a state rather than to secede from it. For example, most black South Africans wanted—and gained—majority control of state power. Turkish and other recent immigrants to Germany worried about their security, seek greater economic opportunities, and hope to become citizens. Native peoples in the Americas want to protect what is left of their traditional lands and cultures from the corrosive influences of modern society. Here we consider some implications of both kinds of ethnic conflict.

The **civil wars** accompanying the dissolution of Yugoslavia into five new states show that subject people's demands for autonomy often escalate into warfare. After Slovenia, Croatia, and Bosnia declared independence in summer 1991, Serbia—the dominant partner in the old Yugoslavian Federation—tried to reestablish its **hegemony** by promoting uprisings by Serbian **minorities** in the latter two states. These Serbs justified their actions by recounting Croat atrocities against Serbs during World War II. They devised brutal and often deadly policies called **ethnic cleansing**, which involved the murder or forced removal of Croatians, Bosnian Muslims, and other minorities from areas in which Serbs lived and prompted hundreds of thousands of refugees to flee to surrounding countries. In Serbia proper the government and local activists severely restricted the activities of Albanian and Hungarian minorities.

One of the longest modern civil wars was waged by the people of the Ethiopian provinces of Eritrea, who supported a war of independence that lasted from the early 1960s until 1991. The Eritrean nationalists received some diplomatic and military support from Middle Eastern states such as Egypt, whereas in the first decade of conflict the imperial Ethiopian government relied heavily on military assistance from the United States. Even the military-led **revolution** that overthrew Emperor Haile Selassie in 1974 did not end ethnic conflict. Instead, the new Marxist military leaders of Ethiopia sought and received support from the Soviet Union to enable them to continue the war against Eritrea. By the end of the 1970s many other ethnic groups in Ethiopia were stimulated into rebellion by the Eritreans, Tigreans, Oromo, and others that culminated in the rebels' triumphal capture of the Ethiopian capital, Addis Ababa, in May 1991.

Unlike the situation in Yugoslavia, there was no serious international effort to check the Ethiopian civil war. No major power recognized Eritrea as an independent state; international organizations regarded the conflict as an internal matter, and there was no media-inspired publicity of atrocities that might have prompted greater action. Only when famine threatened the region did the Ethiopian government allow humanitarian assistance but then prevented distribution of the aid in rebel-held areas.

Following thirty years of warfare, the moderate policies of the new revolutionary government allowed for a peaceful reconciliation. The government made and kept a commitment to hold referendums in 1993 to set up autonomous regional governments or, in the case of Eritrea, to allow full independence. The Eritrean referendum in April 1993 resulted in a 99.8 percent vote in favor of independence. Eritrean independence was accepted by the Ethiopian government, and the new state immediately received diplomatic recognition from the United States and many other countries.

But new sources of ethnic tension soon cropped up. Some Eritreans living in the Ethiopian capital were forced to leave the country, with retaliatory threats by Eritreans to expel Ethiopians. Political and economic tensions escalated until May 1998, when the two countries began a deadly two-year war over some scraps of disputed territory. The Eritrea-Ethiopia conflict, like that between Muslims and Hindus in the Indian subcontinent, shows that separation is not a perfect solution for ethnic tensions because it may lead to future conflicts within and between states.

[...]

Enduring Conflicts, Changing International Responses

We cannot entirely blame the explosion of ethnic conflict in the early 1990s on the end of the Cold War. Figure 13.1 shows clearly that the extent of conflicts worldwide between ethnic groups and states increased steadily from 1950 to 1989, before the Cold War ended. Thus we need to identify other factors that contributed to that explosion. We begin with three Third World examples, which may offer some clues to why some ethnic conflicts were neither affected by nor indirect by-products of Cold War confrontations.

In the 1970s the newly independent African states of Uganda and Equatorial Guinea experienced intense ethnopolitical conflict that had little relationship to the tensions produced by the Cold War. Dictators Macias Nguma of Equatorial Guinea (1968–1979) and Idi Amin of Uganda (1971–1979) each sought to consolidate power by killing thousands of their ethnic and political rivals. These horrifying events elicited no substantive response from the United Nations and few condemnations from individual states. Amin and Macias were virtually free to kill people they defined as enemies, in part because their countries were of little consequence to either the United States or the Soviet Union.

The third case was Rwanda, in which during a genocide in 1994 800,000 to 1 million Tutsis and moderate Hutus perished. When Tutsi exiles of the Rwandan Patriotic Front launched a major invasion from bases in Uganda in 1993, Hutu armies and militias responded with counterattacks. Intermittent negotiations led to the Arusha Accords, but the mobilization of Hutu militias continued. In neighboring Burundi, massacres following a 1993 coup led to a massive exodus of some 342,000 refugees to Rwanda. Militant Rwandan Hutus sought to undermine the Arusha Accords. They probably arranged the downing of the aircraft that carried the presidents of Rwanda and Burundi, Juvenal Habyarimana and Cyprien Ntaryamira, back from peace talks in Tanzania on April 6, 1994. This signaled the beginning of a killing spree in which Belgian peacekeepers and the moderate Rwandan prime minister, Agathe Uwilingiyimana, were among the first to die. Ethnic Tutsis were the primary targets. In the next 100 days, some 800,000 people were killed by marauding Hutu militias, encouraged by their leadership and hate propaganda. In July 1994, Tutsi rebels seized the capital, declared victory, and named a Hutu president. At the end of July Tanzania recognized the new government and Western powers promised aid. But killings continued in Hutu-dominated refugee camps in Zaire.

What these three cases show is that despite warnings of impending disasters, especially in Rwanda, Western powers had little or no interest in intervening. UN peacekeepers in Rwanda were poorly armed and few in number, and their mandate was to remain impartial.

Could more have been done? [...] We believe the international community has an obligation to protect the rights of minorities, beginning with protecting the most basic rights to life and security. For example, and from our point of view, the civil wars and ethnic killings in the breakaway states of former Yugoslavia could have been preempted by early and active international mediation that would have led to guaranteed independence and security for all newly emerging states in the region and to commitments from all parties to protect the rights of each state's ethnic peoples. But the international community is only gradually acquiring the legal principles, political will, and foresight to respond effectively to such conflicts.

In the three cases described above, the consequences of colonialism were a major impediment to decisive action. Colonial subjects in Africa and Asia had few rights, and many ethnic groups were trapped within artificial boundaries imposed by the departing colonial power. Faced with challenges from peoples of different cultures and kinships, most leaders of newly independent Third World countries opted to accept existing boundaries, insisting on absolute sovereignty and the inviolability of territorial borders. This insistence on the right to conduct internal affairs without outside interference gave unscrupulous dictators like Macias and Amin freedom to commit atrocities against their subjects in the name of "nation building." In Rwanda and Burundi, French favoritism, U.S. disinterest, and the UN's self-imposed limited mandate conspired to allow unscrupulous leaders to exploit ethnic tensions.

If the United Nations and the superpowers were indifferent to ethnic conflict and mass murder in peripheral states of the Third World, could regional organizations have responded? Many such deadly episodes occurred in the member states of the Organization of African Unity (OAU, founded in 1963) and the Organization of the Islamic Conference (which represents all states that have significant Muslim populations). But these organizations have usually been politically divided and have had few resources; thus, they have seldom responded to ethnic warfare and severe human rights violations in member states. The OAU, for example, was limited by its charter to mediating conflicts between African states, not within them. In 1981 and 1982, the OAU made its first effort at active peacekeeping when it sent a multinational force to help de-escalate a civil war between communal rivals in Chad; the effort was largely a failure. Partisan support for Rwandan rebels by Uganda did little to defuse the situation. After the Arusha Accords, the OAU verbally condemned international inaction, but had little more to offer than postconflict negotiations.

The impotence of Third World regional organizations combined with the reluctance of the superpowers during the Cold War era to interfere in the internal affairs of states that had little impact on global competition virtually ensured that most ethnic conflicts would remain domestic affairs, even if they led to gross violations of human rights. However, and despite Rwanda, we think that since 1991 the United Nations and the last remaining superpower, the United States, have taken more vigorous action against human rights violators and aggressive states.

[...]

The expanded role of the United States is illustrated by the dispatch of U.S. troops returning from the Gulf War to assist flood victims in Bangladesh in April and May 1991 and by the U.S.-led mobilization of reluctant states to intervene militarily in Iraq during the 1991 Gulf War in a renewed spirit of collective responsibility.

[...]

Regional organizations in the Third World are also taking a more active role in response to internal conflicts. Their leaders are involved in drafting and arguing for extensions to the human rights conventions that would allow for some exceptions to the rule of nonintervention. In the early 1990s, for example, the OAU established a new mechanism for conflict resolution and prevention that, in effect, redefined the OAU doctrine of noninterference in the affairs of member states. The OAU now monitors elections, makes periodic assessments of emerging conflict situations, and sends envoys to countries in which serious crises are brewing. For example in early 1993 the OAU sent a sixty-man observer mission to Rwanda to monitor a cease-fire between rival Hutu and Tutsi armies, but it had neither political nor military clout.

Nongovernmental organizations (NGOs) such as Amnesty International, Human Rights Watch, and the International Crisis Group also play a role by calling attention to ethnic conflict and repression. Activists have lobbied their respective governments and the United Nations to take active roles in supporting humanitarian efforts, have denounced various interventions, and have reported human rights violations to international agencies.

CONCLUSION

We have shown that the "explosion" of ethnopolitical conflicts at the end of the Cold War was, in fact, a continuation of a trend that began as early as the 1960s. It is a manifestation of the enduring tension between states that want to consolidate and expand their power and ethnic groups that want to defend and promote their collective identity and interests. The breakup of the USSR and power shifts elsewhere within the state system have opened up opportunities for ethnic groups to pursue their interests. Coincidentally, the CNN-led explosion of global news coverage has increased public awareness of the human dimensions of these conflicts and thus has contributed to pressures on policymakers to take constructive action.

Recent developments send encouraging signals to those who are concerned about checking the rise of ethnopolitcal conflict and human rights abuses such as ethnic cleansing. For the first time since World War II, the United Nations has begun to realize the vision of its founders: New leadership in the UN, notably Boutros Boutros-Ghali, past secretary general, and Kofi Annan, the current secretary general, have tried to change the role of the UN from reactive to proactive in its role as peacekeeper, intervener, arbiter, and mediator in communal and regional conflicts. A consensus is emerging that the United Nations should establish minimum standards of global security through collective decision making. Of course, the UN's ability to work for world security is directly dependent upon its ability to influence the outcome of emerging ethnic or nationalistic conflicts. However, the continuing caution apparent among most member states over enhancing UN military capabilities signals those who stir up ethnic hatred that they may face a minor roadblock, rather than a major obstacle.

[...]

NOTES

1. The study is detailed in Ted Robert Gurr, *Peoples Versus States: Minorities at Risk in the New Century* (Washington, DC: U.S. Institute of Peace Press, 2000). Current information can be accessed on the project's website, www.cidcm.umd.edu/inscr/mar or, alternatively, www.minoritiesatrisk.com. Five rules were used for identifying groups to be included in the study: (1) Only countries with populations greater than 500,000 were analyzed; (2) only groups that numbered 100,000 or exceeded 1 percent of the population of a country were included; (3) ethnic groups that live in several adjoining countries were counted separately within each country; (4) divisions within an ethnic group within a country were not counted separately—for example, Native Americans in the United States were analyzed as one group, not as three hundred plus separate tribes; (5) twenty-five minorities with political or economic advantages were included [...].

2. Quoted in "Clinton Seeks Foreign Policy Bearings in Post Cold War Fog," *Washington Post*, October 17, 1993, p. A28.

✗ NO
The Banality of "Ethnic War"
JOHN MUELLER

On December 7, 1941, as it is commonly put, "the Japanese" attacked Pearl Harbor. No one of course takes this expression literally to suggest that the entire population of Japan, or even a major portion of it, directly participated in the assault. Rather it is understood to mean that some of Japan's military forces, ordered into action by Japan's government and perhaps supported to varying degrees by the Japanese population, launched the attack. In discussions of ethnic war, by contrast, such distinctions are often missing. When we say "the Serbs" and "the Croats" are engaged in ethnic war, the implication frequently is that those two groups have descended into a sort of Hobbesian war of all against all and neighbor against neighbor.

In this article I assess the violence that took place in the former Yugoslavia and in Rwanda in the 1990s and argue that the whole concept of "ethnic warfare" may be severely misguided. Specifically, insofar as it is taken to imply a war of all against all and neighbor against neighbor—a condition in which pretty much everyone in one ethnic group becomes the ardent, dedicated, and murderous enemy of everyone in another group—ethnic war essentially does not exist. I argue instead that ethnic warfare more closely resembles nonethnic warfare, because it is waged by small groups of combatants, groups that purport to fight and kill in the name of some larger entity. Often, in fact, "ethnic war" is substantially a condition in which a mass of essentially mild, ordinary people can unwillingly and in considerable bewilderment come under the vicious and arbitrary control of small groups of armed thugs.

[...]

Because the violence in Yugoslavia and Rwanda was carried out chiefly by small, ill-disciplined, and essentially cowardly bands of thugs and bullies, policing the situation would probably have been fairly easy for almost any organized, disciplined, and sizable army. An extreme aversion to casualties and a misguided assumption that the conflicts stemmed from immutable ethnic hatreds, however, made international military intervention essentially impossible until the violence appeared to have run its course.[1]

ETHNIC WARFARE IN CROATIA AND BOSNIA

Two explanations are commonly given for the wars in the former Yugoslavia. One is that elemental and ancient ethnic hatreds had only temporarily and superficially been kept in check by communism and that with its demise, murderous nationalism erupted. This perspective has been developed most famously and influentially by Robert Kaplan, who described the Balkans as "a region of pure memory" where "each individual sensation and memory affects the grand movement of clashing peoples," and where the processes of history and memory were "kept on hold" by communism for forty-five years, "thereby creating a kind of multiplier effect for violence."[2] The other explanation holds that the violence was a reaction to continuous nationalist propaganda spewed out by politicians and the media, particularly on Serbian television, that played on old fears and hatreds. As a Belgrade journalist put it to an American audience, "You must imagine a United States with every little television station everywhere taking exactly the same editorial line—a line dictated by David Duke. You too would have war in five years."[3]

The Shallowness of Militant Nationalism in Yugoslavia

Actually, support for militant nationalism in Yugoslavia was not all that deep even at the time of its maximum notice and effect in the early 1990s. The rise of some militant nationalists in elections during that period stemmed less from their wide appeal and more from their ability to manipulate the system and from the disarray of their opposition. In their key victories in 1990, Franjo Tudjman's nationalists in Croatia massively outspent the poorly organized opposition, using funds contributed by well-heeled militants in the Croatian diaspora—particularly in North America. And their success was vastly exaggerated by an electoral system, foolishly designed by the outgoing communists, that handed Tudjman's party 69 percent of the seats with only 42 percent of the vote. In the same election, less than a quarter of the Serbs in Croatia voted for their nationalist party. The same sort of distortions, though to a lesser degree, took place in the elections in Bosnia. In early elections in Serbia, Slobodan Milošević controlled the media and essentially bought the vote by illegally using public funds—hardly a sign of enormous public appeal, and an act that was foolhardy as well because it greatly accelerated the breakup of the country Moreover, like Tudjman's party, Milošević's party was comparatively well organized and widely based and had an enormous advantage under the election rules. Although it garnered less than half the vote, it gained 78 percent of the seats. Milošević's fortunes were further enhanced because Kosovo Albanians boycotted the election, allowing his party to win that area.[4]

A poll conducted throughout Yugoslavia in the summer and autumn of 1990, even as nationalists were apparently triumphing in elections, more accurately indicates the state of opinion after centuries of supposed ethnic hatreds and after years of nationalist propaganda. The question, "Do you agree that every (Yugoslav) nation should have a national state of its own?" elicited the following responses: completely agree, 16 percent; agree to some extent, 7 percent; undecided, 10 percent; do not agree in part, 6 percent; and do not agree at all, 61 percent.[5]

At times, particularly in Serbia during the rise of Milošević, militant nationalists were able to orchestrate huge public demonstrations, which have often been taken to suggest their popular appeal. But in general it is unwise to take large, noisy crowds, which clearly are heavily self-selected, as representing public opinion more generally.[6] Moreover, much of the crowd behavior in Yugoslavia in the early 1990s was manipulated—Milošević's party often paid mobs with free food, transportation, and liquor.[7] And if crowd behavior is to be taken as indicative of wider attitudes, it should be pointed out that even the poorly organized opposition was able to mount massive demonstrations in 1991 and 1992 in Zagreb, Belgrade, and Sarajevo.[8]

Finally, the casual notion that each ethnic or national group in Yugoslavia (or indeed anywhere) is united by deep bonds of affection is substantially flawed. Serbs in Serbia have expressed little affection for the desperate and often rough rural Serbs who have fled to their country from war-torn Croatia and Bosnia.[9] Indeed, as Christopher Bennett argues, in profound contrast with Kaplan, after World War II the "great divide within Yugoslav society was increasingly that between rural and urban communities, not that between peoples."[10]

Armed Thugs and the Banality of "Ethnic Warfare" in Yugoslavia

The violence that erupted in Yugoslavia principally derived not from a frenzy of nationalism—whether ancient or newly inspired—but rather from the actions of recently empowered and unpoliced thugs. Politicians may have started the wars, and they may have whipped up a fair amount of hatred. But the effective murderous core of the wars were not hordes composed of ordinary citizens ripped loose from their repression or incited into violence against their neighbors. Rather the politicians found it necessary to recruit thugs and hooligans for the job.

Significantly, the Serbian (or Yugoslav) army substantially disintegrated early in the hostilities. There may well have been hatreds, and there surely was propaganda. But when ordinary Serb soldiers were given an opportunity to express these presumed proclivities or to act in response to the ingenious televised imprecations in government-sanctioned violence, they professed they did not know why they were fighting and often mutinied or deserted en masse.[11] Meanwhile, back in Serbia young men reacted mainly by determined draft-dodging. Some 150,000 or more quickly emigrated or went underground. In one city, only two of the 2,000–3,000 "volunteers" expected in a call-up showed up, and in several towns there were virtual mutinies against conscription. Overall, only 50 percent of Serbian reservists and only 15 percent in Belgrade obeyed orders to report for duty.[12]

Because Serbs from Serbia proper were unwilling to fight outside their own republic, Belgrade had to reshape its approach to the wars in Croatia and Bosnia in major ways. As a Serbian general put it, modification of Belgrade's military plans was made necessary by "the lack of success in mobilisation and the desertion rate."[13] Part of the solution involved arming the locals, particularly in Serb areas of Croatia and Bosnia.[14] But in general the fighting quality of the militaries, especially initially, was very poor: There was a lack of discipline, ineffective command and control, and, especially in the case of the Serbs, a reluctance to take casualties. Such deficiencies, as Steven Burg and Paul Shoup observe, "led all sides to rely on irregulars and special units."[15]

[...]

As Warren Zimmermann observes, "the dregs of society—embezzlers, thugs, even professional killers—rose from the slime to become freedom fighters and national heroes." Robert Block notes that "gangsters, outlaws, and criminals have had a special place in the war in the former Yugoslavia. Their skills in organizing people and their ruthlessness made them natural choices for Balkan rabble-rousers looking for men to defend cities or serve as nationalist shock troops." And David Rieff points out that "one of the earliest, deepest, and most pervasive effects of the fighting" was "to turn the social pyramid on its head.... Simple boys from the countryside and tough kids from the towns found that their guns made them the ones who could start amassing the Deutschemarks and the privileges, sexual and otherwise."[16]

There was also Rambo-like affectation: Each fighter dressed as if "he had been cast as a thug by a movie director," observes Block. Indeed, one Serbian paramilitary unit called itself "the Rambos" and went around in webbed masks and black gloves with black ribbons fetchingly tied around their foreheads.[17] Naser Orić, a muscular and charismatic former bodyguard who became the Muslim warlord of Srebrenica, and, until 1995, its protector, liked to wear leather jackets, designer sunglasses, and thick gold chains. Members of the Muslim paramilitary group the "Black Swans," which sometimes served as the bodyguard for Bosnia's president when he ventured outside Sarajevo, wore a round patch depicting a black swan having intercourse with a supine woman.[18]

Thus, as Susan Woodward notes, "paramilitary gangs, foreign mercenaries, and convicted criminals roamed the territory under ever less civil control." And "war crimes," observes Norman Cigar, were their "primary military mission."[19] Vladan Vasilijević, an expert on organized crime, says that most of the well-documented atrocities in Bosnia were committed by men with long criminal records. And a United Nations (UN) commission notes a "strong correlation" between paramilitary activity and reports of killing of civilians, rape, torture, destruction of property, looting, detention facilities, and mass graves.[20]

[...]

A COMPARISON: RWANDA

I have stressed the importance of vicious and opportunistic, but often substantially nonideological, criminals and criminal-like elements in the development of the wars in Croatia and Bosnia. This approach seems much sounder than ones that seek to explain the wars as conflicts in which murderous communal rage, exploding from pent-up ancient hatreds or the cynical manipulation of malevolent, short-sighted politicians, induces a Hobbesian conflict of all against all and neighbor against neighbor. There are doubtless instances, however, in which the Hobbesian vision comes closer to being realized. The 1994 genocide inflicted by ethnic Hutus against Tutsis in Rwanda may be a case in point. Closer examination, however, suggests a number of similarities with the wars in Croatia and Bosnia.

Much of the writing about the genocide, in which some 500,000 to 800,000 perished in a matter of weeks—mostly by being hacked to death with machetes or hoes—gives the impression that the conflict was one of all against all, friends against friends, neighbors against neighbors, even Cain against Abel. Friends and neighbors (and even brothers perhaps) did kill each other, but it seems that by far the greatest damage, as in Croatia and Bosnia, resulted from the rampages of murderous thugs.

Far from a spontaneous eruption, the basic elements of the genocidal process had been planned for years by Hutu extremists who were substantially in charge of the ruling party, the government bureaucracy, and the police.[21] Throughout the country Hutus and Hutu police were urged—or ordered—to engage in the killing, and many do seem to have responded enthusiastically. Joining was the Presidential Guard, numbering 700–1,500 men, and the Hutu army, which consisted of some 50,000 men, most of them hastily recruited in the previous few years from land-less peasants, the urban unemployed, and foreign drifters who had chiefly signed up not for ideological reasons, but rather for the guaranteed food and drink (each man was entitled to two bottles of beer a day, a luxury by Rwandan standards) and for the opportunity to loot, because pay was low and irregular.[22]

Finally, there was the Interahamwe, militia bands that had been created and trained by Hutu extremists. As Philip Gourevitch points out, the Interahamwe had its genesis in soccer fan clubs, and it recruited jobless young men who were "wasting in idleness and its attendant resentments," and who tended to see the genocide as a "carnival romp."[23] Moreover, their ranks were expanded by hordes of opportunists once the genocide began. Gérard Prunier notes that a "social aspect of the killings has often been overlooked": As soon as the killing groups "went into action, they drew around them a cloud of even poorer people, a *lumpenproletariat* of street boys, rag-pickers, car-washers, and homeless unemployed. For these people the genocide was the best thing that could ever happen to them. They had the blessings of a form of authority to take revenge on socially powerful people as long as these were on the wrong side of the political fence. They could steal, they could kill with minimum justification, they could rape, and they could get drunk for free. This was wonderful. The political aims pursued by the masters of this dark carnival were quite beyond their scope. They just went along."[24] "Drunken militia bands," notes Gourevitch, "fortified with assorted drugs from ransacked pharmacies, were bused from massacre to massacre."[25] There were about 1,700 "professional Interahamwe" who received training and uniforms, and thousands or tens of thousands joined up (sometimes under coercion) after the genocide began.[26]

As in Yugoslavia, criminals were released from jail to participate in the destruction,[27] and the prospect for enrichment by looting was vastly escalated during the genocide and was used as a specific incentive by the leaders—many of whom were happy to take booty as well.[28] The killers were fully willing to murder fellow Hutus suspected of not being loyal to the cause, and they often forced other Hutus, on pain of instant death, to join the killings.[29] Others participated by manning roadblocks or by pointing out local Tutsis to the marauding *genocidaires*. "I didn't have a choice," one cooperating priest pointed out, "It was necessary to appear pro-militia. If I had had a different attitude, we would all have disappeared."[30]

Many Hutus, however, did hide and protect Tutsi neighbors and sometimes strangers despite the pressure, and despite the fact that the punishment for such behavior could be instant, brutal death.[31] The number of Hutus who did so probably was as high as the number who, under pressure from the often drunken and always-murderous *genocidaires*, indicated where some Tutsis might reside or be hiding.[32] Most of the others, it appears, simply withdrew whether in approval or disapproval of the cataclysm surrounding them: "We closed the door and tried not to hear," said one.[33]

Although an extensive study by Human Rights Watch ventures no direct estimates, it does suggest at various points that the killers numbered in the "tens of thousands."[34] A study by African Rights in London amasses a detailed listing of those in the Hutu elite who directed the genocide and comes up with 600 or 700 names.[35] As indicated earlier, the Presidential Guard comprised some 700–1,500, the army perhaps 50,000, and the Interahamwe militias another 50,000. A year after defeating the genocidal regime, Tutsi forces had 33,000 people incarcerated under suspicion of participating in the genocide—a figure that later rose to at least 125,000.[36]

It may be reasonable to suggest from all this that there were some 50,000 hardcore killers. This would easily be enough to have accomplished the genocide: If each of these people killed one person a week for the course of the 100-day holocaust, more than 700,000 would have perished. This number would represent some 2 percent of the male Hutu population over the age of thirteen. That is, 98 percent of the male Hutu population older than thirteen was not in this group.

It is possible that 200,000 participated in the massacres, though this is likely to be a rather high figure that would include people who, under pressure from the hard-core *genocidaires*, did nothing more than point out where local Tutsi lived or simply manned roadblocks under orders. This would still represent less than 9 percent of the Hutu male population over the age of thirteen. (Though by all accounts very much outnumbered by men and boys, women and girls did join in the genocide. In addition, boys younger than thirteen also often participated.[37] If these groups are added to the base, the percentages would be much lower.)

In some sense, of course, these are astoundingly high figures. In a normal year, by comparison, the proportion of males older than thirteen who committed murder in Rwanda was probably something like 1 in 2,000. Nonetheless, a situation in which more than 90 percent of the over-thirteen male Hutu population did not participate in killings hardly seems to justify the notion that the situation was one of all against all or neighbor against neighbor. As in Croatia and Bosnia, the chief dynamic of the depredations seems to have been furnished by marauding bands of violent, opportunistic, and often drunken thugs.

CONCLUSIONS

This analysis of the experiences in the former Yugoslavia and Rwanda suggests that ethnicity is important in "ethnic wars" more as an ordering device than as an impelling force; that the violence would probably have been fairly easy to police; that the wars did not necessarily derive from the ethnic peculiarities of those regions; and that the wars were by no means inevitable. In addition, some of the wars' key dynamics may have considerable applicability to other violent conflicts.

Ethnicity Is Important Only as an Ordering Device

Michael Ignatieff compares the conditions that prevailed in the former Yugoslavia to a Hobbesian state of nature.[38] But the experience in Yugoslavia and in Rwanda calls this image into question. People did not descend into the war of "every man against every man" that Hobbes so vividly depicted and so ardently abhorred. What happened in Croatia, Bosnia, and Rwanda did resemble a Hobbesian state of nature, but it came about not because people generally gave into murderous enmity, but because they came under the arbitrary control of armed thugs. Ethnicity proved essentially to be simply the characteristic around which the perpetrators and the politicians who recruited and encouraged them happened to array themselves. It was important as an ordering device or principle, not as a crucial motivating force.

[...]

International Policing Could Probably Have Been Effective

Hobbes's greatest mischief comes from his solution to the problem he invents. He assumes that *every* person is, at base, "radically insecure, mistrustful of other men, and afraid for his life." Therefore the only way out of the mess is for everyone permanently to surrender to an authoritarian ruler, one who primarily values glory and stability over doctrinal orthodoxy or ideological purity, and one who will maintain the necessary force to keep all people from once again giving in to their natural proclivities for isolation, hostility, and insensitivity to the rights of others.[39]

But the experience in the former Yugoslav and Rwanda suggests that this monumental—perhaps even impossible—task is hardly required. Most people most of the time do not have much difficulty getting along and creating useful rules and patterns of conduct that allow them to coexist peacefully.[40] Police may be needed, even necessary, to maintain order, but they need not normally be numerous. Nor does their control need to be Leviathan-like, because they mainly need simply to protect the many from the few, rather than everyone from everyone else as Hobbes would have it.

It follows that policing the situation in Yugoslavia and in Rwanda would not have been the major challenge often anticipated. Essentially, the intimidating, opportunistic thugs were successful mainly because they were the biggest bullies on the block. But, like most bullies (and sadists and torturers), they substantially lacked organization, discipline, coherent tactics or strategy, deep motivation, broad popular support, ideological commitment, and essentially, courage.[41] Consequently, if confronted by a military force with these qualities, their most likely reaction would be to flee. And, to a considerable degree, this seems to be what happened both in Yugoslavia and in Rwanda.

[...]

As in Yugoslavia, the marauders in Rwanda were put down fairly easily when confronted with a reasonably coherent military force. Several thousand refugees were saved in a Kigali stadium because the United Nations Assistance Mission to Rwanda, which Prunier characterizes as "the powerless UN 'military' force," simply forbade the murder squads entry. And when the Tutsis eventually were able to get their comparatively capable army into the country, they had to battle for the capital city, but took over the rest of the country with a minimum of fighting. For the most part, Hutu authorities, like their counterparts in the former Yugoslavia, simply ordered their forces to flee when confronted with military force.[42]

[...]

What Happened in Yugoslavia and Rwanda Could Happen Anywhere

If my assessment is essentially correct, it suggests that what happened in Yugoslavia and Rwanda is not unique, but could happen just about anywhere. The Serbian writer Aleksandar Tisma has gloomily concluded from his country's tragedy that "there are civilized people and less civilized people. Here in the Balkans, people don't belong to the civilized but to the less civilized."[43] But the wars in Yugoslavia did not break out because the peoples there are "less civilized." When criminals and sadists are given free rein, they can easily debase the conditions of life.

And thugs are everywhere—at least in small numbers—and only small numbers are necessary if the conditions are ripe. England may seem rather tranquil and well ordered in many respects, but it is also the home of some of the world's most notorious soccer hooligans. Canada often seems to be a nation of eminently reasonable people, but that is not the conclusion one would draw from watching a hockey game. Denmark may today remind people mainly of Hans Christian Andersen and little mermaids, but it once was the home of world-class marauders, and it seems unlikely that that propensity has been fully bred out of the race in the intervening centuries.[44] Moreover, as various studies have suggested, it is often possible to get ordinary people to participate in acts of considerable cruelty when they are placed, voluntarily or involuntarily, in a supportive environment—ideological or ethnic hatred is by no means necessary for this capacity to emerge.[45] Under the right conditions, thugs can rise to a dominant role, others can lend a hand or withdraw into terrified isolation or studied indifference, and any place can degenerate into a Bosnia or a Rwanda.

What Happened in Yugoslavia and Rwanda Was Not Inevitable

The catastrophes that engulfed Bosnia, Croatia, and Rwanda did not have to happen. They emerged not out of inevitable historic necessities, but were instigated and orchestrated by designing politicians and local extremists who, however, often did not know how to control the violent processes they had set into motion.

Yahya Sadowski finds that cultural strife is found about as much in developed countries as in poorer ones, but that such strife is less likely to turn violent in prosperous societies. From this he concludes that economic advancement tends to reduce cultural violence.[46] But it seems, rather, that the actions of leading politicians and police organizations are most important in keeping ethnic and cultural conflict from leading to major violence. Prosperous societies do seem to do better in this regard than poorer ones (which in fact is probably one of the reasons for their comparative prosperity). Prosperity may therefore be beneficial if it helps to develop competent governments and police forces, but wealth itself is not the key operative factor. Thus it is entirely possible to imagine Bosnian-like chaos in prosperous Quebec or Northern Ireland if the Canadian or British authorities had attempted to deal with cultural conflicts by encouraging murderous rampage rather than through patient policing and political accommodation.

On the other hand, because of sound political policies, ethnic violence has been avoided in Bulgaria and Romania even though those countries are hardly more developed than Serbia or Bosnia. And the experience in Macedonia, where political leaders have sought calm accommodation, suggests that the disasters in the more prosperous areas of the former Yugoslavia, far from being inevitable, could almost certainly have been avoided if politicians and police had behaved more sensibly.[47]

[...]

In the end, the basic operation—and the fundamental banality—of much ethnic violence is neatly summed up in a Bosnian expression: "Teško narodu kad pametni ucute, budale progovore, a fukare se obogate." That is, "It is difficult for the people when the smart keep quiet, fools speak out, and thugs get rich."[48] The mistaken—even racist—notion that an entire ethnic group is devotedly out to destroy another ethnic group can in such cases shatter any ability to perceive nuance and variety, and it can be taken to suggest that efforts to foster elite accommodation are essentially irrelevant and therefore bound to prove futile. Further, the all-against-all image can discourage policing because it implies that the entire ethnic group—rather than just a small, opportunistic, and often cowardly subgroup—must be brought under control.

NOTES

1. I am concerned here with ethnic violence and warfare—a condition in which combatants arrayed along ethnic lines seek to kill each other—not particularly with ethnic hatreds. It is important to distinguish common, knee-jerk, and sometimes hateful ethnic slurs—no matter how unpleasant and politically incorrect their expression may often be—from prejudice that is expressed in violence. As James D. Fearon and David U. Laitin have pointed out, ethnic violence is actually exceedingly rare when one considers how many Archie Bunkers there are in the world and how many opportunities there are for it to occur. Fearon and Laitin, "Explaining Interethnic Cooperation," *American Political Science Review*, Vol. 90, No. 4 (December 1996), pp. 716–717. Some analysts argue that "conflicts among nations and ethnic groups are escalating." Samuel P. Huntington, "Why International Primacy Matters," *International Security*, Vol. 17, No. 4 (Spring 1993), p. 71. Others believe "there is a virtual epidemic of armed civil or intranational conflict." See David A. Hamburg, *Preventing Contemporary Intergroup Violence* (New York: Carnegie Corporation of New York, 1993). But such wars and conflicts did not increase in number or intensity in the 1990s. See Yahya Sadowski, *The Myth of Global Chaos* (Washington, D.C.: Brookings, 1998); Ernest J. Wilson and Ted Robert Gurr, "Fewer Nations Are Making War," *Los Angeles Times*, August 22, 1999. p. M2; Steven R. David, "Internal War: Causes and Cures," *World Politics*, Vol. 49, No. 4 (July 1997), pp. 552–576; and James D. Fearon and David D. Laitin, "Weak States, Rough Terrain, and Large Scale Ethnic Violence since 1945," paper presented at the annual meeting of the American Political Science Association, Atlanta, Georgia, September 25, 1999. Rather, what is new is that some of these wars and conflicts have taken place in Europe, an area that had previously been free from substantial civil warfare for nearly half a century. However, militant nationalism—whether violent or not—may well already have had its day in Central and Eastern Europe. Hypernationalists (and even some that are not so hyper), who sometimes appeared threateningly formidable at the polls in the early 1990s, have been reduced in elections in many places to the point of extinguishment.

2. Robert D. Kaplan, "A Reader's Guide to the Balkans," *New York Times Book Review*, April 18, 1993, pp. 1, 30–32. See also Robert D. Kaplan, "History's Cauldron," *Atlantic Monthly*, June 1991, pp. 93–104; and Kaplan, *Balkan Ghosts: A Journey through History* (New York: St. Martin's, 1993). For Kaplan's more recent doomsaying, now focused also on Africa, see his "The Coming Anarchy," *Atlantic*, February 1994, pp. 44–76. For a devastating critique of the argument, see Noel Malcolm, "Seeing Ghosts," *National Interest*, Summer 1993, pp. 83–88. See also V.P. Gagnon, Jr., "Ethnic Nationalism and International Conflict: The Case of Serbia," *International Security*, Vol. 19, No. 3 (Winter 1994/95). pp. 133–134; Russell Hardin, *One for All: The Logic of Group Conflict* (Princeton, N.J.: Princeton University Press, 1995), chap. 6; Sadowski, *Myth of Global Chaos;* and Brian Hall, "Rebecca West's War," *New Yorker*, April 15. 1996, p. 83. For Kaplan's more recent reflections, see his "Reading Too Much into a Book," *New York Times*, June 13, 1999, pp. 4–17.

3. Quoted in Noel Malcolm, *Bosnia: A Short History* (New York: New York University Press, 1994), p. 252. On this argument, see, for example, Christopher Bennett, *Yugoslavia's Bloody Collapse* (New York: New York University Press, 1995), pp. viii, 10, 242; Warren Zimmermann, *Origins of a Catastrophe: Yugoslavia and Its Destroyers* (New York: Times Books, 1996), pp. 120–122; Christopher Cviić, "A Culture

of Humiliation," *National Interest,* Summer 1993, p. 82; Jack Snyder and Karen Ballentine, "Nationalism and the Marketplace of Ideas," *International Security,* Vol. 21, No. 2 (Fall 1996), pp. 25–30; Michael Ignatieff, "The Balkan Tragedy," *New York Review of Books,* May 13, 1993, p. 3; Noel Malcolm, "The Roots of Bosnian Horror Lie Not So Deep," *New York Times,* October 19, 1998; Tim Judah, *The Serbs: History, Myth, and the Destruction of Yugoslavia* (New Haven, Conn.: Yale University Press, 1997), pp. 285, 309; and Peter Maass, *Love Thy Neighbor: A Story of War* (New York: Vintage, 1996), p. 227.

4. On Tudjman's spending, see Susan L. Woodward, *Balkan Tragedy: Chaos and Dissolution after the Cold War* (Washington, D.C.: Brookings, 1995), pp. 119, 229; Bennett, *Yugoslavia's Bloody Collapse,* p. 199; Lenard J. Cohen, *Broken Bonds: Yugoslavia's Disintegration and Balkan Politics in Transition,* 2d ed. (Boulder, Colo.: Westview, 1995), p. 95; Marcus Tanner, *Croatia: A Nation Forged in War* (New Haven, Conn.: Yale University Press, 1997), p. 222; and David Binder, "Gojko Susak, Defense Minister of Croatia Is Dead at 53," *New York Times,* May 5, 1998, p. A25. On Tudjman's electoral success, see Bennett, *Yugoslavia's Bloody Collapse,* p. 127; Woodward, *Balkan Tragedy,* pp. 117–119; Laura Silber and Allan Little, *Yugoslavia: Death of a Nation* (New York: Penguin, 1997), p. 90; and Cohen, *Broken Bonds,* pp. 99–100. On the Serb vote in Croatia, see Gagnon, "Ethnic Nationalism and International Conflict," p. 155; and Bennett, *Yugoslavia's Bloody Collapse,* p. 127. Somewhat similarly, a large portion of those Serbs in Bosnia who lived outside areas controlled by Serb nationalists voted with the Muslims for independence from Serbia in a 1992 referendum; see Gagnon, "Ethnic Nationalism and International Conflict," p. 63. On Bosnia, see Steven L. Burg and Paul S. Shoup, *The War in Bosnia-Herzegovina: Ethnic Conflict and International Intervention* (Armonk, N.Y.: M.E. Sharpe, 1999), pp. 50–51, 57. On Serbia, see Gagnon, "Ethnic Nationalism and International Conflict," p. 154; Bennett, *Yugoslavia's Bloody Collapse,* p. 121; Brian Hall, *The Impossible Country: A Journey through the Last Days of Yugoslavia* (New York: Penguin, 1994), p. 48; Woodward, *Balkan Tragedy,* pp. 130, 448–449; Mladjan Dinkic, *The Economics of Destruction* (Belgrade: Video Nedeljnik, 1995), pp. 30, 61–66; see also Judah, *The Serbs,* p. 260. On vote percentages, see Cohen, *Broken Bonds,* p. 158. On the Albanian vote, see Woodward, *Balkan Tragedy,* p. 121.

5. Laslo Sekelj, *Yugoslavia: The Process of Disintegration* (Highland Lakes, N.J.: Atlantic Research and Publications, 1992), p. 277.

6. Thus, because anti-Vietnam War demonstrators in the 1960s in the United States were predominantly young, most commentators came to hold that young people were more opposed to the war than older people; yet poll data clearly show the opposite to have been the case. John Mueller, *War, Presidents, and Public Opinion* (New York: Wiley, 1973), pp. 136–140.

7. Bennett, *Yugoslavia's Bloody Collapse,* p. 98.

8. On Zagreb, see "Yugoslavia: Death of a Nation," Discovery Channel, 1995. On Belgrade, see Gagnon, "Ethnic Nationalism and International Conflict," pp. 157–158; Silber and Little, *Yugoslavia,* chap. 9; Judah, *The Serbs,* p. 174; and Chuck Sudetic, *Blood and Vengeance: One Family's Story of the War in Bosnia* (New York: W.W. Norton, 1998), p. 85. On Sarajevo, see Judah, *The Serbs,* p. 211; and Robert J. Donia and John V.A. Fine, Jr., *Bosnia and Hercegovina: A Tradition Betrayed* (New York: Columbia University Press, 1994), p. 1.

9. Christine Spolar, "Lesser Serbs in Greater Serbia: Refugees of Croatia Fighting Find Little Welcome from Fellow Serbs," *Washington Post,* May 15, 1995, p. A36; Woodward, *Balkan Tragedy,* p. 364; Stephen Kinzer, "Yugoslavia Deports Refugee Serbs to Fight for Rebels in Bosnia and Croatia," *New York Times,* July 6, 1995, p. A6; and Roger Cohen, *Hearts Grown Brutal: Sagas of Sarajevo* (New York: Random House, 1998), p. 296.

10. Bennett, *Yugoslavia's Bloody Collapse,* p. 63. See also Woodward, *Balkan Tragedy,* pp. 238, 241; Ignatieff, "Balkan Tragedy," p. 4; John R. Bowen, "The Myth of Global Ethnic Conflict," *Journal of Democracy,* Vol. 7, No. 4 (October 1996), pp. 3–14; and Sadowski, *Myth of Global Chaos,* pp. 78–80. Interestingly, in his discussion of the Bosnian war, Peter Maass observes that "to a surprising extent, this was a war of poor rural Serbs against wealthier urban Muslims, a Deliverance scenario." Maass, *Love Thy Neighbor,* p. 159. Donia and Fine note that it was the "relatively uneducated armed hillmen, with a hostility toward urban culture and the state institutions (including taxes) that go with it" who proved "susceptible to Serbian chauvinist propaganda," "allowed themselves to be recruited into Serb paramilitary units," and formed a significant portion of those shelling Bosnia's cities. Donia and Fine, *Bosnia and Hercegovina,* p. 28. See also Fearon and Laitin, "Weak States, Rough Terrain."

11. Norman Cigar, "The Serbo-Croatian War, 1991: Political and Military Dimensions," *Journal of Strategic Studies,* Vol. 16, No. 3 (September 1993), pp. 317–319; Woodward, *Balkan Tragedy,* p. 238; Bennett, *Yugoslavia's Bloody Collapse,* p. 167; Ed Vulliamy, *Seasons in Hell: Understanding Bosnia's War* (New York: Simon and Schuster, 1994), p. 19; Miloš Vasić, "The Yugoslav Army and the Post-Yugoslav Armies," in David A. Dyker and Ivan Vejvoda, eds., *Yugoslavia and After: A Study in Fragmentation, Despair, and Rebirth* (London: Longman, 1996), p. 128; Burg and Shoup, *War in Bosnia-Herzegovina,* p. 51; Gagnon, "Ethnic Nationalism and International Conflict," p. 162; Silber and Little, *Yugoslavia,* p. 177; Tanner, *Croatia,* p. 269; and Judah, *The Serbs,* pp. 185, 189.

12. Jasminka Udovicki and Stojan Cerovic, "The People's Mass Murderer," *Village Voice,* November 7, 1995, p. 27; Stipe Sikavica, "The Collapse of Tito's Army," in Jasminka Udovićki and James Ridgeway, eds., *Yugoslavia's Ethnic Nightmare* (New York: Lawrence Hill, 1995), p. 138; Cigar, "Serbo-Croatian War," p. 315; Tanner, *Croatia,* p. 270; Judah, *The Serbs,* p. 185; and Burg and Shoup, *War in Bosnia-Herzegovina,* p. 51. See also Silber and Little, *Yugoslavia,* p. 177; and Gagnon, "Ethnic Nationalism and International Conflict," p. 162. See also Silber and Little, *Yugoslavia,* p. 177. In all communist countries, certainly including Yugoslavia, people were determinedly subject to decades of communist propaganda in the media. Yet, as history has shown, many—probably most—failed in the end to be convinced by it. If media promotion could guarantee lasting impact, all Yugoslavs would today be worshiping Tito, and all Americans would be driving Edsels. For a discussion, see John Mueller, *Policy and Opinion in the Gulf War* (Chicago: University of Chicago Press, 1994), pp. 129–136. Warren Zimmerman observes, "My most difficult task has been to convey the conviction that all Yugoslavs weren't the bloodthirsty extremists so ubiquitously visible in Western news accounts. Most of the people my wife and I met in six years of living in Yugoslavia were peaceful and decent, without a trace of the hostility on which nationalism feeds.... What amazed me was how many Yugoslavs resisted the incessant racist propaganda." Zimmerman, *Origins of a Catastrophe,* p. xi; see also pp. 209–210.

13. Tanner, *Croatia,* p. 269. See also United Nations Commission of Experts, *Final Report of the United Nations Commission of Experts Established Pursuant to Security Council*

Resolution 780 (1992), Annex III. A Special Forces, ed. M. Cherif Bassiouni, December 28, 1994, par. 29.

14. Burg and Shoup, *War in Bosnia-Herzegovina,* p. 130; and Judah, *The Serbs,* pp. 170–172, 192–195.

15. Burg and Shoup, *War in Bosnia-Herzegovina,* p. 137. There were at least eighty-three of these groups operating in Croatia and Bosnia: fifty-six Serb, thirteen Croat, and fourteen Muslim, with 36,000–66,000 members. See UN Experts, *Final Report,* par. 14.

16. Zimmermann, *Origins of a Catastrophe,* p. 152. Block, "Killers," p. 9. Rieff, *Slaughterhouse,* p. 130. Reportage by Peter Maass is peppered with such phrases as "drunken hillbillies," "death and thuggery," "they don't wear normal uniforms, they don't have many teeth," "the trigger fingers belonged to drunks," "the Bosnians might be the underdogs, but most of their frontline soldiers were crooks," "bullies," massive oaf," foul-smelling warlord," "mouthing the words, 'Bang, you're dead,' through rotten teeth," "an unshaven soldier would point his gun at a desired item and grunt," "only drunks and bandits ventured outside," "goons with guns," "Serb soldiers or thugs—and the difference is hard to tell." See Maass, *Love Thy Neighbor,* pp. 6, 7, 16, 30, 42, 48, 61, 69, 77, 79, 80, 85. Reporter Ed Vulliamy describes them as "boozy at their best, wild and sadistic at their worst" or as "toothless goons" with "inflammable breath." See Vulliamy, *Seasons in Hell,* pp. 19, 46.

17. Block, "Killers"; UN Experts, *Final Report,* par. 291; and Cohen, *Hearts Grown Brutal,* p. 126.

18. Burg and Shoup, *War in Bosnia-Herzegovina,* p. 137; and UN Experts, *Final Report,* at par. 142.

19. Woodward, *Balkan Tragedy,* pp. 254, 356, 485; and Cigar, "Serbo-Croatian War," p. 323. See also Mischa Glenny, *The Fall of Yugoslavia: The Third Balkan War* (New York: Penguin, 1993), p. 185; Chuck Sudetic, "A 'Wild East' Revival in Serbian-Held Croatia," *New York Times,* September 21, 1992, p. A6; Cheryl Benard, "Bosnia: Was It Inevitable?" in Zalmay M. Khalilzad, ed., *Lessons from Bosnia* (Santa Monica, Calif.: RAND Corporation, 1993), pp. 18–25; Vulliamy, *Seasons in Hell,* pp. 307–316; and Bob Stewart, *Broken Lives: A Personal View of the Bosnian Conflict* (London: HarperCollins, 1994), pp. 318–319. See also Rieff, *Slaughterhouse,* p. 83; Ignatieff, *Warrior's Honor,* p. 131; and Sikavica, "Collapse of Tito's Army," p. 138. Vulliamy quotes Reuters reporter Andrej Gustinčić: "Gangs of gun-toting Serbs rule Foča, turning the once quiet town into a nightmare landscape of burning streets and houses.... Some are members of paramilitary groups from Serbia, self-proclaimed crusaders against Islam and defenders of the Serbian nation, others are wild-eyed local men, hostile towards strangers and happy to have driven out their Muslim neighbors. No one seems to be in command, and ill-disciplined and bad-tempered gunmen stop and detain people at will." See Vulliamy, *Seasons in Hell,* pp. 90–91. Many of the "wild-eyed local men," according to another report, were local criminals who "donned uniforms and took part enthusiastically in the subsequent looting." See Julian Borger, "Friends or Foes?" *Guardian Weekly,* January 19, 1997, p. 23. Similarly, the town of Bosanski Novi was ruled by five roaming Serbian armed groups, the most brutal of which was a well-known local mafia known as the "Spare Ribs" that had donned uniforms. See Judah, *The Serbs,* p. 227.

20. On Vasilijevic, see Firestone, "Serb Lawmaker Is Called Vicious Killer." UN Experts, *Final Report,* par. 21.

21. Gérard Prunier, *Rwanda Crisis: History of a Genocide* (New York: Columbia University Press, 1995), p. 169; and African Rights, *Rwanda: Death, Despair, and Defiance*, rev. ed. (London: African Rights, 1995), pp. 51–52.

22. Prunier, *Rwanda Crisis*, pp. 113, 242–243; and African Rights, *Rwanda*, pp. 49, 65.

23. Philip Gourevitch, *We Wish to Inform You That Tomorrow We Will Be Killed with Our Families: Stories from Rwanda* (New York: Farrar, Straus and Giroux, 1998), p. 93.

24. Prunier, *Rwanda Crisis*, pp. 231–232. See also Allison Des Forges, *"Leave None to Tell the Story": Genocide in Rwanda* (New York: Human Rights Watch, 1999), pp. 11, 261.

25. Gourevitch, *We Wish to Inform You*, p. 115.

26. African Rights, *Rwanda*, pp. 55, 61–62, 114.

27. Gourevitch, *We Wish to Inform You*, p. 242.

28. African Rights, *Rwanda*, pp. 55, 61–62, 114.

29. Prunier, *Rwanda Crisis*, p. 247; African Rights, *Rwanda*, chap. 14; and Gourevitch, *We Wish to Inform You*, pp. 307, 309.

30. Prunier, *Rwanda Crisis*, pp. 253–254; and Gourevitch, *We Wish to Inform You*, p. 136.

31. African Rights, *Rwanda*, pp. 1017–1022.

32. Prunier, *Rwanda Crisis*, p. 253; and Des Forges, *"Leave None to Tell the Story,"* pp. 11, 260–262.

33. Des Forges, *"Leave None to Tell the Story,"* p. 262.

34. Ibid., pp. 2, 16, 260, 262.

35. African Rights, *Rwanda*.

36. Gourevitch, *We Wish to Inform You*, p. 242.

37. Bill Keller, "In Mozambique and Other Lands, Children Fight the Wars," *New York Times*, November 9, 1994, p. A14.

38. Ignatieff, "Balkan Tragedy."

39. Robert P. Kraynak, *History and Modernity in the Thought of Thomas Hobbes* (Ithaca, N.Y.: Cornell University Press, 1990), pp. 165, 176, 179.

40. On this issue, see Bruce L. Benson, "The Spontaneous Evolution of Commercial Law," in Daniel B. Klein, ed., *Reputation: Studies in the Voluntary Elicitation of Good Conduct* (Ann Arbor: University of Michigan Press, 1997), pp. 165–189; Robert C. Ellickson, *Order without Law: How Neighbors Settle Disputes* (Cambridge, Mass.: Harvard University Press, 1991); and John Mueller, *Capitalism, Democracy, and Ralph's Pretty Good Grocery* (Princeton, N.J.: Princeton University Press, 1999), chap. 4.

41. Judah observes of Bosnian Serb General Ratko Mladić that "his war was a coward's war. He fought few pitched battles but managed to drive hundreds of thousands of unarmed people out of their homes," and he also questions Mladić's mental stability. Judah, *The Serbs*, pp. 230–231. On this latter issue, see also Robert Block, "The Madness of General Miadic," *New York Review of Books*, October 5, 1995, pp. 7–9; and Jane Perlez, "A Grim Turn for 2 Embattled Serb Leaders," *New York Times*, December 15, 1995, p. Al.

42. Prunier, *Rwanda Crisis*, pp. 254, 268, 377; Gourevitch, *We Wish to Inform You*, pp. 156–157; and Alan J. Kuperman, "Rwanda in Retrospect," *Foreign Affairs*, Vol. 79, No. 1 (January–February 2000), pp. 94–118.

43. Quoted in Jane Perlez, "Balkan Voice of Reason and Despair," *New York Times*, August 14, 1997, p. B1.

44. On the murderous rivalries of motorcycle gangs in tranquil Denmark, see Stephen Kinzer, "Biker Wars in the Land of 'The Little Mermaid,'" *New York Times*, May 6, 1996, p. A4. In this case, however, the thugs are taken to be an aberrant "social pathology" and they are not held to be typical of the entire national spirit as so often happens in Kaplanesque discussions of the Balkans.

45. Stanley Milgram, *Obedience to Authority: An Experimental View* (New York: Harper and Row, 1975); Philip C. Zimbardo, Craig Haney, Curtis Banks, and David Jaffe, "The Mind Is a Formidable Jailer," *New York Times Magazine*, April 8, 1973. pp. 38ff; Christopher R. Browning, *Ordinary Men: Reserve Police Battalion 101 and the Final Solution in Poland* (New York: HarperCollins, 1998); and Fred E. Katz, *Ordinary People and Extraordinary Evil: A Report on the Beguilings of Evil* (Albany: State University of New York Press, 1993).

46. Sadowski, *Myth of Global Chaos*, pp. 174–176.

47. In 1991 Robert Kaplan declared that "Macedonia is once again poised to erupt. Never in half a century has there been so much anger in Macedonia, as its people wake up from a Communist imposed sleep.... Unable to stand on its own, like its more populous and historically grounded neighbor Serbia, Macedonia could implode under the pressures of Albanian nationalism from the west and Bulgarian nationalism from the east. And this is to say nothing of the pressures of Greek nationalism from the south.... The various popular convulsions in the Balkans are inexorably converging on Macedonia.... It is a tragic yet fascinating development. Rarely has the very process of history been so transparent and cyclical." Kaplan, "History's Cauldron," p. 104. See also his "Ground Zero: Macedonia: The Real Battleground," *New Republic*, August 2, 1993, p. 15. Inspired by such wisdom, applications of the now-popular notion of "preventative diplomacy" would have concentrated on exactly the wrong place in the early 1990s. On Bulgaria, see Venelin I. Ganev, "Bulgaria's Symphony of Hope," *Journal of Democracy*, Vol. 8, No. 4 (October 1997), pp. 125–139. On Romania (and also Slovakia), see Robert H. Linden, "Putting on Their Sunday Best: Romania, Hungary, and the Puzzle of Peace," *International Studies Quarterly*, Vol. 44, No. 1 (March 2000), pp. 121–145.

48. Cohen, *Hearts Grown Brutal*, p. 297.

POSTSCRIPT

No matter the causes behind so-called ethnic wars, there is good reason to be concerned that civil conflicts of this sort appear to be on the upswing. The persistence of unresolved colonial-era grievances and artificial borders will continue to cause problems of internal legitimacy and cohesion in many developing states. Continuing violence in Darfur, Iraq, and elsewhere pits rival groups against one another in bloody conflicts that claim staggering numbers of lives. What is more, public cynicism, the relative dysfunction of the United Nations Security Council, and the reticence of the United States and its allies to intervene in these civil conflicts since the invasion of Iraq hinder any attempts to bring an end through armed interventions or diplomacy.

However, the diagnosis of the causes of ethnic strife is certainly an important consideration in thinking through possible solutions to the problem. If ethnic awareness is a deep-seated and significant cause of civil conflict, then it is likely advisable to accept ethnic diversity as a given and promote power-sharing, federalism, and in extreme cases partition as a solution. If mere criminality and individual manipulation of ethnic awareness is the real culprit, then institutions of global justice such as the criminal tribunals held for Yugoslavia and Rwanda, the Special Court for Sierra Leone, or the International Criminal Court (or some form of alternative justice mechanism such as truth commissions) seem to be the more logical choice.

Suggested Additional Readings

Alker, Hayward R., Ted Robert Gurr, and Kumar Rupesinghe, eds. *Journeys through Conflict: Narratives and Lessons* (Oxford: Rowman & Littlefield, 2001).

Anderson, Benedict. *Imagined Communities: Reflections on the Origin and Spread of Nationalism,* revised edition (New York: Verso, 1991).

Crawford, Beverly, and Ronnie D. Lipschutz, eds. *The Myth of "Ethnic Conflict": Politics, Economics, and "Cultural" Violence* (Berkeley: International and Area Studies, 1998).

Horowitz, Donald. *Ethnic Groups in Conflict* (Berkeley: University of California Press, 1985).

_____. *The Deadly Ethnic Riot* (Berkeley: University of California Press, 2001).

Gurr, Ted Robert. *Peoples versus States* (Washington, DC: US Institute of Peace Press, 2000).

Ignatieff, Michael. *Blood and Belonging: Journeys into the New Nationalism* (Toronto: Viking, 1993).

Kaufman, Stuart J. *Modern Hatreds: The Symbolic Politics of Ethnic War* (Ithaca: Cornell University Press, 2001).

Lake, David A., and Donald S. Rothchild. *The International Spread of Ethnic Conflict: Fear, Diffusion and Escalation* (Princeton: Princeton University Press, 1998).

Saideman, Stephen M. *The Ties that Divide: Ethnic Politics, Foreign Policy, and International Conflict* (New York: Columbia University Press, 2001).

Saideman, Stephen M., David J. Lanoue, Michael Campenni, and Samuel Stanton. "Democratization, Political Institutions, and Ethnic Conflict," *Comparative Political Studies,* 35, no. 1 (February 2002): 103–129.

InfoTrac® College Edition

Search for the following articles in the InfoTrac® database:

Bercovitch, Jacob. "Managing Internationalized Ethnic Conflict: Evaluating the Role and Relevance of Mediation," *World Affairs,* 166, no. 1 (Summer 2003): 56–68.

Gurr, Ted Robert. "Ethnic Warfare on the Wane," *Foreign Affairs,* 79, no. 3 (May–June 2000): 52–57.

Kurth, James. "Religion and Ethnic Conflict—In Theory," *Orbis,* 45, no. 2 (Spring 2001): 281–294.

For more articles, enter:
"ethnic conflict," "ethnic politics," "genocide," or "tribalism" in the keyword search.

Web Resources

MINORITIES AT RISK

www.cidcm.umd.edu/inscr/mar

The Minorities at Risk project based at the University of Maryland assesses the status of more than 280 minority groups in countries around the world.

UNITED NATIONS DEPARTMENT OF PEACEKEEPING OPERATIONS

www.un.org/Depts/dpko/dpko

The United Nations has responded with mixed success to many of the explosive ethnic conflicts of the post–Cold War period.

THE INTERNATIONAL CRIMINAL COURT

www.icc-cpi.int

Founded by the Rome Statute of 1998, the International Criminal Court (ICC) is a permanent and independent body that was established to try crimes of genocide, crimes against humanity, and war crimes. While many major international actors have not ratified the Statute, the ICC continues to increase in profile as prominent perpetrators are indicted.

Is Democratization Conducive to Development?

✔ **YES**

AMARTYA SEN, "Democracy as a Universal Value," *Journal of Democracy,* 10, no. 3 (1999): 3–17

✘ **NO**

ADRIAN LEFTWICH, "On Democracy and Development: A Contradiction in the Politics of Economics," *New Political Economy,* 7, no. 2 (2002)

In a well-known comparative text, *The Third Wave,* Samuel Huntington identified the expansion of democracy in three successive historic waves. The first wave began with the broad extension of the franchise beginning in the United States and Britain in the nineteenth century and ended with the period of retrenchment under the communist and fascist governments of the 1920s and 1930s. The second wave arose among former colonial societies in the developing world and crested in 1962. The reversal that came in many developing countries following the second wave arose amid numerous military coups and the associated imposition of authoritarian rule in countries as diverse as Pakistan, Congo, Nigeria, Brazil, and Argentina.

Typically, reversal of democratic rule was and is justified by military juntas on the basis of prior instability, governmental crisis, and crises of internal security. Incoming military dictators such as Gamal Abdel Nasser in Egypt, Mohamed Ayub Khan in Pakistan, Mobutu Sese Seko in Zaire (now the Democratic Republic of Congo), and Augusto Pinochet in Chile among many others sought to bring modernization to their countries. Many adopted patterns of import-substitution industrialization (or ISI) in order to gain through rapid development of key industries. Others, in East Asia, developed a model known as the "developmental state" whereby governments coupled economic management with export-oriented growth. In the case of Latin American countries such as Brazil, Argentina, Uruguay, and Chile, the overturn of democracy was coupled with these modernization strategies and the employment of a special class of technocrats in the government in a pattern that Guillermo O'Donnell has called "bureaucratic authoritarianism". In their early years, many of these modernizers achieved high levels of economic growth, helping to justify the limitation of democracy.

During the 1980s and 1990s, many of these authoritarian regimes came into disrepute and lost domestic and external support. A massive debt crisis threatened the continued pursuit of statist industrialization policies. The end of the Cold War eliminated the rivalry that had made it possible for many governments to ply support from each of the superpowers. In the case of Argentina, a disastrous war fought with the United Kingdom over the Falkland Islands caused the regime to collapse. These states joined the third wave of democratization that according to Huntington had begun with Portugal in 1974 and spread throughout Eastern Europe and Latin America.

However, democratization has brought mixed results in several of the third wave democracies. Some have returned to the instability that had led to military intervention in the first place. Domestic instability has beset Nigeria since the restoration of democratic rule in 1999. Argentina has suffered a major economic downturn and economic crisis. Wary of the chaotic policy changes and uncertainty that accompany democratic rule, many countries have seen a full or partial reversal of democratic reforms and contestation. In Latin America, soft authoritarian regimes under populist leaders have come to power. In Thailand, the military stepped in to depose a controversial and allegedly corrupt democratic government in late 2006.

In each of these cases, military governments restate the case made by the dictatorships and bureaucratic authoritarian governments of the 1970s and 1980s. Democracy invites crippling debates over internal differences in divided societies of the Third World. It tends to contribute to corruption as politicians use favours and government handouts to consolidate their voting base. It provides the opportunity for alternating governments to engage in massive policy shifts that undermine economic planning and thereby constrain the process of industrialization in developing societies.

On the other hand, the most successful and prosperous economies in the world are run by democratic governments. There is good reason to believe that the very free market of ideas that underpins a properly functioning democracy also contributes to innovation, cooperation, and respect for contracts and the rule of law, which help to build a modern economy. There is therefore no reason to believe that a country cannot modernize under a democratic regime.

In the following selections, the debate over the relative merits of democracy in development hinges on the functionality of democracy for development. Amartya Sen, an Indian economist and former Nobel Prize winner in Economics, famously defends the importance of democracy as a vital component of a fully developed economy and society. For Sen, India in particular is exemplary of the ways in which a developing country can benefit through the messy and occasionally tortuous route taken by democratic politics. For this reason, democracy is a "universal" value that is desired and functional for all societies, whether developed or developing. Adrian Leftwich, on the other hand, contends that democracy is inherently conservative and that therefore democratic governments are unable to make the bold decisions necessary to effect rapid improvement in economic performance.

✔ **YES**
Democracy as a Universal Value
AMARTYA SEN

In the summer of 1997, I was asked by a leading Japanese newspaper what I thought was the most important thing that had happened in the twentieth century. I found this to be an unusually thought-provoking question, since so many things of gravity have happened over the last hundred years. The European empires, especially the British and French ones that had so dominated the nineteenth century, came to an end. We witnessed two world wars. We saw the rise and fall of fascism and Nazism. The century witnessed the rise of communism, and its fall (as in the former Soviet bloc) or radical transformation (as in China). We also saw a shift from the economic dominance of the West to a new economic balance much more dominated by Japan and East and Southeast Asia. Even though that region is going through some financial and economic problems right now, this is not going to nullify the shift in the balance of the world economy that has occurred over many decades (in the case of Japan, through nearly the entire century). The past hundred years are not lacking in important events.

Nevertheless, among the great variety of developments that have occurred in the twentieth century, I did not, ultimately, have any difficulty in choosing one as the preeminent development of the period: the rise of democracy. This is not to deny that other occurrences also have been important, but I would argue that in the distant future, when people look back at what happened in this century, they will find it difficult not to accord primacy to the emergence of democracy as the preeminently acceptable form of governance.

The idea of democracy originated, of course, in ancient Greece, more than two millennia ago. Piecemeal efforts at democratization were attempted elsewhere as well, including in India.[1] But it is really in ancient Greece that the idea of democracy took shape and was seriously put into practice (albeit on a limited scale), before it collapsed and was replaced by more authoritarian and asymmetric forms of government. There were no other kinds anywhere else.

Thereafter, democracy as we know it took a long time to emerge. Its gradual—and ultimately triumphant—emergence as a working system of governance was bolstered by many developments, from the signing of the Magna Carta in 1215, to the French and the American Revolutions in the eighteenth century, to the widening of the franchise in Europe and North America in the nineteenth century. It was in the twentieth century, however, that the idea of democracy became established as the "normal" form of government to which any nation is entitled— whether in Europe, America, Asia, or Africa.

The idea of democracy as a universal commitment is quite new, and it is quintessentially a product of the twentieth century. The rebels who forced restraint on the king of England through the Magna Carta saw the need as an entirely local one.

In contrast, the American fighters for independence and the revolutionaries in France contributed greatly to an understanding of the need for democracy as a general system. Yet the focus of their practical demands remained quite local—confined, in effect, to the two sides of the North Atlantic, and founded on the special economic, social, and political history of the region.

Throughout the nineteenth century, theorists of democracy found it quite natural to discuss whether one country or another was "fit for democracy." This thinking changed only in the twentieth century, with the recognition that the question itself was wrong: A country does not have to be deemed fit *for* democracy; rather, it has to become fit *through* democracy. This is indeed a momentous change, extending the potential reach of democracy to cover billions of people, with their varying histories and cultures and disparate levels of affluence.

It was also in this century that people finally accepted that "franchise for all adults" must mean all—not just men but also women. When in January of this year I had the opportunity to meet Ruth Dreyfuss, the president of Switzerland and a woman of remarkable distinction, it gave me occasion to recollect that only a quarter century ago Swiss women could not even vote. We have at last reached the point of recognizing that the coverage of universality, like the quality of mercy, is not strained.

I do not deny that there are challenges to democracy's claim to universality. These challenges come in many shapes and forms—and from different directions. Indeed, that is part of the subject of this essay. I have to examine the claim of democracy as a universal value and the disputes that surround that claim. Before I begin that exercise, however, it is necessary to grasp clearly the sense in which democracy has become a dominant belief in the contemporary world.

In any age and social climate, there are some sweeping beliefs that seem to command respect as a kind of general rule—like a "default" setting in a computer program; they are considered right *unless* their claim is somehow precisely negated. While democracy is not yet universally practiced, nor indeed uniformly accepted, in the general climate of world opinion, democratic governance has now achieved the status of being taken to be generally right. The ball is very much in the court of those who want to rubbish democracy to provide justification for that rejection.

This is a historic change from not very long ago, when the advocates of democracy for Asia or Africa had to argue for democracy with their backs to the wall. While we still have reason enough to dispute those who, implicitly or explicitly, reject the need for democracy, we must also note clearly how the general climate of opinion has shifted from what it was in previous centuries. We do not have to establish afresh, each time, whether such and such a country (South Africa, or Cambodia, or Chile) is "fit for democracy" (a question that was prominent in the discourse of the nineteenth century); we now take that for granted. This recognition of democracy as a universally relevant system, which moves in the direction of its acceptance as a universal value, is a major revolution in thinking, and one of the main contributions of the twentieth century. It is in this context that we have to examine the question of democracy as a universal value.

THE INDIAN EXPERIENCE

How well has democracy worked? While no one really questions the role of democracy in, say, the United States or Britain or France, it is still a matter of dispute for many of the poorer countries in the world. This is not the occasion for a detailed examination of the historical record, but I would argue that democracy has worked well enough.

India, of course, was one of the major battlegrounds of this debate. In denying Indians independence, the British expressed anxiety over the Indians' ability to govern themselves. India was indeed in some disarray in 1947, the year it became independent. It had an untried government, an undigested partition, and unclear political alignments, combined with widespread communal violence and social disorder. It was hard to have faith in the future of a united and democratic India. And yet, half a century later, we find a democracy that has, taking the rough with the smooth, worked remarkably well. Political differences have been largely tackled within the constitutional guidelines, and governments have risen and fallen according to electoral and parliamentary rules. An ungainly, unlikely, inelegant combination of differences, India nonetheless survives and functions remarkably well as a political unit with a democratic system. Indeed, it is held together by its working democracy.

India has also survived the tremendous challenge of dealing with a variety of major languages and a spectrum of religions. Religious and communal differences are, of course, vulnerable to exploitation by sectarian politicians, and have indeed been so used on several occasions (including in recent months), causing massive consternation in the country. Yet the fact that consternation greets sectarian violence and that condemnation of such violence comes from all sections of the country ultimately provides the main democratic guarantee against the narrowly factional exploitation of sectarianism. This is, of course, essential for the survival and prosperity of a country as remarkably varied as India, which is home not only to a Hindu majority, but to the world's third largest Muslim population, to millions of Christians and Buddhists, and to most of the world's Sikhs, Parsees, and Jains.

DEMOCRACY AND ECONOMIC DEVELOPMENT

It is often claimed that nondemocratic systems are better at bringing about economic development. This belief sometimes goes by the name of "the Lee hypothesis," due to its advocacy by Lee Kuan Yew, the leader and former president of Singapore. He is certainly right that some disciplinarian states (such as South

Korea, his own Singapore, and postreform China) have had faster rates of economic growth than many less authoritarian ones (including India, Jamaica, and Costa Rica). The "Lee hypothesis," however, is based on sporadic empiricism, drawing on very selective and limited information, rather than on any general statistical testing over the wide-ranging data that are available. A general relation of this kind cannot be established on the basis of very selective evidence. For example, we cannot really take the high economic growth of Singapore or China as "definitive proof" that authoritarianism does better in promoting economic growth, any more than we can draw the opposite conclusion from the fact that Botswana, the country with the best record of economic growth in Africa, indeed with one of the finest records of economic growth in the whole world, has been an oasis of democracy on that continent over the decades. We need more systematic empirical studies to sort out the claims and counterclaims.

There is, in fact, no convincing general evidence that authoritarian governance and the suppression of political and civil rights are really beneficial to economic development. Indeed, the general statistical picture does not permit any such induction. Systematic empirical studies (for example, by Robert Barro or by Adam Przeworski) give no real support to the claim that there is a general conflict between political rights and economic performance.[2] The directional linkage seems to depend on many other circumstances, and while some statistical investigations note a weakly negative relation, others find a strongly positive one. If all the comparative studies are viewed together, the hypothesis that there is no clear relation between economic growth and democracy in either direction remains extremely plausible. Since democracy and political liberty have importance in themselves, the case for them therefore remains untarnished.[3]

The question also involves a fundamental issue of methods of economic research. We must not only look at statistical connections, but also examine and scrutinize the *causal* processes that are involved in economic growth and development. The economic policies and circumstances that led to the economic success of countries in East Asia are by now reasonably well understood. While different empirical studies have varied in emphasis, there is by now broad consensus on a list of "helpful policies" that includes openness to competition, the use of international markets, public provision of incentives for investment and export, a high level of literacy and schooling, successful land reforms, and other social opportunities that widen participation in the process of economic expansion. There is no reason at all to assume that any of these policies is inconsistent with greater democracy and had to be forcibly sustained by the elements of authoritarianism that happened to be present in South Korea or Singapore or China. Indeed, there is overwhelming evidence to show that what is needed for generating faster economic growth is a friendlier economic climate rather than a harsher political system.

To complete this examination, we must go beyond the narrow confines of economic growth and scrutinize the broader demands of economic development, including the need for economic and social security. In that context, we have to look at the connection between political and civil rights, on the one hand, and the prevention of major economic disasters, on the other. Political and civil rights give people the opportunity to draw attention forcefully to general needs and to demand appropriate public action. The response of a government to the acute suffering of its people often depends on the pressure that is put on it. The exercise of political rights (such as voting, criticizing, protesting, and the like) can make a real difference to the political incentives that operate on a government.

I have discussed elsewhere the remarkable fact that, in the terrible history of famines in the world, no substantial famine has ever occurred in any independent and democratic country with a relatively free press.[4] We cannot find exceptions to this rule, no matter where we look: the recent famines of Ethiopia, Somalia, or other dictatorial regimes; famines in the Soviet Union in the 1930s; China's 1958-61 famine with the failure of the Great Leap Forward; or earlier still, the famines in Ireland or India under alien rule. China, although it was in many ways doing much better economically than India, still managed (unlike India) to have a famine, indeed the largest recorded famine in world history: Nearly 30 million people died in the famine of 1958-61, while faulty governmental policies remained uncorrected for three full years. The policies went uncriticized because there were no opposition parties in parliament, no free press, and no multiparty elections. Indeed, it is precisely this lack of challenge that allowed the deeply defective policies to continue even though they were killing millions each year. The same can be said about the world's two contemporary famines, occurring right now in North Korea and Sudan.

Famines are often associated with what look like natural disasters, and commentators often settle for the simplicity of explaining famines by pointing to these events: the floods in China during the failed Great Leap Forward, the droughts in Ethiopia, or crop failures in North Korea. Nevertheless, many countries with similar natural problems, or even worse ones, manage perfectly well, because a responsive government intervenes to help alleviate hunger. Since the primary victims of a famine are the indigent, deaths can be prevented by recreating incomes (for example, through employment programs), which makes food accessible to potential famine victims. Even the poorest democratic countries that have faced terrible droughts or floods or other natural disasters (such as India in 1973, or Zimbabwe and Botswana in the early 1980s) have been able to feed their people without experiencing a famine.

Famines are easy to prevent if there is a serious effort to do so, and a democratic government, facing elections and criticisms from opposition parties and independent newspapers, cannot help but make such an effort. Not surprisingly, while India continued to have famines under British rule right up to independence (the last famine, which I witnessed as a child, was in 1943, four years before independence), they disappeared suddenly with the establishment of a multiparty democracy and a free press.

I have discussed these issues elsewhere, particularly in my joint work with Jean Dr'eze, so I will not dwell further on them here.[5] Indeed, the issue of famine is only one example of the reach of democracy, though it is, in many ways, the easiest case to analyze. The positive role of political and civil rights applies to the prevention of economic and social disasters in general. When things go fine and everything is routinely good, this instrumental role of democracy may not be particularly missed. It is when things get fouled up, for one reason or another, that the political incentives provided by democratic governance acquire great practical value.

There is, I believe, an important lesson here. Many economic technocrats recommend the use of economic incentives (which the market system provides) while ignoring political incentives (which democratic systems could guarantee). This is to opt for a deeply unbalanced set of ground rules. The protective power of democracy may not be missed much when a country is lucky enough to be facing no serious calamity, when everything is going quite smoothly. Yet the danger of insecurity, arising from changed economic or other circumstances, or from uncorrected mistakes of policy, can lurk behind what looks like a healthy state.

The recent problems of East and Southeast Asia bring out, among other things, the penalties of undemocratic governance. This is so in two striking respects. First, the development of the financial crisis in some of these economies (including South Korea, Thailand, Indonesia) has been closely linked to the lack of transparency in business, in particular the lack of public participation in reviewing financial arrangements. The absence of an effective democratic forum has been central to this failing. Second, once the financial crisis led to a general economic recession, the protective power of democracy—not unlike that which prevents famines in democratic countries—was badly missed in a country like Indonesia. The newly dispossessed did not have the hearing they needed.

A fall in total gross national product of, say, 10 percent may not look like much if it follows in the wake of a growth rate of 5 or 10 percent every year over the past few decades, and yet that decline can decimate lives and create misery for millions if the burden of contraction is not widely shared but allowed to be heaped on those—the unemployed or the economically redundant—who can least bear it. The vulnerable in Indonesia may not have missed democracy when things went up and up, but that lacuna kept their voice low and muffled as the unequally shared crisis developed. The protective role of democracy is strongly missed when it is most needed.

[...]

UNIVERSALITY OF VALUES

If the above analysis is correct, then democracy's claim to be valuable does not rest on just one particular merit. There is a plurality of virtues here, including, first, the *intrinsic* importance of political participation and freedom in human life; second, the *instrumental* importance of political incentives in keeping governments responsible and accountable; and third, the *constructive* role of democracy in the formation of values and in the understanding of needs, rights, and duties. In the light of this diagnosis, we may now address the motivating question of this essay, namely the case for seeing democracy as a universal value.

In disputing this claim, it is sometimes argued that not everyone agrees on the decisive importance of democracy, particularly when it competes with other desirable things for our attention and loyalty. This is indeed so, and there is no unanimity here. This lack of unanimity is seen by some as sufficient evidence that democracy is not a universal value.

[...]

Some who dispute the status of democracy as a universal value base their argument not on the absence of unanimity, but on the presence of regional contrasts. These alleged contrasts are sometimes related to the poverty of some nations. According to this argument, poor people are interested, and have reason to be interested, in bread, not in democracy. This oft-repeated argument is fallacious at two different levels.

First, as discussed above, the protective role of democracy may be particularly important for the poor. This obviously applies to potential famine victims who face starvation. It also applies to the destitute thrown off the economic ladder in a financial crisis. People in economic need also need a political voice. Democracy is not a luxury that can await the arrival of general prosperity.

Second, there is very little evidence that poor people, given the choice, prefer to reject democracy. It is thus of some interest to note that when an erstwhile Indian government in the mid-1970s tried out a similar argument to justify the alleged "emergency" (and the suppression of various political and civil rights) that it had declared, an election was called that divided the voters precisely on this issue. In that fateful election, fought largely on this one overriding theme, the suppression of basic political and civil rights was firmly rejected, and the Indian electorate—one of the poorest in the world—showed itself to be no less keen on protesting against the denial of basic liberties and rights than on complaining about economic deprivation.

To the extent that there has been any testing of the proposition that the poor do not care about civil and political rights, the evidence is entirely against that claim. Similar points can be made by observing the struggle for democratic freedoms in South Korea, Thailand, Bangladesh, Pakistan, Burma, Indonesia, and elsewhere in Asia. Similarly, while political freedom is widely denied in Africa, there have been movements and protests against such repression whenever circumstances have permitted them.

THE ARGUMENT FROM CULTURAL DIFFERENCES

There is also another argument in defense of an allegedly fundamental regional contrast, one related not to economic circumstances but to cultural differences. Perhaps the most famous of these claims relates to what have been called "Asian values." It has been claimed that Asians traditionally value discipline, not political freedom, and thus the attitude to democracy must inevitably be much more skeptical in these countries. I have discussed this thesis in some detail in my Morganthau Memorial Lecture at the Carnegie Council on Ethics and International Affairs.[6]

It is very hard to find any real basis for this intellectual claim in the history of Asian cultures, especially if we look at the classical traditions of India, the Middle East, Iran, and other parts of Asia. For example, one of the earliest and most emphatic statements advocating the tolerance of pluralism and the duty of the state to protect minorities can be found in the inscriptions of the Indian emperor Ashoka in the third century B.C.

Asia is, of course, a very large area, containing 60 percent of the world's population, and generalizations about such a vast set of peoples is not easy. Sometimes the advocates of "Asian values" have tended to look primarily at East Asia as the region of particular applicability. The general thesis of a contrast between the West and Asia often concentrates on the lands to the east of Thailand, even though there is also a more ambitious claim that the rest of Asia is rather "similar." Lee Kuan Yew, to whom we must be grateful for being such a clear expositor (and for articulating fully what is often stated vaguely in this tangled literature), outlines "the fundamental difference between Western concepts of society and government and East Asian concepts" by explaining, "when I say East Asians, I mean Korea, Japan, China, Vietnam, as distinct from Southeast Asia, which is a mix between the Sinic and the Indian, though Indian culture itself emphasizes similar values."[7]

Even East Asia itself, however, is remarkably diverse, with many variations to be found not only among Japan, China, Korea, and other countries of the region, but also *within* each country. Confucius is the standard author quoted in interpreting Asian values, but he is not the only intellectual influence in these countries (in Japan, China, and Korea for example, there are very old and very widespread Buddhist traditions, powerful for over a millennium and a half, and there are also other influences, including a considerable Christian presence). There is no homogeneous worship of order over freedom in any of these cultures.

[...]

The monolithic interpretation of Asian values as hostile to democracy and political rights does not bear critical scrutiny. I should not, I suppose, be too critical of the lack of scholarship supporting these beliefs, since those who have made these claims are not scholars but political leaders, often official or unofficial spokesmen for authoritarian governments. It is, however, interesting to see that while we academics can be impractical about practical politics, practical politicians can, in turn, be rather impractical about scholarship.

It is not hard, of course, to find authoritarian writings within the Asian traditions. But neither is it hard to find them in Western classics: One has only to reflect on the writings of Plato or Aquinas to see that devotion to discipline is not a special Asian taste. To dismiss the plausibility of democracy as a universal value because of the presence of some Asian writings on discipline and order would be similar to rejecting the plausibility of democracy as a natural form of government in Europe or America today on the basis of the writings of Plato or Aquinas (not to mention the substantial medieval literature in support of the Inquisitions).

Due to the experience of contemporary political battles, especially in the Middle East, Islam is often portrayed as fundamentally intolerant of and hostile to individual freedom. But the presence of diversity and variety *within* a tradition applies very much to Islam as well. In India, Akbar and most of the other Moghul emperors (with the notable exception of Aurangzeb) provide good examples of both the theory and practice of political and religious tolerance. The Turkish emperors were often more tolerant than their European contemporaries. Abundant examples can also be found among rulers in Cairo and Baghdad. Indeed, in the twelfth century, the great Jewish scholar Maimonides had to run away from an intolerant Europe (where he was born), and from its persecution of Jews, to the security of a tolerant and urbane Cairo and the patronage of Sultan Saladin.

[...]

WHERE THE DEBATE BELONGS

I have tried to cover a number of issues related to the claim that democracy is a universal value. The value of democracy includes its *intrinsic importance* in human life, its *instrumental role* in generating political incentives, and its *constructive function* in the formation of values (and in understanding the force and feasibility of claims of needs, rights, and duties). These merits are not regional in character. Nor is the advocacy of discipline or order. Heterogeneity of values seems to characterize most, perhaps all, major cultures. The cultural argument does not foreclose, nor indeed deeply constrain, the choices we can make today.

Those choices have to be made here and now, taking note of the functional roles of democracy, on which the case for democracy in the contemporary world depends. I have argued that this case is indeed strong and not regionally contingent. The force of the claim that democracy is a universal value lies, ultimately, in that strength. That is where the debate belongs. It cannot be disposed of by imagined cultural taboos or assumed civilizational predispositions imposed by our various pasts.

NOTES

1. In Aldous Huxley's novel *Point Counter Point,* this was enough to give an adequate excuse to a cheating husband, who tells his wife that he must go to London to study democracy in ancient India in the library of the British Museum, while in reality he goes to see his mistress.

2. Adam Przeworski et al., *Sustainable Democracy* (Cambridge: Cambridge University Press, 1995); Robert J. Barro, *Getting It Right: Markets and Choices in a Free Society* (Cambridge, Mass.: MIT Press, 1996).

3. I have examined the empirical evidence and causal connections in some detail in my book *Development as Freedom,* forthcoming from Knopf in 1999.

4. See my "Development: Which Way Now?" *Economic Journal* 93 (December 1983); *Resources, Values, and Development* (Cambridge, Mass.: Harvard University Press, 1984); and my "Rationality and Social Choice," presidential address to the American Economic Association, published in *American Economic Review* in March 1995. See also Jean Dr'eze and Amartya Sen, *Hunger and Public Action* (Oxford: Clarendon Press, 1987); Frances D'Souza, ed., *Starving in Silence: A Report on Famine and Censorship* (London: Article 19 International Centre on Censorship, 1990); Human Rights Watch, *Indivisible Human Rights: The Relationship between Political and Civil Rights to Survival, Subsistence and Poverty* (New York: Human Rights Watch, 1992); and International Federation of Red Cross and Red Crescent Societies, *World Disaster Report 1994* (Geneva: Red Cross, 1994).

5. Dr'eze and Sen, *Hunger and Public Action.*

6. Amartya Sen, "Human Rights and Asian Values," Morgenthau Memorial Lecture (New York: Carnegie Council on Ethics and International Affairs, 1997), published in a shortened form in *The New Republic,* 14–21 July 1997.

7. Fareed Zakaria, "Culture Is Destiny: A Conversation with Lee Kuan Yew," *Foreign Affairs* 73 (March–April 1994): 113.

✗ NO
On Democracy and Development: A Contradiction in the Politics of Economics
ADRIAN LEFTWICH

I

Insofar as they are analytically isolable from other social processes, all political systems are best understood as systems of power in that they generate, legitimize, distribute, and seek to control (political) power in different ways. Likewise, economic systems are best understood as systems of wealth in that they, too, generate, legitimize, distribute, and seek to control wealth in different ways. In practice, of course, systems of power and wealth overlap and, in doing so, coincide, complement, balance or conflict with each other, or a mix of these. From the point of view of achieving social stability, the macro-political trick is to maintain some kind of equilibrium between them. For stability can be threatened where wealth and power are concentrated in the same hands (as in pre-revolutionary France or Russia and in much of Latin America during the twentieth century), thus provoking pervasive popular opposition. Equally, stability can be threatened where wealth and power are concentrated in different hands, provoking the politics of stand-off or worse (as in Malaysia in the 1960s and Nicaragua in the 1980s), or in the barely suppressed tension between wealth and power in post-apartheid South Africa. It is this relation between systems of power and systems of wealth, crudely stated, and its implications for the political economy of development that is my concern, plus the associated imperative of bringing political science to the core of development studies, and vice versa.[1]

II

However uncomfortable a thesis it may be, I argue that democracy (especially, but not only, in its more limited but almost universally practised representative and Schumpeterian form[2]) is a conservative system of power. Democracy (at least in its liberal form) is also, of course, radical in that no other political systems have promoted and protected individual political rights and civil liberties to the same extent.[3] In their struggles to define, win, or protect such rights in the political domain, countless millions of people have died or suffered appallingly at the hands of authoritarian regimes. These are the human dramas that illustrate so powerfully the 'narrative' of the struggle for democratization from the late-eighteenth century to the present. This should never be underestimated.

But whatever the virtues of their radical properties, stable and hence enduring democracies are conservative systems of power. As Przeworski[4] observes, '[S]ocial and economic conservatism may be the necessary price for democracy.'

There are at least two important respects in which this is the case. First, while democracies have established the principle and practice of at least some civil and political rights in their political systems (though not all, such as gender equality, have been fully implemented), they have not, to the same extent, been able to define, agree upon, or institutionalize social and economic rights (although the record of some democracies, especially social democracies, in these matters is generally better than most authoritarian regimes). Such rights (which the Chinese, at least before the end of the 'iron rice bowl' era, called 'subsistence rights'), include job security, universal and equal access to health and welfare systems, and adequate pension. There are, again, many reasons for this, but as a general rule it is in the nature of governments in democracies to tread warily when seeking to extend their political power in the public domain into the private domain of the system of wealth which would inevitably be required to foot the bill. This is a point to which I will need to return substantively when discussing the developmental implications of democracies or the prospects for developmental democracy.

Democracy may be considered 'conservative' in a second—and perhaps more troubling—sense, at least from a developmental point of view. Democracies have great difficulty in taking rapid and far-reaching steps to reduce structural inequalities in wealth which new democratic governments (as in post-apartheid South Africa) or born-again (and again) democratic governments (as in Brazil or the Philippines) may have inherited, whether they be based on class, colour, ethnicity, religion, or a combination of them. In short, and uncomfortably, the system of power that democratic politics represents seldom promotes the politics of radical change in the system of wealth though this may be vital for establishing developmental momentum, especially in late developing societies. Democracies, that is, have few of the characteristics of what David Apter long ago referred to as 'mobilization' systems, as opposed to 'reconciliation systems.'[5] And this is one of the key reasons why the relationship between democracy and development is so problematic and often tense. For consolidated democratic politics is characteristically the politics of accommodation, compromise and the centre; and its political logic is generally therefore necessarily consensual, conservative and incremental in the change it brings about. For many that is its virtue; for others, its vice.

III

Why should democracy be a conservative system of power? To answer this is to remember the complex structural conditions that underpin and, indeed, define democratic politics. There are many, including, first, a variety of forms of legitimacy—geographic, constitutional, and political. Geographical legitimacy involves citizens accepting their physical place in the territorial state in which they live (which Chechens, Basques, Sri Lankan Tamils, and Southern Sudanese, for example, do not) and not wanting to secede or establish irredentist movements. Likewise, constitutional legitimacy requires acceptance of the political system—that is, the constitutional provisions that provide a durable set of rules for the political game and that distribute and control power in acceptable and hence legitimate ways. These are intensely difficult to establish, as the complex constitutional bargaining in South Africa after 1991 illustrated, and—if not sufficiently acceptable—can easily produce democratic breakdown (often repeated), as in Ulster, Fiji, many parts of post-colonial sub-Saharan Africa, Lebanon, or countless other societies. Finally, political legitimacy entails agreement that the outcome of the political game, according to the operation of its rules, is and remains fair. The absence of such agreement brought about the end-game for Mr. Marcos in the Philippines in 1986 and Mr. Milošević in Serbia in 2000, and deep doubts about fairness of the 1992 election brought uneasy post-electoral politics for President Moi in Kenya.

Such multifaceted legitimacy has never been easy to establish or sustain. Commonly, one or more of its elements (geographic, constitutional, or political) has been missing, deficient, or just plain weak. Moreover, such legitimacy has proved to be very difficult (though not impossible, as in India, though even there it is highly conditional and under both religious and regional threat) to institutionalize in societies where poverty is gross and pervasive, where wealth and income inequality is not only bruising but also not declining, and where the social order is sharply striated by ethnic, religious, or racial cleavages.[6] And already, from these few infrastructural preconditions for democracy, it can be seen why and how democratic politics veer toward procedural conservatism.

But two further intimately related and balancing binary operational conditions of democratic politics make it almost certain that democracy will normally be a conservative system of power. These operational conditions are first, and most simply, that losers must accept the outcome of the political game, knowing that they have the right to come again, within a given and constitutionally stipulated period of time (usually in a range from two to six years' time). Losers cannot return to the gun, the foco, or the bomb (if that is what they did before democratization).

The distinguished American political scientist, Adam Przeworski, has theorized democratization as 'a process of institutionalizing uncertainty, of subjecting all interests to uncertainty.'[7] By definition, no one can know the outcomes of electoral politics. But while this may be true at some level of theory, it is seldom true in practice, for it is highly unlikely that any group or party would come to accept the rules of the electoral game if it knew that losing meant that it or the interests it represented would lose *too* much. In short, no group or interest would enter the democratic political game if it believed that one possible outcome of electoral defeat would result in its effective elimination, politically or otherwise. Thus the quid pro quo for the first operational condition (losers' acceptance of defeat) constitutes the second of the two balancing binary operational conditions for democratic endurance, namely that winners must exercise restraint. Democratic electoral victory is not the same as a licence for the winners to undermine, attack, or eliminate the vital interests or resources of the losers; on the contrary, there are significant limits to what they can do with their newly won power.

This condition means that sustained and sustainable democratic politics thus depends on victorious parties exercising restraint when in government, although the temptation (and sometimes the developmental or egalitarian need) is often to rewrite the policy book. That is to say, new or born-again democracies are more likely to consolidate and prosper if the new government does not pursue highly contentious policies too far or too fast, especially where these policies seriously threaten other major interests. Indeed, such agreed limits on policy change are often established *before* democratization can be completed, in the course of negotiations about the rules of the game, and are thus part of that process itself.[8] The case of Venezuela aptly illustrates this when, in 1958, two extraordinary 'pacts' (the Worker-Owner Accord and the Pact of Punto Fijo) were concluded amongst the three main parties, excluding the Communist Party.[9] These pacts ('pacted' democracy) framed the directions and limits of policy change and effectively tied the major parties into a consensus on the broad limits of developmental policy choice and provided for a sharing of power which, for almost 30 years, sustained democracy in Venezuela, something rare in Latin America during the period. They did so by guaranteeing that the main parties would all have a stake in the government and that neither they nor their supporters would ever lose too much through electoral defeat.

IV

The problem is that *development* is both by definition and in practice a radical and commonly turbulent process that is concerned with often far-reaching and rapid change in the structure and use of wealth, and which—if successful—must transform it. But the prospects of combining such transformation in the structure of wealth with democracy are slim. For in laying the foundations for, or re-starting, development (certainly the kind of rapid and catching-up development so urgently needed in so many societies), it is inevitable that non-consensual steps will have to be taken, especially where a new developmentally committed regime comes to power facing a legacy of immense inequality in the structure of wealth and opportunity (illustrated dramatically by the cases of South Africa or the Philippines after the fall of Marcos).

Land reform is a good example of the kind of non-consensual step often necessary, since it is widely recognised that this can be an important condition for both rural and industrial development. But landowners in general do not consent to land reform! As in Latin America and Asia, they have often constituted a very powerful interest with intimate connections to the dominant parties and the state. In consequence, Third World democracies have seldom been effective in overcoming such vested rural interests to achieve the restructuring of both rural wealth and power which land reform is designed to bring about. Land reform failed in the Philippines after the restoration of democracy in 1986,[10] and proved impossible in Pakistan under the Bhutto regime in the 1970s.[11] Indian democracy too has had very little success in pushing through national land reforms (though some states, such as Kerala, have been more successful). Moreover, at the level of more general redistributive policy and practice in India, there has been '... hardly any significant taxation of agricultural income and wealth.'[12] Indeed, the general attempt in India under the dominance of Congress governments for almost 30 years to organize development of what was in effect a 'continental political economy, more empire than nation,' was undertaken '... with one arm tied behind its back by its commitment to liberal democracy,' as Herring puts it,[13] producing relatively limpingly slow development as reflected in what Raj Krishna once described as 'the Hindu rate of growth.'[14]

V

In conclusion, under *most* circumstances, the rules and operational conditions of stable democratic politics will tend to restrict policy to incremental and accommodationist options. On the other hand, developmental requirements (whether liberal or radical) will be likely to pull politics and policy in the direction of quite sharp (and, for some, unpleasant) changes affecting the structure of wealth of the society and hence important interests within it. It is this structural contradiction between the conservative requirements of stable democratic survival and the urgent transformative imperatives of late development that makes the combination of democracy and development so difficult, and that makes the establishment and continuity of democratic developmental states so rare. For these reasons, no one should hold their breath for an imminent great leap forward in development performance in the Third World, following contemporary western insistence on democratization as a condition for growth (and aid). Effective development will not depend on regime type, but on the character of the state, whether democratic or not. But that is a different story.

NOTES

1. Adrian Leftwich, *States of Development* (Polity Press, 2000).

2. J. A. Schumpeter, *Capitalism, Socialism and Democracy* (Unwin, 1965), p. 269.

3. R.G. Gastil, *Freedom in the World, 1985–6* (Greenwood Press, 1986) and C. Humana, *World Human Rights Guide,* 3rd edition (Oxford University Press, 1992).

4. Adam Przeworski, 'Democracy as a Contingent Outcome of Conflicts,' in J. Elster and R. Slagstad (Eds.), *Constitutionalism and Democracy* (Cambridge University Press, 1988).

5. David Apter, *The Politics of Modernization* (University of Chicago Press, 1965).

6. Adam Przeworski, et al., *Sustainable Democracy* (Cambridge University Press) and Adam Przeworski, M. Alvarez, J.A Cheibub, and F. Limongi, 'What Makes Democracies Endure?' *Journal of Democracy,* 7, no. 1 (1996): 39–55.

7. Adam Przeworski, 'Some Problems in the Study of the Transition to Democracy,' in: G. O'Donnell, et al. (Eds.), *Transitions from Authoritarian Rule. Comparative Perspectives* (Johns Hopkins Press, 1986), p. 58.

8. S.P. Huntington, 'How Countries Democratize,' *Political Science Quarterly,* 106, no. 4 (1991/1992): 609–615.

9. Jennifer McCoy, 'The State and the Democratic Compromise in Venezuela,' *Journal of Developing Societies,* 4 (1988): 85–133.

10. B.J. Kerkvliet, 'Land Reform in the Philippines Since the Marcos Coup,' *Pacific Affairs,* 47 (1974): 286–304; and J. Moran, 'Patterns of Corruption and development in East Asia,' *Third World Quarterly,* 20, no. 3 (1999): 569–587.

11. R.J. Herring, 'Zulfika Ali Bhuto and the "Eradication of Feudalism" in Pakistan,' *Comparative Studies in Society and History,* 21, no. 4 (1979): 519–557.

12. Pranap Bardhan, *The Political Economy of Development in India* (Basil Blackwell, 1984), p. 46 and chapter 6.

13. Ronald J. Herring, 'Embedded Particularism: India's Failed Developmental State' in Meredith Woo-Cumings (Ed.), *The Developmental State* (Cornell University Press, 1999), pp. 306–334.

14. S. Corbridge and J. Harriss, *Reinventing India* (Polity Press, 2000), p. 173.

POSTSCRIPT

Scholars such as Adrian Leftwich envision the restoration of the "developmental state" as a viable alternative in developing societies. In these cases, development is the key preoccupation of the state, rather than democratic participation. Developmental states are better able to set rules by which economies can become robust and well-ordered, as indicated among single-party and soft authoritarian states in East Asia in the latter part of the 1980s as well as under the bureaucratic-authoritarian model. It is argued that the singleness of purpose of these developmental states provides a useful context in which the state can pursue proper economic development. Thus, the developmental state is more effective in providing the kind of stability desired by international lending and aid agencies that seek to improve governance processes as a condition for continued support.

Most international donors do not share this ambiguity about the importance of democratic development to proper governance processes in the developing world. They tend to associate higher levels of democratic participation and contestation with higher levels of transparency and accountability within government. This is by no means universally proven, given the evident problems of chronic corruption and instability in developing societies with democratic governments.

Suggested Additional Readings

Barsh, Russel Lawrence. "Democratization and Development," *Human Rights Quarterly,* 14, no. 1 (February 1992): 120–134.

Bueno de Mesquita, Bruce, and George W. Downs. "Democracy and Development," *Foreign Affairs,* 84, no. 5 (September–October 2005): 77–81.

Chua, Amy. *World on Fire: How Exporting Free Market Democracy Breeds Ethnic Hatred and Global Instability* (New York: Doubleday, 2003).

Huntington, Samuel P. *The Third Wave: Democratization in the Late Twentieth Century* (Norman: University of Oklahoma Press, 1991).

Krieckhaus, Jonathan. "Democracy and Economic Growth: How Regional Context Influences Regime Effects," *British Journal of Political Science,* 36, no. 2 (April 2006): 317–342.

O'Donnell, Guillermo. *Bureaucratic Authoritarianism: Argentina 1966–1973 in Comparative Perspective* (Berkeley: University of California Press, 1988).

Oxhorn, Philip, and Graciela Ducatenzeiler. *What Kind of Democracy? What Kind of Market? Latin America in the Age of Neoliberalism* (University Park: Pennsylvania State University Press, 1998).

Sen, Amartya. *Development as Freedom* (New York: Knopf, 1999).

InfoTrac® College Edition

Search for the following articles in the InfoTrac® database:

Grugel, Jean. "Democracy and Civil Society in the Third World," *Journal of Development Studies,* 34, no. 4 (April 1998): 174–175.

Ma, Shu-Yun. "The Rise and Fall of Bureaucratic Authoritarianism in Chile," *Studies in Comparative International Development,* 34, no. 3 (Fall 1999): 51–65.

For more articles, enter:
"democratization and development," "authoritarianism," or "developmental state" in the keyword search.

Web Resources

FREEDOM HOUSE

www.freedomhouse.org

Freedom House is one of the best-known pro-democracy thinktanks and advocates for human rights. It engages in regular assessment and ranking of all countries based on measures of political and economic freedom.

OVERSEAS DEVELOPMENT INSTITUTE—DEVELOPMENTAL STATES

www.odi.org.uk/speeches/states_06/1stFeb/index.html

This site contains an online overview and video footage of Adrian Leftwich's elaboration on the role of the developmental state.

GLOBAL POLICY FORUM—DEVELOPMENT, DEMOCRACY & HUMAN RIGHTS

www.globalpolicy.org/socecon/develop/democracy/index.htm

This site contains links to many articles regarding the interrelated issues of liberal democracy and development.

PART FIVE

GLOBAL RESOURCES AND THE ENVIRONMENT

Is the World Bank's approach to sustainable development adequate?

Can genetically modified food help solve global food needs?

Is the World Bank's Approach to Sustainable Development Adequate?

✔ **YES**
WORLD BANK, "Pathways to a Sustainable Future," from the *World Development Report 2003*

✗ **NO**
LIANE SCHALATEK AND BARBARA UNMÜSSIG, "The WDR 2003: A Strenuous Tale of Missed Opportunities," in Liane Schalatek, et al., *Managing Sustainability World Bank-Style: An Evaluation of the World Development Report 2003* (Berlin: Heinrich Böll Foundation, 2002)

In 1972, the Conference on Human Environment marked the first significant effort to place environmental issues more firmly on the international agenda. Held in Stockholm, the meetings were important because they focused international attention on environmental problems and encouraged states to cooperate to find solutions. They also laid the groundwork for the creation of the UN Environmental Program (UNEP), which is responsible for monitoring the environment, raising global awareness of environmental problems, encouraging practices that are environmentally friendly, and urging other UN agencies and states to cooperate on environmental matters.

This conference was followed later by the establishment of the World Commission on Environment and Development, often referred to as the Brundtland Commission, after the prime minister of Norway, Gro Harlem Brundtland, who chaired the committee. The commission was charged with examining the relationship between two important objectives: safeguarding the environment and promoting economic growth. After extensive consultations, the commission presented its report, *Our Common Future,* in 1987. The key concept of the achievement of both goals was "sustainable development," which the commission defined as "development that meets the needs of the present without compromising the ability of future generations to meet their own needs" (*Our Common Future,* p. 43). The intent of this concept was to find ways in which states could create economic growth and alleviate poverty while simultaneously protecting the environment and not destroying a society's "natural capital."

The Brundtland Report was followed was five years later by the Rio Summit, or as it was formally known, the United Nations Conference on Environment and Development. This landmark conference in turn was followed up ten years later in 2002 with the World Summit on Sustainable Development in Johannesburg,

South Africa. Although these conferences helped keep environmental issues on the international agenda, the status of the notion of "sustainable development" in actual development planning processes often remained precarious. For a long time, many developing countries remained skeptical of the idea. Many feared that northern environmental activism posed a threat to their development goals and hopes for immediate economic growth. Some even suggested that such environmental pressures from the industrialized countries constituted a new form of "eco-imperialism."

However, with a combination of pressures from environmental activists, global institutions, donor governments, and scientific bodies, the relationship between the environment and development has gradually received more attention. Although the international conferences on the environment have been successful in negotiating new treaties and conventions dealing with various dimensions of the environmental issue, critics have suggested that there still is a long way to go in ensuring that the environment receives adequate attention in development planning.

Often the environment is still seen as a separate, stand-alone concern, not firmly embedded within development planning processes, and only loosely related to wider social and economic agendas. In addition, the concept of sustainable development is still often seen as focusing only on strictly "environmental" issues rather than something that encompasses economic, social, and environmental dimensions. The problem is not unlike the one encountered in relating gender and development. Just as it was found to be insufficient to merely add a "women's" dimension to an existing development project, so too environmental analysts have argued that just adding an "environmental audit" to your project planning was insufficient to achieve sustainable development.

Thus, some have called for a greater effort to "mainstream" environmental concerns into the activities of development agencies and organizations. This means that environmental and sustainability questions need to be incorporated, not just into planning specific projects, but into the broader understanding of the relationship between the environment and social and economic policies.

One agency that has been criticized by environmental activists is the World Bank. In the past, many of the large-scale projects funded by the World Bank, such as the Three Gorges Dam project in China, have garnered widespread criticism for the negative repercussions on the environment. In the 1990s, environmentalists also argued that the Structural Adjustment Programs (SAPs) instituted by IMF and the World Bank in many countries led to policies that also had negative environmental consequences.

In response to this criticism, the World Bank created as early as 1987 an environment department that established detailed environmental impact assessments for all its projects and lending programs. In addition, in 2003, the World Bank took a further step in "mainstreaming" the notion of "sustainable development" by making it the focus of its annual *World Development Report*.

In the introduction to this report, the World Bank notes:

> Any serious attempt at reducing poverty requires sustained economic growth in order to increase productivity and income in developing countries. But there is more to development than just economic growth—much more. This Report argues that ensuring sustainable development requires attention not just to economic growth but also to environmental and social issues. Unless the transformation of society and the management of the environment are addressed integrally along with economic growth, growth itself will be jeopardized over the longer term.

The report also notes that it will take a "comprehensive, longer term, and dynamic view of sustainability, with a clear focus on poverty reduction."

The launch of the *2003 World Development Report,* with the title *Dynamic Development in a Sustainable World,* was scheduled to take place at the World Summit on Sustainable Development (WSSD) in August 2002. It was intended to represent the World Bank's first contribution to the international discussion about sustainable development. Given the importance of the World Bank as major international development agency, and its influence over the discourse of the international development community, the unveiling the Bank's "up-to-date" thinking about an environmentally, socially, and economically balanced development is worth careful attention. In the first reading, we present an excerpt from the *2003 World Development Report.* In the second reading, the two researchers, Liane Schalatek and Barbara Unmüssig from the Heinrich Böll Foundation, provide a critical assessment of the World Bank's approach to sustainable development. They find that the report falls far short of what needs to be done to develop a truly sustainable approach to development.

✔ **YES**
Pathways to a Sustainable Future
WORLD BANK

Accelerated growth in productivity and income can eliminate poverty and enhance prosperity in developing countries. This growth needs to be achieved at the same time critical ecosystem services are improved and the social fabric that underpins development is strengthened. A close look at what is happening on the ground reveals both cause for concern and cause for hope.

Concern stems from evidence that getting the world on a sustainable path is problematic:

- In many developing countries, productivity is low, growth is stagnant, and unemployment is high.

- The number of people living on less than $1 a day (1.2 billion) is dropping but it is still a challenge, and more people are living on fragile lands.

- Income inequality is rising. Average income in the wealthiest 20 countries is 37 times that in the poorest 20 countries—twice the ratio in 1970.

- Many of the poorest countries are wracked by civil conflict, with animosities deep and prolonged.

- Stress on the environment is increasing. Fisheries are being overexploited, soils degraded, coral reefs destroyed, tropical forests lost, air and water polluted.

- The financial transfers to address these issues are far from adequate, even though the resources are available.

Hope springs from the genuine progress made already in boosting average per-capita incomes in developing countries and reducing infant mortality and illiteracy rates—and from the greater awareness of the problems that remain. Disparate groups now agree that the current development path, though possible for a while, is not sustainable. Science and technology are providing some answers, but they will not be sufficient without complementary changes in institutions. The world community, in confronting some of the challenges, is grappling with new strategies and goals:

- Development agencies are shifting to more participatory and holistic approaches with a medium-term perspective, through the Comprehensive Development Framework (CDF) and focused poverty reduction strategies, backed by actions on the ground through partnerships, broader inclusion in the preparation of assistance strategies, and some shifts in lending and grant aid.

- The private sector is more committed to sustainable development, with greater use of triple-bottom-line accounting by firms and greater use of environmental and social criteria by investors.

- Governments and civil society are supporting the Convention on Biodiversity, the Convention to Combat Desertification, the Convention on Climate Change, and the Millennium Development Goals. And civil society is demanding more public and private accountability.

Although encouraging, these advances are small relative to the many challenges of sustainable development. Sustainability requires thinking long term, but acting now—it also requires coordination. This Report recognizes the importance of economic incentives and policies in changing behavior, but it does not focus on specific policies or organizational designs. (Nor does it evaluate projections based on different policy or organizational scenarios.) Instead it argues that well known and appropriate policies have not been adopted or implemented because of distributional problems and institutional weaknesses, and that sustainable development with faster growth and higher productivity, capable of eliminating poverty and achieving a more just and sustainable development path, requires much stronger institutions. To support improvements in well-being, these institutions would need to manage a broader portfolio of assets and adapt to new problems and opportunities. Technologies and preferences will change, and resource allocation and distribution issues cannot be neatly separated.

Managing risk is important. Not all risks are insurable. Not all irreversible changes are bad, but some are. For the assets most at risk—the natural and social—markets cannot provide the basic coordinating functions of sensing problems, balancing interests, and executing policies and solutions. These types of assets have impacts, good and bad, that extend beyond individual transactions and thus require coordination to promote good spillovers and minimize the bad. This coordination reveals the need for institutions that are capable of organizing dispersed interests, confronting vested interests, and ensuring credible commitments in execution.

This Report shows that rising income can facilitate but not guarantee better environmental and social outcomes by permitting countries to simply "grow out of" pollution or civil conflict. It also shows that low income does not condemn people to a deteriorating environment or social climate. What makes the difference? Public action, through competent institutions.

Mobilizing institutional responses is more difficult for some problems than others. Problems with impacts and risks that are diffuse and long term (such as climate change and biodiversity loss) are less readily perceived and appreciated than those immediately felt and measured (i.e., some forms of local air and water pollution and deforestation). Assets that are public goods or common property goods—such as clean air, forests, fisheries, and water—are a challenge to manage sustainably. The reason is that private property rights are difficult to assign or enforce, or if improperly designed they fragment and undermine the underlying joint functions of an asset—say, an interconnected ecosystem. In addition, the concerns of the poor and powerless are less likely to attract the attention of society's many institutions than those of strong and vested interest groups. That is why greater equality in access to assets and voice makes a difference in the kinds of environmental and social concerns that society addresses.

This Report argues that, for countries and local communities, extreme inequalities in assets, power, and voice are corrosive, linked, and self-perpetuating. When the poor lack voice and a stake in society, social assets (such as trust) and environmental assets (on which the poor depend) are eroded, stability is undermined, and the ability to solve economic, social, and environmental problems (that require collective action) dissipates.

As the world comes to resemble a single community, these lessons may apply even at the global level. At the very least, inequality and the lack of hope for the poorest countries will inhibit attempts at solving global problems—not just the current preoccupations with cross-border spillovers of conflict and terrorism, but also the currently unimagined problems that will require global cooperation 20 or 50 years hence. That is why ending global poverty is much more than a moral imperative—it is the cornerstone of a sustainable world.

The next 20 to 50 years are a demographic window of opportunity, created by the deceleration of population growth rates and the decline in dependency ratios. This period will also witness completion of the urban transition in most countries. The demographic transition will permit greater savings if the working age population has jobs and investment opportunities. The urban transition will facilitate income generation, but over the next 50 years it will also require massive investments. Many of these investments are likely to be long-lived—so getting them right by incorporating environmental and social concerns in their design now is critical.

Even the next 15 years (2003–2018) could bring a record period of economic growth in developing countries. Driven by growth in China and India, income in the low- and middle-income countries will almost double—accounting for more than a third of the 60 percent increase in world output. This period offers the opportunity to lay the foundation for inclusive growth—which will require confronting barriers to change. Institutions that can manage the social and economic transitions, by partially compensating losing interests, are much easier to create in rapidly growing economies than in economies where inclusion requires a battle over stagnant shares. For many countries whether the opportunities generated by new growth are inclusive, or whether they lock in vested interests and exclusive institutions, will depend on decisions taken in the next few years.

ACTING TODAY

This Report outlines actions that can be taken now to improve the ability of institutions to identify, adopt, and implement policies that facilitate growth while addressing critical environmental and social issues.

Institutional and Sectoral Approaches Are Complementary

Sustainable development requires action across many sectors and disciplines, including water, energy, health, agriculture, biodiversity, and others. In a companion document, the World Bank sets forth some recommendations and action plans to advance sectoral goals.

This Report takes a different approach—but one intended to complement and support the sectoral perspectives. Its message is that proposing and endorsing a set of action plans are important first step, but realizing them requires an institutional apparatus that cuts across sectors. Achieving all the broad sectoral goals will involve problem diagnosis, decisions with distributional consequences, and coordinated and sustained commitments to action. These functional capabilities require general improvement in coordinating institutions within and across countries.

Making progress on the sectoral issues, for example, requires first a better understanding of local conditions and a better ability to diagnose local problems. Domestic and international institutions will be required to fund and implement R&D where local capacities are deficient. Second, some difficult distributional issues must be resolved: How to divide the water among claimants? How to allocate health resources among preventive, primary, and secondary care? What sort of land uses to permit, for whom, if environmental processes are to be maintained? Without institutions that represent fairly the interests of dispersed and (usually) voiceless interests, institutions affecting these sectors are prone to capture by vested interests, and they are unlikely to implement efficient or equitable solutions. Third, commitment problems loom large. Health and water services often deteriorate after costly initial investments for lack of routine funding and maintenance. This speaks to the challenge of organizing beneficiaries for sustained commitments.

This Report shows that even with imperfect institutions it is possible—indeed imperative—to build now on the many institutional innovations already out there that show the way forward.

Many, if not all, of the institutional innovations cited in this Report already show signs of being replicable and capable of being scaled up to meet the challenges ahead. For example, the pilot experience with security of tenure in *favelas* in Brazil is being extended to hundreds of thousands of households. The multi-stakeholder pilot pollution disclosure programs in China have moved from 2 pilot municipalities to 13; countrywide implementation is currently under discussion. The village initiative in Morocco is being replicated in a dozen other villages. The forest concession program in Cameroon has created a constituency for expanding it to other sectors. There is much creativity under way with initiatives emerging from the public sector, the private sector, and civil society. An enabling environment is needed to encourage such initiatives, to facilitate partnerships, and to help mobilize the resources needed to scale up promising activities within countries, and across countries.

Picking up Signals Early

Being sensitive to early signs of problems, especially from the fringes, is important if society is to avoid costly crises later. HIV/AIDS is a case in point. In the early stages of the epidemic, HIV/AIDS received little attention since no one knew how contagious it was or the trajectory of future costs. By now, with the evidence available, all countries should have programs to identify the problem early and to stay ahead of the epidemic. The same is true for environmental issues–the status of biodiversity, air pollution, lead in gasoline, or the drawdown of acquifers in arid regions.

Creating information for constituencies and constituencies for information. There is a need for significant investment in information and indicators at global and local levels, where this information would find users and audiences. The initiative must go well beyond current attempts to devise indicators of sustainable development, including summary indexes that try to capture sustainable development in a single headline number. If society is to sustain development, it needs good indicators, but it also needs individuals and groups who demand and use detailed and quality information to solve problems, and others who produce information to meet that demand. Summary indicators should rest on a solid foundation of supporting data.

Environmental and social problems are easy to misdiagnose when there is a lack of reliable, current, and geographically disaggregated information. For many important aspects of the environment, global conditions or trends are worrisome, but society lacks the detailed data to monitor, diagnose, and manage the problems at local, national, and global levels. Data for the social sphere are similarly limited. For most countries, reliable, up-to-date, spatially disaggregated information is lacking on poverty and many other social concerns (health, education, crime).

These data gaps inhibit understanding of–and consensus on–the impacts of policy reforms, national and international, on poverty in the developing world. They also impede the formulation and execution of strategies to combat desertification, other forms of ecosystem degradation, and biodiversity loss. And they muddy the discussion of the nature and impacts of global inequality. Fortunately, rapid changes in communication and information technology make it more feasible to gather this information through a combination of surveys, reports from ground observers, and information from satellites and other sensors. As information costs continue to plummet, the scope for expanding the collection of this kind of information is immense. Innovative information systems can track and deter industrial polluters (as in Indonesia's PROPER system) and illegal deforestation and forest fires (as in Mato Grosso's environmental control system).

Although information provision can sometimes be a catalyst for change, the most effective systems are those that create constituencies for information. The constituencies may be public agencies that use the information to plan and assess strategies for pollution control, crime prevention, or public health delivery. Or they may be civil society organizations that use information to mobilize dispersed interests. It is demand by users that stimulates and maintains the production of relevant, reliable information.

This Report proposes an intensive global effort to develop and fund a program to fill data gaps, which would include:

- More local poverty, health, and education data linked to national totals.
- More spatially disaggregated data on economic and environmental health conditions for the analysis of local problems and impacts.
- More coupling of satellite-based remote sensing data with local "ground-truthing" information, to measure the extent and quality of land under different types of habitat or land cover.
- More monitoring of soil degradation, its causes and impacts.
- More effort at measuring hydrological conditions.
- More investments in geospatial information, such as the availability of infrastructure services, and accurate current maps of road networks.
- More coordination and augmentation of national efforts to monitor the Millennium Development Goals, to increase comparability, and to provide desirable levels of frequency and geographic detail.

Balancing Interests

To equitably and efficiently balance interests within a society, two elements are necessary: first, getting everyone fairly represented at the bargaining table; second, facilitating negotiation once everyone is there. For many problems at the level of the community or nation—especially those relating to environmental and social issues—the responsibility lies with the government. But governments vary in their capacity to undertake these tasks. An expanding set of institutional tools can assist or complement governments in balancing interests, and they can assist citizens in ensuring that their governments are fair and responsive in doing so. These tools become even more important at the international level, where they must substitute for government. It is fundamentally difficult to balance interests in heterogeneous societies. But taken together, in a context of increasingly democratic institutions and decreasing costs of information and communication, these tools give some hope.

Transparency, performance reporting, and accountability. Often the biggest barrier to balancing interests is an imbalance in the power or influence of parties. Devices for accountability—including transparency and performance reporting—are useful tools for countering the tendency of entrenched interests to capture institutions or to be unresponsive to dispersed or less powerful interests. Providing this kind of information helps level the playing field for negotiation, since less powerful interests will typically have poorer access to information. Performance reporting can also help governments, companies, and other organizations understand the effectiveness and impacts of their own actions, for instance:

- *National reporting*—transparency in fiscal affairs, reliability of legal institutions, and adequacy of environmental impact reviews—can all provide the information and incentives necessary to improve governance and the balancing of interests. Examples include the recent International Monetary Fund Codes of Good Practice on transparency in fiscal, monetary, and financial policies, and WTO requirements on subsidy reporting. Another example is the Aarhus Convention—a voluntary commitment to environmental transparency. National reporting requirements under the WTO, multinational environmental agreements, and other international treaties can help nations track and manage their own compliance processes and help build confidence among parties to forge agreements.

- *Independent audits of public programs*—especially programs related to the management of public assets, such as land, water, forests, minerals, and fisheries and the regulation of pollution—can deter corruption and promote better management of environmental resources. Regular audits of national environmental assets can be useful in detecting and diagnosing problems. Public ratings of governments' transparency and corruption can affect investment and provide a check on government capture by vested interests. Assessment of the distributional impact of government expenditures provides an essential basis for renegotiating them.

- *Performance reporting for cities and local governments* provides a tool for citizens to ensure that governments are responsive to public needs and are equitably and efficiently implementing agreed-on programs in health, sanitation, water supply, public safety, and other areas of public concern.

- *Performance reporting by private firms*—financial, environmental, and social—helps society to identify actors with disproportionately large impacts, both good and bad, and to understand trade-offs and complementarities between economic performance, and economic, environmental, and social performance.

Forums and networks for negotiation. Governments and civil society can seek ways to facilitate negotiation between affected parties. For instance, Colombia's regional environmental authorities have set up structured negotiations between water polluters and water users to help determine tolerable levels of pollution. Participatory budgeting has transformed the budgetary process in more than 80 Brazilian cities. At the international level, the Convention on Long-Range Transboundary Air Pollution forums on air pollution and the Global Environment Facility-sponsored transboundary diagnostic assessments for international waters provide structured means of assessing options. These forums become more effective when they build up social capital through dense networks of trust and information linking technical experts, government officials and legislators, civil society, and special interests.

Compensation and incentives. Even win-win outcomes usually have a loser—a party whose losses are outbalanced by social gains. Basic principles for balancing interests therefore include minimizing the losses, compensating losers, or providing incentives that reconcile private and social objectives.

One way to do this in the environmental sphere is through market-based permits. Where actors have different costs of complying with social objectives, trading rights or obligations can substantially reduce compliance costs for individuals and for society as a whole. Assignment of valuable permit rights (pollution permits, fishery quotas) is also a means of compensating potential losers and ensuring participation in a reformed system. When the potential losers are wealthy interests, however, there may be an unavoidable trade-off between equity and cooperation.

Certification systems are another means of aligning private and social incentives. Certification of firms helps investors identify companies with better environmental and social performance, thus promoting incentives for more socially responsible behavior. Certification of financial institutions (including private banks, bilateral export-import banks, and multilateral development banks) can promote standards for assessing the environmental and social impacts of investment projects. Certification of products (wood, coffee, fish, beach resorts, garments) can allow consumers and investors to reward firms that employ environmentally and socially sustainable production processes. Certification of diamonds and other lootable commodities can be part of a strategy to avert civil conflict over point-source wealth. [...]

Implementing

Implementing and executing policies and programs requires appropriate institutional capacity. Mention of capacity-building evokes respect and approval—but not always excitement or enthusiasm. It has usually been seen as an add-on to projects and programs with other, more important purposes. It is often identified with failed technical assistance projects that relied heavily on the ephemeral input of foreign consultants. The same is true of monitoring and evaluation, another project add-on that often fails to be executed with rigor or to provide much insight. Yet institutional competence, especially the ability to learn, is crucial to efficient use of development investments and to solving the coordination problems described in this Report.

Promoting capacity-building and problem-solving in the developing world. The need to emphasize long-term capacity-building has been recognized for more than a decade. Yet, despite technical cooperation grants of $201.3 billion over 1990–2001, progress in institution-building in developing countries has been disappointing. Most of those funds, to be sure, have been devoted to project preparation. Such investments may have been effective in achieving project goals through reliance on expatriate inputs, but at the cost of forgone opportunities to bolster local capacity. There are failures, too, in the demand for institution-building.

Often, lack of ownership, lack of government interest in bolstering capacity, and pressures for rent-seeking have kept competent institutions from taking root.

Several new approaches could help place learning and institutional development at the core of sustainable development efforts—that is, projects and programs designed around institutional development, rather than vice versa. These approaches recognize that capacity-building is not accomplished in a few years and thus is not well suited to lending for individual projects or adjustment programs. These approaches also recognize that capacity has a strong social capital component, involving not just people but enduring networks that link policymakers, experts, civil society, and the private sector. And these approaches generate virtuous circles when information and indicators are made available to groups that demand and act on that information.

The new approaches use a variety of new types of learning organizations to stimulate both the demand for and supply of institutional skills; they include:

- *Think-and-do tanks,* policy analytic and action-oriented organizations that build links (twinning) to universities and think tanks in other developing countries and in the developed world, to government line agencies in their own countries, and to local governments and community organizations working on the ground.

- *Scientific research organizations,* based in the developing world, that combine local and global expertise and help to nurture "policy entrepreneurs" at home in both scientific and policy worlds.

- *Learning networks* for sharing knowledge, such as the Union of Capital Cities of Ibero-America—real-time, demand-driven learning networks run by national and international associations of mayors, local government officials, and city practitioners share experiences among their members and other cities through the Internet and workshops.

- *CSOs for monitoring and evaluating government and corporate performance.* These groups that independently monitor and report on government and corporate expenditures and activities have proliferated recently. They can help improve government and corporate accountability, create incentives for monitoring and evaluation within government and corporations, and mobilize public demand for institutional improvements.

- *Mainstreaming monitoring and evaluation functions inside government agencies.* Responding to both internal and public demand for increased efficiency and accountability, some governments are improving internal capabilities for monitoring and evaluating programs and projects.

Donors and multilateral development banks can support the evolution of this intellectual ecosystem of organizations that learn—and apply that learning to improving policies and projects. Donors can support these organizations, through direct funding and twinning arrangements on a large scale. These are long-term efforts that bear fruit over a decade or two as the institutions train people, enhance the prestige of necessary but neglected professions, such as policy analysis, and build dense networks of trust and knowledge. Funding must be committed over periods much longer than traditional projects, and funders must accept that the impacts of these investments, though potentially enormous, will be deferred and difficult to quantify. Donors can also design projects with learning as a central output, providing hands-on monitoring, evaluation, and implementation experience to learning organizations.

Expanding the scope of global assessment institutions to address emerging issues. At the transnational and global level, assessment institutions such as the IPCC have shown their value in forging consensus on the problems and the options for addressing them. More institutions like the IPCC are needed to address the new global problems that continue to emerge all the time. For instance, questions at the intersection of trade and environment are sure to proliferate, as the discussion of product certification illustrates. Trade policy is an area where more systematic analysis of options might help in forging agreements. Deepening scientific knowledge exposes overlooked transnational environmental processes. For instance, there is increasing attention to the global nitrogen cycle and its effect on marine ecosystems. Technical change, too, brings new problems and risks as well as opportunities. Balancing the environmental risks and benefits of genetically modified organisms is a clear example. And social changes require ongoing and forward-looking attention. For instance, intensifying pressures for international migration have far-reaching ramifications. In all of these areas, there is a strong argument for concerted international attention—and for achieving some consensus on the relevant issues.

Ensuring Greater Inclusion

Increased voice and major increases in substantive democratization. Inclusiveness can be expanded through significant changes in governance that increase representation and accountability, such as empowering local government through well-designed decentralization reforms; electing rather than appointing mayors (Mexico City); replacing military with elected regimes (Cubatão), or empowering groups excluded from decisionmaking—women, indigenous people, and other disadvantaged groups, who may be in the majority.

Better distribution of access to assets. Dynamic growth and development processes create more assets and new types of assets. It will be much easier to increase inclusiveness by ensuring that the poor and disenfranchised, as well as the middle class, have greater access to these newly created assets. How? By increasing access to education, which build human capital; by expanding market-based rural land reforms to increase smallholders' access to agricultural land and complementary assets (water, roads, and knowhow); by expanding the provision of secure tenure (protection from arbitrary eviction) in urban slums or other informal urban settlements; by increasing access to knowledge (the new asset frontier). Any remaining need to improve access to assets by redistributing existing assets must be based on carefully designed measures that balance interests so that good institutions that enable people and assets to thrive can emerge.

ONGOING DIALOGUE: A GLOBAL VISION AND ACCORD

To overcome the barriers to solving collective problems more rapidly and systematically requires mutual commitments by developing and developed countries to a bold global vision and accord. This vision requires a massive and steady effort to eliminate poverty and to protect and manage a broader portfolio of assets that will ensure the well-being of future generations.

A Global Vision

Today the lessons of history are clearer than ever, for instance:

- Prosperity and well-being, like peace, are indivisible and must be shared if they are to be maintained.

- Two generations—fifty years—are enough to eliminate poverty and to move to a more sustainable development path.

But negotiating this great transformation in the next 20 to 50 years requires a renewed commitment by all countries—developed and developing—to this overarching common vision. The vision is ambitious, but achievable. Many small, poor countries—Denmark, Ireland, Japan, Malaysia, Norway, and the Republic of Korea—have made the leap at different times from illiteracy and mass poverty to literacy and affluence within two generations. They were late industrializers in a global economy already dominated by giants. The European Union shows how the prospect of mutually beneficial integration can induce poorer countries to adopt higher standards of environmental and economic management while the richer ones provide resources and help to boost capacity. The experience of the Dust Bowl in the United States shows how small, individual states could not solve their problems without the migration opportunities offered by other states, or the channeling of knowledge and financial resources from other states that helped to restore economic health over many decades.

The European Recovery Program (the Marshall Plan) after World War II showed how mobilizing resources on a grand scale can build economies and transform enmity into partnership. The architects of the Marshall Plan accepted the challenge of tackling "hunger, poverty, desperation, and chaos" by rebuilding a continent in the interest of political stability, social development, and a healthy world economy. They had learned the hard lessons of history: the Treaty of Versailles ending the First World War in 1919 had imposed unilateral conditions and enforced severe reparations on the vanquished, paving the way for political extremism. The designers of the Marshall Plan avoided these mistakes and paved the way for peace. The Treaty of Versailles courted conflict. The Marshall Plan broke a vicious cycle of poverty and regret; it supported economic reconstruction and social order; and it injected money and ideas to rebuild Europe and herald more than 50 years of unprecedented peace, prosperity, and partnership.

Balancing interests and forging credible commitments for the long haul is difficult at the national level but even more so at the global level. Yet it is increasingly necessary because national action is insufficient to deal with the scale of spillovers (box 15.1) generated by a more interconnected world and global economy. So increased global coordination is necessary to expand the capacity and opportunities of the weaker segments of the global community. A self-enforcing global accord may be required to get the commitment to finance such a scaled-up effort, to build capacity to use the funds wisely, and to take on difficult reforms in developing as well as industrial countries.

BOX 15.1

A BIG PUSH—TO ADDRESS SPILLOVERS AND SEIZE OPPORTUNITIES

The many global challenges are deeply linked—to each other and to local concerns. So are their solutions. Managing global spillovers, both environmental and social, and taking advantage of a window of opportunity over the next 20–50 years, will require a big push by global institutions—and by national and local institutions.

There are important biophysical links among the spillovers.

- Deforestation, an important cause of biodiversity loss, contributes to climate change. Climate change, in turn, puts stress on ecosystem resources, including grazing lands, water resources, and coral reef fisheries that nourish some of the world's poorest people. It transforms grazing lands to desert. And it threatens cities and coastal populations with more storms and flooding.

- Poverty alleviation and global growth are linked to biodiversity conservation. In the poorest countries, good governance is necessary to protect renewable resources and the people who depend on them—and it is a prerequisite for the ecosystem management organizations advocated here. Furthermore, vigorous local and global development may pull farm populations away from forest lands that are marginal for agriculture but valuable for environmental services. So faster development and the creation of better institutions may avert the sacrifice of valuable ecosystems for ephemeral gain.

- Atmospheric greenhouse gas concentrations cannot be stabilized if the poor countries follow the same emissions path as the developed countries—even if the developed countries were to cut their emissions to zero. Global sustainability requires that all countries work together to pursue long-term paths to low emissions. But equity, and international cooperation, require that greenhouse gases be stabilized without jeopardizing the development aspirations of poor countries.

- Trade and other internationally negotiated policies can affect poverty, biodiversity loss, greenhouse gas emissions, and other global environmental spillovers such as nitrogen emissions and toxins. Coordination at the international level and actions at the national level are important to pursue synergies among goals and avoid unintended consequences. Social spillovers, from institutional and environmental weakness, also tightly bind the interests of rich and poor nations and motivate common interests in sustainable development.

- Infectious diseases are a global concern. Urbanization and faster travel speed the transmission of disease, increasing the chances of epidemics. The misuse of antibiotics— overuse in wealthy countries and underuse in poor ones—stimulates faster evolution of microbes, against which there is a diminishing supply of fall-back drugs.* And human populations—particularly the poor, displaced to fragile lands—are in closer contact with disease reservoirs in forests and wetlands and among domestic animals.

- Poverty contributes to civil conflict and the potential collapse of the state, with transnational impacts. Poverty and the failure of governance are strong risk factors for civil conflict. Nations that experience conflict are at great risk of relapse. Domestic conflicts often have international repercussions, as refugees and violence spill across borders. And terrorism and crime take root in a state vacuum.

- Income disparities create strong pressures for migration, and when these pressures meet closed borders, tensions arise. One study estimates that each 10 percent increase in the foreign-to-local wage difference increases emigration by 1 per thousand population in African countries.† Historically, such labor movements have been powerful avenues of poverty alleviation. But strong migration pressures, combined with a growing population and blocked outlets, lead to tensions and fuel the illegal market in smuggling people, estimated at $7 billion a year.‡

* WHO (2001).
† Hatton and Williamson (2001).
‡ NIC (2000).

A Global Accord

There is growing recognition of the need for mutual commitments and for accelerated improvements in key development indicators. Support for the Millennium Development Goals, which propose to cut the proportion of people in extreme poverty by half by 2015 is now widespread. The goals set ambitious quantitative targets for reducing hunger, increasing primary schooling, improving health, promoting gender equity, and ensuring environmental sustainability. One calculation puts the cost of meeting just the nonenvironmental targets at $40 to $70 billion a year above the current $50 billion in development assistance. Another estimate puts the cost of reaching the environmental goals over a longer period at $25 billion per year.

The recent International Conference on Financing for Development in Monterrey also confirmed the need for more aid, trade, and debt forgiveness by industrial countries, in tandem with domestic reforms in developing countries to increase domestic resource mobilization and facilitate foreign direct investment.

The recent proposal for the New Partnership for Africa's Development (NEPAD) is also based on an arrangement in which developing countries take responsibility for improved governance, and industrial countries help through more aid, debt forgiveness, and market access. The Council of the European Union's proposed Global Deal has many of the same elements.

In the spirit of these initiatives and to maintain the momentum of the Millennium Development Goals beyond 2015, this Report calls for extending the following goals:

- To fully eliminate global poverty, and

- To put the global economy on a more sustainable development path by the middle of this century.

The two features added to existing initiatives are a deeper target over a longer time horizon, and a greater focus on institutional development. It will require 10 or 20 years—starting now—to build up the institutions that can help shift trajectories from unsustainable to sustainable paths over the next 50 years. Many of these long-horizon initiatives will yield benefits in the medium term in support of the Millennium Development Goals. But because many future problems cannot be foreseen, it is important that institutional foundations be strong and that a process and a framework be developed that are robust in picking up new signals, balancing a broader range of interests, and maintaining commitments to the global vision.

At a modest 3 percent annual rate of growth, the global economy in 50 years will be four times the size it is now. Will that larger economy generate less environmental and social stress than the much smaller economy does today? Most of the physical capital required for the economy 50 years hence has not yet been created. This provides an opportunity to incorporate inclusiveness and sustainability criteria in new investments now. The potential is there to shift development paths, provided institutions that adapt and implement better policies can be put in place.

For development strategies and development assistance, this means placing a greater emphasis on:

- Identifying vicious circles that keep the pace of growth low and the distribution of assets unequal—and developing strategic interventions to break these vicious circles.

- Investing in projects, programs, and initiatives that bring about better, more inclusive institutions and ensure systematic learning.

Greater inclusion, better information flows, more transparency, and wider forums for balancing interests will help to improve the functioning of global and local institutions to fight poverty and promote sustainability. Investments in global poverty reduction and in greater inclusiveness will help ensure the representation of all interests in the design of the new and improved institutions.

There is no understating the difficulty of these challenges. Nor is there an easy solution. Social inertia is great, and institutional change can take decades. Overcoming the inertia to tackle these difficult problems—the fears and risks of unilateral action—requires coordination. The Report suggests mutually reinforcing ways to catalyze institutional change, to mobilize dispersed constituencies, and to support capacity development. The core components of a global accord include:

- *Building capacity to use resources wisely.* It is now well established that the effectiveness of development assistance—indeed, of all investment—depends greatly on the quality of economic policies and the reliability and capability of market and nonmarket institutions. But there is a lot more to building capacity than technical assistance, as discussed in this chapter's earlier section titled "Implementing."

- *Providing the necessary funding.* Capital markets (foreign direct investment and private financing) can cover much of the funding required to shift to a more sustainable path if appropriate policies are in place. For example, they can cover investment in new and replacement capital (buildings and equipment) to improve energy efficiency and meet the demands of an urban population that will double. But expanded domestic resources and development assistance will be needed to cover the part of these costs that involve the provision of local, national, and global public goods. Institution building is one of these public goods. The estimated funding requirements for the Millennium Development Goals would not be enough to support a broader and deeper agenda of institution-building. There are some rough estimates of the resources that can to be freed up say, by eliminating perverse subsidies in industrialized and developing countries and redirecting them to support institutional building and the investment requirements of a shift to a more sustainable path. However, a serious data and analytic effort is needed to confirm this information at greater levels of detail, country by country.

- *Undertaking difficult reforms* for both the developed and the developing world.

Main Responsibilities of Developing Countries

A development strategy that emphasizes inclusiveness, shared growth, and better governance places large demands on leaders in developing countries. They must commit to better economic, social, and environmental management—and thus to better governance. To manage their resources, and what they receive from outside, they need to:

- *Strengthen institutions.* The rule of law and good governance allow families and firms to have confidence—in other words, to save and invest.

- *Broaden inclusiveness in the access to assets.* Schooling, health care, and provision of environmental assets that protect health, market-based rural land reform, and regularization of urban tenure (providing protection from eviction without due legal process) all promote asset generation for the poor.

- *Increase transparency.* An open and verifiable flow of information is important to tighten accountability in government and the private sector through such steps as opening procedures for bidding, strengthening meritocracy in the civil service, and making sure that public and corporate budgeting and resource management are governed by law, open to the public, and under proper oversight institutions.

The success of the reforms would be long term; they would secure opportunities and voice for families and their children so they can save, invest, and engage in their communities. But good policies, to be sustained, will require committed support and the legacy of reversals and stalemates is stunning. Research on aid and policy shows that aid is not worth much without good policies and institutions; in fact, it can even be harmful. Research also shows that good policies and institutions are essential to growth and development. This Report has argued that often but not always good policies presuppose good institutions, and these take time to evolve. Funds and assistance will not be available without the conviction that there is capacity to use them effectively. But capacity-building requires patient investment to remove critical barriers because its payoffs are large but take time to be realized. Fundamental reforms require better institutions, which evolve slowly. These requirements are interlinked. So developing country leaders need to know that they will have long-term, reliable support from the larger development community. Without such support—and the quid pro quo on reform to support it—many developing countries will remain in cycles of promise and disappointment. With support, these cycles can be broken.

Main Responsibilities of Developed Countries

Enabling developing countries to develop more rapidly through increased aid, trade, migration, and access to knowledge and technology will place big demands on leaders and voters in developed countries. The actions required of them include:

- *Increase aid and make it more effective.* Developed countries should strengthen the ability of developing countries to pursue sustainable development by providing development assistance that supports public goods and attracts private investment.

- *Reduce debt.* This has started under the Heavily Indebted Poor Countries Debt (HIPC) Initiative, and it is essential to go farther for all developing countries by agreeing on poverty reduction strategies and improving accountability.

- *Open agricultural, industrial, and labor markets.* Developed country trade barriers impede exports from developing countries and undermine the livelihoods of the poor. Unrestricted access to developed country markets in textiles and clothing could yield $9 billion a year, and access to agricultural markets $11.6 billion a year.

- *Improve developing country access to technology and knowledge.* Implement incentives to promote the transfer and dissemination of technologies to developing countries—including those for climate mitigation, disease prevention, and agricultural development. Support more research on crops, vaccines, and adaptation strategies that would improve the livelihood for poor people.

Joint Responsibilities of Developing and Developed Countries

Together the developed and developing countries must address the most urgent problems facing humanity. Their joint responsibility is to *establish a global partnership to set the rules for making rules and the modalities of burden sharing.* As the world becomes more interconnected—environmentally, economically, socially—new institutions and rules must be agreed on and implemented. These will include rules for international trade; rules to avert conflict; rules on migration; rules governing the use of the biosphere; and rules affecting property rights in ideas, technological processes, and genetic information. The consequences will be enduring. If these institutions are to be effective, the rules for making rules have to be fair—in process and in outcome.

There is a role for all actors in the global system: Governments of developing, transition, and developed nations; provinces, cities, and local communities; civil society organizations; private firms; individuals.

- All governments can improve the accountability of public agencies and the provision of information about social and environmental conditions—to improve the ability of the general public and civic groups to identify problems, balance interests fairly, and come up with solutions.

- Civil society organizations can help to aggregate the voices of dispersed interests and provide independent verification of public, private, and non-governmental performance. Academia needs to be recognized as a key actor in learning, monitoring, and evaluating.

- The private sector can advance economic, social and environmental objectives by helping to construct a framework that provides appropriate incentives for firms to be accountable in all three dimensions.

If the global community sees merit in such an accord, the accord's elements will need more careful work over the next few years to develop an implementable program that can adjust to contingencies without undermining the promise of the accord.

ONGOING DIALOGUE: SOME OPEN QUESTIONS

To make more headway on the accord and to define a process and framework that is "fair" will require dealing with some global issues of sustainable development that remain the subject of heated debate. Mentioned here are four important and controversial topics whose resolution has important policy and institutional implications, requiring credible global assessments.

When Is Consumption Overconsumption?

Concern is often expressed about "overconsumption" in wealthy countries and about the threats to sustainability of increasing levels of global consumption. But what kind of consumption qualifies as overconsumption, why is it harmful, and what should be done about it? Does overconsumption imply that there should be a limit on total global consumption (and that as a result, the already high levels of consumption in developed countries need to be reduced to enable increased consumption in poor countries)? On these questions there is little clarity.

One interpretation of overconsumption is that it refers to the environmental externalities associated with consumption at higher levels of per capita income. For example, carbon dioxide emissions, and their contribution to climate change, are highly correlated with consumption of electricity, home heating, transport services, and energy-intensive manufactured goods—all of which tend to increase strongly with income. In these cases, the *over* prefix is justified, since the externalities are by definition inefficient (there is no balancing of costs against benefits) and usually inequitable (wealthier people impose the damages upon poorer people). But the overall level of consumption is not the source of the problem. It is the combination of the specific consumption mix and the production processes that generates the externality. And for these there are well-established policy prescriptions from public finance.

Another interpretation of overconsumption, much more difficult to document, has to do with social externalities. People judge the adequacy of their consumption—clothing, automobiles, housing—in part against norms set by others. If this is true, consumption takes on some of the aspects of an arms race. What are the policy implications? Mutual restraint is needed (a coordination problem par excellence) to shift resources from competitive individual consumption to consumption of public goods. But these externalities need to be much better understood before there can be any agreement on the actions to address them.

What Is the Future of Agriculture and Genetically Modified Organisms?

Despite great promise for improving the agriculture of the poor, biotechnology in general and transgenics research in particular have barely begun to address the problems of the poor. Some applications generate little controversy, such as marker-assisted genetic selection. Others, such as the creation of transgenic organisms, have generated much concern about food safety and potential environmental impacts.

Comfort with the new technology is determined in large measure by societies' comfort with their scientific and food safety institutions and their feelings about emerging concentrations of economic power in multinational "life-sciences" corporations. Solutions to these complex issues are all playing out against a backdrop of globalization-related uncertainty, which has left many people unsettled over their capacity to control their lives and their environment. It is the rural poor in developing countries who most need access to these new agricultural technologies. The precautionary principle tells us that we should err on the side of caution, look at alternatives, and ensure a fully transparent and democratic process. This requires more clearly sorting what is known from current science from what is not, so that the political process can act more effectively. [...]

* * *

This Report argues that the lack of assets, opportunity, and effective voice for large segments of the population blocks the emergence of general welfare-enhancing policies, impedes growth, and undermines the potential for positive change. At the national level, it robs us of the talents of those left out in society. And at the international level, it deprives us of the contribution poor countries can make to a more just and sustainable future. A more sustainable development path is more socially inclusive; it enables societies to transform and solve collective action problems. The challenge, now and in the future, is to develop the courage and commitment to manage the processes that underpin human life and well-being and to bring about a transformation that improves the quality of the environment, strengthens our social fabric, and enhances the quality of people's lives. The more people heard, the less assets wasted.

✗ NO
The WDR 2003: A Strenuous Tale of Missed Opportunities
LIANE SCHALATEK AND BARBARA UNMÜSSIG

INTRODUCTION: LET'S TALK ABOUT SUSTAINABILITY, SHALL WE?

It's very strenuous and technical reading, this year's World Bank World Development Report (WDR). Quite abstract and thus obviously written more for a small "insider community" of academic experts rather than the larger interested audience for which it claims to be intended, the WDR 2003, aptly titled *Dynamic Development in a Sustainable World*, is the timely contribution of the Washington "Knowledge Bank" for the World Summit on Sustainable Development (WSSD) in Johannesburg, incorporating the World Bank's newest take on the topic of sustainable development.

Since it was first popularized at the Earth Summit in Rio de Janeiro in 1992 as the guiding principle of ecologically mindful development, the concept of sustainable development has become more and more imprecise, allowing for an astonishing spectrum of often competing and contradictory definitions, ultimately culminating in conceptual laissez-faire and political insignificance. The WDR 2003, however, does not acknowledge the decade-long protracted career of an often misused concept. Likewise, the Report neglects to acknowledge the World Bank's own contribution in blurring the definition of sustainability as used in the Brundlandt Report of 1987 by reinterpreting it clandestinely and insufficiently as *sustainable growth*. Instead, the Report is satisfied with merely pointing out challenges to sustainability and with listing possible solutions in an abstract and disconnected way.

NO NEW WAY OF DOING WORLD BANK BUSINESS...

The WDR 2003 aims to break away from old ways of thinking and formalistic modes of doing business—including those utilized by the World Bank itself in its day-to-day operations. But readers expecting the unconventional, even visionary will be sorely disappointed. True, in comparison to its Rio-counterpart, the WDR 1992 *Development and the Environment,*[1] the WDR 2003 is undoubtedly more differentiated and comprehensive. The WDR 1992 focused almost exclusively on certain "win-win" scenarios (e.g. the reduction of ecologically damaging subsidies) while issuing at the same time repeated stern warnings about ultimately unavoidable "either-or" choices between income growth and environmental quality.

In contrast, the WDR 2003 attempts to distance itself from the neoclassical economic theory allowing for the full substitution of natural, human, intellectual and social assets with capital assets. Rather, the report stipulates the complementarity of these assets and the necessity of their equitable and just distribution and acknowledges that markets cannot provide environmental and social assets, which have been traditionally undervalued or underprovided and viewed as if they were infinitely renewable. The Report promises a new economic concept combining ecology, social equity and long-term development prospects on a par with economic efficiency. Yet, at the same time the WDR presents a long-term development framework, which invariably relies on productivity growth as the motor for development, primarily in developing countries but also in the industrialized OECD world.

This unchanging mantra repeatedly collides not surprisingly with the texts' sections discussing the limits on the use of natural resources. "The WDR 2003 should at least question whether global economic integration is an adequate institutional context for policies enhancing net wealth creation and poverty alleviation," criticizes the renowned American environmental economist Herman Daly (see his contribution in this *World Summit Paper*, pp. 19–23).

NEW INSTITUTIONS: WHERE ARE THE BLUEPRINTS?

Central to the argumentation of the WDR 2003 is the existence of adequate institutions (which in the WDR's wide definition encompass organizations, rules and norms, regimes, and formal and informal networks alike). Institutions of every kind are indispensable to pick up the right signals, ensure the ability to act collectively and to balance common against individual and vested interests. The Report explains the rather disappointing and sobering post-Rio sustainability record with missing or weak institutions. This, in the analysis of the WDR 2003, is particularly striking with respect to poverty alleviation. The eradication of poverty worldwide is postulated correctly as the cornerstone of a global sustainable development strategy and the Report convincingly makes the causal link between the existence of strong institutions and guaranteed rights and participation for the world's poor and underprivileged. In the Report's own words: "Empowering poor and disenfranchised people, the most excluded members of society, makes for stronger institutions that support longer term sustainable development."

Alas, it must disappoint and dishearten any reader of the WDR 2003 to discover that the Report fails to go into any detail about the reform of existing organizations and regimes and the creation and mandate of new competent institutions it so strongly advocates. "The Report thus makes no recommendation on specific policies or organizational designs," the WDR 2003 draft is in a haste to point out in an introductory chapter. Well, shouldn't this be the main purpose of a 200-plus-page exercise supposedly reflecting the World Bank's most progressive thinking? At the very least, a prominent World Bank publication timed specifically for the WSSD should elaborate on the Bank's own understanding of its role in an optimal global governance framework adequately endowed to promote and enforce sustainable development. But the WDR 2003 doesn't even do this. And it also shies away from addressing a fundamental dilemma of intergovernmental cooperation in international institutions, namely how to deal with states (read specifically the United States with its dislike of multilateral organizations) too powerful to allow themselves to be bound by any international rules.

THE OECD-WORLD'S RESPONSIBILITY: WHAT DOES GLOBAL EQUITY HAVE TO DO WITH IT?

The Bank's most important annual publication has several other glaring short-comings. The politically highly explosive question about the industrial nations' responsibility for and their role in global sustainability efforts is only asked with respect to economic consequences and focuses mainly on the developed countries' relationship with their lesser developed neighbors. Accordingly, the Report's recommendations to increase official development assistance (ODA), to reduce or forgive Southern countries' unsustainable and non-repayable debts, to improve market access for developing country products, and to facilitate and widen technology transfers are said to be in the best economic interest of the OECD world.

At no time does the Report acknowledge these suggestions for asset transfers and development opportunities for what they really are: a moral obligation in the name of global equity and but a first installment of payments for the North's mounting ecological debt vis-à-vis the global South. And at no time does the Report even come close to suggesting that in a world of finite natural resources, industrial nations might have to curtail their future consumption and economic growth in order to create development space for poor countries.

This is just one more example of the WDR's failure to consequently think through its own lines of argumentation. Otherwise the Report—in truly touting a new economic concept taking into consideration social equity, ecological awareness and long-term sustainable development prospects—would have to challenge industrialized countries to set an example for the rest of the world in drastically reorienting their own economies, foremost their unsustainable production and consumption patterns, and their societies in a more ecologically viable fashion. Mentioning the North's persistent system of perverse subsidies (in agriculture, fisheries, forestry, and fossil and nuclear energy) as something to be abolished as the WDR does in this context is, although correct, certainly not enough. And even this mention lacks political bite.

WHY EVEN CONSIDER CRITICAL SELF-REFLECTION?

Regrettably, the WDR 2003 also misses a unique chance for a self-critical reflection and an honest evaluation of the sustainability record of the World Bank's own projects and programs. This and a realistic institutional look ahead would have given moral authority, precedent- and trend-setting strength and courageous vision to an institution which prides itself quite often (and in some areas even correctly) in being a "bench-marking" development agency.

To be quite frank, the World Bank's record provides more than enough opportunities for such self-critical soul-searching. One is tempted to mention structural adjustment programs (SAPs): To this day, they are exempted from the Bank's own environment and social safeguard policies—no peanuts, considering that they make up an average of more than 30 percent of all World Bank loans. One could further point to big infrastructure, energy and extractive industry projects like dams, pipelines or mines with frequently disastrous social and ecological impacts. After a drop in the number of these projects in the early nineties, big infrastructure projects are now back in the name of a reorientation of Bank operations towards greater customer satisfaction and increased efficiency (and many recipient countries despise social and environmental strings attached to World Bank loans[2])—at the expense of social and environmental standards.

As a result of this "customer-is-king" attitude, the fairly advanced social and environmental safeguard and operational policies (OPs), the Bank boosted in the 1980s, got significantly "watered down" in the last decade or so in the course of several OP revisions. For example, the recently revised OP on resettlement did away with the stipulation that those villagers forcefully resettled due to a dam or other major infrastructure project would be compensated land-for-land.

The Bank's own Operations Evaluation Department (OED) chastised the institution just last year[3] for a decline in its environmental performance. Budgets for environment projects have been cut; environmental impact assessments (EIAs) are frequently scrimped on or they are executed too late in the project cycle to have any measurable influence; internal capacity-building measures, particularly for staff in the Bank's country and regional offices, have been reduced; lastly, and most importantly, environmental sensibility and accountability is still not mainstreamed within the institution with the Bank's own environment department finding itself frequently marginalized and with practically no influence over the Bank's operations. In a "Memorandum to the Executive Directors and the President" from March 21, 2001, the OED review stated: "Internally, environmental sustainability was not adequately integrated into the Bank's core objectives and country assistance strategies. Intellectually, the linkages between macroeconomic policy, poverty alleviation, and environmental sustainability were not explicitly forged. In sum, the institution's environmental efforts have not been consistent nor have they been held to uniform quality standards."

The WDR 2003 makes no mention of the Bank's environmental score card with the below-passing grades the institution received from the OED. Nor does it give any indication how the internal administrative structures of the World Bank would have to be changed in order to actually bring the Bank's operative business on the one-way-only road to ecological sustainability.

The World Bank's Sore Record on Participatory Processes

Talking about the World Bank's sustainability score-card of the past decade, one cannot omit the preliminary record of the poverty reduction strategy papers (PRSPs)[4]–the supposed shining examples of participatory and holistic development strategies that are becoming more and more important as the dominant framework for multilateral as well as bilateral development cooperation, since the PRSP approach is supposed to offer the framework for the integration of all (macro- and micro-)economic reforms and poverty reduction policies. More often than not, they equate mere consultation of multiple stakeholders with real participation and with ownership of the entire process and either neglect sustainability criteria completely or relegate their consideration to the distant future.[5]

In many PRSPs, ecological problems are considered to be direct results of population growth and poverty. Thus, it is especially worrisome that most PRSPs' focus on economic growth as key to poverty alleviation, disregarding both social and environmental impacts of this one-dimensional strategy. The PRSPs' dominant aim is to increase export production, mostly through cash crops in the agricultural sector and a concentration on extractive industries and fossil fuel exploitation. Export diversification or food security as valuable development goals are mostly neglected; the negative trade-offs of such an export-oriented growth strategy for environmental and natural resource protection are scarcely, if at all, discussed. On the contrary, many PRSPs explicitly acknowledge that a stronger export-orientation of commercial agriculture and natural resource exploitation (fossil fuels, metals, forestry etc.) in all likelihood will lead to increased ecological impacts, without devising and integrating strategies on how to reduce or prevent them.[6]

With all of the WDR's focus on having the voices of poor and disenfranchised people heard and on the necessity for institutions to pick up on signals, the World Bank's own sore record on participatory processes involving the Bank weighs even heavier. The World Bank effectively disengaged itself from the World Commission on Dams (WCD) after a five-year-participatory process, when the conclusions about the wide-spread social and environmental impacts of the Bank's financing of large dams came out sharply critical of the World Bank.[7] Similarly, the World Bank tried to ignore findings by the multi-country Structural Adjustment Participatory Review Initiative (SAPRI), set up with World Bank participation in 1997, when it concluded that economic adjustment programs mandated by the Bank largely failed to achieve results in poverty reduction, instead increasing impoverishment by devastating local small and medium-sized industries, damaging the environment, reducing food security and undermining the viability of small farms.[8] The legitimacy of the currently ongoing Extractive Industries Review (EIR), modeled after the WCD, is already questioned by many NGOs worried about attempts to minimize inputs from civil society. They demand an opening up of the process, greater transparency and independence of the process and guidelines for mandatory follow-up implementation of civil-society recommendations.[9]

An Approving Nod to an Expanded Notion of Poverty

On the positive side, the WDR 2003 expands the notion of poverty significantly, going way beyond the politically chosen arbitrary definition of people living on less than a US$1 a day. More realistically, the WDR includes those 2.8 billion people worldwide who have to make an existence on US$2 per day. Its urgent demands for the disenfranchised in rural areas and urban slum dwellings include the call for land rights and secure tenure primarily, but also for access to basic health and education services, natural resources and a political voice and vote. It is in this context that the authors show the most guts, politically speaking.

Yet, once again, abstract recommendations of World Bank researchers are not squared with the Bank's own policy practice, in this case its Private Sector Development (PSD), Rural Sector Development (RSD) and Water Resources Sector (WRS) strategies. The World Bank's heavy focus on private sector involvement in the provision of these basic services, for which access is deemed so essential in order to improve the lot of the poor, is likely to result in diminished access for the underprivileged as user-fees are frequently implemented in the name of "cost-recovery." In many developing countries (e.g. in Cochabamba in Bolivia, in Ghana and the Philippines), hundreds of thousands of people have protested on the streets against privatization measures of essential services as mandated by World Bank programs. The World Bank's continued development focus on private sector involvement in essential services is an open contradiction to the calls for inclusiveness, participation and the "voice-and-vote-for-the-poor"-mantra the WDR 2003 incessantly repeats.

Not Just "Women's Special Role," Women's Political and Economic Reality

The Report makes some passing references, particularly in the chapter dealing with the population living in fragile ecosystems, about both obstacles and opportunities for women in development. Yet, a detailed analysis of the specific situation and role of women and gender roles in the context of sustainable development, be it in efforts to eradicate poverty or to protect global natural resources and biodiversity, is mostly missing—quite alarming for an organization which just recently spent significant research and policy efforts in devising a plan of action for integrating gender into its development assistance work.[10] Such an analysis would have to include the specific role of women as keepers of traditional knowledge, as guardians of biological diversity through the practice of collecting and keeping indigenous plant seeds, the overproportional victimization of women in export-processing zones as a result of trade liberalization policies, the necessity to redress glaring gender-discrimination in land tenure, property and family rights, the effects on food security and subsistence agriculture of the commercialization of agriculture, and the impacts of reduced government responsibility for public services through privatization in the health, education and water sector on women. These implications, however, are at best hinted at in the WDR 2003; redress is sought mostly via micro-credits, education and capacity-building without getting to the core of economic and power realities that discriminate against women.

Similarly, the HIV/AIDS epidemic in many parts of the developing world is mentioned almost as a side note, but not given the explicit consideration it warrants as being one of the major impediments to development it constitutes in too many regions of the world.

FOCUS ON LIVING SPACES, NOT RESOURCE REDISTRIBUTION

The WDR 2003 attempts to sketch out problem solutions to be implemented during the next 30 to 50 years by focusing on three distinct typified living spaces, not nations or geographic regions. This comes in very handy for an apolitical discussion of sustainability by conveniently excluding the bleak reality of political power struggles and conflicts about resource distribution.

Among the three living spaces identified and analyzed are fragile ecosystems, often in remote rural areas, which currently form the livelihood for some 1.3 billion people depending mostly on natural resources for their survival. The WDR laments rightfully the fact that their own governments, the international community, but also empirical science have neglected to focus systematically on these fragile living spaces and the rural poor and asks for long-term investment interest in these regions of the world. Community-based local actions and know-how coupled with capacity-building, training, generous non-repayable grants and ecological early-warning-systems are seen as the key factors to improve the social, ecological and political situation in fragile ecosystems.

For all rural areas in developing countries, including fragile ecosystems, the Report advocates the consideration of genetically modified crops. Touting the benefits of e.g. drought-resistant plants, the Report, while acknowledging its legitimacy, effectively proposes the suspension of the internationally accepted precautionary principle (one major achievement of the Rio Earth Summit and since then codified in international environmental law) in the poorer regions of the world. The WDR 2003 states with confidence that "[i]n Africa, in many marginally viable agricultural areas the alternatives have been largely exhausted. For farmers in these areas modified crops which can better survive prolonged drought, or improve diets through micronutrient enrichment may be among the few realistic options." In doing so, it cites an international consensus about the utility of GM crops that, frankly, just does not exist, conveniently toning out the chorus of concerned scientists, development experts and community activists from all over the world. They just don't agree with the scientifically unproven contention of big agro-businesses like Monsanto—and the World Bank's statement in the WDR—"that risks from transgenics can be managed."

Commercial Agriculture over Food Security

In rural areas with the potential for commercial agriculture, the WDR 2003 propagates staunchly the intensification of agriculture. Quite interesting is the reasoning the WDR uses to advocate the shift from food security-based, predominantly subsistence agriculture to export crop-focused commercial agriculture in these areas. Thankfully, the authors didn't stoop so low as to use alleged global food and nutritional shortages as their justification, as many proponents of genetically engineered organisms (GMOs) do. The WDR team indeed acknowledges that distribution failures (in World Bank lingo: "insufficient purchasing power in the hands of the poor"), not food production shortages, are at the heart of persistent hunger for some 800 million people worldwide. Instead, the WDR argues that the commercialization of more existing agricultural areas will prevent the uncontrolled extension of extensive "slash-and-burn" farming on pristine "frontier" lands, and thus stem the continued loss of biodiversity. The above-mentioned PRSPs, the majority of which are currently in preparation, do not have to rely on such spectacular argumentation acrobatics: They unabashedly count on export-oriented agriculture to generate the foreign exchange needed to service developing countries' foreign debt burden.

One wonders whether it's a mere oversight, or, more worrisome, a sign of a complete lack of problem awareness, but a detailed analysis and debate about the ecological and social implications of the proposed intensified agriculture strategy is simply nowhere included in this section of the WDR. Apparently, the WDR's focus on perceived, but not yet realized commercial opportunities leaves no discussion room for the harsh realities of industrialized agricultural production. These include the invariable domination of farming by agro-businesses with the displacement of tens of thousands of small family farmers without alternative ways of making a living, a push for genetically modified food crops with health and environmental implications and the intensive use of fertilizers, herbicides and pesticides. The latter not only increases small farmers' dependence and debt burden, but also harms the environment (e.g. by polluting increasingly scarce freshwater resources), which the WDR claims to protect by intensifying commercial agriculture in many rural areas in the first place.

Freshwater scarcity is given special consideration in this chapter of the WDR—although the Report neglects, once again, to think through the implications for sustainability of its own recommendations. With commercial agriculture being the world's biggest user of freshwater through irrigation and export-crops usually more in need of excessive irrigation than traditional and subsistence farming methods, water scarcity will likely be worsened, not lessened. To deal with water scarcity, the WDR recommends a property rights regime, which would "price" water and establish private water user associations, effectively limiting the public's participation in private sector water delivery schemes and endangering the access of the poor to water.

Land rights for small and medium-sized farmers under such a scenario are supposed to be guaranteed through land reform, albeit not one based primarily on equity and economic justice (e.g. by reform policies that take into account traditional land use rights of indigenous groups) but on the vagaries of the market. Given current negative experiences (an example would be the ongoing market-based land reform in Brazil, which has met with widespread resistance amid claims of disadvantaging the poor, indigenous and landless) such an assumption seems overly optimistic, if not outright naïve.

All these WDR "visions" for the development of rural areas not very surprisingly echo the core points of the World Bank's draft Rural Sector Development Strategy, which has come under heavy criticism from civil society for its misguided approach neglecting basic sustainability considerations.[11]

Urban Centers: Incubators for Innovation and Change?

In cities and towns, the Report euphorically discovers the "incubators" of innovation and change with opportunities to provide jobs and improved quality of life. As the most important prerequisite for the realization of the potential of urban centers, however—as the Report points out—security of tenure and availability of land for new low income settlement are needed that would give urban slum dwellers and rural migrants the chance to stay and make a living in urban centers. With an expected doubling of the urban population worldwide within the next 30 years, this demand takes on a pressing significance.

While the WDR discusses the necessity to generate jobs in urban centers, no mention is made of core labor standards and rights as defined by the International Labor Organization (ILO), which should form the standard of job creation, particularly through foreign direct investment. The existing problems in the so-called export-processing zone (wage discrimination against women or indigenous workers, unhealthy and unsafe working conditions, obstacles to union organizing and collective bargaining to name but a few) and the resulting race-to-the-bottom for workers' wages because of increased competition among developing countries for the same kind of labor-intensive manufacturing jobs are likewise not considered.

GLOBAL ISSUES: WHO'S ENFORCING EQUAL ADHERENCE TO STANDARDS AND INTL. RULES?

On an equal par with poverty alleviation, the WDR 2003 lists halting climate change, desertification and biodiversity protection as the most pressing issues, the latter primarily through local resource management sponsored by national and international institutions. Agreeing on the nature and causes of transboundary problems is seen as the first important step, with institutions tasked to provide the forum for fostering consensus on diagnosis and action. Socially responsible behavior of public and private entities is supposed to be achieved through standards, certification and performance reporting.

Not addressed in the WDR is the critical issue of how to guarantee enforceability of and mandatory adherence to these currently mostly voluntary programs and what global institutions, new or existing ones, could and should have authority to hold all public and private entities equally accountable. This is particularly important with respect to global economic governance, where the rules are undoubtedly rigged in favor of the industrialized countries. Likewise, the WDR wages no proposal on how the tensions between many existing institutions and regimes, particularly between economic and environmental agreements, e.g. the World Trade Organization (WTO) and the Convention on Biological Diversity (CBD), should be reconciled and addressed.

Climate Change: Reverse Current Energy Usage Now!

On the positive side, with respect to climate protection, the Report emphasizes the urgent need for a quick reversal of current energy usage trends with convincing seriousness. It even explicitly suggests the special responsibility of industrial nations for both a reduction of their own emissions and for co-financing global adjustment measures for poor countries most affected by ongoing climate change, e.g. the rise of sea water levels. Yet, an open criticism of the OECD world, especially the United States as the world's most profligate emitter of greenhouse gases, is missing as is an outspoken support of the WDR team for the Kyoto Protocol—even though the Protocol with its institutionalized international cooperation and explicit reduction targets as well as innovative trading mechanisms is an excellent example for the kind of institutions the WDR stresses we need to strengthen in order to address sustainable development on a global level.

Regarding climate change as well as other areas of environmental protection, one is struck by the WDR's unwavering trust in the regulative power of economic instruments as remedy *after* ecological damages have occurred, while prevention and precaution are getting short shrift. Obviously not quite freed yet from the interpretation in the WDR 1992, its Rio+10-sibling, the WDR 2003 still seems to subscribe to the notion that a certain amount of environmental destruction is an unavoidable corollary of economic development, something to be fixed eventually. Markets are also seen as both inevitable and best suited to deal with environmental problems stemming from scarce resources (e.g. freshwater). The solution: attribute property rights speedily before informal markets could make a mess out of orderly private sector involvement!

DEMOCRATIC INSTITUTIONS: THE STILL ELUSIVE QUEST

Realizing the vision of sustainable development and poverty eradication worldwide by 2050 necessitates in the view of the WDR authors a global partnership, which has to be based on massive ODA, a global division of burden and of negative impacts, a regulatory framework for global public goods and enduring and democratic institutions. It is noteworthy that the WDR 2003 hammers repeatedly on the need for continued and increased ODA, although the "gold standard" of ODA, the 0.7 percent of gross national product (GNP) target, is not explicitly mentioned. However, in a nod to the United States, the WDR's authors cannot help themselves but echo some of the recent-most calls for more aid effectiveness and lastly aid selectivity. With this, a WDR 2003 focused on poverty eradication and inclusiveness risks harming people and nations needing help the most by dangerously giving legitimacy to those forces that aim to divide developing countries and societies into aid-deserving good performing ones and bad performing undeserving ones, which can only expect limited support from the global financial community.

The WDR's repeated sales pitch for more democratic institutions is indeed a most fundamental one. Although not likely intended by the authors, it nevertheless points a shaming spotlight on the current untenable praxis of undemocratic decision-making in many international institutions, including the Bretton Woods Twins, the International Monetary Fund (IMF) and the World Bank.

For example, under the World Bank's new disclosure policy, which took effect in January of this year, the minutes of Executive Board Meetings are still not released to the public; project documents are only released after decisions have been made, effectively forestalling any efforts of local or national civil society groups to have their concerns heard and considered in World Bank actions; and the World Bank's Country Assistance Strategies (CAS), the Bank's strategic plan for a country, still is inaccessible to concerned citizens.[12]

Representation on the decision-making World Bank Executive Board of 24 is far from "one-country-one-vote," but instead more a "one-dollar-one-vote" with all of sub-Sahara Africa just being represented by 2 executive directors (EDs), while five of the G7 countries have their own ED and the United States as largest shareholder effectively retains veto power via a blocking minority of votes. Add to it that the heads of international financial institutions are to this day nominated in a kind of gentlemen's agreement of wheeling and dealing among the most powerful nations. Indeed, truly democratic international financial institutions are still an elusive quest...

THE CALL FOR GOOD GOVERNANCE: IS THE BUSINESS SECTOR EXEMPT?

While calling on a global partnership and international collaborative efforts, the WDR authors just don't want to admit that the notion of international cooperation as the panacea in dealing with environmental problems is but possibly the biggest mirage of the post-Rio process and the sustainability concept. If you want to achieve ecological and social sustainability, you have to finally acknowledge the accompanying social and economic, local, regional and international conflicts and have to offer concrete, if politically controversial ways of dealing with them.

If the WDR 2003 had taken this premise to heart, it would have had to reflect more explicitly throughout the entire Report on the role of the private sector, especially the role of transnational corporations (TNCs) and their position of power and capital might within the existing global economic framework. This is the more blatant a shortcoming of the WDR 2003 as private sector and foreign direct investments and market mechanisms continue to be heralded by World Bank economists, including the WDR authors, as the most fundamental factors for achieving development, poverty alleviation and sustainability in the global South. The WDR's unabashed endorsement of the private sector as the "savior" for global development (read: economic growth)—and the call to national governments to generate a strong investment climate "as core component of sustainable development"—has to be also seen in the context of the World Bank's new Private Sector Development and Rural Sector Development strategies, which are currently in the process of being finalized. Both aim to reduce the role of the state in national economies in favor of private sector participation in the provision of essential services like water, health care, electricity and education as well as agricultural development using the World Bank's aid and lending projects as means to promote privatization of these sectors. Public sector privatization is likely to be picked up at the WSSD with the endorsement of public-private initiatives ("Type II outcomes") in these areas.

In the view of the WDR authors, the business sector's contribution to a global compact on sustainability would consist of creating market incentives for (voluntary) adherence of the private sector to social and environmental objectives and of "lobbying vigorously for the growth that will create new markets"—as if powerful transnational companies need to be asked to! No word here about the need for strong institutions (e.g. a regulatory framework for corporate accountability, which civil society groups are demanding as part of the WSSD Plan of Action) to reign in corporate power and which could enforce mandatory adherence to strict sustainability guidelines. A report which declares *good governance* (accountability, transparency, functioning democratic institutions and rule of law) to be the linchpin of global sustainability and obligates countries, especially in the South, to adhere to it should not shy away from demanding the same social, political and ecological responsibility from the global business community.

CONCLUSION: WE EXPECTED MORE...

The WDR 2003 closes by listing several unanswered questions in the global sustainability debate, which demand an urgent, yet still elusive international consensus: When is consumption overconsumption? What is the future of agriculture and of genetically modified organisms? What are the prospects for global migration?

It is admittedly not easy to find solutions to these and other questions and to give plausible answers. But the WDR 2003 does not even make the honest attempt and is afraid to wage the open participation in a global debate which the Report proclaims it wants to stimulate. This is undoubtedly the biggest weakness of the Report. All too frequently it is content with recognizing and listing problems in technocratic accuracy without daring to suggest concrete proposals on how to implement possible solutions. For Johannesburg—and as the primary contribution of the World Bank for the World Summit on Sustainable Development—we would have expected more from the "Knowledge Bank's" flagship publication.

NOTES

1. The complete text of the WDR 1992 is available on the World Bank website at http://wwwwds.worldbank.org/servlet/WDS_Ibank_Servlet?pcont=details&teid=00017 8830_9810191106175.

2. The Three-Gorges-Dam project in China would be a case in point. China withdrew its loan request for the project from the World Bank after the Bank, under massive pressure from civil society groups, insisted on strict adherence to its safeguard policies, particularly on resettlements, for this project.

3. OED Review of the Bank's Performance on the Environment, CODE2001-0029.

4. PRSPs have been developed and used since 1999 in connection with debt relief efforts under the initiative for highly indebted poor countries (HIPCs). PRSPs are supposed to delineate country-owned plans developed nationally with wide-spread civil society participation that outline a long-term development strategy and specify how money from debt relief would be spent to reduce poverty. By April 2002, 10 full and some 42 interim-PRSPs had been submitted for final IMF/World Bank approval and consideration.

5. PRSPs are "country-owned," meaning they are written by national governments and then submitted to the IMF or the World Bank. This country-ownership is in fact undermined by the need for national governments to gain ultimate IFI approval for their poverty reduction strategies. In many cases, because of capacity-problems of poorer governments, IMF and World Bank staff played a dominant role in the genesis of the strategy papers. Not surprisingly then, PRSPs in most cases effectively reflect official IMF and World Bank neoliberal policy recommendations. Preliminary records also show that often civil society input and recommendations for alternative development strategies have not been reflected in the finished PRSPs.

6. This section draws heavily on Miriam Walther, *Armutsstrategiepapiere (PRSP). Neuanfang in der Strukturanpassungspolitik von IWF und Weltbank?*, World Economy, Ecology & Development (WEED), Mai 2002, Bonn.

7. For information from a civil society point of view on the World Commission on Dams and the World Bank's role in it, see the documentation from the International Rivers Network (www.irn.org/wcd). The WCD website is http://dams.org.

8. For civil society comments on SAPRI and the World Bank's participation in it, see documentation collected by the Structural Adjustment Participatory Review Initiative Network (SAPRIN) at www.saprin.org. The World Bank's SAPRI website can be found at http://www.worldbank.org/research/sapri/.

9. For a critical NGO assessment of the ongoing EIR, see http://www.seen.org/pages/ftr/eiranalysis.shtml. The official EIR website is www.eireview.org.

10. For the World Bank's gender mainstreaming strategy, see The World Bank, *Integrating Gender into the World Bank's Work—A Strategy for Action*, Washington, January 2002; the World Bank report *Engendering Development—Through Gender Equality in Rights, Resources, and Voice* (published in January 2001 by Oxford University Press) provides strong empirical evidence of gender-based inequalities that act as impediments to equitable development.

11. For a civil society critique of the World Bank's Rural Development Strategy, see for example http://www.panna.org/campaigns/docsWorldBank/docsWorldBank_020614.dvhtml.

12. For information on the World Bank's information disclosure policy, see the Bank's website at http://www1.worldbank.org/operations/disclosure/. For a summary critique of the shortcomings of the new disclosure policy, see information collected by the Washington-based Bank Information Center at http://www.bicusa.org/policy/InfoDisclosure/moreinfo.htm.

POSTSCRIPT_____

The World Bank's annual *World Development Report* is a significant document. As the world's most important multilateral development agency, the World Bank and its report often influence the terms of the ongoing debates regarding development. A survey of the themes of these annual reports shows how the World Bank has tried to address the "cutting edge" themes in development debates. Certainly the *World Development Report 2003* sought to position the World Bank as an important shaper of opinion at the United Nations Summit on Sustainable Development.

The Bank's report identifies many of the challenges facing the developing world. The report estimates that by 2050 fully two-thirds of the world will be in cities. Three-quarters of the world's population will be living within 100 kilometres of the sea. There will be enormous pressures on housing, water, and energy supplies. The coastal ecosystems will face increased pressures. As estimated 1.3 billion people will live on fragile lands, such as wetlands, slopes, or arid zones, which cannot fully sustain yet.

Despite these challenges the report strikes a positive and hopeful note. It suggests that it will be possible to meet these challenges and reduce poverty and increase life expectancy while also promote increased economic growth and expanded trade. Is it possible to strike these balances? Can you promote both liberal free market solutions to development problems while also preserving the environment and ensuring sustainability? How successful is the *World Development Report 2003* in putting the World Bank at the forefront of thinking on sustainable development?

Suggested Additional Readings

Adams, William. *Green Development: Environment and Sustainability in the Third World* (London: Routledge, 1990).

Broad, Robin. "The Poor and the Environment: Friends or Foes?" *World Development*, 22, no. 6 (1994): 811–822.

Burg, Jericho. "The World Summit on Sustainable Development: Empty Talk or Call to Action?" *Journal of Environment and Development*, 12, no. 1 (2003): 111–120.

Clapp, Jennifer, and Peter Dauvergne. *Path to a Green World: The Political Economy of the Global Environment* (Cambridge: MIT Press, 2005).

Elliot, Jennifer A. *An Introduction to Sustainable Development* (London: Routledge, 2006).

LePrestre, Philippe. *The World Bank and the Environmental Challenge* (Selingsgrove, PA: Susquehanna University Press, 1989).

Markandya, Anil, and Kirsten Halsnaes. *Climate Change and Sustainable Development, Prospects for Developing Countries* (London: Earthscan Publications, 2002).

Rees, William. "Globalization and Sustainability: Conflict or Convergence?" *Bulletin of Science, Technology and Society,* 22, no. 3 (2002): 249–268.

Zoe, Young. *A New Green Order: The World Bank and the Politics of the Global Environment Facility* (London: Pluto Press, 2003).

InfoTrac® College Edition

Search for the following articles in the InfoTrac® database:

Collison, Beth. "The World Bank and Women's Sustainable Economic Development: A Beautiful Marriage or a Contradiction in Terms?" *Canadian Woman Studies,* 23, no. 1 (Fall–Winter 2003): 22–28.

"Global Growing Pains; Sustainable Development; Does the World Bank's Prescription Make Sense?" *Global Agenda,* (August 21, 2002).

Husted, Brayan W. "Culture and Ecology: A Cross-national Study of the Determinants of Environmental Sustainability," *Management International Review,* 45, no. 3 (July 2005): 349–371.

Varma, Adarsh. "Climate Change and Sustainable Development, Prospects for Developing Countries," *Journal of Development Studies,* 40, no. 5 (June 2004): 184–186.

For more articles, enter:
"sustainable development," "environment and development," or "World Bank" in the keyword search.

Web Resources

INTERNATIONAL INSTITUTE FOR SUSTAINABLE DEVELOPMENT

www.iisd.org

IISD is a Canadian organization based in Winnipeg dedicated to promoting discussion of issues related to sustainable development. Be sure to check their searchable online research library.

SD GATEWAY

www.sdgateway.net

The SD Gateway provides access to online information collected by members of the Sustainable Development Communications Network. You can access some 1200 documents on sustainable development here.

DEVELOPMENT ALTERNATIVES NETWORK

www.devalt.org

This is a network of organizations promoting issues related to the environment and sustainable development.

AGORRA FOUNDATION

www.agorrafoundation.org

The Agorra Foundation provides a forum for discussion relating to environmental protection and sustainable development. Their site contains a number of briefing papers on various aspects of sustainability.

THE GREEN CROSS OPTIMIST

www.optimistmag.org/gb/0000/index.php

This is the site for a Swiss-based online magazine focusing on various issues related to the promotion of a truly sustainable and equitable development.

PROSUS, CENTRE FOR DEVELOPMENT AND THE ENVIRONMENT

www.prosus.uio.no/english/about_prosus/

This centre at the University of Oslo, Norway, disseminates information on research directed toward sustainable development and on the debate concerning global ethics.

Can Genetically Modified Food Help Solve Global Food Needs?

✔ **YES**
GREGORY CONKO AND C.S. PRAKASH, "Can GM Crops Play a Role in Developing Countries?" *PBI Bulletin, Issue 2* (2004)

✘ **NO**
INDEPENDENT SCIENCE PANEL, "Why GM Free?" Executive Summary of the Report, *The Case for a GM Free World*

The question of whether world food production levels are adequate to meet the expected demand for food, especially in developing countries, is a subject of ongoing debate. While some analysts have focused on the political and economic obstacles to an adequate and fair distribution of existing food production, others have looked at ways that scientific research can contribute to future food availabilities. In this issue, we look particularly at the promise of biotechnology research to resolve the problem of food availability by technological advances in production. Can genetically modified food provide a vital weapon in the fight against hunger in developing regions, especially in regions like Africa? Advances in biotech research now make it possible for scientists to genetically modify seeds, allowing drought- and disease-resistant crops to be grown even on previously infertile lands. In addition, genetic modifications can be used to significantly improve the nutritional levels of existing crops.

Proponents of genetically modified food argue that only by supporting and investing in biotechnical innovation will developing countries have a reasonable chance of becoming agriculturally self-sufficient and achieve a sustainable level of food security. Biotech crops can produce multiple benefits, including the improvement of crop yields, higher nutritional values from existing yields, and overall reduced cost of production. By using newly engineered disease- and drought-resistant varieties, less effort and expense are needed for irrigation, fertilizers, and pesticides. Thus, the new high tech breeds of crops will also contribute to an environmentally sustainable level of agricultural production capable of meeting future food needs without putting undue stress on the ecosystem.

Despite these promises, the issue of genetically engineered food crops has become intensely controversial, perhaps more so in Europe than in North America. On the one hand, critics are concerned that the high cost of research and development and the tendency for biotechnological control to be held by a small number of firms raise important questions of accessibility and equity. Biotechnology is an area where the use of patents and commercial licences are all pervasive, giving the firms undertaking the research the legal means to protect their investments. By asserting their intellectual property rights, a few biotech firms, largely controlled by large Western corporations, can seriously limit the access that poorer, developing countries have to the new seed types.

Since the biotech research field is driven by desire of corporations to enhance their profits, critics argue that the research often focuses on developing new varieties of crops like wheat, corn, and other temperate crops, grown by more affluent farmers in the North who can pay for the higher cost of genetically modified seeds. GM research has focused less on common staples, such as yams and plantains, which are widely used in developing countries. Intellectual property rights laws restrict the access that poor countries have to these new technologies while the high costs of research reduces the possibility for developing country scientists to develop their own alternatives. Because a relatively small number of GM companies, like Monsanto, control the biotech research, it is feared that these companies may too easily control seed markets and force many local farmers out of business altogether. Thus, it is argued that better means need to be developed to ensure that developing countries have affordable access to these new emerging technologies.

Other critics have focused on the safety concerns relating to the development of GM crops. Genetically modified foods are unnatural and they introduce genetic alterations that cannot be achieved by conventional breeding techniques. These innovations potentially introduce changes in foods that may have unknown long-term side effects on our health. By shifting away from conventional plant breeding techniques toward synthetically created breeds, the degree of biodiversity needed for long-term sustainable agriculture may be undermined. Anti–GM food activists make two points: traditional farmers lose their livelihoods and long-term health risks will exist.

Others contend that the GM debate misses the main point altogether. The problem of hunger is not the availability of food. The world can produce already what it needs. The problem of hunger is more related to distribution and unequal economic and political power structures. Poverty, not an absolute lack of food, is the real issue. Even if biotechnological innovations significantly boost the world's food production, unequal distribution of economic power will still prohibit large numbers of people from being able to purchase the food they need.

At the heart of this issue is the question of the extent to which technological innovations can help us address development problems that also have complex economic, political, and environmental dimensions. In the following debate, we have two sharply contrasting positions. Gregory Conko and C.S. Prakash are co-founders of AgBioWorld Foundation. This is a non-profit organization, based in Auburn, Alabama, which "aims to provide science-based information on agricultural biotechnology issues to various stakeholders across the world." AgBioWorld's purpose is to demonstrate the benefits that biotechnology holds for improving living conditions in developing countries. In their essay, Conko and Prakash set out to show how biotechnology is effectively assisting in the struggle against global hunger.

The second reading is the Executive Summary of a longer report issued by a group called the Independent Science Panel, based in London, England. The ISP states that it brings together "scientists working in genetics, biosciences, toxicology and medicine, and other representatives of civil society who are concerned about the harmful consequences of genetic modifications of plants and animals and related technologies and their rapid commercialisation in agriculture and medicine without due process of proper scientific assessment and of public consultation and consent." The reading presents a summary of the arguments that the ISP developed in a 136-page report released in 2003.

✔ **YES**

Can GM Crops Play a Role in Developing Countries?

GREGORY CONKO AND C.S. PRAKASH

In 2002, while more than 14 million people in six drought-stricken southern African countries faced the risk of starvation, efforts by the U.N.'s World Food Programme were stifled by the global "GM" food controversy. Food aid, containing kernels of bioengineered corn from the United States, was initially rejected by all six governments, even though the very same corn has been consumed daily by hundreds of millions in North and South America and has been distributed by the World Food Programme throughout Africa since 1996.

Four of those governments later accepted the grain on condition that it be milled to prevent planting, but Zimbabwe and Zambia continue to refuse to this day, and recently Angola also joined this group. Zambian President Levy Mwanawasa said his people would rather starve than eat bioengineered food, which he described as "poison." The actually starving Zambian people felt differently, though. One news report after another described scenes of hungry Zambians rioting and overpowering armed guards trying to release tens of thousands of tons of the corn locked away in warehouses by the government.

This is one of the tragic consequences of global fearmongering about recombinant DNA technology and bioengineered crops. Although many varieties that are of use to resource-poor farmers in less developed countries are at very early stages of the development process, even ones that have already been commercialized in such countries as Canada and the United States are being kept from farmers by governments skeptical of "genetic modification".

In the most fundamental sense, however, all plant and animal breeding involves—and always has involved—the intentional genetic modification of organisms. And though critics of recombinant DNA believe it is unique, there have always been Cassandras to claim that the latest technology was unnatural, different from its predecessors, and inherently dangerous.

As early as 1906, Luther Burbank the noted plant breeder said that, "We have recently advanced our knowledge of genetics to the point where we can manipulate life in a way never intended by nature. We must proceed with the utmost caution in the application of this new found knowledge," a quip that one might just as easily hear today regarding recombinant DNA modification.

But just as Burbank was wrong to claim that there was some special danger in knowledge or technology, so are today's skeptics wrong to believe that modern genetic modification poses some inherent risk. It is not genetic modification per se that generates risk. Recombinant DNA-modified, conventionally modified, and unmodified plants could all prove to be invasive, harm biodiversity, or be harmful to eat. It is not the technique used to modify organisms that makes them risky. Rather risk arises from the characteristics of individual organisms, as well as how and where they are used.

That is why the use of bioengineering technology for the development of improved plant varieties has been endorsed by dozens of scientific bodies. The UN's Food and Agriculture Organization and World Health Organization, the UK's Royal Society, the American Medical Association, and the French Academies of Medicine and Science, among others, have studied bioengineering techniques and given them a clean bill of health. Moreover, bioengineered crop plants may be of even greater value in less developed countries than in industrialized ones.

In a report published in July 2000, the UK's Royal Society, the National Academies of Science from Brazil, China, India, Mexico, and the U.S., and the Third World Academy of Science, embraced bioengineering, arguing that it can be used to advance food security while promoting sustainable agriculture. "It is critical," declared the scientists, "that the potential benefits of GM technology become available to developing countries." And an FAO report issued in May 2004 argued that "effective transfer of existing technologies to poor rural communities and the development of new and safe biotechnologies can greatly enhance the prospects for sustainably improving agricultural productivity today and in the future," as well as "help reduce environmental damage caused by toxic agricultural chemicals."

Today, some 740 million people go to bed daily on an empty stomach, and nearly 40,000 people—half of them children—die every day due to hunger or malnutrition-related causes. Despite commitments by industrialized countries to increase international aid, Africa still is expected to have over 180 million undernourished citizens in 2030, according to a report published this year by the UN Millennium Project Task Force. Although bioengineered crops alone will not eliminate hunger, they can provide a useful tool for addressing the many agricultural problems in Africa, Asia, Latin America, and other poor tropical regions.

Indeed, recombinant DNA-modified crops have already increased crop yields and food production, and reduced the use of synthetic chemical pesticides in both industrialized and less developed countries. These advances are critical in a world where natural resources are finite and where hundreds of millions of people suffer from hunger and malnutrition. Critics dismiss such claims as nothing more than corporate public relations puffery. However, while it is true that most commercially available bioengineered plants were designed for farmers in the industrialized world, the increasing adoption of biotech varieties by underdeveloped countries over the past few years demonstrates their broader applicability.

Globally, bioengineered varieties are now grown on more than 165 million acres (67.7 million hectares) in 18 countries, such as Argentina, Australia, Brazil, Canada, China, India, Mexico, the Philippines, South Africa, and the United States, according to the International Service for the Acquisition of Agri-Biotech Applications (ISAAA). Nearly one-quarter of that acreage is farmed by some 6 million resource-poor farmers in less developed countries. Why? Because they see many of the same benefits that farmers in industrialized nations do.

The first generation of biotech crops—approximately 50 different varieties of canola, corn, cotton, potato, squash, soybean, and others—were designed to aid in protecting crops from insect pests, weeds, and plant diseases. As much as 40 percent of crop productivity in Africa and Asia and about 20 percent in the industrialized countries of North America and Europe is lost to these biotic stresses, despite the use of large amounts of insecticides, herbicides, and other agricultural chemicals. Poor tropical farmers may face different pest species than their industrial country counterparts, but both must constantly battle against these threats to their productivity.

That's why South African and Filipino farmers are so eager to grow bioengineered corn resistant to insect pests, and why Chinese, Indian, and South African farmers like biotech insect-resistant cotton so much. Indian cotton farmers and Brazilian and Paraguayan soy growers didn't even wait for their governments to approve biotech varieties before they began growing them. It was discovered in 2001 that Indian farmers were planting seed obtained illegally from field trials of a biotech cotton variety then still under governmental review. Farmers in Brazil and Paraguay looked across the border and saw how well their Argentine neighbors were doing with transgenic soybean varieties and smuggling of bioengineered seed became rampant.

When the Indian government finally approved bioengineered cotton in 2002 for cultivation in seven southern states it proved to be highly successful. A study conducted by the University of Agriculture in Dharwad found that more insect damage was done to conventional hybrids than to the bioengineered variety and that the bioengineered cotton reduced pesticide spraying by half or more, delivering a 30–40 percent profit increase.

During the 2002–2003 growing season, some Indian cotton farmers saw no increased yield from the more expensive biotech varieties, but droughts during that year generated harsh conditions throughout India's southern cotton belt. Many growers of conventional crop varieties also suffered unanticipated and tragic crop losses. Most of the farmers who grew bioengineered cotton decided to plant it again in 2003, however, and total planted acreage grew from approximately 1 million acres in 2002–2003 to an estimated 3.3 million acres in 2003–2004.

When the planting of bioengineered soybean was provisionally legalized in Brazil for the 2003–2004 growing season, over 50,000 farmers registered their intent to plant it—including almost 98 percent of the growers in the southernmost state of Rio Grande do Sul, where the soybeans originally bred for Argentine climatic conditions will grow best. What is especially noteworthy is that the government decree did not legalize commercial sales of the biotech soybean, it only authorized the planting of illegal seed already in the possession of farmers. Thus, by registering their intent to grow the bioengineered variety, farmers were informing the government of their prior guilt.

There are few greater testaments to the benefits of biotechnology than the fact that thousands of poor farmers are willing to acknowledge having committed a crime just to gain access to the improved varieties. The clear lesson is that, where bioengineered varieties become available (legal or not), most farmers themselves are eager to try them.

"When the Indian government finally approved bioengineered cotton in 2002 ... it proved to be highly successful."

There is even evidence that biotech varieties have literally saved human lives. In less developed nations, pesticides are typically sprayed on crops by hand, exposing farm workers to severe health risks. Some 400 to 500 Chinese cotton farmers die every year from acute pesticide poisoning because, until recently, the only alternative was risking near total crop loss due to voracious insects. A study conducted by researchers at the Chinese Academy of Sciences and Rutgers University in the U.S. found that adoption of bioengineered cotton varieties in China has lowered the amount of pesticides used by more than 75 percent and reduced the number of pesticide poisonings by an equivalent amount. Another study by economists at the University of Reading in the U.K. found that South African cotton farmers have seen similar benefits.

The productivity gains generated by bioengineered crops provide yet another important benefit: they could save millions of acres of sensitive wildlife habitat from being converted into farmland. The loss and fragmentation of wildlife habitats caused by agricultural encroachment in regions experiencing the greatest population growth are widely recognized as among the most serious threats to biodiversity. Thus, increasing agricultural productivity is an essential environmental goal, and one that would be much easier in a world where bioengineering technology is in widespread use.

Opponents of biotechnology argue that organic farming can reduce pesticide use even more than bioengineered crops can. But organic farming practices are less productive, because there are few effective organic controls for insects, weeds, or pathogens. Converting from modern, technology-based agriculture to organic would mean either reducing global food output significantly or sacrificing undeveloped land to agriculture. Moreover, feeding the anticipated population of eight or nine billion people in the year 2050 will mean increasing food production by at least 50 percent.

As it is, the annual rate of increase in food production globally has dropped from 3 percent in the 1970s to 1 percent today. Additional gains from conventional breeding are certainly possible, but the maximum theoretical yields for most crop plants are being approached rapidly. Despite the simplistic claims made by critics of plant technology, providing genuine food security must include solutions other than mere redistribution. There is simply no way for organic farming to feed a global population of nine billion people without having to bring substantially more land into agricultural use. Dramatically improving crop yields will prove to be an essential environmental and humanitarian goal.

We have already realized significant environmental benefits from the biotech crops currently being grown, including a reduction in pesticide use of 20 million kg in the U.S. alone. A 2002 Council for Agricultural Science and Technology report also found that recombinant DNA-modified crops in the US promote the adoption of conservation tillage practices, resulting in many other important environmental benefits: 37 million tons of topsoil preserved; 85 percent reduction in greenhouse gas emissions from farm machinery; 70 percent reduction in herbicide run-off; 90 percent decrease in soil erosion; and from 15 to 26 liters of fuel saved per acre.

And, as we have seen, while the first generation of bioengineered crops was not designed with poor tropical farmers in mind, these varieties are highly adaptable. Examples of the varieties that now are being designed specifically for resource-poor farmers include virus-resistant cassava, insect resistant rice, sweet potato, and pigeon pea, and dozens of others. Chinese scientists, leaders in the development of both bioengineered and conventional rice have been urging their government to approve commercialization of their biotech varieties that have been thoroughly tested and ready for market for several years.

The next generation of products, now in research labs and field trial plots, includes crops designed to tolerate climatic stresses such as extremes of heat, cold, and drought, as well as crops designed to grow better in poor tropical soils high in acidity or alkalinity, or contaminated with mineral salts. A Mexican research group has shown that tropical crops can be modified using recombinant DNA technology to better tolerate acidic soils, significantly increasing the productivity of corn, rice and papaya. These traits for greater tolerance to adverse environmental conditions would be tremendously advantageous to poor farmers in less developed countries, especially those in Africa.

Africa did not benefit from the Green Revolution as much as Asian and Latin American nations did because plant breeders focused on improving crops such as rice and wheat, which are not widely grown in Africa. Plus, much of the African dry lands have little rainfall and no potential for irrigation, both of which play essential roles in productivity success stories for crops such as Asian rice. And the remoteness of many African villages and the poor transportation infrastructure in landlocked African countries make it difficult for African farmers to obtain agricultural chemical inputs such as fertilizers, insecticides and herbicides—even if they could be donated by aid agencies and charities. But, by packaging technological inputs within seeds, biotechnology can provide the same, or better, productivity advantages as chemical or mechanical inputs, but in a much more user-friendly manner. Farmers could be able to control insect pests, viral or bacterial pathogens, extremes of heat or drought and poor soil quality, just by planting these crops.

And the now-famous Golden Rice, with added beta carotene, is just one of many examples of bioengineered crops with improved nutritional content. Indian scientists have recently announced development of a new high protein potato variety available for commercial cultivation. Another team of Indian scientists, working with technical and financial assistance from Monsanto, is developing an improved mustard variety with enhanced beta carotene in its oil. One lab at Tuskegee University is enhancing the level of dietary protein in sweet potatoes, a common staple crop in sub-Saharan Africa. Researchers are also developing varieties of cassava, rice, and corn that more efficiently absorb trace metals and micronutrients from the soil, have enhanced starch quality, and contain more beta-carotene and other beneficial vitamins and minerals.

Ultimately, while no assurance of perfect safety can be made, breeders know far more about the genetic makeup, product characteristics, and safety of every modern bioengineered crop than those of any conventional variety ever marketed. Breeders know exactly what new genetic material has been introduced. They can identify where the transferred genes have been inserted into the new plant. They can test to ensure that transferred genes are working properly and that the nutritional elements of the food have been unchanged. None of these safety assurances have ever before been made with conventional breeding techniques. We have always lived with food risks. But modern genetic technology makes it increasingly easier to reduce those risks.

Societal anxiety over the new tools for genetic modification is, in some ways, understandable. It is fueled by a variety of causes, including consumer unfamiliarity, lack of reliable information on the current safeguards in place, a steady stream of negative opinion in the news media, opposition by activist groups, growing mistrust of industry, and a general lack of awareness of how our food production system has evolved over time. But saying that public apprehension over biotechnology is understandable is not the same as saying that it is valid. With more than thirty years of experience using recombinant DNA technology, and nearly two decades worth of pre-commercial and commercial experience with bioengineered crop plants, we can be confident that it is one of the most important and safe technologies in the plant breeder's toolbox. It would be a shame to deny biotechnology's fruits to those who are most in need of its benefits.

✗ NO
Why GM Free?
INDEPENDENT SCIENCE PANEL

1. GM CROPS FAILED TO DELIVER PROMISED BENEFITS

The consistent finding from independent research and on-farm surveys since 1999 is that GM crops have failed to deliver the promised benefits of significantly increasing yields or reducing herbicide and pesticide use. GM crops have cost the United States an estimated $12 billion in farm subsidies, lost sales and product recalls due to transgenic contamination. Massive failures in Bt cotton of up to 100% were reported in India.

Biotech corporations have suffered rapid decline since 2000, and investment advisors forecast no future for the agricultural sector. Meanwhile worldwide resistance to GM has reached a climax in 2002 when Zambia refused GM maize in food aid despite the threat of famine.

2. GM CROPS POSING ESCALATING PROBLEMS ON THE FARM

The instability of transgenic lines has plagued the industry from the beginning, and this may be responsible for a string of major crop failures. A review in 1994 stated, "While there are some examples of plants which show stable expression of a transgene these may prove to be the exceptions to the rule. In an informal survey of over 30 companies involved in the commercialisation of transgenic crop plants.... almost all of the respondents indicated that they had observed some level of transgene inaction. Many respondents indicated that most cases of transgene inactivation never reach the literature."

Triple herbicide-tolerant oilseed rape volunteers that have combined transgenic and non-transgenic traits are now widespread in Canada. Similar multiple herbicide-tolerant volunteers and weeds have emerged in the United States. In the United States, glyphosate-tolerant weeds are plaguing GM cotton and soya fields, and atrazine, one of the most toxic herbicides, has had to be used with glufosinate-tolerant GM maize.

Bt biopesticide traits are simultaneously threatening to create superweeds and Bt-resistant pests.

3. EXTENSIVE TRANSGENIC CONTAMINATION UNAVOIDABLE

Extensive transgenic contamination has occurred in maize landraces growing in remote regions in Mexico despite an official moratorium that has been in place since 1998. High levels of contamination have since been found in Canada. In a test of 33 certified seed stocks, 32 were found contaminated.

New research shows that transgenic pollen, wind-blown and deposited elsewhere, or fallen directly to the ground, is a major source of transgenic contamination.

Contamination is generally acknowledged to be unavoidable, hence *there can be no co-existence of transgenic and non-transgenic crops.*

4. GM CROPS NOT SAFE

Contrary to the claims of proponents, GM crops have not been proven safe. The regulatory framework was fatally flawed from the start. It was based on an *anti-precautionary* approach designed to expedite product approval at the expense of safety considerations. The principle of 'substantial equivalence', on which risk assessment is based, is intended to be vague and ill-defined, thereby giving companies complete licence in claiming transgenic products 'substantially equivalent' to non-transgenic products, and hence 'safe'.

5. GM FOOD RAISES SERIOUS SAFETY CONCERNS

There have been very few credible studies on GM food safety. Nevertheless, the available findings already give cause for concern. In the still only systematic investigation on GM food ever carried out in the world, 'growth factor–like' effects were found in the stomach and small intestine of young rats that were not fully accounted for by the transgene product, and were hence attributable to the transgenic process or the transgenic construct, *and may hence be general to all GM food.* There have been at least two other, more limited, studies that also raised serious safety concerns.

6. DANGEROUS GENE PRODUCTS ARE INCORPORATED INTO CROPS

Bt proteins, incorporated into 25% of all transgenic crops worldwide, have been found harmful to a range of non-target insects. Some of them are also potent immunogens and allergens. A team of scientists have cautioned against releasing Bt crops for human use.

Food crops are increasingly used to produce pharmaceuticals and drugs, including cytokines known to suppress the immune system, induce sickness and central nervous system toxicity; interferon alpha, reported to cause dementia, neurotoxicity and mood and cognitive side effects; vaccines; and viral sequences such as the 'spike' protein gene of the pig coronavirus, in the same family as the SARS virus linked to the current epidemic. The glycoprotein gene *gp120* of the AIDS virus HIV-1, incorporated into GM maize as a 'cheap, edible oral vaccine,' serves as yet another biological time-bomb, as it can interfere with the immune system and recombine with viruses and bacteria to generate new and unpredictable pathogens.

7. TERMINATOR CROPS SPREAD MALE STERILITY

Crops engineered with 'suicide' genes for male sterility have been promoted as a means of 'containing,' i.e., preventing, the spread of transgenes. In reality, the hybrid crops sold to farmers spread both male sterile suicide genes as well herbicide tolerance genes *via pollen.*

8. BROAD-SPECTRUM HERBICIDES HIGHLY TOXIC TO HUMANS AND OTHER SPECIES

Glufosinate ammonium and glyphosate are used with the herbicide-tolerant transgenic crops that currently account for 75% of all transgenic crops worldwide. Both are systemic metabolic poisons expected to have a wide range of harmful effects, and these have been confirmed.

Glufosinate ammonium is linked to neurological, respiratory, gastrointestinal and haematological toxicities, and birth defects in humans and mammals. It is toxic to butterflies and a number of beneficial insects, also to the larvae of clams and oysters, *Daphnia* and some freshwater fish, especially the rainbow trout. It inhibits beneficial soil bacteria and fungi, especially those that fix nitrogen.

Glyphosate is the most frequent cause of complaints and poisoning in the UK. Disturbances of many body functions have been reported after exposures at normal use levels.

Glyphosate exposure nearly doubled the risk of late spontaneous abortion, and children born to users of glyphosate had elevated neurobehavioral defects. Glyphosate caused retarded development of the foetal skeleton in laboratory rats. Glyphosate inhibits the synthesis of steroids, and is genotoxic in mammals, fish and frogs. Field dose exposure of earthworms caused at least 50 percent mortality and significant intestinal damage among surviving worms. Roundup caused cell division dysfunction that may be linked to human cancers.

The known effects of both glufosinate and glyphosate are sufficiently serious for all further uses of the herbicides to be halted.

9. GENETIC ENGINEERING CREATES SUPER-VIRUSES

By far the most insidious dangers of genetic engineering are inherent to the process itself, which greatly enhances the scope and probability of horizontal gene transfer and recombination, the main route to creating viruses and bacteria that cause disease epidemics. This was highlighted, in 2001, by the 'accidental' creation of a killer mouse virus in the course of an apparently innocent genetic engineering experiment.

Newer techniques, such as DNA shuffling, are allowing geneticists to create in a matter of minutes in the laboratory millions of recombinant viruses that have never existed in billions of years of evolution. Disease-causing viruses and bacteria and their genetic material are the predominant materials and tools for genetic engineering, as much as for the intentional creation of bio-weapons.

10. TRANSGENIC DNA IN FOOD TAKEN UP BY BACTERIA IN HUMAN GUT

There is already experimental evidence that transgenic DNA from plants has been taken up by bacteria in the soil and in the gut of human volunteers. Antibiotic resistance marker genes can spread from transgenic food to pathogenic bacteria, making infections very difficult to treat.

11. TRANSGENIC DNA AND CANCER

Transgenic DNA is known to survive digestion in the gut and to jump into the genome of mammalian cells, raising the possibility for triggering cancer.

The possibility cannot be excluded that feeding GM products such as maize to animals also carries risks, not just for the animals but also for human beings consuming the animal products.

12. CaMV 35S PROMOTER INCREASES HORIZONTAL GENE TRANSFER

Evidence suggests that transgenic constructs with the CaMV 35S promoter might be especially unstable and prone to horizontal gene transfer and recombination, with all the attendant hazards: gene mutations due to random insertion, cancer, reactivation of dormant viruses and generation of new viruses. This promoter is present in most GM crops being grown commercially today.

13. A HISTORY OF MISREPRESENTATION AND SUPPRESSION OF SCIENTIFIC EVIDENCE

There has been a history of misrepresentation and suppression of scientific evidence, especially on horizontal gene transfer. Key experiments failed to be performed, or were performed badly and then misrepresented. Many experiments were not followed up, including investigations on whether the CaMV 35S promoter is responsible for the 'growth-factor-like' effects observed in young rats fed GM potatoes.

In conclusion, GM crops have failed to deliver the promised benefits and are posing escalating problems on the farm. Transgenic contamination is now widely acknowledged to be unavoidable, and hence there can be no co-existence of GM and non-GM agriculture. Most important of all, GM crops have not been proven safe. On the contrary, sufficient evidence has emerged to raise serious safety concerns, that if ignored could result in irreversible damage to health and the environment. GM crops should be firmly rejected now.

POSTSCRIPT

From the previous discussion, it is clear that the role of genetically modified organisms (GMOs) as a potential solution to the food deficits of developing countries remains highly contentious. An equally contentious issue is the role of the genetically modified food should play in international food aid programs. The United States, the world's leading food aid donor, is also the largest donor of genetically modified food aid. In 2002, it shipped significant amounts of such food aid, particularly maize, to southern Africa. Despite experiencing serious food shortages, a number of southern African countries refused to receive the food aid. Part of the reason was over concerns about the negative health risk of GMOs. But they were also concerned that the genetically modified food aid would contaminate local crops, thus making it difficult to export to Europe in the future. In Europe, the opposition to GMOs has been much stronger and the European community has banned imports of genetically modified food. In turn, the United States refused to provide the countries that refused the maize with alternative non-genetically modified food aid.

Some accused the United States of using their food aid program to create markets for the new strains of food that they could not market in Europe. In response, the United States criticized African leaders for their shortsightedness and suggested that they had acted irresponsibly in refusing much needed aid at time when many were suffering from starvation conditions. At the same time, the US complained the Europe's moratorium of GMO food imports was unnecessarily contributing to hunger in Africa.

Given the contentious nature of GMO foods, what is an appropriate food aid policy to follow? If large numbers of people are vulnerable to starvation, would it not be better to use the food aid to save their lives? Or, does the imposition of GMO foods on recipients governments constitute another form of imperialism?

Suggested Additional Readings

Braman, Sandra. "Informational Meta-Technologies, International Relations, and Genetic Power: The Case of Biotechnologies," in James N. Rosenau and J. P. Singh, eds., *Information Technologies and Global Politics* (Albany: State University of New York, 2002), pp. 91–112.

Charles, Daniel. *Lords of the Harvest: Biotech, Big Money, and the Future of Food* (Cambridge: Perseus, 2001).

Clapp, Jennifer. "The Political Economy of Food Aid in an Era of Agricultural Biotechnology," *Global Governance*, 11, no. 4 (October-December 2005): 457–485.

———. "Unplanned Exposure to Genetically Modified Organisms: Divergent Responses From the Global South," *Journal of Environment and Development,* 15, no. 1 (March 2006): 3–21.

Cohen, Joel I. "Poorer Nations Turn to Publicly Developed GM Crops," *Nature Biotechnology*, 23, no. 1 (January 2005): 27–33. http://www.ifpri.org/pubs/articles/2005/naturebiotech.pdf

Conway, G. *The Doubly Green Revolution: Food for All in the Twenty-first Century* (Ithaca, NY: Comstock Publishing Associates, 1998).

Dossier, P. *Miracle or Menace? Biotechnology and the Third World* (Washington: The Panos Institute, 1990).

Fukuyama, Francis. "Gene Regime," *Foreign Policy*, no. 129 (March/April 2002): 57–63.

Morris, Michael L., et al. "Potential Impacts of Biotechnology-Assisted Selection on Plant Breeding Programs in Developing Countries," in Philip G. Pardey, ed., *The Future of Food* (Washington: IFPRI, 2001), pp. 197–218.

Parrlberg, Robert. "The Global Food Fight," *Foreign Affairs*, 79, no. 3 (2000): 24–38.

——. *The Politics of Precaution: Genetically Modified Crops in Developing Countries* (Baltimore: Johns Hopkins University Press, 2001).

Pinstrup-Andersen, Per, and E. Schioler. *Seeds of Contention: World Hunger and the Global Controversy over GM Crops* (Baltimore: Johns Hopkins University Press, 2001).

Radin, John W. "How Safe Are Genetically Engineered Crops," *Agricultural Research*, 52, no. 9 (September 2004).

Snell, Marilyn Berlin. "Against the Grain: Why Poor Nations Would Lose in a Biotech War on Hunger," *Sierra* (July/August, 2001): 30–33.

InfoTrac® College Edition

Search for the following articles in the InfoTrac® database:

Aubert, Jean-Eric. "NGOs on GMOs: The Reasons for Resistance," *OECD Observer* (April 2000): 47.

Jefferson, Valeria. "The Ethical Dilemma of Genetically Modified Food," *Journal of Environmental Health*, 69, no. 1 (July–August 2006): 33–34.

Pringle, Peter. "Hunger and the Biotech Wars," *World Policy Journal*, 20, no. 2 (Summer 2003): 43–50.

For more articles, enter:
"GMOs" and "genetically modified plants" or "genetically modified foods" in the keyword search.

Web Resources

AGBIOWORLD

www.agbioworld.org

This is a pro-GMO website run by C.S. Prakash. It contains a large number of articles and reports that look at the benefits of biotechnology research.

INDEPENDENT SCIENCE PANEL

www.indsp.org

ISP is an organization composed of scientists who are opposed to the use of genetically modified foods. The site contains a number of their reports, including the full 136-page report on "The Case for a GM-Free Sustainable World."

FRIENDS OF THE EARTH EUROPE

www.foeeurope.org/GMOs/Index.htm

This section of the Friends of the Earth Europe website contains information on the European campaign against GMOs. It also contains a number of position papers and briefs on GMOs.

BIOTECH BASICS

www.biotechbasics.com

This website is run by Monsanto, the leading corporation involved in biotechnological research in agriculture. The site provides updates on biotechnological developments in various parts of the world.

GREENPEACE INTERNATIONAL

www.greenpeace.org/international/campaigns/genetic-engineering

This page on the website of Greenpeace International contains news items and articles about their anti-GMO campaign.

INTERNATIONAL CENTRE FOR GENETIC ENGINEERING AND BIOTECHNOLOGY

www.icgeb.trieste.it/biosafety

ICGEB describes itself as an autonomous, international, intergovernmental organization with the special mandate "to promote the safe use of biotechnology world-wide and with special regard to the needs of the developing world." The site contains considerable information on efforts to establish regulations ensuring the safe use of GMOs.

BIOWATCH SOUTH AFRICA

www.biowatch.org.za

Biowatch South Africa is a South African NGO that focuses on issues relating to biological diversity, genetic engineering, and sustainable livelihoods.

Contributor Acknowledgments

The editors wish to thank the publishers and copyright holders for permission to reprint the selections in this book, which are listed below in order of appearance.

Issue 1

Henry Veltmeyer, "Development and Globalization as Imperialism," *Canadian Journal of Development Studies*, 26, no. 2 (2005), 89–106.

Economic Commission for Latin America and the Caribbean, *Globalization and Development* (New York: ECLAC, 2002), 17–27. The United Nations is the author of the original material.

Issue 2

Martin Wolf, *Why Globalization Works* (New Haven, CT: Yale Nota Bene, 2005), 138–172.

Robert Isaak, *The Globalization Gap: How the Rich Get Richer and the Poor Get Left Further Behind*: 1e, (Upper Saddle River, NJ: Prentice-Hall, 2005), 183–202.

Issue 3

Laure Waridel, *Coffee with Pleasure: Just Java and World Trade* (Montreal: Black Rose Books, 2002), 93–115. Reprinted with kind permission of Black Rose Books, *www.blackrosebooks.net*.

Gavin Fridell, "The Fair Trade Network in Historical Perspective," *Canadian Journal of Development Studies*, 25, no. 3 (2004), 411–428.

Issue 4

Paul Krugman, "In Praise of Cheap Labor," found at http://web.mit.edu/krugman/www/smokey.html.

John Miller, "Why Economists Are Wrong About Sweatshops and the Antisweatshop Movement," from *Challenge*, vol. 46, no. 1 (January/February 2003), 93–122. © M.E. Sharpe, Inc. Reprinted with permission.

Issue 5

George Ayittey, "Smart Aid for Africa," *African Dialogue Series*, No. 773 (2005), www.utexas.edu/conferences/africa/ads/773.html.

Moses Ochonu, "The Case for Debt Cancellation and Increased Aid to Africa," *The Nigerian Village Square* (2005) www.nigeriavillagesquare.com/content/view/1137/55.

Issue 6

Copyright © 2000 by Hernando de Soto. Reprinted by permission of Basic Books, a member of Perseus Books Group.

Alan Gilbert, "On the Mystery of Capital and the Myths of Hernando de Soto," *International Development Planning Review*, 24, no. 1 (2002): 1–16.

Issue 7

Brian Ames, et al. *Macroeconomic Policy and Poverty Reduction*, International Monetary Fund, August 2001.

Adam Davidson-Harden. *"An 'Empty Glass': How the Bretton Woods Institutions Sustain and Exacerbate Poverty."* © Nelson, a division of Thomson Canada Limited, 2007.

Issue 8

Courtesy of the Canadian International Development Agency (CIDA). Excerpts from CIDA Development Report 2004–05. Found at www.tbs-sct.gc.ca/rma/dpr1/04-05/CIDA-ACDI/CIDA-ACDId45_e.asp. Reproduced with the permission of the Minister of Public Works and Government Services, 2005, being the copyright holder.

Dexter Samida, "A Hand Out Instead of a Hand Up: Where Foreign Aid Fails," *Public Policy Sources*, No. 30 (1999), Fraser Institute Occasional Papers Series, www.fraserinstitute.ca.

Issue 9

Sakiko Fukuda-Parr, "Millenium Development Goals: Why They Matter," From *Global Governance: A Review of Multilateralism and International Organizations*, vol. 10, #4. Copyright © 2004 by Lynne Rienner Publishers, Inc. Used with permission of the publisher.

Michael Clemens and Todd Moss, "What's Wrong with the Millennium Development Goals," *Center for Global Development*, 2004.

Issue 10

Peter Uvin, "On High Moral Ground: The Incorporation of Human Rights by the Development Enterprise," *Praxis: The Fletcher Journal of Development Studies*, XVII (2002).

Hugo Slim, "Making Moral Low Ground: Rights as the Struggle for Justice and the Abolition of Development," *Praxis: The Fletcher Journal of Development Studies*, XVII (2002).

Issue 11

Aruna Rao, *Making Institutions Work for Women*, 2006, Development 49 (1), (63–67) © 2006 Society for International Development. Reproduced with permission of Palgrave Macmillan.

Rebecca Tiessen. "What's New about Gender Mainstreaming? Three Decades of Policy Creation and Development Strategies." *Canadian Journal of Development Studies*, Volume 26, 2005.

Issue 12

"Executive Summary," *Our Common Interest, Report of the Commission on Africa*, pp. 13–17.

Richard Sandbrook, "Africa's Great Transformation?" *Journal of Development Studies, 41*, 6 (August 2005), 118–125. Reprinted by permission of the publisher, Taylor & Francis Ltd, www.tandf.co.uk/journals.

Issue 13

Barbara Harff and Ted Robert Gurr, *Ethnic Conflict in World Politics*, Boulder: Westview Press, 2004, 1–17.

John Mueller, "The Banality of 'Ethnic War,'" *International Security* 25 (1), Summer 2000, 42–70.

Issue 14

Amartya Sen, "Democracy as a Universal Value," *Journal of Democracy* 10(3), 1999, 3–9, 13–16. © National Endowment for Democracy and The Johns Hopkins University Press. Reprinted with permission of The Johns Hopkins University Press.

Adrian Leftwich, "On Democracy and Development: A Contradiction in the Politics of Economics." *New Political Economy*, vol. 7, no. 2, 2002.

Issue 15

World Bank, *World Development Report 2003*. © The International Bank for Reconstruction and Development/ The World Bank.

The WDR 2003: A Strenuous Tale of Missed Opportunities by Liane Schalatek and Barbara Unmüssig, Heinrich Böll Foundation. Taken from *Managing Sustainability World Bank-Style, An Evaluation of the World Development Report 2003*.

Issue 16

Gregory Conko and C.S. Prakash, "Can GM Crops Play a Role in Developing Countries?" *PBI Bulletin*, Issue 2 (2004).

Independent Science Panel, "Why GM Free?", Executive summary of the Report, *The Case for a GM Free World*, www.indsp.org/ISPreportSummary.php.